BRITISH FILM
CHARACTER ACTORS

BRITISH FILM CHARACTER ACTORS

Great Names and Memorable Moments

Terence Pettigrew

David & Charles
Newton Abbot London

Barnes & Noble Books
Totowa, New Jersey

British Library Cataloguing in Publication Data

Pettigrew, Terence
   British film character actors
   1. Moving-picture actors and actresses – Great
   Britain – Biography
   I. Title
   791.43'028'0922   PN1998.A2
   ISBN 0 7153 8270 5

Library of Congress Cataloguing in Publication Data

Pettigrew, Terence.
   British film character actors.
   1. Moving-picture actors and actresses – Great
   Britain
   I. Title
   PN1998.A2P475   1982   791.43'028'0922   82–3912
   ISBN 0–389–20289–4   AACR2

This edition first published in 1982
in Great Britain by
David & Charles (Publishers) Limited
Brunel House Newton Abbot Devon

First published in the USA 1982 by
Barnes & Noble Books
81 Adams Drive, Totowa, New Jersey, 07512

Phototypeset by ABM Typographics Ltd, Hull.
and printed in Great Britain by
Redwood Burn Limited, Trowbridge, Wilts

Contents

Introduction

The art of the character actor is eloquently summarised by the performance of Alec Guinness as Fagin in *Oliver Twist,* in which the character seems to take over so profoundly that the performer's own personality disappears completely. In Guinness's case, the accent is on 'actor'. John Mills, Denholm Elliott, Richard Attenborough, Laurence Olivier, Peter Sellers and Peter Ustinov can be found mostly on that side of the fence, too.

But equally significant in any review of the actor's art are the 'characters', that is, actors who give us in film after film minor variations of the same persona. Harry Andrews, Ian Carmichael, John Gregson, Leslie Phillips, Kenneth More, Trevor Howard, Alastair Sim, Cecil Parker are among the dozens who regularly turn up with little or no disguise. As with Guinness and company, their boldly defined, resoundingly flesh-and-blood characterisations have created the backbone of the British film since the end of World War II.

Character actors, like babies, therefore, arrive in all shapes and sizes. There is no clear division between stardom and character 'actordom' other than the certainty that not all stars are character actors, nor are all character actors necessarily stars.

As to the actors discussed in this book, bearing in mind the constraints on space which publishers must exercise, I have, in a number of cases, included lesser known names at the expense of established stars, particularly international superstars whose careers are already comprehensively documented elsewhere. For example, Dirk Bogarde and Sean Connery are world stars in the widest sense, as are Richard Burton and Michael Caine. But whereas their careers have been scrutinised in magazines and individual biographies to a far greater extent than their inclusion in *British Film Character Actors* could ever hope to match, references to the work of actors like Harry Andrews, Ian Bannen, Gordon Jackson and Alastair Sim lie mostly tucked away on microfilm and in yellowing news clippings.

By including these along with a broad spectrum of dependable supporting actors such as George Cole, Michael Hordern, Sidney James and Michael Medwin, interwoven with the career highlights of actors who are, or once were, stars known best for great 'character' performances – for example, Alan Bates, Peter Finch, Richard Harris, Trevor Howard and Jack Hawkins – I believe the right balance has been maintained. And certainly the original concept of the book, which was to provide an informative digest on the careers of Britain's best-loved character actors, and not merely another superstars' showcase, has been preserved.

Inevitably, since space denies the inclusion of everyone I would have liked to bring in, there are omissions which won't please everyone. To the many admirers of Michael Gough, Nigel Davenport, James Hayter, Leo Genn, Robert Flemyng and others I can only stress the unavoidability of their exclusion, which is in no way a comment on their very fine abilities.

Finally, I would like to draw particular attention to the fact that, unless clearly shown otherwise in the text, all references to each actor contained in this book relate expressly to the characters they have portrayed in films and to their performances. In the interest of brevity, and to avoid unnecessary confusion, the actors are referred to by their own names and not by the names of the characters played in the films discussed.

Under no circumstances should any comment made about an actor in the context of explaining or reviewing a particular film or an individual performance, or of describing the character being played, be taken as a reference to any actor in his capacity as a private individual, and any such interpretation is contrary to the intentions of the author and to the spirit of the book.

TERENCE PETTIGREW

Harry Andrews

Harry Andrews could be rather good at urging jaded battalions to fight on. That rich fruity voice belonged in the open air, hemmed in by mortar fire and the acrid chorus of battle. One can imagine the dead hopping obediently to life the moment Andrews made it compulsory.

In or out of uniform, he emanates authority. The profile seems to have been carved from the least accessible areas of the Eiger. Add a hint of ornamental Toby jug and you have what Michael Billington describes as his 'massive, oak-like presence'.

His debut film – after some two decades of stage work, predominantly Shakespearean – was *The Red Beret* (1953, Terence Young), an entertaining Anglo-US adventure drama set among a platoon of wartime paratroopers. Andrews' dour RSM, in charge of Alan Ladd, Donald Houston and others, had most of the good lines and stole the show.

Ladd must have bribed him to appear in *The Black Knight* (1954, Tay Garnett), the silliest yarn ever to come out of Camelot. Andrews played a nobleman whose castle is plundered by Normans, and Ladd, looking about as olde Englishe as a cheeseburger, does his familiar Shane routine from inside a suit of armour.

'If Ahab has his way neither thee nor me will see home again' Leo Genn warns Andrews in *Moby Dick* (1956, John Huston), an intermittently interesting adaptation of Herman Melville's powerful novel. Both are members of Gregory Peck's whaling crew, and Genn's fears that their captain's weird obsession about killing the Great White Whale will scuttle them all are not, as it happens, very far off the mark. In the final-reel confrontation with Moby Dick all go under except lowly mariner Richard Basehart, through whom the entire saga is subjectively recalled.

Huston abandoned the heavy symbolism of the original book in favour of making a rattling good sea yarn, and I certainly would not argue with this decision although his choice of Gregory Peck as Ahab – more in view of the actor's established persona than through any fault one can find in Peck's acting – did at the time come under fire. It would be interesting to see what a more sensitive and less self-conscious director would make of the story's more cerebral qualities.

Harry Andrews has played most officer types

as well as a gallery of hard-bitten NCOs. He was the Air Force chief behind the fjord raids in *633 Squadron* (1964, Walter Grauman), a Whitehall defence official in *Battle of Britain* (1969, Guy Hamilton), a brigadier in *Play Dirty* (1968, Andre de Toth), and a lieutenant-colonel in *Too Late the Hero* (1970, Robert Aldrich). Among his better known non-coms were the platoon sergeant in *A Hill in Korea* (1956, Julian Aymes), and a detention camp RSM in *The Hill* (1965, Sidney Lumet).

He had a good part alongside John Mills in *Ice Cold in Alex* (1958, J. Lee-Thompson), as an Army sergeant chased by Germans across the Libyan desert in a beat-up ambulance. A little way on they pick up a stranded South African officer, Anthony Quayle, whom Andrews suspects is a German spy because he is unable to make a fire in the desert Allied troops-style; there is also the matter of a mysterious shoulder-pack which Quayle never leaves out of his sight.

Trailing him into the desert one evening, Andrews has his suspicions confirmed – the pack contains a radio transmitter. But before they reach safety in British-held Alexandria, Quayle has shown that a German can also be a good guy, and it is Andrews' presence of mind, in snatch-

Harry Andrews in *Ice Cold in Alex* (1958)

ing Quayle's identity tags moments before he is marched off by redcaps, which saves him from a firing squad.

Andrews' arrogant, unimaginative police chief in India during the time of the Raj causes the fuss in *The Long Duel* (1967, Ken Annakin). His closed fist attitude towards the natives provokes them into a rebellion under Yul Brynner. Further mishandling fans the trouble into large-scale shoot-outs. Andrews reckons he can subdue the rebels with additional firepower, but resident British governor Maurice Denham favours the more restrained approach of another police officer, Trevor Howard. Andrews sourly insists that, given the extra troops he requested, he would have brought Brynner to heel without Howard's interference, but the flaw in his argument is that, most of the time, he behaves like an idiot.

He could be a proper swine, too, as in *I'll Never Forget Whatshisname* (1967, Michael Winner), in which he played a randy Cambridge don who keeps porno movies in his What-The-Butler-Saw machines. He was a snide baronet – another oily snake performance – in *Man at the Top* (1974, Mike Vardy), a dud-squib Joe Lampton adventure with Kenneth Haigh as the blunt Yorkshire swinger. Haigh is snared into a shady business deal involving Andrews by his lordship's nubile but otherwise dull wife, Nanette Newman, and when Andrews turns out to be a transparently decadent creep Haigh stitches him up so tightly that all poor Andrews can do is play the wounded armadillo and – for the sake of appearances – feign upper-crust bonhomie till his teeth hurt. Critic John Gillett noted that Haigh's 'coarse, chip-on-the-shoulder gruffness and wearying pop-eyed charm soon fall flat' but added: 'Harry Andrews' steely banked-down performance is a decided asset'.

In *The Ruling Class* (1972, Peter Medak) Andrews again played an aristocrat, but an agreeably nutty one whose suicide in the opening sequences, clad in longjohns, ballerina skirt and regimental jacket, is a genuine loss far too early in a film which, though witty in snatches is mostly heavy going, a victim of its own cleverness. Arthur Lowe was particularly good as Andrews' bolshie servant. In *Night Hair Child* (1971, James Killy), a moderate shocker, Andrews played a boarding school headmaster reluctant to divulge why he had to expel the cherub-faced Mark Lester. Stepmother Britt Ekland is also worried about young Mark – with

good reason, for behind those bland angelic eyes he is as knotted as leftover spaghetti. The film has a number of conventional surprises, but saves the best one till the end, when Miss Ekland, by way of recompense for all the trouble he has caused her, gleefully nudges him under a passing car.

Andrews' knobbly face is impossible to disguise – he must be a make-up department's nightmare – yet it has never kept him out of work. The blemishes make his characters all the more believable, and since Andrews has a reputation for tackling almost anything, it's a help when he starts off looking so reassuringly flesh-and-blood, such as, for instance, in *Country Dance* (1969, J. Lee-Thompson), where he plays Peter O'Toole's landowner-neighbour.

He had a silly role, though no sillier than any of the other actors, in *Theatre of Blood* (1973, Douglas Hickox), as one of the critics circle murdered by deranged Shakespearean ham actor Vincent Price. Andrews is lured to an empty proscenium by Diana Rigg, as Price's daughter, where the curtain is waiting to go up on *The Merchant of Venice*, with Andrews, reading Antonio's lines, doomed to become an unwilling heart donor at the point where the evil, leering Shylock claims his pound of flesh. In *The Four Feathers* (1977, Don Sharp) Andrews played the long-suffering father of dishonoured army officer Beau Bridges, and in *The Big Sleep* (1977, Michael Winner), he played the butler of a wealthy old eccentric who hires Robert Mitchum, alias private eye Philip Marlowe, to help sort out the confusing mess of murder and blackmail which his family has landed in.

Andrews made two above-average films with James Coburn. In *The Internecine Project* (1974, Ken Hughes) he played a slightly odd masseur at a posh gentleman's club who loves cats and despises women – 'they're all whores!' – and is used by Coburn to dispose of Christiane Kruger, a job which he tackles with sickly relish. Traces of Hitchcock are glimpsed in the scene where he strangles her in the shower. The sophisticated daisy-chain of killings – each assassin becomes, in turn, the next assassin's victim – are organised by Coburn, a departing CIA agent who needs to close the file permanently on his undercover activities in London. Andrews' pleasure from his grisly task is short-lived, for soon afterwards, a timid, bespectacled Ian Hendry springs from the bushes and bashes his head in as he lets himself into his gloomy, cat-infested apartment.

8

Harry Andrews (left), Allan Cuthbertson (centre) and Nigel Patrick in *The Informers* (1963)

With Coburn again he made *Sky Riders* (1976, Douglas Hickox), a pictorially elegant thriller about the rescue of kidnap victims from a seemingly unreachable heavily guarded mountaintop fortress – unreachable, that is, until Coburn and some daredevil hang-glider chums drop in from nearby mountain peaks. Andrews was a go-between in a smuggling enterprise to whom Coburn hands over a suspicious-looking package, whose contents are not discussed but mention of Beirut implies hard drugs, before embarking on the kidnap rescue. The airborne sequences, as the intrepid rescue team cruise in and around picturesque mountains and soar like hand-painted eagles over lush green valleys, are beautiful to watch and provide poetic pauses between bursts of explosive action. As the laconic hero James Coburn, brandishing two immaculate rows of teeth set in a not unpleasantly corroded face, was everything his fans might expect.

When bowler-hatted Whitehall types were needed, Andrews could usefully fill in. He was Michael Craig's Intelligence chief in *Modesty Blaise* (1966, Joseph Losey), and double-agent Laurence Harvey's boss in *A Dandy In Aspic* (1968, Anthony Mann) – the former being comic strip hokum, the latter slowly asphyxiating in its own pretentiousness. In *The Mackintosh Man* (1973, John Huston), a *39 Steps*-type spy thriller with interesting Irish backgrounds, Andrews was a top civil servant who recruits agent Paul Newman and later, uncharacteristically, allows himself to be rubbed out by the opposition.

Harry Andrews
b. 1911. Rough-hewn but gentle-voiced ex-Shakespearean stage actor who has specialised in films (since 1953) in forceful, authoritative figures, often in uniform. Film debut, as dour Scots RSM in *The Red Beret*, a World War II drama, established blueprint for dozens of similar solid supporting roles.

1953 *The Red Beret* (RSM)	*A Nice Girl Like Me* (Savage)
1954 *The Black Knight* (Earl of Yeonil)	*The Seagull* (Sorin)
The Man Who Loved Redheads (Williams)	*Country Dance* (Brigadier Crieff)
1956 *A Hill in Korea* (Sergeant Payne)	*Destiny of a Spy* (General Kirk)
Moby Dick (Stubb)	*The Night They Raided Minsky's* (Rachel's
Alexander The Great (Darius)	Father)
1957 *Saint Joan* (John de Stogumber)	1970 *Entertaining Mr Sloane* (Ed)
1958 *I Accuse* (Major Henry)	*Wuthering Heights* (Mr Earnshaw)
Ice Cold In Alex (Sergeant Tom Pugh)	*Too Late the Hero* (Lt-Col Thompson)
1959 *The Devil's Disciple* (Major Swindon)	1971 *Night Hair Child* (Dr Kessle)
A Touch of Larceny (Captain Graham)	*I Want What I Want* (Father)
Solomon and Sheba (USA) (Baltor)	*Nicholas and Alexandra* (Grand Duke
1960 *In the Nick* (Chief Williams)	Nicholas)
Circle of Deception (Captain Rawson)	*Burke and Hare* (Dr Knox)
1961 *The Inspector* (Ayoob)	*The Nightcomers* (Master of the House)
1962 *Reach For Glory* (Captain Curlew)	*The Ruling Class* (13th Earl of Gurney)
1963 *Nine Hours to Rama* (General Singh)	1972 *Man of La Mancha* (Inn Keeper/
The Informers (Superintendent Beswick)	Governor)
1964 *Nothing But the Best* (Horton)	1973 *Theatre of Blood* (Trevor Dickman)
The System (Larsey)	*The Mackintosh Man* (Mackintosh)
633 Squadron (Air Vice Marshal Davis)	*The Final Programme* (John)
The Truth About Spring (Sellers)	1974 *The Internecine Project* (Albert Parsons)
1965 *The Hill* (RSM Bert Wilson)	*Last Days of Man on Earth* (John)
Sands of the Kalahari (Grimmelman)	*Man at the Top* (Lord Ackerman)
1966 *Modesty Blaise* (Sir Gerald Tarrant)	1976 *Sky Riders* (Auerbach)
The Jokers (Marryatt)	*The Prince and the Pauper* (Hertford)
The Night of the Generals (Governor)	*Candleshoe* (not in cast list)
1967 *The Long Duel* (Superintendent Stafford)	*Equus* (Harry Dalton)
I'll Never Forget Whatshisname (Gerald	1976 *The Blue Bird* (Oak)
Sater)	1977 *The Four Feathers* (General David
The Deadly Affair (Inspector Mendel)	Feversham)
1968 *The Charge of the Light Brigade* (Lord	*The Big Sleep* (Vincent Norris)
Lucan)	*Death on the Nile* (Barnstaple)
A Dandy in Aspic (Fraser)	1978 *Superman* (2nd Elder)
Play Dirty (Brigadier Blore)	*Medusa Touch* (Assistant Commissioner)
1969 *The Southern Star* (Kramer)	1980 *SOS Titanic* (Captain Edward J. Smith)
Battle of Britain (Top Civil Servant)	*Hawk the Slayer* (High Abbot)

Richard Attenborough

Richard Attenborough has given heart to successive generations of plain, round-faced boys from whose ranks he rose to become one of the film industry's more durable assets. That dissolute choirboy look clung on till middle age; he was stumpy, low on charm and had a tendency to lisp. But he went on to become Sir Richard Attenborough – boss of Capital Radio and chairman of the British Film Institute – proof that anyone can attain the glittering prizes.

Anyone, that is, with Attenborough's singu-

lar dedication, appetite for hard work, and skill in avoiding the typecast-trap. His progress from 'simpering baby-faced idiot' roles (Attenborough's own description) to international acclaim has not been easy, yet his work is significant on several levels: his acting (and notably in this context, his association with the Boultings); his executive partnership with Bryan Forbes; and latterly his impressive, though sometimes longwinded, directorial feats.

Attenborough came to attention in the late

1940s as the cruel but cowardly razor thug in *Brighton Rock* (1947, John Boulting), a landmark in British films for its imaginative use of exterior locations – Brighton seascape, streets and racetrack – as integral parts of the action. In *The Guinea Pig* (1948, Roy Boulting) he was a bright grammar-school type who wins a scholarship to a public school – intellectually holding his own but socially out of his depth.

In *In Which We Serve* (1942, Noel Coward, David Lean) he was a cowardly naval rating who deserts his post under fire, and in *Morning Departure* (1950, Roy Baker) he was another flustered little rotter, a stoker who panics inside a crippled submarine. 'You're useless to me and a menace to everyone on board – GET OUT!' shouts Captain John Mills, momentarily forgetting that what Attenborough would like most, at that precise moment, *is* to get the hell out! In the end, as one of the last four left behind with no chance of rescue, he manages to come to terms with his fate, becoming in fellow-seaman James Hayter's view 'a real good 'un!'

He played yet another Cockney seaman in *The Gift Horse* (1952, Compton Bennett), a civvy-street trade union organiser able to quote Navy Regulations from cover to cover. An inborn distrust of officer types inhibits him from requesting compassionate leave after learning that his mother is dying, but a word in the right ear from sympathetic fellow sailor Bernard Lee gets him packed off ashore anyway. Following a raid on an enemy-held port, Attenborough is among the prisoners rounded up, and promptly acquaints his Nazi captors with the small print on the Geneva Convention.

Trevor Howard made a splendidly gritty ship's captain, a war-weary old seadog with a suspiciously vulnerable soft centre, and the film was as competent a pastiche of shore and shipboard drama as anything the period offered, but it was Attenborough, gratefully clutching his chance to set adrift that 'orrible misfit character, who appeared to put in most of the hard work.

With *The Gift Horse*, Attenborough confirmed suspicions that had emerged through his performance in *Morning Departure*, that he was an actor with a future provided the right sort of role could be found. The problem was finding it – physically he was all wrong to be a hero, facially he was too ordinary to make a career as a villain, and there was nothing about his personality that ran to natural laughter.

After marking time in several weak melo-

Richard Attenborough, 1952

dramas like *Eight O'Clock Walk* (1954, Lance Comfort) and *The Ship That Died of Shame* (1955, Basil Dearden) – in which suggestions of the little runt surfaced again with, in the latter, Attenborough as a malevolent, two-timing smuggler – and in a few limp comedies such as *Father's Doing Fine* (1952, Henry Cass) and *The Baby and the Battleship* (1956, Jay Lewis), the Boultings handed his career a badly-needed lifeline with *Private's Progress* (1956, John Boulting), the first of several Boulting brothers satires.

His *Private's Progress* role, a breezy con man, was repeated in the equally successful *I'm All Right, Jack* three years later. Attenborough and Dennis Price were sleazy management types exploiting the workers in order to cop a fat missiles contract from an equally unscrupulous Arab. As the plot appears about to pay off, their Arab accomplice chortles in triumph: 'We appear to have the bird by the bush in the hand.' But their delight, along with their hopes of becoming rich, collapses as the workers, prompted by Ian Carmichael, link arms to foil them.

Attenborough's association as producer with screenwriter Bryan Forbes created several impressive works, notably *The Angry Silence* (1960, Guy Green) with Attenborough as a trade unionist cruelly victimised for refusing to join a strike call, and *The League of Gentlemen* (1960, Basil Dearden), an intelligent adroitly-handled story of variously down-at-heel Army types turning to crime. As well as producing, Attenborough appeared in front of the cameras, as a member of the gang.

He produced, but made no appearance in *Whistle Down the Wind* (1961, Bryan Forbes), a charming, offbeat allegorical comedy, written and directed by Forbes, about three likably over-imaginative children in a remote Yorkshire farming community who mistake a bearded fugitive holed up in their father's barn for Jesus Christ. The following year, Attenborough produced and Forbes directed *The L-Shaped Room* (1963) a gloomy 'who's-been-sleeping-in-my-bed' drama set in Notting Hill bedsitter-land, with Leslie Caron and Tom Bell as a pair of jaded lovers.

In front of the cameras, with Forbes again providing the words, Attenborough was the smug, prickly Welsh bard with a passion for Virginia Maskell in *Only Two Can Play* (1961, Sidney Gilliatt), a juicy tongue-in-cheek romantic comedy, with Peter Sellers as a randy, down-at-heel librarian married to Miss Maskell but lusting after amorous socialite Mai Zetterling.

Attenborough was in the big-budget *The Great Escape* (1963, John Sturges) with Steve McQueen, James Coburn and Charles Bronson, three of the original 'Magnificent Seven'. It also had the director of the 'Seven', John Sturges. Though based on Paul Brickhill's book, the film bears only token resemblance to it. Attenborough played a senior RAF officer who organises a mass breakout right under enemy noses – or, to be more exact, under their barbed wire. Over seventy Allied officers initially get away, but fifty of them, including Attenborough and the POW's intelligence officer Gordon Jackson, are later rounded up and machine-gunned by peevish Gestapo officers.

The film was exciting enough but low on subtlety, as one might have expected from its Hollywood tough guy line-up. Historical accuracy was a casualty in the undignified scramble for US box office appeal – hence all the prisoners played by American stars appear as colourful,

Richard Attenborough (left) keeps a sharp lookout for his fellow robbers Terence Alexander and Keiron Moore in *The League of Gentlemen* (1960)

free-wheeling hotshots who either get clean away or survive to try again, and the Britishers, sober and sheep-like, are good only at delivering solemn eulogies and getting caught.

Attenborough was excellent in *Guns At Batasi* (1964, John Guillerman) as a wax-moustached RSM based in an African state on the verge of civil war. When a disloyal black officer attempts to seize power by murdering the native commanding officer, and Attenborough gives sanctuary to the badly-wounded CO – who has survived the murder attempt by crawling off into the bush – the British forces are sucked into a violent confrontation with the rebels. Attenborough's bull-necked professional soldier is about as pleasant as a ropeburn and is ably summed up by visiting parliamentarian Flora Robson who, believing his principles to be an inadequate reason for getting them all wiped out by rampaging troops, scornfully tells him: 'The only way you'll ever fulfil yourself is to die in action!'.

Attenborough was physically all wrong for the gaunt, bespectacled 1950s mass-murderer John Christie in *10 Rillington Place* (1970, Richard Fleischer), a flat, tasteless retelling of the grisly events leading to Christie's arrest. Even with elaborate make-up, he was unmistakably Attenborough. There might have been some point to it had an attempt been made to come to grips with Christie's ghoulish personality, or an explanation offered as to how this latter-day Jekyll-and-Hyde managed to elude justice for so long. But Attenborough's grim, zombie-like performance gave nothing away.

Attenborough has directed several elegant set-pieces, always with a tendency to overdress. *Young Winston* (1972), showing the early days of the Great Man, was satisfying on several levels. Bolt's *Oh! What a Lovely War* (1969) and *A Bridge Too Far* (1976, Richard Attenborough) suffered through an excessive number of star guest appearances – it was like being force-fed with chocolate pudding. Economies all round might have made them more appetising. Nevertheless, Attenborough has demonstrated coherence and flair in portraying major events in history – seen again in the recent *Gandhi* (1981) – and no-one can accuse him of shying away from a tough challenge.

Richard Attenborough

b. 1923. Deceptively versatile actor-producer-director, whose early-career cowardly, nervy characteristics took years to outgrow. After acting career downturn in late '50s, formed Beaver Films with Bryan Forbes, and produced many stylish successes – *The Angry Silence* (1960), *The League of Gentlemen* (1960) in which he also starred, and *Whistle Down the Wind* (1961). Has directed many fine historical superdramas, such as *Young Winston* (1972), *A Bridge Too Far* (1976) and *Gandhi* (1981) with flair and vision. Married to former actress Sheila Sim.

1942 *In Which We Serve*
1943 *Schweik's New Adventures*
1944 *The Hundred Pound Window*
1945 *Journey Together* (David Wilton)
1946 *A Matter of Life and Death* (English Pilot)
     School For Secrets (Jack Arnold)
1947 *The Man Within* (Francis Andrews)
     Dancing with Crime (Ted Peters)
     Brighton Rock (Pinky Brown)
1948 *London Belongs to Me* (Percy Boon)
     The Guinea Pig (Jack Read)
1949 *Boys In Brown* (Jackie Knowles)
     The Lost People (Jan)
1950 *Morning Departure* (Stoker Snipe)
1951 *Hell Is Sold Out* (Pierre Bonriet)
     The Magic Box (Jack Carter)
1952 *The Gift Horse* (os 'Dripper' Daniels)
     Father's Doing Fine (Dougal)
1954 *Eight O'Clock Walk* (Tom Manning)
1955 *The Ship That Died of Shame* (George Hoskins)
1956 *The Baby and the Battleship* ('Knocker' White)
     Private's Progress (Cox)
1957 *Brothers in Law* (Henry Marshall)
     The Scamp (Stephen Leigh)
1958 *Dunkirk* (John Holden)
     The Man Upstairs (Peter Watson)
     Sea of Sand (Trooper Brody)
1959 *Danger Within* (Captain Bunter Phillips)
     Jet Storm (Ernest Tilley)
     SOS Pacific (Whitey)
     I'm All Right, Jack (Sidney de Vere Cox)
1960 *The Angry Silence* (Tom Curtis)
     The League of Gentlemen (Edward Lexy)
1961 *Only Two Can Play* (Probert)
     All Night Long (Rod Hamilton)
     Whistle Down the Wind (produced)
1962 *The Dock Brief* (Fowle)
     The L-Shaped Room (produced)
1963 *The Great Escape* (USA) (Bartlett, Big 'X')
1964 *Seance on a Wet Afternoon* (Billy Savage)

The Third Secret (Alfred Price-Gorham)
Guns at Batasi (RSM Lauderdale)
1965 Flight of the Phoenix (USA) (Lew Moran)
1966 The Sand Pebbles (USA) (Frenchy)
1967 Doctor Dolittle (Albert Blossom)
1968 Only When I Larf (Silas)
The Bliss of Mrs Blossom (Robert Blossom)
1969 Oh! What a Lovely War (co-produced and directed)
David Copperfield (Mr Tungay)
The Magic Christian (Oxford Coach)
1970 The Last Grenade (General Charles Whiteley)
10 Rillington Place (John Reginald Halliday Christie)

Loot (Truscott)
A Severed Head (Palmer Anderson)
1972 Young Winston (directed)
1975 Brannigan (Commander Swann)
Ten Little Indians (Judge)
Conduct Unbecoming (Major Lionel Roach)
Rosebud (USA) (Sloat)
1976 A Bridge Too Far (directed)
1977 The Chess Players (India) (General Outram)
1978 Magic (directed)
The Human Factor (Colonel John Daintrey)
1981 Gandhi (directed)

Stanley Baker

'Mine is a hell of a face,' Stanley Baker once said. 'But it keeps me in work because there aren't many like it!' In the early days he was like William Bendix with brains, a lower order tyrant with a rugged physique and a short fuse. He stuck out like a festered thumb, and was shaping up nicely as a competent Hollywood-style 'heavy' before his bosses smoothed him out to internationalise his appeal. It did the trick and made him a star, but in the transformation some of that splendid, raw cutting edge disappeared.

He won attention as the bullying first officer in The Cruel Sea (1952, Charles Frend) – 'I'm the first lieutenant round here and don't you forget it!' Married junior officers returning from shore leave have to put up with Baker's nasty moods and taunts about 'buns in the oven' – a naval euphemism for unwanted pregnancy. Before long, he is doubled up with a suspected duodenal ulcer which prompts Denholm Elliott, an erstwhile victim of his bullying, to suggest with mock sympathy that perhaps he has a bun in the oven. Baker is taken off the ship for an operation, and peace is restored.

He was Alan Ladd's gutsy paratroop instructor in The Red Beret (1953, Terence Young), an early casualty when his parachute fails to open. Ladd dunked him in a hole in the Antarctic at the end of Hell Below Zero (1954, Mark Robson), adapted from Hammond Innes' novel The White South, for attempting some crude surgery – with an ice pick – on Ladd's tempting blonde head. Another watery grave awaited him in

Campbell's Kingdom (1957, Ralph Thomas), also from a novel by Hammond Innes, as a brutish contractor opposed to neighbour Dirk Bogarde's intrusive oil excavations.

Traces of a conscience surfaced for Baker in The Good Die Young (1954, Lewis Gilbert), an unrelentingly gloomy thriller in which he is one of a trio of misfits enticed into robbery and murder by aristocratic swine Laurence Harvey. Baker was the sympathetic one, a disfigured boxer on the skids, who is shot in the back by Harvey as he attempts to warn the police that Harvey is armed and dangerous.

Thereafter, the 'heavy' element was frequently diluted to reveal the man within, not always, in my view, a fair exchange. In Hell Drivers (1957, Cy Endfield) Baker was a paroled ex-convict looking after his crippled young brother, David McCallum, and side-stepping trouble from a psychopathic driver in a truck company in order to hold down an honest job. Muzzled by caution and concern for his brother and a need to avoid trouble, Baker was dull compared to the eye-rolling, slur-voiced villain of the piece, Patrick McGoohan. The harsh, uncompromising milieu of a trucker's life, the cheap rented accommodation, transport cafés and the like, is honestly observed. Wilfred Lawson, as a gnarled old trucker, adds his customary touch of gallows humour.

In one scene, perched in the passenger seat like a noxious pixie, he urges Baker to jeopardise life and limb in a mad race along narrow country

Stanley Baker (right) with Anthony Steel in *Checkpoint* (1956)

roads to beat McGoohan to the loading point. Baker hesitates, knowing that riding the crown of a winding narrow lane at this speed is a recipe for disaster should anything be coming the opposite way. It's a possibility which Lawson, with a toothy cackle, refuses pointblankly to contemplate.

As Henry Tudor, Baker led the overthrow of *Richard III* (1955, Laurence Olivier), a brief spot notable for the performance of his Adam's apple. He played a wandering merchant seamen who signs on with Victor MacLaglen's salvage crew in *Sea Fury* (1958, Cy Endfield) and becomes romantically involved with MacLaglen's sexy, young Spanish fianceé – a thoughtfully restrained performance which, in fairness, any competent actor might have done equally well.

In *The Angry Hills* (1959, Robert Aldrich), a tough spy thriller set in wartime Greece, Baker was a Nazi agent trying to suppress information useful to the Allies held by slippery US war correspondent Robert Mitchum. By coincidence, the role of the war correspondent was originally intended for Alan Ladd, an actor instrumental

in giving Baker some valuable screen exposure in the early days.

Bible aficionados will know that *Sodom and Gomorrah* (1962, Robert Aldrich) are not Irish expletives but ancient cities renowned for their decadence. Director Robert Aldrich attempted to draw some kind of parallel between ancient and modern self-destructive societies, but the lesson was about as coherent as two drunks explaining their failure to win a three-legged race. Baker went back to his grass roots, as a baleful, bearded bad guy.

He captained the airliner that Richard Attenborough planned to explode in *Jet Storm* (1959, Cy Endfield), a dull, good-guy role that effectively smothered his surly talents. He was in better form as a wartime infantry captain in *Yesterday's Enemy* (1959, Val Guest), leading a doomed patrol through Jap-ridden Burmese jungles. And better still in *The Criminal* (1960, Joseph Losey), a tense atmospheric thriller, as a gaolbird with a key to hidden loot who is double-crossed and eventually killed by ruthless gangland associates.

In *Blind Date* (1959, Joseph Losey) Baker was a police inspector investigating the murder of a one-time mistress of an influential Foreign Office official. The chief suspect is a struggling Dutch artist, played by Hardy Kruger, who has been giving the woman painting lessons. Because of its sensitive nature Baker's superiors want the case against Kruger wrapped up expediently; there are veiled promises of promotion should the matter be resolved to the department's satisfaction. Luckily for Kruger, however, Baker cares more for truth than self-advancement, and defies the wrath of senior colleagues to nail the real culprit.

Also in plain clothes, he was the working-class copper confronting a gun-toting neurotic holed up in a schoolroom in *Violent Playground* (1958, Basil Dearden). Baker was a genuine man of the streets, waging a private war not only against urban crime but against the conditions which breed it. Filmed documentary-style on the streets of Liverpool, *Violent Playground* has pace and realism and pulls off that cinematic rarity – depicting delinquency without plunging into hysterics every other frame.

Baker led the defence of Rorke's Drift against 4,000 angry tribesmen in *Zulu* (1963, Cy Endfield), an overdressed, tedious film notable only for its belated acknowledgement of the star qualities of Michael Caine, seen in his first major role as Baker's plummy-voiced second-in-command. In his last major film, *Innocent Bystanders* (1972, Peter Collinson), Baker was an ageing secret agent whose nerve is suspect and whom his departmental bosses are ready to sacrifice to the KGB in exchange for a high-ranking fugitive Russian scientist. Scripted by James Mitchell, creator of TV's *Callan*, from which the film at times seems to borrow rather heavily – notably in the depicted cynicism of the central character and the sadistic challenge he faces from within his own department – *Innocent Bystanders* proved a worthwhile epitaph, a tough, physical thriller of the kind Baker made his name with.

Stanley Baker

1928-1976. Tough guy actor with a gentle side. Film debut in *Undercover* (1943). Formed Oakhurst Productions and became producer, notably *Zulu* (1963) and *Robbery* (1967) in which he starred. Knighted in 1975.

1949 *All Over the Town* (uncredited)
1950 *Your Witness* (uncredited)
1951 *The Rossiter Case* (Joe)
   Cloudburst (uncredited)
   Home to Danger (Willie Dougan)
   Captain Horatio Hornblower (Mr Harrison)
1952 *Whispering Smith Hits London* (uncredited)
1953 *The Cruel Sea* (First Officer Bennett)
   The Red Beret (Breton)
   The Telltale Heart (short) (Edgar Allan Poe)
1954 *Hell Below Zero* (Erik Bland)
   The Good Die Young (Mike)
   Beautiful Stranger (Louis Galt)
   Knights of the Round Table (Modred)
1955 *Richard III* (Henry Tudor)
1956 *Child In the House* (Stephen Lorimer)
   A Hill In Korea (Corporal Ryker)
   Checkpoint (O'Donovan)
1957 *Hell Drivers* (Tom Yately)
   Campbell's Kingdom (Owen Morgan)
1958 *Violent Playground* (Sgt. Truman)
   Sea Fury (Abel Hewson)
1959 *The Angry Hills* (Konrad Heisler)
   Yesterday's Enemy (Captain Langford)
   Jet Storm (Captain Bardow)

Stanley Baker gets a bullet in the chest in *Violent Playground* (1958)

Blind Date (Inspector Morgan)
1960 *Hell is a City* (Insp Martineau)
The Criminal (Johnny Bannion)
1961 *The Guns of Navarone* (CPO Brown)
1962 *A Prize of Arms* (Turpin)
The Man Who Finally Died (Joe Newman)
Sodom and Gomorrah (Astarogh)
1963 *Zulu* (also co-produced) (Lt John Chard)
1965 *Dingaka* (Tom Davis)

1967 *Sands of the Kalahari* (also co-produced) (Bain)
Accident (Charley)
Robbery (also co-produced) (Paul Clifton)
1968 *Where's Jack* (Jonathan Wild)
1969 *The Games* (Bill Oliver)
1970 *The Last Grenade* (Maj Harry Grigsby)
Perfect Friday (Mr Graham)
1972 *Innocent Bystanders* (John Craig)

Ian Bannen

Ian Bannen, we're told, chose acting instead of becoming a monk. The brothers' loss was our gain. Among the true connoisseurs of naturalistic acting, the relatively unsung Bannen is a force to reckon with. He's a stealthy performer, with limpid eyes and the well-scrubbed good looks of a head prefect; but Bannen can make us forget those looks when he turns on the emotional high tension that is a measure of his skill, which seems equally unstretched whether he's attempting raffish louts, wheedling-type idiots or rather intense nice guys.

His film career began in 1956, in the Boulting Brothers' *Private's Progress*, as one of the platoon. He played a workman in *The Long Arm* (1956, Charles Frend), an Ealing drama about the pursuit of an elusive safecracker by Superintendent Jack Hawkins. Bannen was thirteenth in the credits list, one above Alec McCowen, an actor similar in style.

He was a member of barmaid Belinda Lee's garrulous Italian family in *Miracle In Soho* (1957, Julian Aymes), a syrupy, lower-orders love story, with John Gregson as Miss Lee's whimsical Irish road-mender boyfriend. 'Miracle' is right – nothing less could transform the grubbiest square mile in London into a scene befitting a Christmas card!

In *Carlton-Browne of the FO* (1959, Roy Boulting) he was a molasses-faced colonial-type king, stirring up the tropical fun with Peter Sellers and Terry-Thomas. Comedy never seemed Bannen's natural stamping ground, but he put up a lively show as the love-lorn student in *A French Mistress* (1960, Roy Boulting). Bannen's problem is that his dream girl, French teacher Agnes Laurent, might also be his own half-sister, due to a long-ago Alpine love-in by his father, school headmaster Cecil Parker. The Boultings

rely on several familiar character actors like Parker, Raymond Huntley and Kenneth Griffith to carry this flimsy confection through to an (almost) satisfactory conclusion, and though they strut their stuff like the troupers they are, the end product seems scarcely worth their efforts.

Bannen had a good part in *The Hill* (1965, Sidney Lumet) as an NCO in the hell-hole military detention camp where bullies and no-goods, suitably striped and pipped, rule the compound. Sean Connery was a rebel prisoner who takes the law into his own hands and kills the sadistic redcap who has caused the death of a fellow prisoner. Bannen played an NCO, disgusted by what is happening but fearful of reprisals if he is seen hobnobbing with the victims – a neat, clipped performance in a tough, thought-provoking film.

He supported George C. Scott in *Jane Eyre* (1970, Delbert Mann) as the sad-eyed vicar with whom Jane, played by Susannah York, finds temporary solace after discovering that Rochester (Scott) is married and thus unattainable. Bannen loses out when passion proves stronger than kindness.

In *Fright* (1971, Peter Collinson) Bannen had a role where he could really work up a lather, as an institutionalised loony who breaks out to revenge himself on ex-wife Honor Blackman, whose current boyfriend, George Cole – understandably in view of Honor's earlier liaison – cannot wait to whisk her abroad. Poor George is a nice enough type and Miss Blackman is certainly no femme fatale – but what matters is that Bannen believes she is, and that's enough to put everyone in the house, including Susan George as a mini-skirted baby-sitter, in fear of their lives.

Fright was one of those creepy-old-house melodramas where none of the window-catches

Ian Bannen (second right) with Marie Burke, Rosalie Crutchley, Peter Illing and Belinda Lee in *Miracle in Soho* (1957)

fit and unseen prowlers lurk asthmatically just out of camera range. Bannen tricks his way into the house where his baby son is being looked after by Miss George, and in his deranged state he imagines that the terrified baby-sitter is his ex-wife and sexually assaults her – at least, that's his excuse! Imaginative camera work throughout puts the audience in the position of Bannen's potential victims, and the soundtrack gives everyday kitchen happenings such as a boiling kettle or a dripping tap a neat prickly menace.

One of Bannen's meatiest roles for ages, as a pathetic child-molester, occurred in *The Offence* (1972, Sidney Lumet). Sean Connery played the long-serving police inspector driven crazy by the years of cruelty and violent death he has witnessed. Bannen's arrest and whining-rat conduct in custody proves too much for Connery's deteriorating mental state, and Connery kills him during a violent interrogation after Bannen has accused him of being a repressed pederast. 'There's nothing I can say to you that you haven't already thought of a million times!' croons Bannen just before Connery erupts. But is the killing caused by justifiable outrage or

murderous self-disgust? That's the question which visiting CID super-hawk Trevor Howard has to grapple with, alas not very invigoratingly.

Ian Bannen
b. 1928. Versatile, virile dependable Scotsborn character player, can be either clean-cut hero, romantic lead or sinister villain with equal impact.

1956 *Private's Progress* (Pte Horrocks)
     The Long Arm (Workman)
1957 *Miracle in Soho* (Filippo Gozzi)
     Yangtse Incident (Bannister)
     The Birthday Present (Assistant)
1958 *A Tale of Two Cities* (Gabelle)
     Behind the Mask (Alan Crabtree)
     She Didn't Say No (Peter Howard)
1959 *Carlton-Browne of the FO* (King Loris)
1960 *Suspect* (Alan Andrews)
     A French Mistress (Colin Crane)
1961 *Macbeth* (Macduff)
1962 *Station Six Sahara* (Fletcher)
1963 *Psyche 59* (Paul)
1964 *Mister Moses* (Robert)

| 1965 | The Hill (Sgt Charlie Harris) | 1973 | The Mackintosh Man (Slade) |

1965   *The Hill* (Sgt Charlie Harris)
       Rotten To the Core (Lt Percy Vine)
       The Flight of the Phoenix (Crow)
1967   *The Sailor from Gibraltar* (Alan)
1968   *Lock Up Your Daughters* (Ramble)
1969   *Too Late the Hero* (Thornton)
1971   *The Deserter* (USA) (Crawford)
       Fright (Brian)
       Jane Eyre (Rev St John Rivers)
1972   *Doomwatch* (Dr Del Shaw)
       The Offence (Baxter)

1973   *The Mackintosh Man* (Slade)
       From Beyond The Grave (Christopher Lowe)
1975   *Bite the Bullet* (USA) (Norfolk)
1976   *Jesus of Nazareth* (TV) (Amos)
1977   *The Sweeney* (Baker)
1979   *Watcher In the Woods* (John Keller)
       Tinker, Tailor, Soldier, Spy (TV) (Jim Prideaux)
1980   *Eye of the Needle* (Godliman)
       Night Crossing (Joseph Keller)

Alfie Bass

In *Alfie* (1966, Lewis Gilbert), Bill Naughton's bitter comedy about the comeuppance of a randy London yobbo played with a raunchy insolence by Michael Caine, Alfie Bass was the nervy sanatorium patient whom Caine befriends during a brief stay there and whose mousey wife falls prey to Caine's mongrel charm. As Bass frets away the final minutes before her visit, Caine blithely suggests she might have taken off with the milkman. When she arrives late, flustered and laden with eggs and marmalade, their conversation is a mess of small talk and awkward silences. 'It's not easy with their sort of mentality,' Caine tells us with an apologetic shrug.

Bass's forte has been for playing whimsical, slightly down-at-heel Cockney characters, whose natural habitat would be the dockland café, the boxing gym or the street market and to whom he added an engaging warmth and sanguinity. Being the authentic Londoner made it easy, he says. And he certainly made it look easy.

Playing basically the same character, Bass has hopped chirpily from drama to comedy and into costume pieces and back like an energised sparrow. With the crossover of cinema audiences to television during the late fifties, Bass switched media too and was an instant success as the resourceful 'Excused Boots' Bisley in the long running *Army Game* TV series, and its patchy TV spin-off *Bootsie and Snudge*, which depicted the amiable layabout adjusting to civvy street in the company of his snobby, overbearing RSM, played by Bill Fraser.

There was a time when no British film seemed complete without Alfie Bass popping up in some guise or other. He was a redcoat in *Holiday Camp* (1947, Ken Annakin), a military hospital orderly in *The Hasty Heart* (1949, Vincent Sherman), a newspaper vendor in *The Galloping Major* (1951, Henry Cornelius), one of the dressing-room retinue in *The Square Ring* (1953, Basil Dearden). The effect of these and other brief appearances was to establish him as a familiar supporting face, and, having made the right impression with a character as authentically London as a pot of jellied eels, Bass's career was set fair for life.

In *The Lavender Hill Mob* (1951, Charles Crichton), Ealing's gentle comedy about a bullion snatch by two genial fellow-lodgers, Bass was their lookout, a timid, minor villain who prefers watching the Test Match to a trip to Paris for a triumphant shareout of the proceeds.

At the *Sailor Beware* (1956, Gordon Parry) nuptials, Bass was the church organist, sneaking furtive puffs on a cigarette between chords of the wedding march; fortunately for Bass, he is tucked tidily out of sight of the groom's bossy, foghorn mum-in-law Peggy Mount. In *A Tale of Two Cities* (1958, Ralph Thomas), he was servant to nobleman Cecil Parker for whose daughter the sad, dissolute Dirk Bogarde, as Sydney Carton, does his 'far, far better thing'; and he ran the junkshop where Dennis Waterman helped out in *Up the Junction* (1967, Peter Collinson).

In Roman Polanski's *Dance of the Vampires* (1967, Roman Polanski) Bass was a Jewish vampire with nothing to fear from a crucifix. When a tasty female victim misguidedly brandishes one in front of him to save her pretty neck, Bass gleefully brushes it aside, grinning: 'Have *you* got the wrong vampire!'

Bass was in one of the more tolerable episodes of *The Magnificent Seven Deadly Sins* (1971,

19

Stanley Holloway (left), Alfie Bass (centre) and Sidney James count up the loot in *The Lavender Hill Mob* (1951)

Graham Stark), as a working-class type out for a leisurely drive with his wife in the ancient family roadster, who encounters head-on in a narrow lane a toffee-nosed twit – that's Ian Carmichael – in a Rolls Royce. The lane is too narrow for either car to pass, and since neither driver will give way, insults and fisticuffs result. When this, too, fails to produce an outright decision, AA and RAC bikemen get involved, each snottily defending his own paid-up member. In the end the crisis, which has been watched throughout with bored cynicism by the protagonists' 'seen-it-all-before' wives, is resolved by a bicycling bobby who declares Bass's car unfit for the road. But as Carmichael gloatingly applauds the decision, he suddenly realises he has been facing in the wrong direction all the time.

Alfie Bass
b. 1921. Whimsical Jewish character actor, predominantly Cockney roles. Film debut *Johnny Frenchman* (1945). Numerous TV roles,

notably Bootsie in *The Army Game* and *Bootsie and Snudge* sequel.

1945 *Johnny Frenchman* (uncredited)
    Brief Encounter (unbilled)
    Perfect Strangers (uncredited)
1947 *Holiday Camp* (Redcoat)
    It Always Rains on Sunday (Dicey Perkins)
1948 *Vice Versa* (Urchin)
    The Monkey's Paw (Manager)
1949 *The Hasty Heart* (Orderly)
    Boys In Brown (Basher)
    Stage Fright (uncredited)
1950 *Man on the Run* (uncredited)
1951 *Pool of London* (Alf)
    Talk of a Million (Lorcan)
    The Galloping Major (Newsboy)
    The Lavender Hill Mob (Shorty)
    High Treason (uncredited)
1952 *Brandy For the Parson* (Dallyn)
    Derby Day (Spider Wilkes)
    The Planter's Wife (Soldier)

Made In Heaven (Mr Jenkins)
1953 Top of the Form (Arty Jones)
The Square Ring (Frank Forbes)
1954 Time Is My Enemy (Ernie Gordon)
The Angel Who Pawned Her Harp
(Lennox)
To Dorothy a Son (Taxi-driver)
The Passing Stranger (Harry)
Make Me an Offer (Fred Frames)
Svengali (Carrell)
1951 Murder By Proxy (Ernie)
The Night My Number Came Up (Soldier)
A Kid For Two Farthings (Alf)
The Bespoke Overcoat (short) (Fender)
1956 Jumping For Joy (Blagg)
Child In the House (Ticket Collector)
Behind the Headlines (Sammy)
A Touch of the Sun (May)
1957 No Road Back (Rudge Haven)
Carry On Admiral (Orderly)

Hell Drivers (Tinker)
1958 A Tale of Two Cities (Jerry Cruncher)
I Was Monty's Double (Man)
I Only Arsked ('Excused Boots' Bisley)
1960 The Millionairess (Fish Curer)
1965 Help! (Doorman)
Doctor In Clover (Fleming)
1966 Alfie (Harry)
The Sandwich Man (Yachtsman)
A Funny Thing Happened on the Way to the
Forum (Gatekeeper)
1967 Dance of the Vampires (Shagal)
A Challenge For Robin Hood (Merchant)
Up the Junction (Charlie)
1971 The Magnificent Seven Deadly Sins
(Spooner)
1976 The Chiffy Kids (Tramp)
Come Play With Me (Kelly)
1977 Revenge of the Pink Panther (Fernet)
1978 Moonraker (Consumptive Italian)

Alan Bates

'For most actors it's enough that they manage one mood with confidence. Alan Bates effects three or four moods at the same time!' So says Michael Cacoyannis, who directed Bates in *Zorba the Greek* (1964). Of the three new-wave young actors swept to prominence in the early 1960s – the others being Finney and Courtenay – Bates had a quality the other two lacked: warmth. Finney was the brash bulldog with a juicy bone between his teeth, Courtenay the wiry stray skulking just out of reach of the dog warden's net, and Bates the moist-eyed collie alert to all the intriguing aromas carried on the wind.

Bates' film credits are relatively short, but multi-coloured. He played Olivier's son in *The Entertainer* (1960, Tony Richardson), but the first film of note was *Whistle Down the Wind* (1961, Bryan Forbes), with Bates as the bearded fugitive holed up in a Yorkshire barn whom three imaginative schoolchildren believe to be Jesus Christ. They obligingly bring him food, and hope, in return, that he will dash off an occasional miracle. When word gets out and Bates is hauled off by the authorities, his plight and treatment merely compound the Christ-like imagery.

A Kind of Loving (1962, John Schlesinger) established Bates as a key performer of his genera-

tion in a role which delineated youthful British working class as sharply as James Dean had captured American juvenile frustration less than a decade before. Bates was a raunchy young draughtsman whose sexual encounters with an attractive but rather dull office-girl, played by June Ritchie, lead to pregnancy and marriage. Tensions increase when circumstances force the young couple to move in with Miss Ritchie's shrewish mother – a real, venom-spitting, mock-genteel better-than-thou performance here from Thora Hird – and the inevitable fights and separations occur, with Miss Ritchie siding with her more forceful mother, and Bates sliding further and further off the marital rails.

When mum-in-law lambasts him for taking advantage of her daughter, Bates tells her, bluntly, that she needed little persuasion. 'If it hadn't been me, it would have been somebody else,' he growls. Later, returning from a drinking spree, he inadvertently vomits all over her new carpet. 'You filthy disgusting article,' she screams at him, but Bates is evidently pleased at having shown her, in the most graphic way the circumstances will allow, exactly how he feels about being her son-in-law.

This was Schlesinger's first big movie, and he crowned it with top performances from a (then)

21

Alan Bates confronts his 'flock' in *Whistle Down the Wind* (1961)

relatively little known cast. Its flavour of Midlands industrial life has Lowry-like whiffs of reality and simplicity, and the emotional troubles of the hard-hit young couple are honestly – and in view of the period, courageously – depicted. Bates was marvellous as the sinful lad caught in the crossfire and June Ritchie equally excellent as the shallow Ingrid.

For me, *A Kind of Loving* is impressively real, and its degree of observation is more shrewdly applied than in either *Room at the Top* or *Saturday Night and Sunday Morning*. For example, the factory dance scene, all phoney bonhomie and with the boss's self-conscious mock-hilarity, is only too horribly true-to-life. 'It came at the end of those films with a similar industrial location but it was the only one of the bunch which dealt with extremely ordinary people!' says Bates.

In *Nothing But the Best* (1964, Clive Donner) he was a ruthless social climber hankering after the boss's daughter and his rival's E-type Jaguar – but not for long, for under the seedy bloodshot eyes of a former member of the genteel set, Bates

acquires the necessary skills to outmanoeuvre his pompous rival and get the girl. En route, however, he is obliged to strangle his one-time mentor – played with twitchy relish by Denholm Elliott – with one of his old school ties, not realising that Elliott was the black sheep of the family he has set his mind on marrying into.

The film cuts off at the point where Elliott's remains, hitherto tidily stashed out of sight in his landlady's basement, are uncovered, and we are left to conjure up for ourselves Bates' ultimate fate. He deserves to shift the blame, and from what we have seen of his nimble-footedness, most probably does – the most likely fall-girl being his ex-landlady, who has known all along that Bates murdered his fellow-lodger but kept quiet about it because Bates was always willing to hop into her bed to keep her happy.

Director Clive Donner keeps the mayhem bubbling at a fast pace, and Bates' spirited conman is such a likable rogue that most people will want him to succeed, beyond the point where the film ends. Despite the obvious temptations a sequel was never made, and this was the right decision.

In *Far From the Madding Crowd* (1967, John Schlesinger), Thomas Hardy's melodramatic view of Wessex rural life during the last century, director Schlesinger chose for three of the four central roles artistes whose works he knew well. Julie Christie, as the rich headstrong Bathsheba Everdene, had been virtually a Schlesinger discovery, in *Billy Liar*; Bates and Peter Finch (as rivals for Miss Christie's hand in marriage) are associated with other important Schlesinger films, *A Kind of Loving* and *Sunday Bloody Sunday*. Terence Stamp was the philandering Grenadier sergeant who gets Miss Christie to the altar while the other two are left dithering at the starting-gate.

Schlesinger's canvas was faithful to Hardy's view of life – sprawling, colourful, tragic. Bates was an honest rustic whose proposal of marriage Miss Christie rejects because she does not love him; Finch as a neighbouring gentleman farmer is no more successful than Bates, but a lot more persistent. To their horror, she marries Stamp, whose one-time fianceé dies in poverty shortly afterwards, giving birth to his child. When Stamp finds out about her fate, his attitude to Miss Christie degenerates into surly contempt, and he vanishes by means of a faked drowning accident.

Seizing what he reckons must be his best chance of catching the rebounding Miss Christie, Finch hosts a lavish party in her honour, but Stamp barges in and humiliates her in full view of the startled locals. Finch retaliates by shooting him, for which he is later hanged. Bates, the least favoured of her three boyfriends of the previous year, is now the only one left, and after a quick reappraisal of her fortunes, she glides smoothly into his gruff but boringly loyal arms.

For a film loaded with 1960s sex symbols, it has curiously little passion, except for Stamp's sensuous sabre-swinging during a courtship romp in the fields. Bates is about as passionate as a boiled sweet and Finch grovels in the dust like a demented ferret. Stamp looks raffish enough in his smart uniform, as if Errol Flynn had sloped off for a quick smoke and got separated from the rest of the Light Brigade, but he is more caricature than real man.

The bare-buff firelit wrestling scene with Oliver Reed obscures several of the real merits of *Women In Love* (1969, Ken Russell). Again, the sense of period is sharply observed as is D. H.

Lawrence's pungent sex-and-class warfare saga in the strident performances of Glenda Jackson and Jennie Linden as the liberated sisters who change the individual destinies of two former school chums. Bates played an intellectual dreamer whose attraction to Miss Linden is so obvious from their first meeting that fiancée Eleanor Bron has every reason to be unsettled. When he explains his flirtation as 'an act of pure spontaneity,' Miss Bron scoffs 'My arse!'

Reed was the son of a bullying pit-owner who would like to redress the effects on the community of his father's mismanagement but instead dumps his stricken conscience into the hot lap of Glenda Jackson, who can nail amorous lads to the floor with shouts of 'How are your thighs? I want to drown in hot, physical naked flesh!' Much of it is bravado, however, for when Miss Jackson is finally shown the way by the amorous Reed, she begins to wish that he would 'love me a little more and want me a little less'. When their romance peters out during a holiday in Switzerland, Reed goes stumbling off into the snowy Alps to die, an act of which Bates would thoroughly approve. Earlier, discussing the incident in which Reed's newly-wed sister had drowned along with her husband in an accident on the family's estate, Bates assures Reed, 'There's nothing wrong with death. Nothing better'.

This is a sombre, moderately successful adaptation of Lawrence's fiery novel, and Ken Russell peppers it with several fiery images. Regrettably, the final result is not nearly as good as the sum of its individual scenes and Bates, in particular, seems unable to develop his character beyond that of a likable pastiche.

The Go-Between (1970, Joseph Losey) reunited Bates with Julie Christie, in L. P. Hartley's turn-of-the-century novel about a cool, aristocratic lady's doomed love for a rough-hewn tenant farmer. Unable to meet socially or contemplate marriage with Miss Christie, he enlists the help of a young house guest, played by Dominic Guard, whose adolescent mind is also much taken by her beauty, to carry notes between the lovers thus making it possible for them to meet in secret. At first the boy is happy to do what he is asked, unaware that the envelopes contain passionate declarations of love, but later after reading one of the letters, his attitude changes. When Miss Christie's coldly disapproving mother – played by Margaret Leighton – confronts him with his duplicity, he leads her to expect'. What people have come to expect are quiet performances of considerable sensitivity, depth and detail, each characterisation individual in its own right, and more than a few of them genuinely astounding.

Alan Bates
b. 1934. Handsome international star since early 1960s 'realism' movies (*The Entertainer, A Kind of Loving, The Caretaker*, etc). Most impressive in reflective, romantically inclined figures (*Far From the Madding Crowd*) or strong-willed loners (*The Fixer*). Frequently works on the stage in Simon Gray plays (*Butley*, etc). Was Henchard in BBC TV's *Mayor of Casterbridge*.

1960 *The Entertainer* (Frank Rice)
1961 *Whistle Down the Wind* (Arthur Blakey)
1962 *A Kind of Loving* (Vic Brown)
1963 *The Running Man* (Stephen Maddox)
      The Caretaker (Mick)
1964 *Nothing But the Best* (Jimmy Brewster)
      Zorba the Greek (Basil)
1966 *Georgy Girl* (Jos)
1967 *Far From the Madding Crowd* (Gabriel Oak)
1969 *Women In Love* (Rupert Birkin)
1970 *The Go-Between* (Ted Burgess)
      The Fixer (Yakov Bok)
1971 *A Day In the Death of Joe Egg* (Brian)
1974 *Three Sisters* (Vershinin)
      Butley (Ben Butley)
      Impossible Object (Harry)
1975 *In Celebration* (Andrew Shaw)
      Royal Flash (Rudi Von Starnberg)
1977 *An Unmarried Woman* (USA) (Saul Keplan)
      The Shout (Charles Crossley)
1978 *The Rose* (USA) (Rudge)
1979 *Nijinsky* (Sergei Diaghilev)
1980 *Very Like a Whale* (Sir Jack Mellor)
1981 *Quartet* (H. J. Heidler)

Alan Bates finds something suspicious on the line in *The Shout* (1977)

Bates' farm where the couple are caught making love. The shock to the lad's senses is more than he can bear.

The film probes with a delicate touch the hypocrisy and tensions underlying the higher echelons of Edwardian society, counterpointing the passion and deceit with leisurely shots of rural England at its most typical, whether bathed in soft-focus sunlight or being gently hosed down by freak storms. David Shipman thought Bates' performance 'as uncertain as his Norfolk accent'.

Early in his career Bates made up his mind to follow his instincts even if it led to obscurity – 'I want every film or play I do to cut across the previous one, that way people won't know what to

Robert Beatty

Robert Beatty once had one of the best groomed – and more famous – thatches in Britain, thanks to a bathroom product which he publicised for years. Now a grizzled senior citizen with hardly a strand missing, he is a walking endorsement of everything the product claimed. Alas, preserving

his once-vigorous career was not so easy for the Canadian leading man with the pleasantly lopsided grin and a jawline contoured like a rusty anchor.

Beatty was a radio star in Canada during the 1930s, but reasoning that stardom in Canada equates with being known to less than 2½ per cent of the world, Beatty came to London and RADA, hoping to up the percentage by at least the same amount. He more than succeeded in this modest ambition, beginning with appearances in several top-line wartime movies including *Dangerous Moonlight* (1941, Brian Desmond Hurst), *49th Parallel* (1941, Michael Powell), *One of Our Aircraft Is Missing* (1941, Michael Powell, Emeric Pressburger) and *San Demetrio London* (1943, Charles Frend).

Of his early post-war films, only *Odd Man Out* (1947, Carol Reed) had the stamp of real quality. In it Beatty was a friend of wounded IRA fugitive James Mason.

In *Her Favourite Husband* (1950, Mario Soldati) Beatty had two roles – of a ripsnorting gangster departed to his native Italy and of his timid, bank clerk lookalike. Release of the film was delayed while censors – believe it or not – debated whether or not to allow a scene where Beatty spanks Jean Kent. He was the villain opposite Walter Pidgeon in *Calling Bulldog Drummond* (1951, Victor Saville), and presented a brief cameo, Lord Beaverbrook, in *The Magic Box* (1951, John Boulting).

His busiest period film-wise began in 1952. He was an IRA villain in *The Gentle Gunman* (1952, Compton Bennett), an ambitious attempt to go against type which failed. A younger actor was needed to play the washed-up boxer with wife and money problems in *The Square Ring* (1953, Basil Dearden), but Beatty was chosen. At the age of forty-four, one would think Beatty's biggest problem would be passing the physical; nevertheless it was a nice idea, set in the dressing room of a provincial boxing promotion. The lifestyles of various boxers are seen in sharp relief – one-time champion Beatty is trying to regain former glories and hold his fragile marriage together; Ronald Lewis is a young Welsh fighter who learns a few dirty tricks the hard way; Maxwell Reed is a crooked fighter who plans to take a dive in the 4th round, but changes his mind; Bill Owen is a jaunty, woman-chasing lightweight worried about damaging his profile.

The dialogue sounds ring-rusty in places – 'Every time you took a beating they were hitting me,' complains Beatty's strung-out wife as the ex-champ gets ready for the contest, but the back-stage atmosphere feels authentic enough, as triumph and tragedy rub together like the spare gumshields in Beatty's overnight bag. Star of this modest but effective museum-piece was Jack Warner, as a sympathetic corner-man.

Warner co-starred with Beatty again later the same year in the excellent *Albert RN* (1953, Lewis Gilbert), a POW escape drama based on fact, in

Robert Beatty (left) on the listening end of James Robertson Justice's advice in *Wings of Danger* (1952)

(Left to right) Robert Beatty, Ferdy Mayne and Anton Diffring in *Where Eagles Dare* (1969)

which a group of prisoners fabricate a dummy which they conceal in a washroom outside the camp. The dummy, suitably uniformed, is carried back to camp replacing one of the workparty – thus fooling the dozy guards – while a real member of the workparty heads for home. Warner was the senior British officer, and Beatty an expatriate Canadian Air Force prisoner.

Beatty was an airline pilot in *Out of the Clouds* (1955, Michael Relph, Basil Dearden), and a worried parent whose small son is sealed inside an airtight bank vault in *Time Lock* (1957, Gerald Thomas). Perhaps his most memorable role of the period was as the womanising Yank on vacation in *The Amorous Prawn* (1962, Anthony Kimmins), a light romantic comedy about a business-minded general's wife, played by Joan Greenwood, who connives with the general's personal staff to convert the Scottish country mansion at which they are staying into a holiday hotel while her husband is absent on War Office business. The plan is to earn extra revenue so that they can afford the cottage of her dreams when he retires. But complications quickly set in, one of them being Beatty, who wants Miss Greenwood all to himself. When the unsuspect-

ing general, played by Cecil Parker, returns to find Beatty chasing his wife round the garden, he sighs, 'Anyone would think this place was a damned hotel!' – unaware, till Miss Greenwood confesses what she has done, that it is!

During the sixties and seventies Beatty's film work was sporadic, to put it kindly. In *Where Eagles Dare* (1969, Brian G. Hutton) he was the target whom commandos Richard Burton and Clint Eastwood are ordered to rescue from the Nazis' Swiss stronghold, supposedly a US Army general, one of Eisenhower's inner circle co-ordinating the Invasion of Europe and so, obviously, a prisoner whose tongue the enemy would like to loosen. After Burton and Eastwood literally storm the place, they discover that Beatty is not a military bigwig but an ordinary dog-soldier elevated to a phoney rank to confuse and rattle the enemy, and succeeding admirably.

He had another one-scene cameo in *Sitting Target* (1972, Douglas Hickox) as a grizzled old gun dealer who equips crazed jailbreaker Oliver Reed with the means to kill the man who has been carrying on an affair with his wife while Reed has been cooped up in prison.

Beatty admits that life has not been an easy

ride all the way, but blames himself primarily for the bumps he has taken, such as his three unsuccessful marriages and his disagreements with the Inland Revenue. In *The Square Ring*, as the aging boxer plunging headlong into yet another crisis, he tells an enterprising novice fighter: 'Sometimes you win, sometimes you lose; there's nothing else to it!' It's Robert Beatty's recipe for life.

Robert Beatty

b. 1909. Craggy Canadian-born leading man during 1940s and 1950s, popular as virile hero in contemporary action films. Star of early TV cops-and-robbers series *(Dial 999)* and hair-care product advertising. Still occasionally pops up in TV drama, barely recognisable behind a grey beard.

1938 *Murder in Soho*
1939 *Mein Kampf, My Crimes*
1941 *Dangerous Moonlight*
     49th Parallel
     One of Our Aircraft Is Missing
1942 *Suspected Person*
1943 *San Demetrio London*
1944 *It Happened One Sunday*
1946 *Appointment With Crime* (Inspector Rogers)
1947 *Odd Man Out* (Dennis)
     Green Fingers (Thomas Stone)
1948 *Against the Wind* (Father Phillip)
     Counterblast (Dr Rankin)
     Another Shore (Gulliver Shiels)
     Portrait From Life (Campbell Reid)
1950 *The Twenty Questions Murder Mystery* (Bob Beacham)
     Her Favourite Husband (Antonio/Leo)
1951 *Captain Horatio Hornblower* (Lieutenant William Bush)
     Calling Bulldog Drummond (Guns)
     The Magic Box (Lord Beaverbrook)
1952 *Wings of Danger* (Nick Talbot)
     The Gentle Gunman (Shinto)
1953 *The Net* (Sam Seagram)
     The Oracle (Bob Jefferson)
     The Square Ring (Kid Curtis)
     The Broken Horseshoe (Dr Mark Fenton)
     Albert RN (Lieutenant Jim Reid)
1955 *Out of the Clouds* (Nick Melbourne)
     Portrait of Alison (Tim Forrester)
1957 *Time Lock* (Pete Dawson)
     Tarzan and the Lost Safari (Tusker Hawkins)
1960 *The Shakedown* (Inspector Jarvis)
1962 *The Amorous Prawn* (Larry Hoffman)
1968 *2001: A Space Odyssey* (Halvorsen)
1969 *Where Eagles Dare* (Cartwright Jones)
1972 *Sitting Target* (Gun Dealer)

Reginald Beckwith

Reginald Beckwith always looked neat and snug behind a counter. That gnomish appearance and prissy manner embodied the popular idea of how minor civil servants, scoutmasters, clergymen, publicans, hotel receptionists, manservants and the like behaved, and during his very active film career, Beckwith played them all. He turned servility into a minor art form and dished it up with an occasional touch of refined mockery worthy of the great clowns.

Though comedy was undoubtedly Beckwith's strongest card, he surfaced regularly in the unlikeliest places. Who would have expected him to turn up as one of Captain Scott's courageous real-life Antarctic explorers, yet there he was, mushing gamely through the snow alongside John Mills and other true-blues in *Scott of the Antarctic* (1948, Charles Frend). Beckwith played 'Birdie' Bowers, the plucky uncomplaining naval officer who perishes with Scott (John Mills) and a third explorer at the end of the long trail, a mere 11 miles from rescue.

Even when a succession of comedy parts made it difficult to take him seriously, Beckwith continued to pop up unexpectedly, sometimes at the expense of the subject material. When, for example, that most innocent of English faces appeared under a Nazi peaked cap in a well-meaning, modestly produced real-life POW drama *The Password Is Courage* (1962, Andrew Stone), the password quickly became something else.

Far from being the dithery little twerp he portrayed, Beckwith was an accomplished stage craftsman and playwright. His *Boys In Brown* was filmed in 1949 with Jack Warner, Dirk Bogarde and Richard Attenborough, and during his career Beckwith produced several stage successes.

Reginald Beckwith (left) stands up for his rights against burly policeman James Copeland in *The Thirty-nine Steps* (1959)

junkman Ronald Shiner out of the clutches of some nasty spivs led by John Slater whom Shiner has antagonised. It was behind-the-counter time yet again in *A Shot in the Dark* (1964, Blake Edwards), as the startled nudist camp receptionist invaded by the Sûreté police after a murder has been committed on the premises. When harrassed police commissioner Herbert Lom starts leaning on everyone in sight, Beckwith shows his consternation but keeps everything else, including his roly-poly self, tastefully under wraps.

Reginald Beckwith

1908-1965. Familiar face, notable for prim, servile cameos. On stage from 1926, and a capable stage writer (eg *The Boys In Brown*, 1940). Film debut in *Freedom Radio* (1941).

As with Alfie Bass, most of Beckwith's appearances were brief, but their sheer frequency wore you down. He was a scoutmaster in *Brandy For the Parson* (1952, John Eldridge), a politician in *Penny Princess* (1952, Val Guest), a photographer in *Innocents In Paris* (1953, Gordon Parry), a vicar in *Charley Moon* (1956, Guy Hamilton). As a railway union official in *The Titfield Thunderbolt* (1953, Charles Crichton), he was one of several voices opposed to an amateur consortium getting a licence to operate its local branch line independently. Characteristically, Beckwith's voice is only timidly raised.

He was a curious choice for Friar Tuck in *Men of Sherwood Forest* (1954, Val Guest), but no worse than the same film's Robin Hood, American light comedy actor Don Taylor. By comparison, Beckwith gave a nugget of a performance as Gregory Peck's fussy aide in *The Million Pound Note* (1954, Ronald Neame).

In the fifties version of John Buchan's *The Thirty-nine Steps* (1959, Ralph Thomas) he was an understanding out-of-the-way publican who shields handcuffed fugitives Kenneth More and Taina Elg during their flight from enemy agents.

In *The Night We Got the Bird* (1961, Darcy Conyers), a mindless farce about a reincarnated parrot, Beckwith was a junk dealer known as Chippendale Charlie, who tries to keep fellow

1948 *Scott Of The Antarctic* (Lieutenant H. R. Bowers)
    My Brother's Keeper (uncredited)
1950 *The Body Said No!* (Benton)
1951 *Mr Drake's Duck* (Mr Boothby)
    Circle of Danger (Oliver)
    Another Man's Poison (Mr Bigley)
1952 *Whispering Smith Hits London* (Manson)
    Brandy For the Parson (Scoutmaster)
    You're Only Young Twice (BBC Commentator)
    Penny Princess (Finance Minister)
1953 *The Titfield Thunderbolt* (Coggett)
    Genevieve (J. C. Callahan)
    Innocents in Paris (Photographer)
1954 *Don't Blame the Stork* (Jonathan)
    The Million Pound Note (Rock)
    Fast and Loose (Tripp-Johnson)
    The Runaway Bus (Collector)
    Dance Little Lady (Poldi)
    Lease of Life (Foley)
    Aunt Clara (Alfie Pearce)
    Men of Sherwood Forest (Friar Tuck)
1955 *The Lyons in Paris* (Captain Le Grand)
    They Can't Hang Me (Harold)
    A Yank in Ermine (Kimp)
1956 *Charley Moon* (Vicar)
    The March Hare (Broker)
    It's a Wonderful World (Manager)
    A Touch of the Sun (Hardcastle)
1957 *Carry On Admiral* (Receptionist)
    These Dangerous Years (Hairdresser)
    Lucky Jim (Porter)
    Night of the Demon (Mr Meek)
    Break in the Circle (Dusty)
1958 *Up the Creek* (Publican)

Next to No Time (Warren)
Rockets Galore (Mumford)
1959 The Captain's Table (Burtweed)
The Horse's Mouth (Captain Jones)
The Thirty-nine Steps (Lumsden)
The Ugly Duckling (Reginald)
The Navy Lark (CNI)
Friends and Neighbours (Wilf Holmes)
Desert Mice (Fred)
Expresso Bongo (Rev Tobias Craven)
1960 Dentist in the Chair (Watling)
Doctor In Love (Wildwinde)
There Was a Crooked Man (Mr Foster)
Bottoms Up (uncredited)
1961 The Girl on the Boat (Barman)
The Night We Got The Bird (Chippendale Charlie)
Five Golden Hours (Brother Geronimo)
Double Bunk (Alfred Harper)
Dentist on the Job (Duff)

The Day the Earth Caught Fire (Harry)
1962 Hair of the Dog (Fred Tickle)
The Prince and the Pauper (Landlord)
Night of the Eagle (Harold Gunnison)
The Password Is Courage (Unteroffizier)
1963 The King's Breakfast (short) (Magician)
Just for Fun (Leader of the Opposition)
Lancelot and Guinevere (Sir Dagonet)
Doctor in Distress (Meyer)
Never Put It In Writing (Lombardi)
1964 Mister Moses (Parkhurst)
A Shot in the Dark (Nudist Camp Receptionist)
1965 Gonks Go Home (Professor)
The Amorous Adventures of Moll Flanders (Doctor)
The Big Job (Registrar)
Thunderball (Kenniston)
How to Undress in Public Without Undue Embarrassment (short)

Ian Carmichael

Ian Carmichael was a central figure in the Boultings' comedies of the fifties. His affable innocent-at-large bore the brunt of their scalpel humour. Carmichael was always the well-bred chap whose refined, olde-worlde values were in conflict with the real world. His bewilderment and sense of alienation provided the comedy, but comedy usually had a serious purpose in the Boultings' scheme of things. Their best work, following on almost chronologically without a break from the decline of Ealing Studios as Britain's top film comedy factory, provided audiences with a welcome continuity of product quality.

After small parts in films like Time Gentlemen Please (1952, Lewis Gilbert) as a PR man, and The Colditz Story (1954, Guy Hamilton) as a Guards officer, Carmichael got a featured role in Simon and Laura (1955, Muriel Box), repeating his stage role as a harrassed TV producer driven nearly mad by the unfortunate casting in his popular happy families soap-opera TV series of a married couple playing husband-and-wife who, away from the cameras, can barely stand the sight of each other. Playing the feuding couple were the habitually excellent Peter Finch and Kay Kendall.

Carmichael became famous as an inept conscript in Private's Progress (1956, John Boulting), and repeated the role in I'm All Right, Jack (1959, John Boulting) after the success of the earlier film had prompted the Boultings and author Alan Hackney to concoct a sequel. His military service over, the Carmichael character fails at several job interviews but is rescued – or so he is allowed to think – by crafty uncle Dennis Price, who offers him a blue-collar job in the family firm.

Carmichael is the tame cat deliberately tossed among the pigeons, the latter being a bunch of bolshie trade unionists led by Peter Sellers, so that Price and his accomplice Richard Attenborough can pull off a lucrative swindle. When Carmichael eventually cottons on and stirs up resistance, he becomes a folk-hero to the working classes. As cheering crowds line the pavement outside the family house, great aunt Margaret Rutherford, chins quivering with pride, declares: 'What a nation we British are when we're stirred'.

The legal profession came under fire in Brothers in Law (1957, Roy Boulting), with Carmichael as a young barrister under fire from both his professional peers and clients. Similarly, university life was the target in Lucky Jim (1957, John Boulting). Carmichael was Janette Scott's husband-to-be in *Happy is the Bride* (1958, Roy Boulting), a flimsy comedy about the traumatic run-up to a rural society wedding. Miss Scott was again the object of his desire in *School for Scoundrels* (1960, Robert Hamer), but when a successful rotter usurps her affections the rather weak-kneed Carmichael enrols at Alastair Sim's one-upmanship academy, which he hopes will transform him into a successful swine. Under Sim's careful tutelage, Carmichael eventually graduates with sufficient dishonours to reinstate himself with the alluring Miss Scott.

With Sim again, he made *Left, Right and Centre* (1959, Sidney Gilliatt), in which a Tory candidate at a by-election – Carmichael – becomes romantically entangled with his political opposite number, sexy Labourite Patricia Bredin. In *Heavens Above* (1963, John Boulting) the Church stepped forward for a few obligatory swipes, with Carmichael in a guest role as a goofy, public school churchman who should have taken over as cleric to a sleepy English hamlet. However, due to an administrative hiccup, the vicar who lands the job is a lowbrow Black Country parson (Peter Sellers) with a distinctly off-beat line in flock-gathering.

From 1963 onwards, Carmichael was having career problems. In his autobiography he notes, 'All I was being offered were variations on the same old bumbling accident-prone clot'. Television came to his rescue with *The World of Wooster*, which reunited him, as the dozy, stammering Bertie, with his one-time Boultings sparring partner Dennis Price, arguably the most perfect of all Jeeveses. Their superb timing and rapport, polished over years of working together, aided by genuinely witty scripts, boosted the series high into the ratings and they made 20 episodes together. Subsequent attempts to televise Wodehouse have lacked that spark which made Carmichael's Wooster so watchable. Later TV series included *Bachelor Father* (1970-71), and for three years he played Lord Peter Wimsey, Dorothy L. Sayers' upper-crust detective (1972-75).

Ian Carmichael

b. 1920. Stage revue star who became 1950s amiable clot in several Boultings comedies. TV work includes Bertie Wooster and Lord Wimsey. Film debut in *Bond Street* (1948).

1948 *Bond Street* (uncredited)
1949 *Trottie True* (uncredited)
      Dear Mr Prohack (uncredited)
1952 *The Ghost Ship* (uncredited)

Ian Carmichael (left) and Arthur Lowe recreate the Basil Radford–Naunton Wayne roles of Caldicott and Childers in the 1978 remake of *The Lady Vanishes*

Ian Carmichael, 1961

Time Gentlemen Please (Public Relations Man)
1953 *Meet Mr Lucifer* (Man Friday)
1954 *The Colditz Story* (Robin Cartwright)
1955 *Storm Over the Nile* (Tom Willoughby)
    Simon and Laura (David Prentice)
1956 *Private's Progress* (Stanley Windrush)
    The Big Money (Willie Frith)
1957 *Brothers In Law* (Roger Thursby)
    Lucky Jim (Jim Dixon)
1958 *Happy is the Bride* (David Chaytor)
1959 *Left, Right and Centre* (Robert Wilcott)
    I'm All Right, Jack (Stanley Windrush)
1960 *School for Scoundrels* (Henry Palfrey)
    Light Up the Sky (Lieutenant Ogleby)
1961 *Double Bunk* (Jack Goddard)
1962 *The Amorous Prawn* (Corporal Sidney Green)
1963 *Heavens Above* (Rev John Smallwood)
    Hide and Seek (David Garrett)
1967 *Smashing Time* (Bobby Mome-Rath)
1971 *The Magnificent Seven Deadly Sins* (Ferris in the 'Pride' episode)
1972 *From Beyond the Grave* (Reginald Warren)
1978 *The Lady Vanishes* (Caldicott)

George Cole

For years, the twin spectres of David Bliss and Flash Harry rattled along behind George Cole's career like old cans tied to a car. Bliss was the radio sitcom series bachelor whom he played for 15 years – 'wholesome to the point of nausea', recalls Cole. Flash Harry was the flamboyant teddy boy parody in five 'St Trinian's' comedies, a character he played well into his forties. Each creation was, in its own way, characteristic of postwar comedy at its least adventurous.

In his early days, Cole always looked as if he had one foot in a sanatorium. He was about as robust as Salvation Army soup. The poor fellow usually meant well, of course, but lack of grit and slow wits made him a natural loser. Nevertheless, he was useful to have around, as the hero's gormless chum or as the heroine's discardable boyfriend.

In *Flesh and Blood* (1951, Anthony Kimmins), a confused melodrama about a Victorian doctor and his ne'er-do-well grandson (both played by Richard Todd), Cole was a dour medical student whose mother chars for spoilt brat Joan Green-wood. Marriage to Miss Greenwood would be a step in the right direction socially, but the lady has other ideas. 'You'll never marry me,' she yells. 'I'm a lady. You came from the gutter!' When Cole resorts to blackmail she poisons him with a medical concoction he has foolishly left lying around.

He was a naval rating trapped inside the doomed submarine in *Morning Departure* (1950, Roy Baker). When Captain John Mills discovers there are not enough escape sets to go round, the decision on who goes and who stays rests on the turn of a card. Cole and Richard Attenborough tie for the last remaining kit, with Cole winning the draw at the second attempt. Attenborough, a weak-willed claustrophobic, kicks up such a fuss about being, in essence, condemned to death on the turn of a card, that Mills suggests it might be better all round if Cole gives up his place to Attenborough, which he instantly agrees to do. Attenborough, however, recovers his nerve and fakes an injury that restores Cole to his rightful place on the escape roster.

31

Bank clerk George Cole (left) has some bad news about his boss's wife's shattered portrait in *Laughter in Paradise* (1951). Ronald Adam is the unamused bank manager

George Cole finds Nadia Gray's table bugged in *Top Secret* (1952)

In *Lady Godiva Rides Again* (1951, Frank Launder), an agreeable if laboured satire on the beauty queen business, Cole was the soggy home-town boyfriend of beauty contestant Pauline Stroud, whom he promptly loses to the cheesecake milieu once she appears to be going places. Grudgingly he takes off after her, hoping to snatch her back from the glamour circuit before all is lost. 'I don't want to see London,' he wails, footloose in the unfamilar, big city. 'I wanted to go to a holiday camp and get brown!'

Cole played a young Ebenezer, before he ages into Alastair Sim, in *Scrooge* (1951, Brian Desmond Hurst), a near-perfect adaptation of Dickens' *A Christmas Carol*. He made several films with Sim who, according to Philip Norman, had semi-adopted Cole at the outset of his career and 'taught him to speak so that he could be understood'. Their other films together included *Laughter in Paradise* (1951, Mario Zampi), *The Green Man* (1956, Robert Day) and three 'St Trinian's' farces in which Sim played both the matron and her sponger of a brother.

Cole was shipwrecked with Joan Collins in *Our Girl Friday* (1954, Noel Langley) along with Kenneth More and Robertson Hare. At no time in his career could Cole be described as the kind of male Miss Collins might be enticed to share a tree house with. In *The Intruder* (1953, Guy Hamilton), a small-scale social drama that uses types rather than people, Cole was an ex-Army corporal who helps his former tank commander Jack Hawkins piece together the tangled lifestory of a one-time decorated trooper from his old unit, played by Michael Medwin, who has fallen on hard times and regressed into petty crime.

He was a sly gypsy in *The Adventures of Quentin Durward* (1955, Richard Thorpe), a sort of chicken in sheep's clothing who nevertheless musters sufficient courage to switch allegiance from villainous employers to Robert Taylor. When Taylor demands to know why he is so dishonourable, Cole explains that it's because he's a gypsy – it's expected of him! When the baddies strike, Cole decamps to a quiet corner where he hopes he won't be noticed, leaving Taylor to broadsword his way to freedom. But fair damsel Kay Kendall has his number and, accused by her of treachery, Cole merely shrugs and asks: 'What d'you expect of the son of a horse-thief?' What, indeed!

Although he appeared in numerous dramas, Cole fared better in comedy, loping onion-faced through an assortment of catastrophes, the patron saint of mediocrity around whom the wise and the wicked could run cruel, tantalising circles. In *Too Many Crooks* (1958, Mario Zampi) he led a troop of hopelessly inept villains whose attempts to blackmail rich rogue Terry-Thomas come unstuck when, instead of kidnapping his daughter, they cart off his wife Brenda de Banzie, a bossy woman whom Terry-Thomas is only too happy to unload. The gang's attempts to extort a ransom get nowhere, but Miss de Banzie, stung by her husband's public admission that she means nothing to him, takes over the gang and promptly leads them to the old boy's loot.

One line is ghastly enough to stand repeating. To kidnap Miss de Banzie, the gang masquerades as undertakers, but returning with her to the hideout, the hearse which they borrowed gets out of control and crashes into the middle of a river. Miss de Banzie is removed from the water-logged coffin and completes the journey in an old van. Cole's wry explanation to gang moll Vera Day as to what went wrong – 'We changed hearses in mid-stream!'

He was Honor Blackman's lover in *Fright* (1971, Peter Collinson), the reason why her psychotic husband escapes from his padded cell seeking revenge. It was one of those atmospheric, creepy-house melodramas where the cameras work harder than the actors, zooming suddenly on to dripping taps and staring up into tense nostrils and skulking outside in the shrubbery. Tension is neatly conveyed and held from the start when mini-skirted baby-sitter Susan George arrives at the isolated Victorian house which Cole shares with Miss Blackman.

An early scene involving Cole and Miss George in awkward small talk, held entirely in long shot from a low-angle camera, purposely keeps the audience at arm's length, making them intruders also. Cole was good as the ordinary-joe lover who wisely keeps a rather low profile in the climactic confrontation between Ian Bannen and Miss Blackman. All he wants is a new job in Brussels and a fresh start with Miss Blackman, but it's a future which Bannen's brutal shadow obscures.

The passage of time has given Cole's closed-fist features a distinct weathering and he remains much in demand on television, favouring crisis-prone, menopausal characters. Memories of Flash Harry surfaced in the TV series *Minder*, which starred Cole as a sticky-fingered Soho character. Dennis Waterman was his 'minder', a one-time boxing hopeful, now Cole's personal strong-arm. *Minder* was a series with a heart, and the relationship between Cole, a showy but inwardly sad character, and Waterman, an amiable tearaway who hungers for self-improvement, echoed on a human level the warts-and-all reality of its bustling London locations.

George Cole

b. 1925.   Likable all-purpose actor whose glum features are better suited to comedy. Film debut in *Cottage To Let* (1941). 1950s radio star in *A Life of Bliss* and many TV roles include minor Soho baron in *Minder*.

1941 *Cottage To Let*
1942 *Those Kids from Town*
1943 *The Demi-Paradise*
1945 *Henry V* (Boy)
      Journey Together (Curly)
1948 *Quartet* (Henry Sunbury)
      My Brother's Keeper (Willie Stannard)
1949 *The Spider and the Fly* (Marc)
1950 *Morning Departure* (ERA Marks)
      Gone to Earth (Albert)
1951 *Flesh and Blood* (John Hannah)
      Laughter in Paradise (Herbert Russell)
      Scrooge (Ebenezer Scrooge, as a young man)
      Lady Godiva Rides Again (Johnny)
1952 *The Happy Family* (Cyril)
      Who Goes There (Arthur Crisp)
      Top Secret (George Potts)
      Folly To Be Wise (Private)
1953 *Will Any Gentleman* (Henry)
      The Intruder (John Summers)
      The Clue of the Missing Ape (formerly *Gibraltar Adventure*) (Gobo)
1954 *Our Girl Friday* (Jimmy Carroll)
      Happy Ever After (Terence)
      Belles Of St Trinian's (Flash Harry)
      An Inspector Calls (uncredited)
1955 *A Prize Of Gold* (Sgt Roger Morris)
      Where There's a Will (Fred Slater)
      The Constant Husband (Luigi Sopranelli)
      The Adventures of Quentin Durward (Hayraddin)
1956 *It's a Wonderful World* (Ken Miller)
      The Green Man (William Blake)
      The Weapon (Joshua Henry)
1957 *Blue Murder at St Trinian's* (Flash Harry)
1958 *Too Many Crooks* (Fingers)
1959 *The Bridal Path* (Sergeant Bruce)
      Don't Panic Chaps (Pte Eric Finch)
      The Pure Hell of St Trinian's (Flash Harry)

1963 *Dr Syn – Alias The Scarecrow* (Sexton Mipps)
       Cleopatra (Flavius)
1964 *One Way Pendulum* (Defence Counsel/Friend)
1965 *The Legend of Young Dick Turpin* (Mr Evans)
1966 *The Great St Trinian's Train Robbery* (Flash Harry)
1970 *The Vampire Lovers* (Morton)
1971 *Fright* (Jim)
1973 *Take Me High* (Bert Jackson)
1974 *Gone in Sixty Seconds* (Atlee Jackson)
1976 *The Blue Bird* (Dog)

Tom Courtenay

'I can't turn it on like some actors. I have to look as I feel,' says Tom Courtenay. As he usually looks as if he's just swallowed some liniment, the question is, might he not be in the wrong profession? 'No,' he says emphatically. That crucified look was the result of nerves in the early days. 'I was chucked into the top in this business bloody young. Half the time I was scared.'

The top, as he calls it, came with his selection to play the Borstal youth in Alan Sillitoe's *The Loneliness of the Long Distance Runner* (1962, Tony Richardson) after the director had spotted him on the London stage as Billy Liar. Courtenay's rawness and his painful lack of presence helped make the slum-kid which he played an Everyman of the 1960s. His near-blank face was a scribbling block on which to sketch all the neuroses and frustrations of the first 'telly-age' generation. Richardson's film is populated with losers – Courtenay himself, his cancer-ridden father, his good-timing mother, even the dour Borstal governor hiding his ineffectiveness behind a string of useless platitudes and clichés. Courtenay falls foul of authority when he robs a bakery – the act is as much a gesture against the Establishment as an attempt to make money – and the film concentrates on authority's feeble efforts to put him back on the rails, via a term in Borstal.

In the film, Courtenay has a single talent, the ability to run long distances, which the governor tries to exploit for his own selfish ends, winning a sports trophy in competition with a nearby public school. Courtenay 'plays ball' with the governor until the actual race, which he deliberately throws, bowing defiantly within sight of the winning post as he lets the others through.

The same wistful vulnerability was there in *Private Potter* (1962, Casper Wrede) with Courtenay as a soldier on active service whose sudden cry of alarm during an ambush gives away the platoon's position. Courtenay is subsequently court-martialled, but claims in defence that the reason he suddenly cried out was that he had seen Jesus Christ.

He was the screen *Billy Liar* (1963, John Schlesinger), the stage role that had won him his first film job. Here again, it might have been the long distance runner daydreaming some much-needed colour and promise into his drab young life. Courtenay's Billy is a lad clutching at straws, the stoutest of which is a Mittyish imagination which allows him to machine-gun his intolerable family, and invent bizarre explanations to get him out of harrassments brought on by even more bizarre conduct.

Everything in Billy's life is damnable. His job at the local undertakers, presided over by a skin-

Tom Courtenay

Tom Courtenay as the lad with the Walter Mittyish imagination in *Billy Liar* (1963), with Julie Christie making her film debut

flint Leonard Rossiter, is in doubt; his engagements to two hard-necked fillies hang over him like a Damoclean sword; and the home scene is eternally turbulent and disordered. Billy's only defence against all this lies in his fertile imagination, and in Julie Christie, making a stunning film debut as a wholly liberated lady who nearly becomes his salvation.

King and Country (1964, Joseph Losey) was intended to shock, in the way that Kubrick's *Paths of Glory*, seven years previously and on a similar theme, had done. Seeing it for the first time recently, one was struck by its unrelenting gloom and the onesidedness of its arguments, factors which make it a weaker film than Kubrick's.

Courtenay played a young soldier court-martialled for desertion during the Passchendaele assault at the height of World War I. Dirk Bogarde was his defending officer. Though the act on which the charge was based was clearly more one of confusion than desertion, justice

has no part, for military discipline must be maintained at all costs. Thus Courtenay, who has had a wretched time in the trenches and in only slightly altered circumstances would be stepping forward for a medal, is condemned to a firing squad to appease the consciences of his senior officers.

Losey handles the tensions well, but his keenness to state his case at times overrides his narrative judgement. The story was horrifying enough without the final agony, the failure of the firing squad to finish off the prisoner, who is despatched by the humane Bogarde as he writhes on the ground, hands and feet bound to a chair. At times, Losey gives us the feeling we are watching self-destructive termites, a feeling heightened by the trench-like passages and squalid little dug-outs which make up the soldiers' quarters.

Courtenay was excellent as the luckless victim, trying to reason his way out of the nightmare but meeting, instead of reason on the other

35

side, blank minds and ugly resentment. Bogarde was first-rate, too, as were the string of supporting actors including Leo McKern as a medical officer, Peter Copley as the colonel-in-charge, and James Villiers as the prosecuting captain.

Poor Courtenay fared little better in *Operation Crossbow* (1965, Michael Anderson), but at least he had the satisfaction of knowing the firing squad is the enemy's. Courtenay was one of three secret agents – the other two were George Peppard and Jeremy Kemp – sent undercover into the Nazis' underground rocket sites to sabotage the entire operation. Shortly after his arrival, Courtenay is recognised by enemy agent Anthony Quayle, and brutally beaten up by the ss in an attempt to get him to disclose details of the mission. When he refuses, Quayle has him shot.

Two more war films – *Night of the Generals* (1967, Anatole Litvak), a tense murder-who-dunnit set among high Nazi brass along with Peter O'Toole and Omar Sharif, and *King Rat* (1966, Bryan Forbes), set in a South East Asia prison camp – wrapped up for the time being Courtenay's military 'period'. He was a cunning spy on the trail of double agent Laurence Harvey in *A Dandy in Aspic* (1968, Anthony Mann, later Laurence Harvey), a routine melodrama which added nothing new to the genre, although the keen personal duel between Courtenay and Harvey provided some cut-and-thrust dialogue from time to time, as when Harvey tells him warningly: 'You died the moment you were born. When your heart stops, it will be a mere formality!' After Mia Farrow has confessed her love for Harvey, Courtenay pulls a wry face: 'He hasn't got a future. None at all,' he insists, and every word is meant.

'You don't get *real* scripts very often in films,' Courtenay once moaned to Sheridan Morley. *Catch Me a Spy* (1971, Dick Clement) proved he had a point. He played an inept Special Branch detective shadowing the wife of a spy who is also

the niece of Shadow Foreign Secretary Trevor Howard. It was a trite and confusingly assembled spy comedy unworthy of these two leading actors of their respective generations.

Courtenay experienced the full horrors of a Soviet prison camp in *One Day in the Life of Ivan Denisovich* (1971, Casper Wrede) and gave a moving performance as a Gulag-style victim of Russian oppression. To get himself physically right, he shed half a stone from his already wiry frame, shaved his head and removed the caps from his front teeth. It was filmed on location 250 miles north of Oslo in temperatures 30 degrees below zero. Courtenay's extra bony frame felt the cold as keenly as Denisovich was supposed to in the film. 'When I shivered I wasn't acting,' he says.

Tom Courtenay
b. 1937. Fragile-looking, morbidly-inclined 1960s kitchen-sink star who came to prominence in *The Loneliness of the Long Distance Runner* (1962) and *Billy Liar* (1963) as gaunt, likable rebel. Also stage lead on London and Broadway. Married briefly to actress-singer Cheryl Kennedy, his co-star in the West End run of Alan Ayckbourn's *Time and Time Again*.

1962 *The Loneliness of the Long Distance Runner* (Colin Smith)
      Private Potter (Potter)
1963 *Billy Liar* (Billy Fisher)
1964 *King and Country* (Hamp)
1965 *Operation Crossbow* (Robert Henshaw)
1966 *King Rat* (Lt Gray)
      Dr Zhivago (Pasha)
1967 *Night of the Generals* (Cpl Curt Hartmann)
      The Day the Fish Came Out (Navigator)
1968 *A Dandy in Aspic* (Gatiss)
      Otley (Gerald Arthur Otley)
1971 *Catch Me a Spy* (Baxter)
      One Day in the Life of Ivan Denisovich (Ivan Denisovich)

Michael Craig

Michael Craig once said: 'Most of the films I appeared in were a load of rubbish'. One cannot argue with that, but an actor with more personality might have done something with them – consider how Dirk Bogarde coped with similar

rubbish in early career. The problem for Craig was a definite lack of substance behind those dreamy looks and refined manners. He was, in a word, underwhelming. One could almost say that he set himself disappointingly low standards which he then appeared hard pushed to maintain. Nor did it help when so many of his lines were gems like: 'Gosh, Martha, shall we go to the pictures on Saturday?' or 'Excuse me, is this seat taken?'

Without appearing to try very hard, one breed of actor can put an unmistakable signature on a film – look at the early Brando, or Stanley Baker. With others, like Craig, appearing to not try very hard is totally the opposite of what is going on, only there's nothing much to show at the end of it. In fairness to Craig, a lot of the material shovelled at him was probably beyond salvaging.

His first important screen role was as Diana Dors' lover in Yield to the Night (1956, J. Lee-Thompson), a story based vaguely on the case of Ruth Ellis, the last woman to face the gallows in Britain. The controversy aroused by the Ellis case did more to bring about the end of capital punishment in Britain than probably any other single event. The film was an eloquent anti-hanging statement and Diana Dors gave a surprisingly moving performance as the tragic murderess. Craig was one of the oil-drillers in Campbell's Kingdom (1957, Ralph Thomas), and partnered police inspector Nigel Patrick on the trail of the murderer of a coloured girl student found dead on Hampstead Heath in Sapphire (1959, Basil Dearden), a film that cleverly used the mechanics of a murder hunt to say something about the roots of racial tensions. As the investigation probes deeper we encounter the inter-racial tensions and resentments simmering just below the surface, and the fictional story, made shortly after the notorious Notting Hill race riots, gains weight from a more honest than usual portrayal of a particularly urgent problem facing urban society, more so now than when the film was made.

In the end, the murderer is revealed as neither a shabby racist nor right wing agitator but a sad, genteel English mother, played by Yvonne Mitchell, who kills for the sake of her son.

Craig wrote the original treatment for The Angry Silence (1960, Guy Green) and showed it to Richard Attenborough while they filmed Sea of Sand (1958, Guy Green) together in Tripoli. Attenborough recalls that, at the time, his acting career was in the doldrums and he was searching for fresh ground. Craig's story line was precisely what he had been looking for. Bryan Forbes sharpened up the script, Attenborough produced and starred as the factory worker who pays dearly for his beliefs, and Craig also starred as Attenborough's buddy, whose loyalty wilts in the heat of conflict but who recovers his grit in time to stand by him.

Craig hit some true notes in Life for Ruth (1962, Basil Dearden), as a Jehovah's Witness who allows his child to die rather than accept a transfusion, despite considerable pressure from the police and their no-nonsense family doctor, played by Patrick McGoohan. As the straight-laced father, stubbornly loyal to his beliefs but quietly hoping for a miracle that will let him off the hook – a miracle that is sadly denied –Craig turns in possibly his best work.

Cone of Silence (1960, Charles Frend) gave us par-for-the-course Craig, as a genial pilot training officer who at first agrees with a court of enquiry verdict that veteran airline pilot Bernard Lee caused a crash, but later changes his opinion. After Lee is killed in a carbon-copy of the first accident Craig carries out his own investigation, which shows that the fault was in the approved take-off procedure, an error which is put right just in time to avert a third disaster.

'I'm sorry to be such an ungrateful bore,' says Julie Andrews, as musical comedy star Gertrude Lawrence, to Craig, a well-connected smoothie who elevates her into top London society to boost both her career and his stage-door johnnie image in Star! (1968, Robert Wise). Miss Andrews is grateful, but not grateful enough to marry him.

Miffed about being turned down for something as nebulous as a dazzling career on both the London and Broadway stages, Craig enlists in the colonial service and is hustled off to India from where he only momentarily reappears. Played by Julie Andrews, an actress singularly lacking in dazzle or even plain, simple warmth, Miss Lawrence comes across as a personality with about as much depth as the skin of a balloon. Daniel Massey, as a young Noel Coward, provides this wishy-washy biopic with its few tolerable moments.

In recent years, Craig has faded from the big screen, and even on the small one his involvements have been rather disappointing. He played a middle-aged man who takes up with a willowy young blonde in a dull-witted sitcom series, and appeared as a ship's captain in BBC-TV's early-evening Triangle series. It would be a great pity if Craig vanished completely. Despite the early shortcomings, there had been signs of his developing belatedly into a spring-cleaned version of the kind of run-down, nose-bleed

character at which Denholm Elliott has become
so accomplished.

One of Craig's most impressive roles to date
was as Peter O'Toole's ex-brother-in-law in
Country Dance (1969, J. Lee-Thompson). Craig
has been married to Susannah York but their relationship is soured by O'Toole's unnatural
jealousy, which Miss York appears to encourage.
Craig, however, still loves her and refuses to be
made a back number, which is fortunate for Miss
York after her possessive brother finally goes
crazy and needs to be institutionalised for his
own protection. In her time of crisis, Craig's de-
voted reassurance points the way out. Craig and
O'Toole compete for the fair Miss York like opposing teams chasing a trophy. O'Toole's dirty
tactics dominate the mid-field early on in the
game, but it is Craig's scrupulously fair, persistent tackling and his ability to keep cool in the
penalty area which gain the deciding point.

Michael Craig
b. 1928. Lightweight leading man, occasionally comedy. Film debut in *Malta Story* (1954).
Wrote original story and also starred in *The
Angry Silence* (1960).

1954 *Svengali* (Zou Zou)
      Malta Story (uncredited)
      The Love Lottery (uncredited)
1956 *The Black Tent* (Faris)
      Yield to the Night (Jim Lancaster)
      House of Secrets (Larry Ellis)
      Eye Witness (Jay Church)
      High Tide at Noon (Nils)
1957 *Campbell's Kingdom* (Bladen)
1958 *The Silent Enemy* (C. S. Knowles)
      Sea of Sand (Captain Cotton)
1959 *Life in Emergency Ward 10* (Dr Stephen
      Russell)
      Sapphire (Inspector Learoyd)
      Upstairs and Downstairs (Richard Barry)
1960 *The Angry Silence* (Joe Wallace)
      Cone of Silence (Captain Hugh Dallas)
      Doctor in Love (Dr Richard Hare)
1961 *Payroll* (Johnny Mellors)
      No, My Darling Daughter (Thomas
      Barclay)
1962 *A Pair of Briefs* (Tony Stevens)
      Mysterious Island (Captain Cyrus
      Harding)
      Life for Ruth (John Harris)
      The Iron Maiden (Jack Hopkins)
      Captive City (Captain Elliott)
1963 *The Stolen Hours* (John Carmody)
1965 *Life at the Top* (Mark)
1966 *Modesty Blaise* (Paul Hagan)
1968 *Star!* (Sir Anthony Spencer)
1969 *Twinky* (Father)
      The Royal Hunt of the Sun (Estete)
      Country Dance (Douglas Dow)
1971 *A Town Called Bastard* (Paco)
1973 *Vault of Horror* (Maitland)
1978 *The Irishman* (Australia) (Paddy
      Doolin)

Peter Cushing

There was always something disturbingly fun-
ereal about Peter Cushing. His face was just a
skull decorated with odd bits of upholstery and
those long bony fingers belong dabbling in gore.
Along with Christopher Lee, Cushing was a cornerstone of the home-grown horror market, a
distinction he earned almost by accident and
one possibly unworthy of his lengthy patronage.

Prior to donning the cloak of the foxy Baron
Frankenstein in 1957, Cushing was shaping up
nicely as a surrogate Basil Rathbone, whose appearance and demeanour he was said to resem-
ble. Both played Sherlock Holmes in *The Hound
of the Baskervilles*, Rathbone in 1938, Cushing
exactly 20 years later, and both were enemies of
Robin Hood – Rathbone as Sir Guy in the 1938
Errol Flynn classic, Cushing as Sheriff of
Nottingham in *Sword of Sherwood Forest* (1960,
Terence Fisher). Cushing lacked the flair and
agility for costume villainy and abandoned it in
favour of the more ethereal kind. A shrewd
move, if *The Black Knight* (1954, Tay Garnett)
was anything to judge by. Cushing, as an evil
Saracen plotting to take over medieval England,
struggled under a layer of chocolate make-up, a
flowing kaftan, and dialogue borrowed from a
Christmas cracker.

A strong impact on television as George Or-

Peter Cushing (left) and Duncan Lamont dissect a few human remains in *Nothing But the Night* (1972)

well's tragic hero of *1984*, probably rescued him from further *Black Knight*-style nasties. He was the sympathetic loser again in *End of the Affair* (1955, Edward Dmytryk), as a stodgy civil servant whose repressed wife, played by Deborah Kerr, has a wartime affair with American author Van Johnson that ends in tragedy.

Of Cushing's Frankenstein portrayals, which began with *The Curse of Frankenstein* (1957, Terence Fisher), John Brosnan, in his book *Horror People,* comments: 'One of the outstanding things about Cushing is that no matter how mediocre or downright dismal the script may be he always manages to give the character he is playing that something extra. He breathes life into characters that would be mere cardboard in anyone else's hands'.

Up to the mid-1960s Cushing popped up in occasional non-horror films, such as *Violent Playground* (1958, Basil Dearden), where he was

a priest. In *Cone of Silence* (1960, Charles Frend) he was a pompous airline routes officer who opposes the re-licensing of veteran pilot Bernard Lee to fly following a crash for which a court of enquiry holds him responsible. When fresh opportunities occur to heap more doubts on Lee's competence, Cushing is in there shovelling faster than anyone. But confronted with his own lack of judgement, he does a neat turn-around and wants the entire matter hushed up.

In horror movies, which make up the bulk of Cushing's screen work since 1965, he has been both demon and demon-catcher, regularly swopping sides without adjusting his performance. He first played Van Helsing to Christopher Lee's *Dracula* in 1958 (Terence Fisher), the start of a chase that endured for 15 years on the screen. By the 1970s the Dracula cycle, in keeping with the media generally, had become more explicit in every way. Victims on sacrificial

40

tables were shown naked and nobody could misinterpret the intention behind thrusting the obligatory stake into a scantily-clad vampire lady.

In *The Satanic Rites of Dracula* (1973, Alan Gibson), one of the last and weakest in the series, police inspector Michael Coles, menaced by a female vampire in a manor house coffin room, lies between her writhing legs as he whacks in the stake. Nothing is left to the imagination – a great failing of the later Hammer-Dracula films. They also transferred the original characters to modern trendy settings, which proved without exception to be disastrous. In *Satanic Rites*, for example, Dracula masquerades as a 1970s property tycoon using motorcycle gangs to trap his victims and pursued in turn by Cushing, an identikit descendant of the original Van Helsing. Even the lines were carelessly thrown together. Listing a vampire's pet aversions, Cushing says: 'it lives in mortal dread of silver'. Lives? Mortal? Not the Drac. that I grew up with.

Later in the film, Cushing says about Dracula: 'Perhaps deep in his subconscious what he wants is an end to it all'. Audiences had already arrived at a similar conclusion, and Cushing whacked in the final stake in *Dracula AD 1972* (Alan Gibson), set incongruously in disco-mad Chelsea, by any reckoning a long haul from Transylvania as the humble bat flies.

Cushing appeared in several horror complications with which his sombre presence was nicely in tune. He was the mysterious customer who puts impoverished tailor Barry Morse into the *Asylum* (1972, Roy Ward Baker), a crude horror compilation that works in patches. The suit Cushing orders has to be made from a special material equipped with supernatural properties to restore his dead son to life. Cushing cannot afford the suit immediately and, because Morse cannot afford to let him have it on tick, the suit is stored on a tailor's dummy at Morse's shop. While Cushing attempts to raise the necessary finance, the garment is raising to life the dummy, whose first and possibly only thought is to make a play for Morse's startled wife.

A brain drain with a difference confronts Cushing in *Horror Express* (1974, Eugenio Martin). He and Christopher Lee were scientists on board an Orient Express on which a visitor from a distant galaxy, dormant inside a 2 million years old fossil, begins running loose, sucking dry the brains and eyeballs of various startled passengers in its quest for knowledge. The beast's trick of hiding inside people makes his detection a little difficult, and near impossible when he pops inside the police chief in charge of the case. When someone has the temerity to suggest that Lee or Cushing might be at the back of it, Cushing declares haughtily: 'Monster? We're British!' – an explanation which is accepted without a murmur. In the end, the creature is destroyed along with a section of the train when signalmen cunningly divert them over a cliff.

'I cannot find my volumes on the folklore of the New Guinea primitives,' wails Cushing in *The Creeping Flesh* (1973, Freddie Francis) after someone has injudiciously tidied his study. Cushing is a scientist dabbling in the origins of man, in whose laboratory a skeleton recomposes on being swabbed down with tap-water. After Cushing has gone into a long explanation as to why it might have happened, glazed-eyed lab assistant George Benson, speaking for the rest of us, declares: 'I don't really understand . . . it's all rather, er, difficult'. Cushing's half-brother Christopher Lee runs a lunatic asylum where brains submerged in brine are put to work operating the fingers of a dismembered hand. Envious of Cushing's professorship, Lee plans to earn scientific acclaim with a revolutionary thesis on the cause and prevention of madness. His own precarious mental state would seem to make him something of an authority on the subject.

In the episodic *Tales from the Crypt* (1972, Freddie Francis) Cushing plays a lonely old recluse who loves children but whose horrid landlord stirs up neighbourhood hatred so that children shun him and he becomes the bewildered target of a vicious smear campaign. Unable to endure – or comprehend – this cruelty, the old man hangs himself on his birthday. But all is not over, for next birthday, there he is, risen but not exactly fresh out of the grave, eye sockets hollow, shuffling up to the real villain of the piece whose heart he snatches clean out of his body before you can say 'aorta'.

In *Dr Terror's House of Horrors* (1964, Freddie Francis) Cushing succeeds in keeping Edgar Allan Poe alive for well over a century in the cellar where, chained to his desk, the poor old boy is still churning out horror stories. Who better to put him out of his misery than Ol' Python-head himself, Jack Palance, on the side of fair play for once and obviously thinking that, after 120 years, it was time Cushing stopped using the same Poe.

Peter Cushing in familiar guise as Dr Frankenstein in *Frankenstein and the Monster from Hell* (1974)

Peter Cushing
b. 1913. Glum-faced horrorflick star, ably projects sincerity in any old rubbish. Made TV history as oppressed victim of state control in 1954 TV version of Orwell's *1984*. From 1958, played numerous Baron Frankenstein and Van Helsing roles and others unworthy of his finely-tuned talents.

1949 *Hamlet* (Osric)
1953 *Moulin Rouge* (Marcel de la Voisier)
1954 *The Black Knight* (Sir Palamides)
1955 *End of the Affair* (Henry Miles)
1956 *Time Without Pity* (Jeremy Clayton)
       Alexander The Great (Memnon)
1957 *The Curse of Frankenstein* (Victor
          Frankenstein)
       The Abominable Snowman (Dr John
          Rollason)
1958 *Violent Playground* (The Priest)
       Dracula (Dr Van Helsing)
       The Revenge of Frankenstein (Victor
          Frankenstein)
1959 *The Hound of the Baskervilles* (Sherlock
          Holmes)
       The Mummy (John Banning)

1960 *The Flesh and the Fiends* (Dr Robert Knox)
       Cone of Silence (Capt Clive Judd)
       The Brides of Dracula (Dr Van Helsing)
       Suspect (Professor Sewell)
       Sword of Sherwood Forest (Sheriff of
          Nottingham)
1961 *The Hellfire Club* (Merryweather)
       Fury at Smugglers Bay (Squire Trevenyan)
       The Naked Edge (Wrack)
       Cash On Demand (Fordyce)
1962 *Captain Clegg* (Dr Blyss)
       The Man Who Finally Died (Dr Von
          Brecht)
1964 *The Garden* (Dr Namaroff)
       Dr Terror's House of Horrors (Dr Sandor
          Schreck)
       The Evil of Frankenstein (Baron
          Frankenstein)
1965 *She* (Major Horace Holly)
       Doctor Who and the Daleks (Dr Who)
       The Skull (Prof Christopher Maitland)
1966 *Island of Terror* (Dr Brian Stanley)
       Daleks – Invasion Earth AD 2150 (Dr Who)
1967 *Frankenstein Created Woman* (Baron
          Frankenstein)
       Night of the Big Heat (Dr Stone)
       Torture Garden (Canning)
       Some May Live (John Meredith)
1968 *The Blood Beast Terror* (Inspector
          Quennell)
       Corruption (Sir John Rowan)
1969 *Frankenstein Must Be Destroyed* (Baron
          Frankenstein)
1970 *Scream and Scream Again* (Major
          Heinrich)
       The Vampire Lovers (General Spielsdorf)
       The House That Dripped Blood (Philip
          Grayson)
       Incense for the Damned (Dr Goodrich)
1971 *I, Monster* (Utterson)
       Twins of Evil (Gustav Weil)
1972 *Asylum* (Smith)
       Dracula AD 1972 (Prof Van Helsing)
       Fear in the Night (Michael Carmichael)
       Nothing But the Night (Sir Mark Ashley)
       Tales from the Crypt (Mr Grimsdyke)
       Dr Phibes Rises Again (Captain)
       Horror Express (Dr Wells)
1973 *The Satanic Rites of Dracula* (Van Helsing)
       Island of the Burning Damned (Dr Stone)
       The Creeping Flesh (Emmanuel Hildern)
       And Now the Screaming Starts (Dr Pope)
       From Beyond the Grave (Shopkeeper)
1974 *Madhouse* (Herbert Flay)

Horror Express (Dr Wells)
The Beast Must Die (Dr Lungren)
Frankenstein and the Monster from Hell
    (Dr Frankenstein)
Legend of the Werewolf (Paul Cataflangue)
The Ghoul (Dr Lawrence)
1975 Shatter (Rattwood)
Trial by Combat (Sir Edward Gifford)
The Devil's Men (Baron Corofax)

1976 At the Earth's Core (Dr Abner Perry)
Battle Flag (Major Von Hackenberg)
Star Wars (Grand Moss Tarkin)
The Uncanny (Wilbur Gray)
1977 Son of Hitler (Heinrich Hussner)
1978 Arabian Adventure (Wazir Al Wurzara)
Touch of the Sun (Commissioner Potts)
1980 A Tale of Two Cities (Dr Manette)
Monster Island (Colderup)

Maurice Denham

Maurice Denham had one of the best known bald heads in British movies. His face was a minor work of art, a bright-eyed pixie face hand-painted on an egg. It could be kindly, sympathetic, gnomish and infinitely expressive. He also had one of the most listenable and controlled English-speaking voices, a legacy from his many years on radio.

He was one of the supports of ITMA, a popular wartime entertainment, the first to use quick-fire gags. Much-Binding-in-the-Marsh established him as a familiar radio character, supporting RAF officer-types Richard Murdoch and Kenneth Horne at an imaginary Air Force station. Denham's catch-phrase – the standard technique used by radio comics to establish immediate recognition by listening audiences – was a breezy, 'Dudley Davenport at your service, sir'.

He was chief of police in Oliver Twist (1948, David Lean), the classic David Lean version with Alec Guinness and Robert Newton, and a zany Nazi spy plaguing dapper diplomats Basil Radford and Naunton Wayne in It's Not Cricket (1949, Alfred Roome, Roy Rich). Denham frequently supported American stars, chosen no doubt for his Englishness and his ability to add depth to a scene beyond the reach of the dialogue. In Time Bomb, also known as Terror on a Train (1952, Ted Tetzlaff), with Glenn Ford, Denham was a bomb disposal expert who sportingly goes up with the threatening device.

He was bumped off, in curious circumstances, at the beginning of Night of the Demon (1957, Jacques Tournier), a neatly-told low-budget occult thriller. The killer is a fearsome devil figure conjured up by Denham's former partner, a mad diabolist. His bereaved daughter, Peggy Cummins, enlists the help of American lecturer on demonology, Dana Andrews, to break the diabolist's power and snare him in one of his own evil traps.

Denham was a pompous flight lieutenant caught up in the Burma jungle war in The Purple Plain (1954, Robert Parrish). He shares a tent with Gregory Peck, a rough-and-ready squadron leader, whom he bores rigid with constant references to his family in England and the 'important job' he had in civvies. Peck is the opposite, bitterly mourning the recent loss of his young bride in an air raid, and dourly suicidal. But on a flight taking Denham across the jungle, when Peck's small plane crash-lands, and a younger officer, played by Lyndon Brook, suffers serious injury, Denham's true colours are revealed. He frets himself silly – 'we might just as soon shoot ourselves and have done with it' – a grim prophecy which he subsequently carries out on himself. Peck fights on to keep his other wounded comrade alive till rescue arrives, and the challenge it creates restores his own appetite for life.

Denham supported Peck again in The Million Pound Note (1954, Ronald Neame), Mark Twain's story of a footloose American loaned a £1 million note by two wacky brothers to test the theory that mere possession of the note will buy a life of grandeur without ever having to cash it. Denham helps prove the validity of the wager.

His career has spanned most genres with equal style from early Huggett comedies to murder melodramas, from costume extravaganzas to horror films. He has often appeared in uniform, mostly as high ranking officials with a likably human touch, or senior coppers with a weathered awareness of the human predicament. He has also been heard without being seen, as the voices of all the different creatures in Animal Farm (1954, John Halas), a spiky cartoon version of George Orwell's allegorical novel. In

Maurice Denham as the eager-to-please cabin steward in *Doctor At Sea* (1955)

comedy, he can be sly and fussy and petulant, but also eager-to-please and cherubic, like the cabin steward in *Doctor At Sea* (1955, Ralph Thomas), fussing over ship's doctor Dirk Bogarde like a maiden aunt, or contentedly absconding to his bunk with three-dimensional pin-ups of Diana Dors.

He had a small part as a French military official in de Gaulle's cabinet in *The Day of the Jackal* (1973, Fred Zinnemann). This tense fast-moving political thriller by Frederick Forsyth tells the inside story of an attempt on the life of the French President in 1962 when the OAS, an outlawed secret army, infuriated by what they regard as de Gaulle's sellout over Algeria, recruit a gentlemanly British assassin, code-named the Jackal. The capture and torture of an OAS lieutenant reveals to the authorities the existence of the Jackal, played with ruthless single-mindedness by Edward Fox. Though the plan is officially dropped, Fox decides to go it alone, switching identities and killing anyone likely to obstruct his target. The final showdown, as Fox gets his victim in his sights and the net closes in, is brilliantly constructed, reminiscent on several levels of John Frankenheimer's *The Manchurian Candidate* (1962).

Denham was the bearded scholar in *Countess Dracula* (1970, Peter Sasdy), a vampire cheapie with lesbian overtones, who stumbles on to the grisly secret of what it is that keeps a nasty old crone looking like Ingrid Pitt. Bathing daily in virgin's blood seems to do the trick, but the disappearance of so many local wenches is making the villagers restless. Denham discovers the answer in old volumes in the castle library, but is killed by the Countess's lover, Nigel Green, before he can raise the alarm.

Maurice Denham
b. 1909. On stage from 1934. Wartime radio comic (*ITMA*, *Much-Binding-in-the-Marsh*) and busy distinctive-voiced character player in films from *Daybreak* (1946).

1946 *Daybreak* (Inspector)
1947 *Take My Life* (Defence Counsel)
    The Upturned Glass (Policeman)
    Holiday Camp (Doctor)
    Jassy (Jim Stones)
    Captain Boycott (Colonel Strickland)
    The End of the River (Defence)
    Dear Murderer (uncredited)
    The Man Within (Smuggler)
1948 *Easy Money* (Inspector Kirby)
    Blanche Fury (Major Frazer)
    Escape (Crown)
    Miranda (Cockle Man)
    Oliver Twist (Chief of Police)
    My Brother's Keeper (Trent)
    London Belongs to Me (Jack Rufus)
    The Blind Goddess (Butler)
    Here Come the Huggetts (Mechanic)
    Look Before You Love (Fosser)
1949 *Once Upon a Dream* (Vicar)
    The Blue Lagoon (Captain)
    It's Not Cricket (Otto Fisch)
    A Boy, a Girl and a Bike (Bill Martin)
    Poet's Pub (Constable)
    Don't Ever Leave Me (Mr Knowles)
    Madness of the Heart (Dr Simon Blake)
    Landfall (Wing Comdr Hewitt)
    The Spider and the Fly (Colonel de la Roche)
1950 *Travellers' Joy* (Fowler)
1951 *No Highway* (Major Pearl)
1952 *The Net* (Carrington)
    Time Bomb (Jim Warrilow)
    Street Corner (Mr Dawson)
1954 *The Million Pound Note* (Reid)
    Eight O'Clock Walk (Horace Clifton)
    The Purple Plain (Flight Lieutenant Blore)
    Carrington VC (Lieut Colonel Reeve)

A hefty drinks bill for monocled Maurice Denham (left) in *The Captain's Table* (1959). Companion Peggy Cummins looks suitably guilty!

	Animal Farm (voices of all the animals)		*The Seventh Dawn* (Tarlton)
1955	*Doctor At Sea* (Easter)		*Hysteria* (Hemmings)
	Simon and Laura (Wilson)		*The Uncle* (Mr Ream)
1956	*Checkpoint* (Ted Thornhill)	1965	*The Legend of Young Dick Turpin*
1957	*Night of the Demon* (Professor Harrington)		(Mr Fielding)
	Barnacle Bill (Mayor Crowley)		*Operation Crossbow* (RAF Officer)
	Campbell's Kingdom (uncredited)		*Those Magnificent Men in Their Flying*
1959	*The Captain's Table* (Major Broster)		*Machines; or How I Flew from London to*
	Man With a Dog (short) (Mr Keeble)		*Paris in 25 Hours and 11 Minutes* (Ferry
1960	*Our Man In Havana* (Admiral)		Skipper)
	Two-Way Stretch (Commander Horatio		*The Nanny* (Dr Beamaster)
	Bennett)		*The Heroes of Telemark* (Doctor)
	Sink the Bismarck (Commander Richards)		*The Alphabet Murders* (Inspector Japp)
1961	*The Mark* (Arnold)		*The Night Caller* (Professor Morley)
	The Greengage Summer (Mr Bullock)	1967	*The Long Duel* (Governor)
	Invasion Quartet (Dr Barker)		*Torture Garden* (Colin's Uncle)
1962	*HMS Defiant* (Mr Goss)		*Danger Route* (Peter Ravenspur)
1963	*The Set-Up* (Theo Gaunt)	1968	*Attack on the Iron Coast* (Sir Frederick
	Paranoic (John Kosset)		Grafton)
	The Very Edge (Crawford)		*Negatives* (Father)
1964	*Downfall* (Sir Harold Crossley)	1969	*Some Girls Do* (Mortimer)

Anton Diffring

Anton Diffring's family name, de Vrient, means friend but in most of his film roles he is about as friendly as a beartrap. Diffring is the bad guy we love to hate, often seen in a Nazi uniform, displaying all the charm of a wrestler's armpit.

He was once on the British side, as a vengeful Pole, one of Alan Ladd's paratroop squad in *The Red Beret* (1953, Terence Young), but thereafter sided mainly with the opposition.

In *Albert RN* (1953, Lewis Gilbert), a well-intentioned and agreeably restrained – till the last reel – POW drama, Diffring was a prison guard who strikes a shady bargain with US airman William Sylvester, ie, briefly turning a blind eye while Sylvester makes his escape in return for the airman's chronometer. Sylvester hands it over, whereupon Diffring kills him, an act which fellow prisoner Anthony Steel later avenges when the Allies storm the camp. Albert, incidentally, was a papier mâché dummy which the prison guards mistake for Steel – an understandable mistake, considering the lifelessness of Steel's acting.

In *Reach for the Sky* (1956, Lewis Gilbert), Diffring was the German officer who recaptures legless flyer Douglas Bader, played by Kenneth More, in a barn after his first escape attempt, a piece of daring which results in the intrepid Britisher's confinement in the 'escape-proof' Colditz camp. By coincidence, Diffring had been a prison guard in an earlier film about the camp, *The Colditz Story* (1955, Guy Hamilton), starring John Mills and Eric Portman.

He popped up as Nazi security officer, guarding Norwegian heavy water installations against sabotage in *The Heroes of Telemark* (1965, Anthony Mann). Kirk Douglas and Richard Harris lead the attackers, a pick-and-mix assortment of zanies and patriots. He was Oscar Werner's fire-raising colleague in the cleverly futuristic *Fahrenheit 451* (1966, François Truffaut), who blows the whistle on him when Werner's interest in books threatens his ability to destroy them. Fortunately for Werner, Diffring's warning comes too late, and Werner succeeds in defecting to a colony where prized literature is memorized word for word and is therefore immune from destruction.

He was a Russian agent in *The Double Man* (1967, Franklin Schaffner), an intriguing spy yarn centring on the kidnap of CIA agent Yul Brynner in Austria and his replacement by an identical look-alike, also Brynner. Diffring masterminds the snatch, but his accomplices botch it, and CIA man Brynner returns to make life hot for his Russian counterpart. Their bitter showdown in a near-deserted ski-lift station, with

Anton Diffring, arch-badman of over a dozen war adventure stories

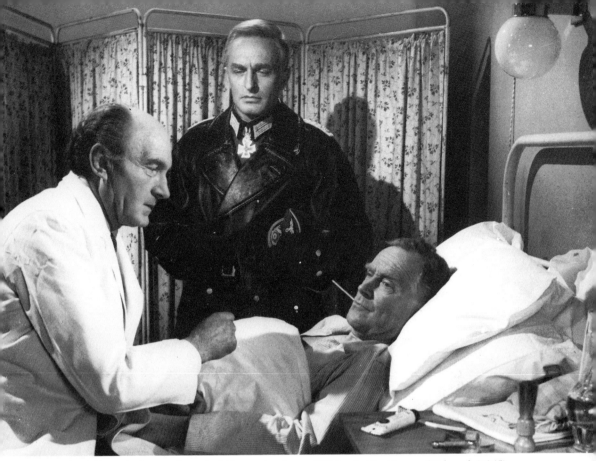

Ralph Michael fakes a bad appendix to fool Nazi major Anton Diffring in *The Heroes of Telemark* (1965).
Doctor Maurice Denham (left) attempts a diagnosis

both claiming to be genuine article and the American having to wager his life to call the imposter's bluff, is breathless enough to make one overlook the plot's basic implausibility. Brynner's Alpine-cool performance helps, too. Diffring offers a toned-down version of his familiar wicked Hun, a portrayal that gets progressively nervous – with good reason – as he becomes less and less able to humour his faceless employers.

In *Where Eagles Dare* (1968, Brian G. Hutton), a humourless but actionful war adventure, Diffring was the SS Commandant of an Alpine fortress holding a top American brasshat, one of the architects of the invasion of Europe, from whom they hope to extract valuable information. Richard Burton and Clint Eastwood are parachute officers assigned the job of getting him out, but it turns out that the American general is an imposter, a docile old GI corporal played by Robert Beatty, set up to dupe the Boche. Diffring seems a reasonable chap, sharing the view of a visiting Reichsmarschall, that an upstart

Gestapo major, Derren Nesbitt, ought to be kept out of things as far as possible, but it cuts no ice with the monosyllabic Eastwood – about whom Pauline Kael once wrote: '(He) has to deliver death because he has no other appeal'. Eastwood calmly disposes of Diffring, Nesbitt and dozens more loyal to the crumbling Fatherland.

Diffring made two far-fetched horror films between 1959-60. As *The Man Who Could Cheat Death* (1959, Terence Fisher) he was a nutty surgeon over 100 years old, kept youthful on yearly gland implants. When his aging mentor suffers a heart attack making further surgery impossible, Diffring's search for youth-giving serum becomes more desperate. At the end, the accumulated years stampede all over him, and his face disintegrates like the contents of a shredded pillowcase.

In *Circus of Horrors* (1960, Sidney Hayers) Diffring played a plastic surgeon whose disfigurement of a titled lady patient sends him on the run. He inherits a rundown circus which he

47

glamourises with criminal girls whom his surgical skills transform into beauties. When they become jealous of each other, and troublesome the way that beautiful ambitious girls can be, Diffring gets rid of them by causing their circus acts to go spectacularly wrong – high wires snap, knives impale, tigers rampage. The stories are junk but Diffring manages to instil his characters, badly written though so many were, with a certain noble despair, which suggests that he may have been a better actor than he has been given credit for.

Anton Diffring

b. 1918. Frequently seen Nazi-style bully or cold-eyed villain in 1950s uniform melodramas. (In real life, a charming and cultured actor.) Still very active in films, though now predominantly on the European scene. Occasional British TV (*The Flambards* etc).

1950 *State Secret* (Policeman)
1951 *Hotel Sahara* (German)
       Appointment with Venus (German)
1952 *The Woman's Angle* (Peasant)
1953 *The Red Beret* (The Pole)
       Albert RN (Hauptmann Schultz)
       Park Plaza 605 (Gregor)
       Operation Diplomat (Schroder)
1955 *Colditz Story* (Capt Fischer)
       I am a Camera (Fritz)

1956 *The Black Tent* (German Officer)
       House of Secrets (Lauderback)
       Reach for the Sky (German Soldier)
       Doublecross (Dimitri Krassin)
1957 *The Traitor* (Joseph Brezzini)
       The Crooked Sky (Fraser)
       Seven Thunders (Col Trautmann)
       Lady of Vengeance (Karnak)
1958 *A Question of Adultery* (Carl Dieter)
       Mark of the Phoenix (Insp Schell)
1959 *The Man Who Could Cheat Death* (Dr
       Georges Bonner)
1960 *Circus of Horrors* (Dr Bernard Schuler)
1961 *Enter Inspector Duval* (Insp Duval)
1963 *Incident at Midnight* (Dr Erik Leichner)
1965 *The Heroes of Telemark* (Major Frick)
1966 *The Blue Max* (Holbach)
       Fahrenheit 451 (Fabian)
1967 *The Double Man* (Berthold)
1968 *Where Eagles Dare* (Col Kramer)
1970 *Zeppelin* (Colonel Johann Hirsch)
1974 *The Beast Must Die* (Pavel)
       Dead Pigeon on Beethoven Street (Mensur)
       The Day the Clown Cried
1975 *Shatter* (Hans Leber)
       The Swiss Conspiracy (Franz Benninger)
1976 *Operation Daybreak* (Reinhard Heydrich)
1977 *Valentino* (Baron Long)
       Return to Munich
1978 *Tusk*
1980 *The Winds of War*

Denholm Elliott

It's even money that Denholm Elliott must come a cropper in *The Sound Barrier* (1952, David Lean). He wants to enlist in the Navy, or perhaps the Commandos – anywhere but the RAF – but hard-boiled plane-maker father Ralph Richardson wants Elliott to continue the family's distinguished flying tradition. Alas, the lad is a big disappointment – in the air he's more like Red Riding Hood than the Red Baron, a timid dyspeptic soul who can barely distinguish a joystick from a length of Blackpool rock. You're either born to fly or you're not – I'm not!' he confides to protective big sister Ann Todd, the night before his first, and last, attempt at solo flying.

Richardson is determined that his jet plane will be first to exceed the speed of sound, despite

the loss of his son and, later in a test flight, the death of son-in-law Nigel Patrick. It's an obsession from which he pulls back in time to avoid becoming a deranged lonely old man.

It has taken Denholm Elliott a long time to mature, but like good wine it's been worth the wait. Maturity has brought colour and dimension to that pallid, true-blue face which anguished and perspired its way through films of the 1950s and 1960s.

Another good example of vintage weak-guy Elliott occurred in *The Cruel Sea* (1953, Charles Frend), in which he was an unhappy junior officer in Jack Hawkins' command whose small-time actress wife, Moira Lister, plays fast and loose with unsavoury theatrical types while Elliott is away. One night he answers the phone and hears someone asking if she has managed to shake off 'that clot of a husband' for the night. Shortly afterwards his ship is torpedoed, and Elliott drowns without putting up much of a struggle, still rankled by his wife's infidelity.

Elliott hated being cast as a supercilious juvenile, a sort of middle-class George Cole – for one thing he was already in his thirties when he made *The Cruel Sea* and had, in fact, been in a German prisoner-of-war camp for three years after being shot down over Germany whilst serving with Bomber Command. Not that he hankered for red-blooded roles, either. He told one reporter: 'I don't think of myself as a hero. I've always been drawn to parts that have a rich and somewhat shady character.'

Elliott has followed his own advice and given some of the sleaziest performances around. He was the seedy dropout who shows Alan Bates how to scale social heights in *Nothing But The Best* (1964, Cliver Donner). When Elliott is refused credit by his bookies, Bates starts an account which, thanks to Elliott's connections, scoops the jackpot. Rather than part with the winnings to Elliott, Bates strangles him with his old school tie.

In *Alfie* (1966, Lewis Gilbert) he was the abortionist who gets rid of Vivien Merchant's unwanted baby in Michael Caine's flat. 'Its a crime against the unborn child . . . not a course to be embarked on lightly,' he says before greedily pocketing the £25 fee and knuckling down to the task. Afterwards Caine panics at the thought of her being left in his sole care and wants Elliott to stay on and see the job through. But Elliott is not in the least interested and feels no responsibility. He leaves a phial of tablets for Miss Merchant – 'two if she sweats' – and vanishes zombie-like into the night.

Here We Go Round the Mulberry Bush (1967, Clive Donner) gave us a different kind of Denholm Elliott, seen here as a happy-go-lucky middle-aged swinger with a sexy daughter, Judy Geeson, and an equally alluring German au pair. The daughter's fresh-faced college beau Barry Evans, envious at his chums having all the girlie action, has his eyelids rolled back during a weekend romp at Elliott's rural pile.

Denholm Elliott (left), as the police inspector, confronts Gene Barry in *Maroc 7* (1966)

Denholm Elliott in *Bad Timing* (1980)

Evans arrives with two pyjama tops and no bottoms – a mistake in the packing department which nonetheless aptly summarises his expectations. The evening is spent draining a variety of Daddy's favourite wine bottles, while Elliott extols the virtues of each glass like a speaking wine brochure. When Evans retires upstairs with Miss Geeson, Elliott, by then rapturously bog-eyed, simply can't understand why anyone would decline 'a rather excellent port'. The bedroom antics are confined to nimble footwork and not much else, with the desirable Miss Geeson passing out drunk before Evans can achieve the otherwise highly likely. There are a few sinister bumps in the night, or rather, the corridor, as Elliott makes his way stealthily towards the au pair's bedroom, and even the coolly composed lady of the house, Maxine Audley, is soon at it, persuading Evans, after lights out, that he really ought to have a (nudge, nudge) nightcap.

It was a breezy, inoffensive romp, time-locked to the Swinging Sixties, and, if one is looking for near comparisons, less pedestrian than the *Carry Ons* (which predate it) whilst, in my view, more palatable than the few *Confessions Of* – which came after. Barry Evans, whose career in films regrettably never took off, was agreeable enough as a kind of working-class Ian Carmichael, determined to lose his innocence and keep his nerve at the same time, whilst Elliott, as the raffish, liberated father, made much more of the material than was actually written.

In *Too Late the Hero* (1969, Robert Aldrich), he was in charge of an ill-assorted platoon given the task of destroying enemy communications on an island overrun by Japs. Under his command are Cliff Robertson, as a Jap-speaking US Marine on loan to the British Army because he can fluently impersonate the enemy, Michael Caine as a resourceful cockney roughneck who resents taking orders that put his life at risk, plus Ian Bannen, Ronald Fraser and Percy Herbert as war-hardened soldiers bedevilled by hordes of small yellow men. The platoon nevertheless reach the offending transmitters, but Robertson refuses to obey Elliott's command to storm the target, on the grounds that he is there to parley Japanese over the wires not kill the existing broadcasters. Elliott is thus forced into an un-characteristic John Wayne act, for which he pays with his life, but not before lurching back to where Robertson sits, in the safety of some trees, and fixing the American with an accusing, wide-eyed, death stare, rather like the one Janet Leigh wore after Anthony Perkins had knifed her to death in the famous shower scene in *Psycho* (1959).

This is too much for Robertson who is im-mediately transformed into a war-comic Jap-hater, and so starry-eyed is he about his new voc-ation that when Caine suggests nipping off in the opposite direction to the gunfire, Robertson chops him in the stomach for having succumbed to such naughty impulses. None of this, alas, is of much interest to Elliott, still dead as a dodo amid the wreckage of several huts. In the same way, one suspects that what happens next is not of great interest to the audience, since it's all too familiar, and the chemistry that the producers hoped for between Caine and Robertson simply never happened.

I also found the notion of Japanese troops broadcasting their threats to the fleeing Britons in perfect English via huge loudspeakers in the jungle a little odd. Anyway, why stop at just talk when a few increased decibels and some tradi-tional Japanese music would, I am sure, have had Caine and his partner leaping into their arms in surrender.

Elliott once told the *Evening News*: 'I would rather stay in the second line. As a character actor you get interesting parts . . . and you're in a very good position to steal the film.' He had a fair crack at doing just that in *The Night They Raided Minsky's* (1968, William Friedkin) as the insidi-ously nasty anti-vice watchdog whose strident

opposition to the notorious burlesque show results in its closure. Elliott cannot reconcile the
complacency of the authorities with the spread
of immorality throughout New York, and pesters
everyone in sight for action. Asked why he is so
hot under the collar he replies indignantly,
'Well, for one thing, all the ladies *jiggle!*'

Denholm Elliott

b. 1922. Juvenile-looking 1950s dogsbody
(*The Sound Barrier* (1952), *The Cruel Sea*
(1953)), who matured during 1960s into appeal-
ingly-repugnant disreputable roles, such as Alan
Bates' mentor – and later murder victim – in
Nothing But the Best (1964). Often seen in smallish,
scene-stealing parts, eg the abortionist in *Alfie*
(1966) or the moralist in *The Night They Raided
Minsky's* (1968). Former husband (before Bill
Travers) of actress Virginia McKenna.

1949 *Dear Mr Prohack* (Ozzie Morfrey)
1952 *The Sound Barrier* (Chris Ridgefield)
      The Holly and the Ivy (Michael Gregory)
      The Ringer (John Lenley)
1953 *The Cruel Sea* (Lieutenant Morell)
      The Heart of the Matter (Wilson)
1954 *They Who Dare* (Sgt Corcoran)
1955 *The Man Who Loved Redheads* (Dennis)
      The Night My Number Came Up (Flight
          Lieutenant MacKenzie)
      Lease of Life (Martin Blake)
1956 *Pacific Destiny* (Arthur Grimble)
1963 *Station Six Sahara* (Macey)
1964 *Nothing But the Best* (Charlie Prince)
      The High Bright Sun (Baker)
1965 *You Must Be Joking* (Captain Tabasco)

King Rat (USA) (Larkin)
1966 *Alfie* (Abortionist)
      The Spy With A Cold Nose (Pond-Jones)
      Maroc 7 (Inspector Barrada)
1967 *Here We Go Round the Mulberry Bush* (Mr
          Beauchamp)
1968 *The Night They Raided Minsky's* (USA)
          (Vance Fowler)
1969 *The Seagull* (Dorn)
      Too Late the Hero (Captain Hornsby)
1970 *The Rise and Rise of Michael Rimmer*
          (Peter Niss)
      The House that Dripped Blood (Charles
          Hillyear)
      Percy (Emmanuel Whitbread)
1971 *Quest for Love* (Tom Lewis)
1972 *Madame Sin* (Malcolm de Vere)
1973 *Vault of Horror* (Diltant)
      A Dolls House (Krogstad)
1974 *Percy's Progress* (Sir Emmanuel
          Whitbread)
      The Apprenticeship of Duddy Kravitz (Friar)
1975 *Russian Roulette* (USA) (Petapiece)
      To the Devil a Daughter (Henry Beddows)
      Robin and Marian (Will Scarlett)
1976 *Voyage of the Damned* (Admiral Cararis)
      A Bridge Too Far (RAF Met Officer)
1978 *The Boys From Brazil* (Sidney Beyman)
1979 *Saint Jack* (William Leigh)
      Game for Vultures (Raglan Thistle)
      Zulu Dawn (Colonel Pulleine)
1980 *Bad Timing* (Stefan Vognic)
      The Sweeney (Jupp)
      Ciba (Skinner)
      Rising Damp (Seymour)
1981 *Raiders of the Lost Ark* (Brody)

Peter Finch

Some actors like, for example, Alan Ladd, lead
colourful, non-conformist lives in front of the
cameras and keep the agonies and self-doubts for
private moments. With Peter Finch it was the
other way round. He often acted as though parts
of him were being fed through a mincer, but
away from the movie set his extravagant
maverick nature broke out into the sunniest of
smiles.

Biographer Trader Faulkner said that long before Finch arrived back in Britain in 1948 – he
was born in South Kensington in 1916 – he had

become a legend in his own lunchtime. His one
reasonable movie part, a miner in Ealing's
Eureka Stockade (1948, Harry Watt), made on
location in Australia, had vanished in the edit-
ing-room, but Sir Laurence Olivier, who had
befriended him in Australia, had invited him to
get in touch if ever he wanted to break into the
British theatre scene, and starts do not come any
more encouraging than that. Harry Watt, his
director on *Eureka Stockade*, got him a small part
as a murderer in *Train of Events* (1949, Basil
Dearden), and he played a captive Australian Air

Stolen moments in a Japanese POW camp for Peter Finch and Virginia McKenna in *A Town Like Alice* (1956)

Force officer – again a one-scene job in the camp sick-bay – in *The Wooden Horse* (1950, Jack Lee), most famous of the wartime escape stories based on Eric Williams' blood-stirring account of the Stalag Luft III breakout.

Finch's career took a significant lurch forward with his sombre, ruminative Sheriff of Nottingham in Disney's *The Story of Robin Hood and His Merrie Men* (1952, Ken Annakin), a performance that forsook the swagger and vowel-rolling villainy of the pre-war Rathbone version in favour of a quietly determined, almost gentlemanly villain. It was a refreshingly new perspective on one of folklore's more celebrated nasties. By contrast, Richard Todd's Robin Hood looked like a garden gnome in a carelessly-made green tunic.

Finch took on Alec Guinness at his own game in *Father Brown* (1954, Robert Hamer), in which he played a smooth master-criminal adept at disguises, several of which he employs in order to outwit Guinness's unrelentingly decent detective-priest. It was a demanding, multi-role performance and Finch was impressive, no

doubt encouraged to be so by the presence of his illustrious co-star. He was less than good in *Simon and Laura* (1955, Muriel Box), Alan Melville's awkwardly pretentious stage comedy about a TV soap-opera couple blisslessly married in real life. Top radio humourists Muir and Norden were roped in to boost the humour, but it was doubtful fodder for Finch. Through the kiss-and-yell antics of Finch and Kay Kendall as the steamy couple, one can detect his genuine unease.

He played an Aussie soldier in Japanese hands in war-torn Malaya in *A Town Like Alice* (1956, Jack Lee), and a free-wheeling swagman with child trouble in *The Shiralee* (1957, Leslie Norman), one of his liveliest roles of the 1950s and one allegedly close to his own character. He played a German battleship captain in *Battle of the River Plate* (1956, Michael Powell, Emeric Pressburger), based on the account of the British naval blockading of the SS *Graf Spee* off the coast of South America during the opening stages of World War II. The film never caught fire, but Finch's thoughtful playing of the doomed officer who prefers suicide in a lonely hotel room to returning home in disgrace succeeds in making the character sympathetic in a way rarely tasted in enemy officer portrayals.

He was a memorable Oscar Wilde in *The Trials of Oscar Wilde* (1960, Ken Hughes), a vibrant extravaganza that contained all the capriciousness and noisy decadence of an impressionist print. The film opens at the height of Wilde's popularity when he was the darling of London society, and traces the ups and downs of his ill-judged affair with the Marquis of Queensberry's unstable son, played by John Fraser, and Queensberry's revenge. Several scenes are quite excellent, such as the distraught Queensberry, Lionel Jeffries, presenting Wilde with a bouquet of rotten fruit and being waspishly told: 'Everytime I smell these I shall think of you.'

When Fraser makes a quip and Finch admits to his cronies that he wishes he had said that, one of them knowingly observes: 'You will, Oscar. You will!' Casting Finch, a well-documented womaniser, in the role of a homosexual was seen at the time – when the public attitude to such subjects was less tolerant than now – as a clever move by the film's producers Warwick Films to forestall any outcry. But in the last analysis it was the quality of Finch's acting, not his much publicised hetero leanings, which ensured the film a trouble-free and, indeed, from all quarters, a warm reception.

Like many top actors Finch preferred not to analyse his craft. He saw acting as a natural extension of living which, like life itself, just happened. 'Many fine actors have a kind of dedication to acting that is born, grows and matures with them,' he once said. 'Others just drift into it, fall in love with it and stick with it. Either way there's no mystery about it.'

No Love for Johnnie (1961, Ralph Thomas) was an unsentimental peep under the lid of British politics, with Finch as an ambitious Socialist MP whose brilliance in the House is counterpointed in his private life by weakness and vanity. The film was nicely in tune with the mood of realism pervading British studios of the period and Finch brought a watchable, care-worn quality to the flawed MP. He was Ann Bancroft's menopausal husband in *The Pumpkin Eater* (1964, Jack Clayton), a superior marriage-on-the-rocks drama which set a high standard for other mid-life marital crisis stories to try to emulate. Scripted by Harold Pinter from Penelope Mortimer's novel, it must have done for the bridal gown trade what the Titanic did for winter cruises.

Two of his more satisfying later roles occurred under John Schlesinger's direction – *Far From the Madding Crowd* (1967) and *Sunday Bloody Sunday* (1971).

In the former, he was rich estate-owner Julie Christie's bachelor neighbour, desperately in love with her but unable to arouse her interest. Her admission that she loves a disreputable Guards sergeant nearly drives him off his head, but when the resulting marriage flops and Miss Christie again needs comforting, Finch comes back into the picture more strongly than before.

At a party he gives in her honour, however, the unwanted husband returns and behaves disgracefully in front of Finch's guests, humiliating Miss Christie by attempting to drag her outside. Finch snatches up his rifle and calmly shoots the intruder. It's a gallant thought, but the law takes a different view, and shortly afterwards we see prison carpenters busily at work on his coffin while Finch broods sadly on what might have been.

In *Sunday Bloody Sunday*, he played a cultured Jewish doctor, again badly wrecked emotionally by an on-off affair with a handsome bisexual. The lad in question also enjoys a few bedtime romps with Glenda Jackson. In the end he departs for New York leaving his unhappy partners to mull over the wreckage.

Both were pictorially elegant 'mood' pictures, and as with his Oscar Wilde performance eleven years previously, Finch achieved, in the latter, close identification with the star-crossed homosexual without the merest hint of effeminacy. He achieved it by projecting up through the outer layers of an apparently normal personality an almost imperceptible despair. His acting had the quality of immaculately diffused lighting –one could enjoy the glow without being in any way conscious of the source.

Finch made his share of stinkers, too, but managed to redeem all but the really hopeless cases with his customary integrity. His final role was Israel Premier Yitzhak Rabin in *Raid on Entebbe* (1976, Irvin Kershner), a documentary flavoured retelling of the commando-style rescue of a group of Israeli hostages from Uganda's main airport during Amin's rule. But Finch's epitaph is considered by most people to have been his Oscar-winning performance in *Network* (1976, USA, Sidney Lumet), in which he played a TV

Peter Finch played an ambitious Socialist MP in *No Love for Johnnie* (1961)

newscaster so disgusted with life that he makes it known during a newscast that he intends to end his life in exactly one week – in full view of the cameras. The network chiefs decide to fire him, but a sudden leap in the ratings rules that out. Instead, he is marketed to a mesmerised audience as a kind of avenging angel, articulating the voice of the demented masses. It was a powerful film, and Finch's best for several years. Ironically, after over two decades of unsuccessfully courting Hollywood, he was dead before finally being admitted on his own terms.

Peter Finch
1916-1977. London-born, Australia-domiciled (till 1948), expressive-eyed leading man, best utilised in romantic, human conflict, contemporary roles. Winner of three British Film Awards and one Oscar. On stage from 1934. Australian film debut: *The Magic Shoes* (1935). British film debut: *Eureka Stockade* (1948).

1938 *Dad and Dave Come to Town*
1939 *Mr Chedworth Steps Out*
1941 *The Power and the Glory*
1944 *Rats of Tobruck*
1945 *Red Sky at Morning* (Michael)
1946 *A Star Is Born* (Paul Graham)
1948 *Eureka Stockade* (John Humffray)
1949 *Train of Events* (Philip Mason)

1950 *The Wooden Horse* (RAAF Officer)
       The Miniver Story (Polish Officer)
1952 *The Story of Robin Hood and his Merrie Men*
       (The Sheriff of Nottingham)
1953 *The Story of Gilbert and Sullivan*
       (Rupert D'Oyly Carte)
       The Heart of the Matter (Father Rank)
1954 *Elephant Walk* (USA) (John Wiley)
       Father Brown (Flambeau)
       Make Me an Offer (Charlie)
1955 *The Dark Avenger* (Count De Ville)
       Passage Home (Captain 'Lucky' Ryland)
       Josephine and Men (David Hewer)
       Simon and Laura (Simon Foster)
1956 *A Town Like Alice* (Joe Harman)
       The Battle of the River Plate (Captain
       Langsdorff)
1957 *The Shiralee* (Jim Macauley)
       Robbery Under Arms (Captain Starlight)
       Windom's Way (Alec Windom)
1958 *The Nun's Story* (Dr Fortunati)
       Operation Amsterdam (Jan Smit)
1959 *Kidnapped* (Alan Breck Stewart)
1960 *The Sins of Rachel Cade* (USA)
       (Colonel Henry Derode)
       The Trials of Oscar Wilde (Oscar Wilde)
1961 *No Love for Johnnie* (Johnny Byrne)
1962 *I Thank a Fool* (Stephen Dane)
       In the Cool of the Day (Murray Logan)
1963 *The Girl With Green Eyes* (Eugene
       Gaillard)
1964 *The Pumpkin Eater* (Jake Armitage)
       First Men in the Moon (Bailiff's Man)
1965 *Judith* (USA) (Aaron Stein)
       The Flight of the Phoenix (USA)
       (Captain Harris)
1966 *10.30pm Summer* (USA/Spain) (Paul)
1967 *Far From the Madding Crowd* (William
       Boldwood)
1968 *The Legend of Lylah Clare* (USA) (Lewis
       Zarkin)
1969 *The Red Tent* (USSR/Italy) (General
       Umberto Nobile)
1971 *Sunday Bloody Sunday* (Dr Daniel Hirsh)
       Something to Hide (Harry)
1972 *England Made Me* (Erich Krogh)
1973 *Lost Horizon* (USA) (Robert Conway)
       Bequest to the Nation (Horatio Nelson)
1974 *The Abdication* (Cardinal Azzolino)
1976 *Network* (USA) (Howard Beale)
1976 *Raid on Entebbe* (USA) (Yitzhak Rabin)
Also directed short film, *The Day* (1960) made in Spain, and appeared as Errol Flynn in US 2-reeler, *The Greatest Mother of Them All* (1969).

Albert Finney

'What a wonderful Friday night,' growls Albert Finney in *Saturday Night and Sunday Morning* (1960, Karel Reisz), when Rachel Roberts, the married lady with whom he has been fooling, announces that she is pregnant. Shortly afterwards he is cornered by two beefy army pals of her husband, who give him a thorough working over. 'They bested me right enough,' he concedes afterwards, but adds chirpily, 'Still, I had my bit of fun!'

Finney always seems to have his bit of fun in his films, which is probably why, despite relatively few appearances, he remains one of our most engaging actors. He represents the rough, gritty, gregarious North, narrow streets, back-to-backs, fish suppers and public bars in much the same way Michael Caine used to characterise the trendier South. Compare the central character of Finney's *Gumshoe* (1972, Stephen Frears) and Caine's *Get Carter* (1971, Mike Klinger), both pacy English echoes of the familiar glossy US gangster product. Finney's sharp-talking bingo caller with notions of being Philip Marlowe weaves rather than shoulders his way through a tangled sub-Chandleresque web complete with its own Fat Man.

In *Get Carter*, Caine was a hard-nosed gangland figure who returns to his native North East to avenge his brother's murder. The killings and violence are graphically – some critics at the time thought gratuitously – depicted, and the film lacks the cleverness and ambivalence of *Gumshoe*.

Although *Get Carter*, using familiar characters and filmed against authentic North East backgrounds, ought to ring more true than *Gumshoe*, which is really nothing more than an affectionate send-up of a dated genre that had, at the time of its decline, already come dangerously close to self parody, the remarkable fact is that it does not. And its mostly due to Finney.

In *Gumshoe*, Finney stays convincingly within his established movie character – colourful, breezy, self-effacing – who happens on this occasion to be a bingo-caller. There are no sides to the character which fall outside our conception of him, so nothing that he is a party to rings fake. Though the Caine character is a close cousin of his self-aware Alfie creation, we are asked to believe that he is a gangster and a killer; but we know the actor too well through various

newspaper items and TV interviews to ever believe he is anything but a popular actor chancing his arm in a different sort of part. And that, for me, relegates *Get Carter* to a lesser kind of experience.

As *Tom Jones* (1963, Tony Richardson) in Fielding's irreverent 18th-century romp, Finney again had his 'bit of fun', although he was conspicuously of the present day in a field of players who might have dropped out of a Hogarth canvas. Finney was a country lad born on the wrong side of the blanket whose climb to social acceptance and the love of high-born Susannah York is very nearly thwarted by unscrupulous rivals and a hangman's noose. Only when director Tony Richardson's self-indulgence runs away with itself, as for example with silent-flick subtitling, freeze-framing, and characters confiding in the camera, does the fun become laboured.

At the end of *The Victors* (1963, Carl Foreman), a sprawling anti-war canvas, Finney was the belligerent Russian soldier who gets involved in a futile argument with a mild but war-scarred US infantryman, George Hamilton, which ends in a savage knife fight in which

Albert Finney adopts the Bogart look as a private eye Eddie Ginley in *Gumshoe* (1972)

55

both are killed. Foreman addresses his message with the subtlety of a teenage graffiti artist, but the pre-credits image of Finney and Hamilton lying dead in a bomb-flattened German town is peppered with raw irony.

Finney holds the attention but his performance lacks the dimension of inner torment as the psychopath in Emlyn Williams' *Night Must Fall* (1964, Karel Reisz) who keeps a victim's mutilated head in a hat box. The opening sequence, Finney enigmatically hacking at something hidden in dense undergrowth, is given a neat, retrospective horror when later in the film we are let into the secret of what he had been doing.

Finney directed and starred as *Charlie Bubbles* (1967), a successful novelist visiting his humble Northern roots following a bereavement. The prodigal son, unstirred by fame and fortune, tries gamely to reinstate himself with faces and attitudes long left behind, but failure and disillusion confront him at every turn. Even his ex-wife, played by Billie Whitelaw, is aloof and recriminatory, and at the end he has to face the painful truth that the gap is unbridgeable.

Finney went in for an elaborate disguise as Hercule Poirot, Agatha Christie's sardonic Belgian detective, in *Murder on the Orient Express* (1974, Sidney Lumet), with puffy cheeks, a curly waxed moustache, hair treatment by courtesy of Mobil and a voice that sounded like Sydney Greenstreet trying to make himself understood in downtown Bruges. Despite the celebrated cast and Finney's skilful impersonation, the excursion was a bit of a sleeper and its cop-out ending

a disappointment. The big question was, did someone sneak into dislikable Richard Widmark's compartment and stab him twelve times, or did twelve people, all with good reason to want him dead, file in singly and each stick him once. The film seemed to opt for the second alternative, but, alas, half-heartedly, like nearly all the big-name performances.

Albert Finney
b. 1936. On stage from 1956. Early examples of 1950s neo-realism acting school, later leading National Theatre player. Popular stage successes include *Billy Liar* and *Luther*. Film debut in *The Entertainer* (1960). Directed as well as starred in *Charlie Bubbles* (1967).

1960 *The Entertainer* (Mick Rice)
     Saturday Night and Sunday Morning (Arthur Seaton)
1963 *Tom Jones* (Tom Jones)
     The Victors (Russian Soldier)
1964 *Night Must Fall* (Danny)
1967 *Charlie Bubbles* (Charlie Bubbles)
     Two for the Road (Mark Wallace)
1970 *Scrooge* (Ebenezer Scrooge)
1972 *Gumshoe* (Eddie Ginley)
1974 *Murder on the Orient Express* (Hercule Poirot)
1977 *The Duellists* (Fouche)
1979 *Wolfen* (N. York)
1980 *Loophole* (Mike Daniels)
     Looker (Larry Rogers)
     Shoot the Moon (George)
1981 *Annie* (Daddy Warbucks)

Bryan Forbes

It comes as no surprise to discover that Bryan Forbes began life as Nobby Clarke from West Ham. Everyone has had a Chalky White or a Nobby Clarke as his best pal at some time, shinning up trees together or collecting newts, and Forbes, with the spiky hair and engaging manner, fits the bill exactly. For the Cockney son of a commercial traveller –'There was no literary or artistic influence there, but I think I found out about people' – Forbes' achievements in films, as actor, writer and director, are formidable. To master any of those skills is praiseworthy but to blaze a trail in all three (all right then, two!)

takes talent way above the ordinary.

Acting came first, beginning with being blown up by a plastic bomb in *The Small Back Room* (1949, Michael Powell), a prisoner-of-war in *The Wooden Horse* (1950, Jack Lee), and a doomed Bomber Command pilot in *Appointment in London* (1952, Philip Leacock). Whatever else he was, Forbes was expendable. Newly married to a second-league American actress, he followed her dog-like to Hollywood, passing up chances to appear in *The Sound Barrier* (1952, David Lean) and *The Holly and the Ivy* (1952, George More O'Ferrall) in roles that would have

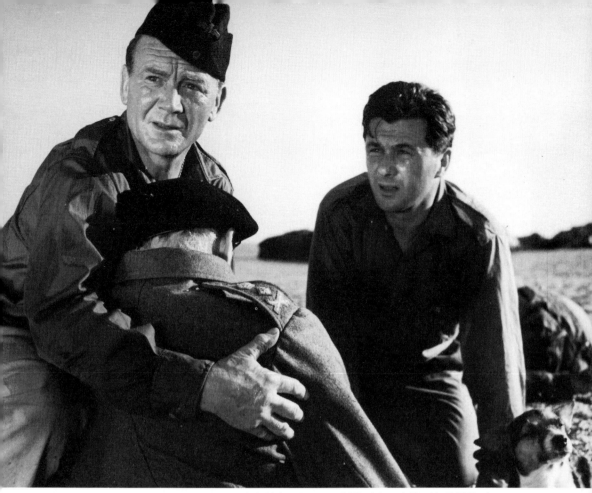

Bryan Forbes (right) and John Mills tend wounded Clifton James in *I Was Monty's Double* (1958), the true story of James' impersonation of Britain's most famous Field Marshal during World War II

established him as a marketable actor. Denholm Elliott substituted for him on both occasions.

Forbes was a Napoleonic Wars matelot, Rock Hudson's side-kick, in *Sea Devils* (1953, Raoul Walsh), and appeared with Gregory Peck in *The Million Pound Note* (1953, Ronald Neame), based on Mark Twain's story about a drifter who is given a million pound note by two scatty brothers, each wagering a bet with the other about the note's impact – on no account must it be broken into – on the drifter's way of life. With the benefit of hindsight, one wonders what Forbes might have done with the script – his lightness of touch might have transformed this average film into an outstanding one.

He got his first crack at writing, under Raoul Walsh's paternal guidance during *Sea Devils*, but the first script he got a credit on was *The Black Knight* (1954, Tay Garnett), an unintentionally hilarious medieval romp with Alan Ladd rescu-

ing Olde England from marauding Normans. Forbes was a late gamble by the producers to salvage something from what had gone ahead, but like an alcoholic's paycheck, it was unsavable.

Between appearances in *Passage Home* (1955, Roy Baker) and *The Extra Day* (1956, William Fairchild), and no doubt in gratitude for his attempts to salvage *The Black Knight*, its producers gave him the job of revamping *Cockleshell Heroes* (1955, José Ferrer), a true-life war adventure in which a party of commandoes sabotage part of the German fleet by fixing limpet mines to the vessels while they are docked. Assault is mounted from a contingent of two-man canoes which bob in and around the enemy warships like flies around a team of plough-horses. Ferrer doubled as director and star, with Trevor Howard as the British adjutant in charge. Forbes kept his credit, but his efforts had been superseded, on Ferrer's say-so, before the cameras rolled.

He appeared briefly with John Mills in the prisoner-of-war escape drama *The Colditz Story* (1954, Guy Hamilton) and again in *It's Great To Be Young* (1956, Cyril Frankel), where Mills was a trendy history teacher trying to keep the school orchestra alive against the wishes of new headmaster Cecil Parker. Forbes had one scene, as a chirpy organ salesman who tries to win an order from Parker. Selling ski-boots to penguins would have been easier.

Invited to co-script *The Baby and the Battleship* (1956, Jay Lewis), a facile comedy about the smuggling of a baby on to a Royal Navy cruiser, again with Mills plus Richard Attenborough, Forbes felt on solid ground after the Ladd and Ferrer fiascos. He also got to know Attenborough, then at a restless point in his acting career, and it proved a meeting of similar minds much to the benefit of the British film industry.

The Angry Silence (1960, Guy Green) was a creditable start to their fledgling partnership, known as Beaver Films, and aptly named, according to Forbes, for the way Attenborough slaved to make the venture a success. Michael Craig's original story line about blue-collar conscience versus industrial mob violence was fleshed out by Forbes into a disturbing statement on the decline of decency and fair play in modern industrial relations. Attenborough produced as well as starred as a factory worker whose refusal to join a strike fuelled by bully-boys and political hotheads ends in tragedy for him. Pier Angeli played his distraught wife and Michael Craig was the fair-weather friend who later marshals the voices of reason.

Forbes appeared in *The Key* (1958, Carol Reed), a salty tale about naval captains William Holden and Trevor Howard and their relationship with Sophia Loren, and made two actionful war movies – *Yesterday's Enemy* (1959, Val Guest) and *The Guns of Navarone* (1961, Carl Foreman). *Yesterday's Enemy,* about a platoon in Burma outnumbered and hounded through hostile jungles by resourceful Japs, was criticised at the time for its depiction of British Army cruelty to the natives in a progressively desperate fight to survive. Nothing is done to soften the harshness of armed conflict on all concerned, and the film delivers its strong anti-war message without flinching from the task. Forbes' appearance in *The Guns of Navarone* was a long way down the cast list as a member of General James Robertson Justice's staff.

With the coming of the 1960s, Forbes' opportunities for screen acting diminished – 'I gave up acting before acting gave me up,' he admits – and he began devoting his considerable talents and energies almost exclusively to writing and directing features for Beaver Films.

He wrote *The League of Gentlemen* (1960, Basil Dearden), which Attenborough produced and acted in as one of an ensemble of ex-Army no-goods fashioned into a skilful assault unit by a shrewd senior officer with a grudge against the Establishment. Their target is a bank. First-rate performances came from Jack Hawkins, as the gang's resourceful leader, Nigel Patrick as an engaging down-at-heel, with Roger Livesey, Attenborough and Norman Bird as other 'gentlemen', and a literate script discusses within the framework of an exciting bank-job story a much more relevant issue – the dangers posed to society by those trained to use arms in defence of its freedoms, when lack of lawful goals or adequate rewards turn those deadly skills against society and its institutions. Forbes turned in his best writing to date – possibly his best writing ever – and the production won stunning reviews everywhere it played. Even after all these years, it has lost none of its nervy vitality.

Forbes' first direction job was *Whistle Down the Wind* (1961), an appealing Christ-fable allegory, based on a novel by Mary Hayley Bell (Mrs John Mills), starring daughter Hayley as the oldest of three rural Yorkshire schoolchildren whose encounter with bearded fugitive Alan Bates is both funny and deeply touching. In his book *Notes For a Life,* Forbes reveals that John Mills and his wife were unhappy about entrusting Hayley's career to a novice director, and at first exercised their power of veto over his taking charge, but later relented. Forbes' directorial debut proved every bit as distinctive as the first film he had written for Beaver, *The Angry Silence,* but in a wholly different sort of way, different enough to make you wonder how two such divergent themes and treatments could possibly originate within the space of less than a year from a single creative source.

The following year saw Forbes redrafting Kingsley Amis' novel *That Uncertain Feeling* as *Only Two Can Play* (1962, Sidney Gilliatt), a runaway success for Peter Sellers, cast as a morose Welsh librarian-drama critic, putting his stamp on things other than books, with producer Attenborough again making a guest appearance, as Sellers' one-time rival for the hand of Sellers' wife and still miffed over his defeat by someone he so obviously regards as an intellectual in-

Bryan Forbes (extreme right) and some of his bank robber friends in *The League of Gentlemen* (1960)

ferior. Attenborough, a local poet and playwright, wows the Swansea literati but gets nowhere in his attempts to squash the wryly disrespectful Sellers. When the old foes meet at a posh party, and Attenborough asks, with a sneer, if he's still peddling trash to the masses,. Sellers replies, 'Yes, are you still writing it?'

Later, Sellers prefers an evening of (attempted) passion with a local councillor's wife – played by Mai Zetterling – to attending the opening night of a dreary amateur stage production, and delivers a pre-written, conciliatory review to his local paper before the curtain goes up. While he cavorts with Miss Zetterling, the theatre is gutted by fire half-way through the performance, an incident damningly ignored in Sellers' so-called review. Though X-rated at the time of its release, changing attitudes have made *Only Two Can Play* respectable without damaging its fine comic balance.

'My films are all about aspects of love,' says Forbes, and *The L-Shaped Room* (1962, Bryan Forbes) dealt with passion and jealously in bedsitter land. Leslie Caron was the girl forced to take a room in a London tenement because she is pregnant. there she meets a footloose writer Tom Bell, and a tender but curiously – for Forbes – sluggish love affair transpires. Considering his earlier triumphs, one must conclude he was tak-

ing a bit of rest during this one. He had a shot at shaping a remake of Somerset Maugham's *Of Human Bondage* (1964, Henry Hathaway) – the original had been made in 1936 with Leslie Howard and Bette Davis – into screenable material. Laurence Harvey played the club-footed medical student, and Kim Novak was the waitress, as ill-matched off the set as the characters they played.

The Wrong Box (1966, Bryan Forbes), set in Victorian England, began as a wild, farcical black comedy – about two aging brothers fighting over an inheritance – but went out of control, something rare in a Forbes film. To be fair, it has several genuinely funny moments and lots of inventive ideas, but in between it is a disappointing mish-mash of tired slapstick routines, big names hamming it up for the sheer hell of it, and guest star appearances, like Tony Hancock's as a bumbling police inspector, which mean nothing very much.

By contrast, there was only one star in Forbes' next film, *The Whisperers* (1967, Bryan Forbes), the gorgeous – for there is no other word for her – Edith Evans, playing an elderly recluse, in a performance more moving and alert than even the most accomplished actress half her age would be capable of.

Forbes took charge of *The Madwoman of Chail-*

lot (1969, Bryan Forbes), replacing John Huston after disagreements over the handling of Giraudoux's play had prompted Huston's withdrawal. Katherine Hepburn was the star – an embarrassingly high-powered line-up had been engaged, including Charles Boyer, Yul Brynner, Paul Henreid, Danny Kaye, Margaret Leighton, Donald Pleasence and Richard Chamberlain – and, as Forbes concedes in his book, 'he would be the foolish man indeed who turned down the chance to direct Miss Hepburn'.

Forbes' initial reservations about following Huston were understandable – Hepburn and Huston were old friends from *The African Queen* and she might conceivably resent anyone, especially a relatively unknown British director, replacing him. But to his considerable relief, Kate pitched in with her customary dedication and tenacity, though alas by themselves these were not enough to save the production from a critical scalding.

In 1969, Forbes took over as Head of Production at EMI, and one of his first sensible acts was to give a worthwhile role to his wife Nanette Newman in *The Raging Moon* (1970, Bryan Forbes), a brilliantly handled bitter-sweet love story about two young paraplegics – Miss Newman and the fast-rising Malcolm McDowell as a crippled sportsman – who enjoy a short, poetic and engagingly defiant romance before Miss Newman's crippling terminal illness, the exact nature of which she conceals from him, takes its course. The humour and pathos are all judiciously measured, like drops in a laboratory test-tube; nevertheless, the quality of Miss Newman's acting, and thus the impact of her character, is such that when the character dies we share McDowell's impotent fury at the waste and hypocrisy of it all.

Bryan Forbes
b. 1926. Unimpressive, sparrow-faced bit-player who subsequently became a major influence in British filming, as script-writer and director. Co-founded Beaver Films with Richard Attenborough in 1959, wrote *The Angry Silence* (1960), *The League of Gentlemen* (1960), *Only Two Can Play* (1962) and *The Whisperers* (1967) among others. Was also production boss of EMI (1969-1971). Previously married to Hollywood fifties starlet Constance Smith, later (and currently) to British actress Nanette Newman, who has appeared in several Forbes successes,

eg, *The Wrong Box* (1966), *The Raging Moon* (1970), *The Stepford Wives* (1974).

1949 *The Small Back Room* (uncredited)
      All Over the Town (Trumble)
      Dear Mr Prohack (Tony)
1950 *The Wooden Horse* (Paul)
1951 *Green Grow the Rushes* (uncredited)
1952 *Appointment in London* (P/O Greeno)
1953 *Sea Devils* (Willie)
      Wheel of Fate (Ted Reid)
      The Million Pound Note (Tod)
1954 *An Inspector Calls* (Eric Birling)
      Up to His Neck (Subby)
      The Colditz Story (Jimmy Winslow)
      The Black Knight (scripted)
1955 *Passage Home* (Shorty)
      Now and Forever (Frisby)
      The Quatermass X-Periment (uncredited)
      The Last Man to Hang (uncredited)
      Cockleshell Heroes (scripted)
1956 *The Extra Day* (Harry)
      It's Great to be Young (Salesman)
      The Baby and the Battleship (Professor)
        (co-scripted)
      Satellite in the Sky (Jimmy)
      The Black Tent (co-scripted with Robin
        Maugham)
      House of Secrets (co-scripted with Robert
        Buckner)
1957 *Quatermass II* (Marsh)
1958 *The Key* (Weaver)
      I Was Monty's Double (scripted)
1959 *Yesterday's Enemy* (Dawson)
      The Captain's Table (co-scripted with
        John Whiting and Nicholas Phipps)
1960 *The Angry Silence* (scripted)
      The League of Gentlemen (scripted)
      Man in the Moon (co-scripted with
        Michael Relph)
1961 *The Guns of Navarone* (Cohen)
      Whistle Down the Wind (directed,
        co-scripted with Keith Waterhouse
        and Willis Hall)
1962 *Only Two Can Play* (scripted) (from
        Kingsley Amis' novel *That Uncertain
        Feeling*)
      Station Six Sahara (co-scripted with Brian
        Clemens)
      The L-Shaped Room (directed, scripted
        from Lynne Reid Banks' novel)
1964 *Of Human Bondage* (scripted from
        Somerset Maugham)
      The High Bright Sun (co-scripted

with Ian Stuart Black)
Seance on a Wet Afternoon (directed, scripted)
A Shot in The Dark (Turk Thrust)
1965 *King Rat* (USA) *(scripted, directed)*
1966 *The Wrong Box* (directed, co-produced with Larry Gelbart)
1967 *The Whisperers* (directed, scripted)
1968 *Deadfall* (directed, scripted)
1969 *The Madwoman of Chaillot* (directed, after John Huston withdrew, from

Jean Giraudoux's play)
1970 *The Raging Moon* (directed, scripted)
1972 *Conduct Unbecoming* (scripted)
1974 *The Stepford Wives* (USA) (directed)
1976 *The Slipper and the Rose* (directed, scripted)
International Velvet (directed, scripted)
1980 *The Sunday Lovers* (scripted British segment)
Hopscotch (USA) (scripted)

Harry Fowler

'You've got sausage on your chin,' says Harry Fowler's mother, Vida Hope, in *Hue and Cry* (1946, Charles Crichton), coolly playing down his teatime declaration that he's on the trail of a gang of criminals. But young Fowler's claim is not moonshine. The serial in his weekly comic is being used to pass information between sections of London's criminal fraternity, against whom he marshals swarms of children who, like well-orchestrated Lilliputians, pursue and collar the villains.

Though something of a museum piece now, *Hue and Cry* has energy to spare, with Fowler's irrepressible Cockney kid leading the charge through sewers and over yawning bomb sites. Its authentic glimpses of early post-war London, still hideously scarred and with not a single tower block in sight – one crowning shot shows St Paul's dominating, as it did for so long, the capital's skyline – add to the film's curiosity value. For the rest of us who simply enjoy an exuberant romp, it still has a lot to commend it, although the sight of Jack Warner as a criminal takes a little adjusting to.

Harry Fowler was, and is, as English as suet pudding, a character first and actor second, though some critics – and with typical frankness, Fowler himself –would put 'actor' much further down the pecking order. True, there may not have been a hungry acting talent striving for recognition, but the chirpiness, the joie de vivre, was real enough.

The Fowler character was neither wholly honest nor irretrievably delinquent, merely wise in the ways of the streets, surviving through a combination of wit and stealth. He had a certain arrogance, but there was an appealing vulner-

ability, too. None of the films he made added up to much, but as genuine slices of London low-life they have their place.

In the early days, in films like *A Piece of Cake* (1948, John Irwin), *Once a Sinner* (1950, Lewis Gilbert) and *I Believe In You* (1952, Basil Dearden), he gave another meaning to the term 'arrested adolescent'. He transplanted easily into Dickensian London as Sam Weller to James Hayter's superb Pickwick in *The Pickwick Papers* (1952, Noel Langley). In *Top of the Form* (1953, John Paddy Carstairs) he played a troublesome schoolboy, but the real trouble here was Fowler's age: at twenty-six he was a bit long in the leg for schoolroom antics.

From cheeky delinquents to spivs and small-time crooks was a small step which Fowler accomplished with scarcely a blink. He played other characters but it was shifty-eyed minor villains with whom he remains closest identified. In *Crooks Anonymous* (1962, Ken Annakin), a mild farce which occasionally manages to tweak the funny bone, he keeps lining up lucrative safe-cracking jobs for Leslie Phillips, a reluctant cracksman who hopes to mend his ways at Wilfrid Hyde White's voluntary correction academy. Phillips wants rehabilitation at any price because he loves Julie Christie, a nightclub stripper. Fowler views Phillips' defection from the criminal ranks as a form of mental aberration and recommends a further course – in psychiatry.

Harry Fowler
b. 1926. Child actor, on radio since 1941. Cheeky wide-boy Cockney roles a speciality. In films since *Those Kids From Town* (1942).

Ex-criminal Leslie Phillips (left) meets old lag-from-the-past Harry Fowler in *Crooks Anonymous* (1962)

1942 *Those Kids From Town*
Salute John Citizen
The Demi-Paradise
Went the Day Well
1943 *Get Cracking*
Don't Take it to Heart
1944 *Champagne Charlie*
Painted Boats
1946 *Hue and Cry* (Joe Kirby)
1948 *A Piece of Cake* (Spiv)
1949 *For Them that Trespass* (Dave)
Now Barabbas was a Robber (Smith)
1950 *Once a Sinner* (Bill James)
She Shall Have Murder (Albert Oates)
1951 *Scarlet Thread* (Sam)
Madame Louise (Clerk)
1952 *I Believe In You* (Hooker)
The Last Page (Joe)
At Home with the Hardwickes (6-part series of short comedies) (Harry Hardwicke)
The Pickwick Papers (Sam Weller)
1953 *Top of the Form* (Albert)

A Day to Remember (Stan Harvey)
1954 *Don't Blame the Stork* (Harry Fenn)
Conflict of Wings (Buster)
Up to His Neck (Smudge)
1955 *Stock Car* (Monty Allbright)
The Blue Peter (Charlie Barton)
1956 *Fire Maidens from Outer Space* (Sydney Stanhope)
Behind the Headlines (Harry)
Home and Away (Sid Jarvis)
1957 *West of Suez* (Tommy)
Booby Trap (Sammy)
Lucky Jim (Taxi-driver)
The Birthday Present (Charlie)
1958 *Soapbox Derby* (Barrow-boy)
The Diplomatic Corpse (Nocker Parsons)
1959 *Idol on Parade* (Ron)
The Heart of a Man (Razor)
The Dawn Killer (Children's 8-part serial) (Bert Irons)
Don't Panic Chaps (Private Fred Ackroyd)

John Gielgud

John Gielgud has said, 'I made a list of all the things I wanted to do. By the time war broke out I had achieved all of them!' In film terms, he had, by then, given a grand total of six wholly negligible performances, two of them silent. The statement tells us more about Gielgud's film star ambitions than about his qualities as an actor.

The latter has never been in dispute. Long before movies learnt to talk, Gielgud was a giant of the classical stage – 'I was brought up on the well-made play,' he says – where his neo-Raphaelite looks, cultured voice and nobly poetic stare had made him the most lionised romantic actor of his generation. With equipment like that he rather sensibly decided there were better uses to put it to than chivying his way to movie stardom. Alongside Olivier, he stands as one of the top Shakespearean actors of the century, having tackled all the 'great' roles, such as Romeo, Hamlet, Antonio, King Lear, Macbeth, Leontes and Prospero. In many of these, Gielgud's highly personal interpretation became the standard for other top actors to follow.

In 1950, he played Cassius in a Stratford-upon-Avon presentation of Shakespeare's *Julius Caesar*. Three years later, the offer came from Hollywood to repeat the role in Joseph Mankiewicz's film version, starring Marlon Brando as Antony. Cassius was one of the conspirators behind the assassination of Caesar whose reign they believe is no longer in the interests of Rome, but when Antony, Caesar's friend and sometime romantic rival, savagely denounces the plot, the murderers in turn become fugitives.

The denunciation speech is a powerful scene for Brando, arguably one of the best ever. Gielgud, the complete perfectionist, later dismissed it as 'a bad imitation of Olivier'.

In *Richard III* (1955, Laurence Olivier) – 'a feast for Shakespeare fans', cooed the *Daily Mirror*, which, of course, devotes a lot of attention to such matters – Gielgud was the Duke of Clarence, Richard's ineffective elder brother callously swept aside in the scramble for the monarchy. Olivier was Richard, the malevolent Duke of Gloucester, who wins the race by a padded nose, and, with so many famous actor-knights in support, it's the kind of visual and vocal treat that occurs only when there's a purple moon.

Gielgud went back to Hollywood to make *The Barretts of Wimpole Street* (1956, Sidney Franklin), playing the heavy father with Jennifer Jones as Elizabeth and the unknown Bill Travers as Robert Browning. Miss Jones' contract required her to be on-screen for at least 75 per cent of the time, which resulted in endless shots of her doing very little, and the film suffered accordingly. 'I was awful,' says Gielgud, too much the gentleman ever to lay blame at the proper door.

He was in Graham Greene's grim adaptation of *St Joan* (1957, Otto Preminger) as an English earl, a rather fey and uninspired performance in a likewise film, and was probably not surprised at the critical thumbs-down that followed. *Becket* (1964, Peter Glenville) was a pleasant contrast, handsomely staged with vigorous redneck performances from Richard Burton as Becket and Peter O'Toole as Henry II, former chums driven apart by religious differences. Gielgud was the Pope whom Becket consults when his rift with Henry threatens the authority of the Catholic Church in England.

Gielgud was one of the fussy, inept brasshats leading the British cavalry into *The Charge of the Light Brigade* (1968, Tony Richardson). His Lord Raglan is a masterpiece of sleepy bewilderment, fussing over minor irritations yet oblivious to the impending annihilation of his regiment. Tony Richardson shows us that defeat was due to the cracks, and the crackpots, in high command, and his canvas quite properly counterpoints the vainglorious posturing of those in charge – who

63

Headmaster John Gielgud and star pupil Malcolm McDowell before McDowell takes to the skies in *Aces High* (1976)

naturally survive the carnage to poke accusing fingers at each other – with shots of lower ranks dying valiantly for a hopeless cause. Over-flashy performances from Trevor Howard and Harry Andrews, as rival higher-ups, are the film's main disappointment. At times, it has more the look of a noisy dressing-up game for ten-year-olds than an authentic slab of British history.

Gielgud was with Howard again in *Eleven Harrowhouse* (1974, Aram Avakian) as boss of a diamond house where James Mason, a dying employee, relatively unrewarded – indeed, scarcely noticed – after years of dog-like service, becomes the inside man in a daring robbery attempt funded by Howard, a shady entrepreneur, and carried out by Charles Grodin. Too glaring an American influence – for an all-too-obvious Stateside market – and, again, hammy performances plus a stupid, slapstick ending, marred an otherwise palatable comedy-thriller.

Gielgud cantered through *Murder on the Orient Express* (1974, Sidney Lumet) as the nasty victim's wing-collared valet, with little to do but look heartily bored, which he almost certainly was. He speaks enthusiastically of *Providence* (1978, Alain Resnais), where he played a crazy old bohemian boozed on white wine, wrestling with an uncompleted novel which is made up of large segments of his early life which he fretfully remembers, plus a few imaginary demons. Very Resnais but not really Gielgud, though it was interesting to see him in a character study tidily removed from either classical acting or his most familiar screen number, those thin-blooded, expensive porcelain types. In America, the *Village Voice* critic abandoned its strongly anti-Establishment habits of a lifetime, and wrote of his performance in *Providence*: 'Gielgud proves again he is the greatest living actor in the English language.'

His appetite for movie work – and, unquestionably, his liking for the money that goes with it – has come late, and he appears to be frantically making up for lost time. His choice of film roles may be suspect – 'rubbish or quality, it doesn't matter,' sighs actor/playwright Alan Bennett – but the talent is weathered in oak and frequently rides above the dross he seems incapable of turning down. Nevertheless, his agreement to appear in the *Penthouse*-financed horror comic *Caligula* (1980, Tinto Brass) must have been extracted under torture, appropriate in the circumstances. Star and title-role player Malcolm McDowell later lambasted the makers for splicing in lots of depravity after he had gone home. Given that he must have known where his salary came from, McDowell's anger sounds self-defensive.

McDowell had earlier appeared with Gielgud in *Aces High* (1976, Jack Gold), a World War I flying adventure with McDowell as a superior example of the kind of pupil headmaster Gielgud likes to groom for the Flying Corps. A younger recruit from the same school, Peter Firth, gets an eye-opener when he is posted at his own request to McDowell's beleaguered squadron in France. Gielgud's former star pupil has been transformed by the toils of war into a hard-drinking, demoralised veteran. Gielgud fans arriving ten minutes late will miss his performance.

He seems unembarrassed by the brevity of his most recent screen appearances, which, for an actor of Gielgud's stature and experience, could be thought demeaning. He was a preacher in *Portrait of the Artist as a Young Man* (1977, Joseph Strick), a brigadier in *The Human Factor* (1979, Otto Preminger), a Cambridge don in *Chariots of Fire* (1980, Hugh Hudson), a hospital chief in *The Elephant Man* (1980, David Lynch) – inconsequential roles effortlessly seen off by a genuine master of the spoken word. His performance in *Arthur* (1981, Steve Gordon) won him an Oscar in 1982.

John Gielgud

b. 1904.   Sepulchral-voiced actor-knight, pre-war Shakespearean theatre star, most effective in classical-romantic leads. Shunned films till early 1950s (he was Cassius to Brando's Antony in *Julius Caesar* (1953)). Latterly hyperactive before the cameras, mostly as snobby, bemused upper-crust figures, entertaining to watch even when indifferently acted (as is often the case, regrettably).

1953 *Julius Caesar* (USA) (Cassius)
1954 *Romeo and Juliet* (Chorus)
1955 *Richard III* (Duke Of Clarence)
1956 *The Barretts of Wimpole Street* (Moulton Barrett)
1957 *St Joan* (Earl of Warwick)
1964 *Becket* (Louis VII)
1967 *Sebastian* (Intelligence Head)
1968 *Charge of the Light Brigade* (Lord Raglan)
1969 *Oh! What a Lovely War* (Count Berchtold)
1970 *Julius Caesar* (Julius Caesar)
1972 *Shoes of the Fisherman* (First Pope)
1974 *Eagle in a Cage* (Lord Sissal)
       Frankenstein (Chief Constable)
       Eleven Harrowhouse (Meecham)
       Gold (Farrell)
       Murder on the Orient Express (Beddoes)
       Galileo (The Old Cardinal)
1976 *Aces High* (Headmaster)
       Joseph Andrews (Doctor)
1977 *Portrait of the Artist as a Young Man* (Preacher)
1978 *Providence* (Clive Langham)
1979 *The Human Factor* (Brigadier Tomlinson)
1980 *Chariots of Fire* (Master of Trinity College)
       Sphinx (Abu Hamdi)
       The Elephant Man (Carr Gomm)
       Caligula (Nerva)
1981 *Lion of the Desert* (Eri Gariani)
       Arthur (USA) (Hobson)
       Brideshead Revisited (TV) (Edward Ryder)

Nigel Green

'War is a criminal enterprise,' Nigel Green tells Michael Caine in *Play Dirty* (1968, André de Toth), a scaled down *Dirty Dozen* caper with a North African oil depot as the target for destruction. Caine has been assigned a platoon of psychopaths, Green and Nigel Davenport included, to destroy the enemy's energy supply. Disguised as Italians, they encounter a group of Arab nomads who offer them tea. Without warning – because their cover is blown – Daven-

Michael Caine (left) once more fails to impress his dour spy-boss, bow-tied and tongue-tied Nigel Green, in *The Ipcress File* (1965)

Nigel Green relaxes with his script on the set of *Deadlier Than the Male* (1966)

port machine-guns the entire encampment. Unaware that anything was wrong, Caine demands an explanation. 'I didn't like the tea,' comes the mocking reply.

Nigel Green was a rugged actor well suited to outdoor escapades. In or out of uniform he was equally authoritative; his range was impressively wide from horror to satire to spy dramas, and there was plenty of variety in the parts he played.

He was Kenneth More's fellow-patient in *Reach for the Sky* (1956, Lewis Gilbert), and it is while on an authorised jaunt in Green's Bentley coupé that More meets tearoom waitress Muriel Pavlow, whom he later marries. In *Corridors of Blood* (1958, Robert Day), he was a police chief and in *Sword of Sherwood Forest* (1960, Terence Fisher), a low-budget Robin Hood story, he played Little John. That solid physical presence came in useful again as Vincent Price's reliable hatchetman in *Masque of the Red Death* (1964, Roger Corman). He also scored well as the regimental colour sergeant in *Zulu* (1963, Cy Endfield) with Stanley Baker and Michael Caine.

Green was Caine's boss, a stony bureaucrat, in *The Ipcress File* (1965, Sidney J. Furie), first and best of the Harry Palmer espionage trilogy. Caine is assigned to Green's department to investigate the disappearance of a number of top Government scientists. His new boss can scarcely believe the character reference that goes with him, which describes Caine as 'insubordinate, insolent, a trickster perhaps with criminal tendencies' – an assessment with which Caine readily agrees. But Green is the real trickster, a ruthless double agent whose associates snatch Caine and use sinister brain-washing techniques to programme him into assassinating a high-ranking Intelligence chief. The plan fails, however, because Caine manages to distract himself during the brainwashing, thereby effectively resisting its effects. His mind stays clear enough to recognise Green for what he is and kill him.

Eva Renzi, as a stranded fashion model caught up in a diamond chase with James Garner and George Kennedy in a remote area of Latin America in *The Pink Jungle* (1968, Delbert Mann), is neatly on target when she suspects there's 'something deadly' about Green, a mysterious, bearded prospector whom they encounter along the way. Green pretends to have a much sought-after map to a spectacular diamond vein but is, in fact, a murderous con man waiting his chance to kill the others. Halfway across a desert he takes off, having first drained off all the water flasks. But Green neglects to keep a sensible distance between his former companions and himself, and when the others catch up with him, Kennedy, an unforgiving soul, bumps him off.

In *Countess Dracula* (1970, Peter Sasdy), Green procures the damsels whose blood keeps Ingrid Pitt in prime condition. Bookworm Maurice Denham dies shortly after uncovering her secret, a loss which Green openly laments. 'Brilliant scholar,' he tut-tuts. 'Read all those books. He knew everything and now he knows nothing.' What Green neglects to mention is that he personally hanged Denham from the library chandelier.

Strange goings-on can be seen in *Gawain and The Green Knight* (1973, Stephen Weeks), a sort of cross between Hereward the Sleepless and Carry On Camelot, with Green as the enigmatic Knight who gatecrashes a rowdy Arthurian knees-up with a challenge to the by now weedy, dissolute knights. 'Is there no man among you who will play my game?' he demands – the game being first crack at his grizzled head with an axe. Failure to dislodge at a single swipe means the challenger has to submit his own dome for identical therapy – and Green has a crazy mean look about him that suggests he is unlikely to muff his shot.

Murray Head, a timid youth elected to have a go – obviously on account of his name – gets shock number one when Green's head parts company from the rest of him, and an even bigger one when the crafty old codger reaches down and plonks it on his shoulders. It's a tough act to follow, and in a half-hearted attempt to sustain our interest – since little else in this silly, forsooth-ridden fairy-tale is likely to – Green pulls a few additional bizarre stunts, such as disappearing into the ground like milk into muesli. John Baxter noted in the *Monthly Film Bulletin* that director Stephen Weeks' dependence on castles and costumes 'leaves the Arthurian revels looking like a fancy dress harvest festival, and his distinguished cast resort, for the most part, to half-hearted mugging'.

Green's equally eccentric behaviour in *The Ruling Class* (1972, Peter Medak) was less obvious because virtually everyone in that high-blown satire was off his head. Green, a Scottish loon convinced he is Jesus Christ, equates divine power with electricity, and having discharged his batteries in a lively dispute with Peter O'Toole – who claims to be God – replenishes his depleted energies by ramming his finger into a light socket. Accused of bungling the creation, Green concedes but without a trace of the humility he expects from others, that our unlovely planet Earth was one of his 'earliest failures'.

Nigel Green

1924-1972.   Burly character support with accent on villainy.

1955 *As Long As They're Happy* (Peter)
1956 *Reach For the Sky* (Streatfield)
1957 *Bitter Victory* (Wilkins)
1958 *Corridors of Blood* (Inspector Donovan)
1960 *Sword of Sherwood Forest* (Little John)
1961 *Man at the Carlton Tower* (Lew Daney)
       The Queen's Guards (Abu Sidbar)
       Pit of Darkness (Jonathan)
1962 *The Spanish Sword* (Baron Breaute)
       Mysterious Island (Tom)
       Playback (Ralph Monk)
       The Man who Finally Died (Hirsch)
1963 *Jason and the Argonauts* (Hercules)
       Zulu (Colour-Sgt Bourne)
       Saturday Night Out (Paddy)
1964 *The Masque of the Red Death* (Ludovico)
1965 *The Ipcress File* (Dalby)
       The Face of Fu Manchu (Nayland Smith)
       The Skull (Wilson)
1966 *Khartoum* (General Wolseley)
       Deadlier Than the Male (Carl Petersen)
1967 *Africa – Texas Style* (Karl Bekker)
       Tobruk (USA) (Colonel Harker)
1968 *Play Dirty* (Colonel Masters)
       Fraülein Doktor (Mathesius)
       The Pink Jungle (USA) (Crowley)
1969 *The Wrecking Crew* (USA) (Count Massimo Contini)
       The Kremlin Letter (Janis alias 'The Whore')
1970 *Countess Dracula* (Captain Dobi)
1972 *The Ruling Class* (McKyle)
       Gawain and the Green Knight (Green Knight)

John Gregson

John Gregson could never understand what all the fuss was about, and vigorously denied that he was a star. 'I don't even look like one,' he protested. 'I just see myself as a handy type to have around.'

Before *Genevieve* (1953, Henry Cornelius), that was how his employers saw him too. His country-fresh good looks and gentle manner were appealing but unexceptional, in roles like, for example, an islander in *Whisky Galore* (1948, Alexander Mackendrick), a member of John Mills' team of explorers, denied the glory of the final assault on the South Pole in *Scott of the Antarctic* (1948, Charles Frend), a pilot officer in *Angels One Five* (1952, George More O'Ferrall), a detective on the trail of the bullion thieves in *The Lavender Hill Mob* (1951, Charles Crichton), a steam train aficionado in *The Titfield Thunderbolt* (1952, Charles Crichton).

But *Genevieve* changed his luck. Gregson achieved stardom as an amiable barrister with a chocolate-box wife, Dinah Sheridan, and a vintage car fetish. The film focused on the annual London to Brighton Old Crocks Race in which Gregson and Kenneth More were eager competitors. Like Gregson's earlier steam train movie, *Genevieve* was an affectionate dig at the Englishman's predilection for antiquated gadgetry, and the deep-seated rivalries, both mechanical and personal, which metallic love affairs provoke among otherwise decent sorts, which both Gregson and More clearly are – before the race gets underway.

By the time they reach Brighton old wounds are rubbed raw, and the return trip develops into a private race, loss of which will mean for Gregson the sale of Genevieve to settle the wager. Despite this, he is too nice a chap to interrupt a talkative old gent who badgers him about the magnificent old car at a road crossing. With Gregson an evident loser, virtue has its reward, when More's wheels get stuck in tramlines on the approach to Westminster Bridge and he is whisked horrified back to suburbia. Genevieve chugs the last few triumphant yards, literally on her own steam.

Gregson reverted to assisting yokels to thwart bureaucracy in *Conflict of Wings* (1954, John Eldridge), a weak comedy about rural East Anglians united in opposition to a War Office scheme to turn an offshore island, well-estab-

lished as a bird sanctuary, into a rocket training site. Gregson was an RAF corporal who sides with hayseeds, but neither the RAF scheme nor the film successfully gets off the ground. In one of the *Three Cases of Murder* (1955, David Eady), Gregson played the more extrovert – and thus more popular with the girls – member of a two-man advertising partnership formed with reticent boyhood chum Emrys Jones. When Jones falls in love with Elizabeth Sellars, Gregson cannot help interfering and soon turns her head with his roguish charm. The former friends become intense rivals, and one evening, after a tremendous row, Gregson returns to the apartment they share, with blood on his hands. With news headlines the morning after shrieking that Miss Sellars has been brutally murdered, it appears Gregson might have a guilty secret.

He denies killing her, but as he is prone to spells of forgetfulness, suspicion surrounds him. The twist in the tale is that the killer is, in fact, the mild-mannered Jones, who, when Gregson traps him into admission of guilt, promptly chucks his accuser down several storeys into the courtyard below. He, of course, has no problem convincing the police that his pal killed himself in a fit of remorse after murdering Miss Sellars, for Gregson has always been their prime suspect.

At the end, Jones is trapped by greed, with a helping nudge from a vigilant barman, played by Alan Badel, who also appears in the two other stories shown. The Gregson-Jones story is the best of the three, and Gregson is excellent as the buccaneering executive who is too charming for his own good.

He captained a midget submarine, one of several engaged in sinking the *Tirpitz*, in *Above Us the Waves* (1955, Ralph Thomas). Gregson's four-man mini-sub gets into difficulties when his depth gauge develops a fault, but he decides to carry on the chase relying wholly on the periscope. He should have heeded the warning signs. Shortly afterwards, his sub's torpedo jams in the launch tube and blows him skyhigh.

Undaunted, Gregson returned to wartime battle stations, again in the Royal Navy, this time up against the *Graf Spee* in *The Battle of the River Plate* (1956, Michael Powell, Emeric Pressburger), a matter-of-fact reconstruction of the famous early-war skirmish between a German pocket battleship and three British cruisers

John Gregson and Dinah Sheridan try to placate the traffic cops in *Genevieve* (1953)

off the coast of South America. Rather than lose dishonourably, the German captain, given a restrained nice-guy touch by Peter Finch, scuttles his own ship and then commits suicide. Our chaps are good sports too – with Gregson and Bernard Lee captaining for us, that was a foregone conclusion – and scarcely a shot is fired in anger. Unfortunately, the whole, beautifully managed escapade has about as much snap as an afternoon snooze at a posh gentleman's club.

In *Jacqueline* (1957, Roy Baker) Gregson swopped his smart uniform for a pair of overalls. He played a feckless Irish shipyard worker with money and family problems – or, to put it more directly, boozing his money causes problems in the family. Gregson drinks because he hates his work and longs for the far-off days when he managed a farm. The film shows how his school-age daughter, a lonely, somewhat over-imaginative little brat, chances her arm for family unity by cajoling a tight-wad landowner into giving her dad a job on the land.

The only thing missing from this tedious rag-bag of Irish aphorisms is a choir of leprechauns singing 'The Rose of Tralee'. Everything recognisably Irish is pulled out of the bag for this one – smart kids, whimsical padres, dissenting mothers-in-law, gruff millionaires, tut-tutting neighbours – and set out like garden gnomes on a seaside landlady's front garden.

Midway through the film, such was its level of penetration and the quality of acting, I began to think I was actually watching garden gnomes. During the mid-fifties bog-flavoured movies were popular, and Rank Studios appointed Gregson as their all-purpose Irishman. It was a role he would repeat uncomplainingly three times in two years: in *Jacqueline* (1957); then in *Miracle in Soho* (1957, Julian Aymes), in which he was an Irish road-mender in London; and finally in *Rooney* (1958, George Pollock), where he played a Dublin dustman, again with a fatal weakness for the bottle. It's easy to see why he was the ideal choice. He certainly looked the part, but more importantly, he conveyed warmth, concern, friendliness and a sense of

John Gregson (left) under starter's orders for a raid behind enemy lines in *Sea of Sand* (1958). Michael Craig anxiously checks his watch

humour without even trying – qualities, one suspects, that were as much Gregson himself as the characters he loaned them to.

His contract with Rank ended after *Rooney*, and Gregson's career took a severe jolt. Irregular featured roles replaced the starring ones, none of them likely to arrest what, to his fans, seemed an inexplicably sudden decline. In *Frightened City* (1961, John Lemont) he was a police inspector patrolling *Miracle in Soho* territory, alas, without the miracle it needed. Gregson and Bruce Seton – of *Fabian of the Yard* fame – were coppers trying to clean the place up, but the gangs have stopped chivying each other, thanks to an influential crooked lawyer, a behind-the-scenes Mister Big, who has shown them that suppressing inter-gang squabbles means more profit all round. The film, shot in black-and-white (a fair measure of the Studio's faith in it), was an early vehicle for Sean Connery, cast as a crime syndicate muscleman.

One of Gregson's last films was *Fright* (1971, Peter Collinson), where he played a psychiatrist helping Honor Blackman over the memory of a murderous assault by psychotic husband Ian Bannen. A cosy outing to a local nightspot is shattered when Bannen escapes from the asylum and barricades himself in his former home with their child and baby-sitter. Gregson contacts the local police and follows Miss Blackman back to the house, which, unknown to either of them, already contains one corpse, and looks like having a couple more before the long night ends.

Television gave him a final flutter, as the home-loving Inspector Gideon of the Yard in *Gideon's Way*, a somewhat timid cops-and-robbers series spun from the 1958 Jack Hawkins film. His last television role, in a thriller series *Dangerous Knowledge* with Patrick Allen, screened only a couple of months after his death from a heart attack in 1975, revived a passing interest in some of his early work.

John Gregson
1919-1975. Handsome, dependable, nice-guy actor, best remembered for comedy roles. On stage from 1947. Film debut: *Saraband for Dead Lovers* (1948). Most important film: *Genevieve* (1953).

1948 *Saraband for Dead Lovers* (unbilled)
　　 Scott of the Antarctic (Petty Officer Green)
　　 Whisky Galore (Sammy MacCodrum)
1949 *Train of Events* (Malcolm Murray-Bruce)
1950 *Treasure Island* (Redruth)
　　 Cairo Road (Coastguard)
1951 *The Lavender Hill Mob* (Farrow)
1952 *Angels One Five* (Pilot Officer 'Septic' Baird)
　　 The Brave Don't Cry (John Cameron)
　　 The Holly and the Ivy (David Patterson)
　　 Venetian Bird (Cassana)
　　 The Titfield Thunderbolt (Gordon Chesterford)
1953 *Genevieve* (Alan McKim)
1954 *The Weak and the Wicked* (Michael)
　　 Conflict of Wings (Bill Morris)
　　 The Crowded Day (Leslie)
　　 To Dorothy a Son (Tony Rapallo)
1955 *Above Us the Waves* (Lieutenant Alec Duffy)
　　 Three Cases of Murder (Edgar Curtain)
　　 Value for Money (Charley Broadbent)
1956 *The Battle of the River Plate* (Captain Bell)
1957 *Jacqueline* (Mike McNeil)
　　 True as a Turtle (Tony Hudson)
　　 Miracle in Soho (Michael Morgan)
1958 *Rooney* (James Rooney)
　　 Sea of Sand (Captain Williams)
1959 *The Captain's Table* (Captain Albert Ebbs)
　　 SOS Pacific (Jack Bennett)
1960 *Faces in the Dark* (Richard Hammond)

Hand in Hand (Father Timothy)
1961 The Treasure of Monte Cristo (Renato)
      Frightened City (Inspector Sayers)
1962 Live Now – Pay Later (Callendar)
      Tomorrow at Ten (Inspector Parnell)

The Longest Day (British Army Padre)
1966 The Night of the Generals (Colonel
      Sandauer)
1971 Fright (Dr Gareth Cordell)
1975 The Tiger Lily (Controller of TV Station)

Kenneth Griffith

When a schoolgirl is murdered in *Revenge* (1971, Sidney Hayers), evidence suggests that shabby tramp Kenneth Griffith could be the killer. Helped by a friend, the victim's parents James Booth and Joan Collins, who run a pub, snatch Griffith, savagely beat him up, and lock him in the cellar – all for nothing, for as it turns out, Griffith is not the murderer. It's an utterly negligible film, apart from Griffith, who spends the entire time trussed up like an oven-ready turkey, yet gives everyone associated with this grubby production an acting lesson to remember.

Griffith was one of our better lower-order nasties. Nervy, mean-minded, deceptively servile and sinister, he was definitely not the type to be left alone with the best silverware. He had the wide, tense eyes of a stag run to ground and the sly, fawning rhetoric of a hot car dealer. Nothing the residual Griffith character did seemed of itself, entirely savoury. Even his most innocent actions had a dubious or cowardly quality, and occasionally he was quite mad.

Although he worked consistently in comedies, it was rare – indeed, almost impossible – for Griffith on his own to be intrinsically funny. Stale-breath characters only provoke laughter when mixed with other ingredients, and in Griffith's case that something else was frequently Peter Sellers. He popped up in several Boultings comedies, including *Private's Progress* (1956, John Boulting) as a scurrilous little private, *Brothers in Law* (1957, John Boulting) as an undertaker, and *I'm All Right, Jack* (1959, John Boulting) as a mealy-mouthed trades union agitator.

In *Blue Murder at St Trinian's* (1957, Frank Launder), when education inspector Richard Wattis wants to hire Terry-Thomas' derelict coaches for the school's trip to Rome – because no other hire operator will oblige – Griffith was the dour handyman who makes the introductions. He was a wireless operator aboard the *Titanic* in *A Night to Remember* (1958, Roy

Baker), and a spoof Hitler – a performance to forget – in *The Two-Headed Spy* (1958, André de Toth).

He played shifty Soho characters in *Expresso Bongo* (1959, Val Guest) and *The Frightened City* (1961, John Lemont) – in the latter he was crippled, limping badly like the script. In *Only Two Can Play* (1962, Sidney Gilliatt), he was Peter Sellers' down-trodden neighbour and colleague, a real simpering performance. He was Sellers' dresser in *The Naked Truth* (1957, Mario Zampi), vigilantly restraining his boss from the wilder excesses of his nature.

Griffith had a small role with Elliott Gould and Donald Sutherland in *S*P*Y*S* (1974,

Wireless operator Kenneth Griffith prepares for a cold bath in *A Night to Remember* (1958), a sensitive reconstruction of the Titanic tragedy

Shabby tramp Kenneth Griffith has his arm twisted by vengeful parent James Booth in *Revenge* (1971)

Irwin Kershner), a satire on the espionage business, unfavourably – and in my view, unfairly – compared with their more famous $M^*A^*S^*H^*$. The two productions, their pace and style, and even the characters portrayed, were wholly dissimilar, and it was clearly a mistake to package the second film in a way that invited such direct comparison. Gould and Sutherland were a pair of bungling French-based CIA agents whom their boss Joss Ackland plans to sacrifice in order to maintain the delicate balance of rubbed-out agents in both the CIA and KGB camps – 'You owe me two!' insists Ackland's cold-eyed Russian opposite number Vladek Sheybal. Ackland assumes responsibility for bumping them off, but after a couple of failed attempts Gould and Sutherland wise up to what's going on and hightail it to London to relieve Kenneth Griffith, an unlikely looking double agent, of a string of microdots that contain details of China's European spy network, possession of which will effectively buy their safety.

One scene has Gould and Sutherland tailing Griffith to a classy restaurant, where he parks his adored King Charles spaniel up at the table beside him and cooingly feeds it expensive titbits. 'That dog's practically human,' observes Gould, to which the exhausted, down-at-heel Sutherland sighs: 'What's so great about being human?' They eventually corner their quarry in a cross-Channel ferry toilet, where Griffith's dumb bodyguard accidentally kills him with a bullet intended for the Americans.

'With a bodyguard like him you don't need an enemy,' is Gould's wry comment when, later, the same fellow, still trying to shoot them, brings down a diminutive French pigeon-fancier. The film is a very free-wheeling, hit-and-miss affair, not unlike Sutherland's romance with French Leftwing terrorist moll, Zou-Zou. Returning one night to the apartment which he occasionally shares with her, Sutherland peels off his clothes, and begins to playfully tickle her feet – only to discover an extra pair nestling beside hers – a graphic illustration of Marxist bed-fellows sharing the same bunk.

In *Jane Eyre* (1971, Delbert Mann), a wholly depressing and largely insensitive trudge across Brontë country in which ninety per cent of the characters are people to avoid, Griffith was the spoilsport who interrupts governess Susannah York's wedding to wealthy landowner George C. Scott with the news that Scott is already married to his sister, a dangerous nutcase under lock and key at Scott's moorland manor – but still, by Griffith's reckoning, a wife. Her problem is hereditary madness and, judging by the spaniel-eyed, moist-lipped look that Griffith wears in the film, he risks going the same way.

The shattering news sends Miss York hotfoot-ing across the slumbering dales into a morbid, stifling dalliance with Ian Bannen. Meanwhile Scott's demented wife, racked by the news that he was about to hook up with another, sets the manor house alight, killing herself and blinding him. It can't have been easy reducing one of English literature's great love stories into an un-distinguished slice of Regency pap, but this lum-bering production seems to have managed it.

Griffith was circus boss Anton Diffring's weedy accomplice who arranges the gory 'acci-dents' in *Circus of Horrors* (1960, Sidney Hayers). He willingly carries out Diffring's in-structions while the boss pays attention to his protective sister, played by Jane Hylton, but when Diffring's interest wanders towards meatier competition – with which the circus seems to be liberally stacked – Griffith decides it's time to wrap up the show. Characteristically, he springs the trap on Diffring from a safe dis-tance.

He gained distinction in the seventies as a documentary-maker of controversial subjects, but the experience has not entirely killed his en-thusiasm for acting. He was one of Richard Burton's mercenaries in *The Wild Geese* (1977, Euan Lloyd), a gay hospital porter whose evil gnome appearance would scare the plumes off any juju man. Griffith is armed to the teeth, and not afraid of a shoot-out with the bad guys. As the platoon dodge their gun-toting pursuers, Griffith valiantly decides to lengthen the gap by standing his ground and downing as many Sim-bas as his sten-gun can handle.

'Come on, my beauties,' he croons as they leap from the bushes right into his line of fire. It's a pleasure to see Old Demon Eyes doing some-thing right for a change.

Kenneth Griffith

b. 1921. 'Little man' specialist with shifty eyes and ingratiating manner. Played in numerous Boultings comedies with Peter Sellers. Latterly, a TV documentary producer specialising in con-troversial historic themes.

1947 *The Shop at Sly Corner* (Archie Fellowes)
1948 *Bond Street* (Len Phillips)
1949 *Forbidden* (Johnny)
1950 *Water Front* (Maurice Bruno)
1951 *High Treason* (Jimmy Ellis)
1954 *Thirty Six Hours* (Henry)
1955 *Track the Man Down* (Ken Orwell)
     The Prisoner (The Secretary)
1956 *1984* (Prisoner)
     Private's Progress (Pte Dai Jones)
     Tiger in the Smoke (Crutcher)
1957 *Brothers in Law* (Undertaker)
     Lucky Jim (Cyril Jones)
     Blue Murder at St Trinian's (Charlie Bull)
     The Naked Truth (Porter)
1958 *A Night to Remember* (Phillips)
     The Man Upstairs (Pollen)
     Chain of Events (Clarke)
     The Two-Headed Spy (Adolf Hitler)
1959 *Tiger Bay* (Choirmaster)
     Carlton-Browne of the FO (Griffiths)
     I'm All Right, Jack (Dai)
     Expresso Bongo (Charlie)
1960 *Circus of Horrors* (Martin Webb)
     Snowball (Phil Hart)
     Suspect (Dr Schole)
1961 *Rag Doll* (Wilson)
     The Frightened City (Wally)
1962 *Only Two Can Play* (Jenkins)
     We Joined the Navy (Orator)
1963 *Heavens Above* (Rev Owen Thomas)
1965 *Rotten to the Core* (Lenny the Dip)
1966 *The Whisperers* (Mr Weaver)
1967 *The Bobo* (Pepe Gamazo)
     Great Catherine (Naryshkin)
1968 *The Lion in Winter* (Player)
1969 *The Assassination Bureau* (Pòpescu)
1971 *Jane Eyre* (Mason)
     Revenge (Seely)
1973 *The House in Nightmare Park* (Ernest Henderson)
1974 *Callan* (Waterman)
     S*P*Y*S (Lippet)
1976 *Sky Riders* (Wasserman)
1977 *The Wild Geese* (Witty)
1980 *The Sea Wolves* (Wilton)

Alec Guinness

Alec Guinness and Ealing Studios were made for each other. Ealing needed Guinness's virtuosity to flesh out their witty satires as much as he needed a studio unlikely to exhaust itself of comic invention. That each flourished without the other is not in question, but when they got together in perfect attunement, sparks flew.

As Fagin in Dickens' *Oliver Twist* (1948, David Lean), an early success, Guinness seemed to shed totally his own persona. Critic Lawrence Shaffer wrote : 'peer and listen as hard as you will, he [Guinness] is nowhere to be found'. Shaffer insists there is a Jekyll-and-Hyde quality to great character acting, and in *Oliver Twist* Guinness's performance comes clearly into this category: 'Jekyll let himself be overwhelmed by Hyde just as Guinness surrendered himself to Fagin'. Surrender was the operative word, also, in *Kind Hearts and Coronets* (1949, Robert Hames), as eight different Guinness characters – the D'Ascoynes – are systematically bumped off by penniless distant cousin Dennis Price in reprisal for the family's having alienated his mother for marrying 'beneath her'.

The murders are carried out with great finesse, while Price rationalises his actions on the soundtrack with dry candour. 'It seemed appropriate that he who had lived within the cannon's roar should die explosively,' comments Price as he downs another Guinness – by detonating his caviare.

In *The Lavender Hill Mob* (1951, Charles Crichton) Guinness was an outwardly passive bank clerk ('no imagination, no initiative,' is how snooty boss Ronald Adam describes him to bank supervisor Archie Duncan) who carries off a million-pound bullion heist with the help of fellow-lodger Stanley Holloway and two back-up villains Alfie Bass and Sidney James. Holloway owns a foundry at which the bullion is converted into innocent-looking paperweights. It's a delightful comedy, mostly tongue-in-cheek, with touches of wild surrealism, such as the gang's caper on the Eiffel Tower, and a nail-biting attempt to board a Channel ferry, frustrated at every turn by a bewildering chain of passport, customs and currency regulations.

Guinness gives the clerk a wafer-thin mock-seriousness, behind which a kind of suppressed mania is clearly visible. His sly bespectacled face, topped with a bowler hat and tailed with a bank-regulation stiff collar, is in almost permanent repose, but one can see in the eyes a hankering for adventure, danger and the fulfilment of dreams – not just dreams of wealth but of flying the cage, of grinding his pompous employers' noses in the dust.

In *Barnacle Bill* (1957, Charles Frend), an Ealing tail-ender lacking the vitality and wit of its more illustrious predecessors, he was a would-be ship's captain prone to sea-sickness (consequently he's never actually been to sea), who takes over a run-down pier and attempts to register it as a ship – a plan daft enough to galvanise the bureaucrats into opposition. Guinness even offers mock cruises for travellers who prefer stay-at-home holidays. A marvellous flashback sequence, in which Guinness impersonates the character's naval ancestors, recalls his multi-faceted performance in *Kind Hearts and Coronets*.

In *The Captain's Paradise* (1953, Anthony Kimmins) he had the best of two worlds, or rather, two countries, as a ferry boat captain with a wife either side of the Gibraltar strait.

Guinness led a bungling group of bank robbers in *The Ladykillers* (1955, Alexander MacKendrick), in a glorious over-the-top performance, all protruding teeth and sham gentility. The gang, masquerading as a string ensemble, take lodgings in a house where all the pictures hang askew due to subsidence and where the water pipes only work when rapped with a mallet – a suitably bizarre setting in which to finalise their plans to rob a Kings Cross security van.

The Last Holiday (1950, Henry Cass) also brims over with delicious ironies. Guinness played one of his meek-little-nobody roles, an unsuccessful farm equipment salesman who discovers, after a medical check-up, that he has only weeks to live. Determined to get something out of life before it vanishes, he blows his savings on a seaside holiday, and once installed at a snobby resort, things start to go miraculously right for him – an eccentric inventor, Wilfrid Hyde White, offers him a partnership, a cabinet minister wants to hire him as an adviser, a junk foods tycoon, Sidney James, is prepared to give him a large chunk of the business, and he wins a small fortune on the horses.

Despairing of the short time he has left, Guinness puts his good fortune at the disposal of others. He forks out £100 to help the no-good husband of a lady whom he fancies, and when the hotel union boss calls a strike, Guinness persuades the residents to fend for themselves.

The film succeeds in threading its way between comedy and pathos without settling too cosily near neither. One is drawn into the hotel milieu without consciously feeling the pull, and Guinness's timid outsider strikes exactly the right note of deadpan wretchedness.

More surrealism surfaced in *The Man in the White Suit* (1951, Alexander MacKendrick), with Guinness as an eccentric textile chemist who creates an indestructable ever-clean synthetic fabric which needs to be cut with an oxyacetylene flame. Initially hailed as a miracle-worker, Guinness soon finds himself ostracised and ridiculed by both management and workers, anxious to suppress the invention because it threatens a slump. It's all neatly summed up for Guinness by his landlady, who also takes in washing, who ticks him off by saying: 'Why can't you scientists leave things alone? What about my washing when there's no washing to do!'

Clad in the wretched suit, Guinness goes into hiding to escape getting one from angry millworkers, but its fluorescent quality makes him easy to spot. The crisis – and Guinness's alienation – ends when the fabric suddenly disintegrates before everyone's eyes – and jubilantly they snatch handfuls of the suit until Guinness is in his shirt-tail. *The Man in the White Suit* is a neat satire on post-war technology with Guinness personifying the mad march of progress, science for science's sake irrespective of the consequences, and getting caught, as technology so often richly deserves to be, with his pants down.

Top box office money-spinner of 1957 was *The Bridge on the River Kwai* (David Lean) from Pierre Boulle's novel, with Guinness as a blinkered CO of a group of Japanese POWs engaged in the construction of a bridge section of the notorious Burma-Siam railway. 'I'll say this for the old man – he's got guts!' says an admiring lower rank as Guinness endures weeks in a punishment hell-hole for reminding the Jap commandant about the Geneva Convention.

Guinness thereafter acquires a blind obsession to construct a bridge that will be a monument to British resource – apparently unaware that the completion of his honourable fantasy will provide a major asset to the enemy. 'Must we work so well? Must we build a better bridge than they could do themselves?' asks a worried James

Alec Guinness as Herbert Pocket in *Great Expectations* (1946)

Donald, as Guinness fusses over it like a broody hen. He even tries to stop Jack Hawkins and William Holden dynamiting it while a trainload of Jap VIPs sit obligingly overhead. Ironically, it is his death fall on to the plunger which blows the bridge sky-high. The conflict between Guinness and Sessue Hayakawa, as the camp commandant, is particularly interesting. Both are characters snipped from the same cloth, obsessive, hardened pros unwilling – or more to the point, unable – to concede an inch.

The conflict is intense on physical, ideological and cerebral levels, with a subdued Guinness just managing to hold the line. When Guinness's obduracy – which lands him in the hold – halts progress on an earlier bridge, Hayakawa attempts to enlist his antagonist's co-operation by releasing him and informing him that failure to complete the structure on time will leave him no alternative but suicide. 'What would you do in my position,' asks Hayakawa, to which Guinness replies impassively, 'I suppose I'd kill myself.' This piece of candour promptly lands him back in the hold.

In *Tunes of Glory* (1960, Ronald Neame) his successor and rival was John Mills, a new-

Alec Guinness shares a thoughtful good-night drink with Odile Versois in *To Paris With Love* (1955)

broom, 'rule book' colonel attempting to take command of a Scottish regiment sloppily run by Guinness, the sly, hard-drinking CO whom he replaces. Mills loses the drawn-out battle of words for the regiment's heart and blows his brains out.

Guinness was Charles I in *Cromwell* (1970, Ken Hughes), a foot-weary trudge through a section of English history best forgotten. Guinness tries to hang on to control of Parliament while Richard Harris, as Cromwell, favours chopping his head off. When they are not hurling threats amid the draperies they are leading their supporters into dispirited sorties in the greenwood. All the main characters are either dull or dislikable, and the dialogue is strictly correspondence-course Shakespeare. At one point Guinness admonishes a court minion with the phrase: 'You make a knave of your King', a line that belongs, surely, to Woody Allen. At the end, Guinness wants to walk instead of ride the short distance to the scaffold because 'the morning air will do

me good'. Not as good, perhaps, as a brisk canter in the opposite direction.

The cornerstone of Guinness's success has been his own near-anonymity. The face seems purposefully nondescript, as if waiting for a character, any but his own, to move in and occupy it. The faces he has donned over the years represent a gallery without equal in the history of screen character acting.

Whether in a supporting role in big budget productions, such as an Arabian prince in *Lawrence of Arabia* (1962, David Lean), the hero's revolutionary brother, later a Commissar in the Red Army, in *Dr Zhivago* (1966, David Lean), the Führer in *Hitler: The Last Ten Days* (1973, Ennio de Concini), or, more recently, the bearded Ben Kenobi in *Star Wars* (1976, George Lucas), or any from the long catalogue of earlier successes, such as Disraeli in *The Mudlark* (1951, Jean Negulesco), the rough-and-ready artist in *The Horse's Mouth* (1958, Ronald Neame) or the

76

cunning, intractable detective-priest in *Father Brown* (1954, Robert Hamer), Guinness gets it absolutely right down to the tiniest observation.

It was this type of meticulous preparation and execution which keeps him so vividly remembered on the strength of a mere handful of films, as the quiet genius of Ealing Studios.

Alec Guinness

b. 1914. Chameleon-like, quietly effective character star whose gallery of faces and mannerisms is practically a blue book for aspiring character players. Played all eight victims in Ealing's *Kind Hearts and Coronets* (1949), thereafter starred in several of the same studio's 1950s winners (*The Lavender Hill Mob*, *The Man in the White Suit*, *The Ladykillers* etc). Also been in several David Lean classics, including *Great Expectations* (1946, his film debut), *Oliver Twist* (1948), *Bridge on the River Kwai* (1957), *Lawrence of Arabia* (1962) and *Dr Zhivago* (1966). Still a key figure in big-budget productions. Was Ben Kenobi in *Star Wars* (1976) and spin-off *The Empire Strikes Back* (1980) and TV's errant spy-catcher George Smiley in Le Carré's *Tinker, Tailor, Soldier, Spy*.

1946 *Great Expectations* (Herbert Pocket)
1948 *Oliver Twist* (Fagin)
1949 *Kind Hearts and Coronets* (Ascoyne d' Ascoyne, Duke of Chalfont, Lady Agatha, General d'Ascoyne, Admiral d'Ascoyne, Lord d'Ascoyne, Henry d'Ascoyne, Canon d'Ascoyne)
A Run for Your Money (Whimple)
1950 *The Last Holiday* (George Bird)
1951 *The Mudlark* (Benjamin Disraeli)
The Lavender Hill Mob (Dutch Holland)
The Man in the White Suit (Sidney Stratton)

1952 *The Card* (Edward Henry Machin)
1953 *The Captain's Paradise* (Captain Henry St James)
Malta Story (Flight Lieutenant Peter Rose)
1954 *Father Brown* (Father Brown)
1955 *To Paris With Love* (Sir Edgar Fraser)
The Prisoner (The Cardinal)
The Ladykillers (Professor Marcus)
1956 *The Swan* (USA) (Prince Albert)
1957 *The Bridge on the River Kwai* (Colonel Nicholson)
Barnacle Bill (William Ambrose)
1958 *The Horse's Mouth* (Gulley Jimson)
1959 *The Scapegoat* (John Barratt/Count Jacques)
1960 *Our Man In Havana* (Jim Wormald)
Tunes Of Glory (Lt Col Jock Sinclair)
1961 *A Majority of One* (USA) (Koichi Asano)
1962 *Lawrence of Arabia* (Prince Feisal)
HMS Defiant (Capt Crawford)
1964 *The Fall of the Roman Empire* (USA) (Marcus Aurelius)
1965 *Situation Hopeless but Not Serious* (Herr Wilhelm Frick)
1966 *Hotel Paradise* (Benedict Boniface)
The Quiller Memorandum (Pol)
Dr Zhivago (Yevgraf Zhivago)
1967 *The Comedians* (USA) (Major Jones)
1970 *Cromwell* (King Charles I)
Scrooge (Jacob Marley)
1973 *Brother Sun, Sister Moon* (Italy) (Pope Innocent III)
Hitler: The Last Ten Days (Adolf Hitler)
1976 *Murder by Death* (James Bensonmum)
Star Wars (Ben [Obi-Wan] Kenobi)
1979 *Raise the Titanic* (John Bigalow)
1980 *The Empire Strikes Back* (Ben [Obi-Wan] Kenobi)
1981 *Little Lord Fauntleroy* (Earl of Dorincourt)

Richard Harris

There's a scene in *Man in the Wilderness* (1971, Richard Sarafian) where Percy Herbert, a trapper who'd 'steal the pennies from his mother's eyes', sits beside a badly-lacerated Richard Harris, who has been crushed by a huge bear. Herbert wants his buddy to die so that he can inherit his rifle, but Harris hangs on, grittily refusing to part with anything. 'Dammit,' snorts Herbert,

'A man ought to know when his time is up!'

Acting-wise, Harris's time has often seemed to be up. With his boorish high spirits providing a ready focus for the gossip columns, his acting talent has avoided serious scrutiny. Despite actively encouraging the wild Irish rover image, he must at times feel a prisoner of it, because his thoughtfulness and sensitivity – he is also an

Richard Harris, 1965

accomplished singer-poet – rarely get a look-in.

His film career started well. Three years after leaving LAMDA he was on his way, as the mutinous first mate in *The Wreck of the Mary Deare* (1959, Michael Anderson) with Gary Cooper and Charlton Heston. His undentable brogue made him a natural for IRA-man Robert Mitchum's hardliner chum in *A Terrible Beauty* (1960, Raymond Stross), an outsider's vision of the Irish troubles which goes to extraordinary lengths to depict the republican cause as a fountain of tolerable idealism. Harris's showy performance makes Mitchum's contribution seem hardly worth getting out of bed for, and Mitchum performs accordingly, like a hippo with sunstroke.

The Long and the Short and the Tall (1960, Leslie Norman) and *The Guns of Navarone* (1961, Carl Foreman) gave Harris tough Army roles. In the former he was an NCO, the resentful target of Private Laurence Harvey's oafish needling, and in the latter he was one of the assault team killed early in the operation. He was one of the mutineers in *Mutiny on the Bounty* (1962, Lewis

Milestone), flogged by Trevor Howard's order for suggesting the disciplinarian captain has authorised the stealing of cheese. Later he redresses the injury by helping Marlon Brando, as Fletcher Christian, suspend Howard's cruel command.

This Sporting Life (1963, Lindsay Anderson) made Harris a star, as an aggressive rugby player in love with his widowed landlady, played by Rachel Roberts. The film's opening scenes are vivid and distressing, where Harris has his front teeth smashed off at gum level in a cowardly assault on the field, and is dragged semi-conscious to a dentist who digs out the roots. This sombre, uncompromising mood never lifts, even in the momentarily tender scenes between Harris and Miss Roberts. Harris brings a gruff, physical power to his role as a brooding loner and Miss Roberts is no less excellent as the embittered widow.

Charlton Heston worked with Harris for a second time in *Major Dundee* (1965, Sam Peckinpah), both as Cavalry officers but with opposing attitudes about the best way to suppress Indians. Heston noted in his diary afterwards that it had 'a smell of a great film in there somewhere among the ruins'. Harris supported Kirk Douglas in *The Heroes of Telemark* (1965, Anthony Mann) as a Norwegian officer, a brittle, precipitous performance unimpaired by reported disagreements between the two stars.

This wasn't the first time Harris's co-stars had felt the sharp edge of his tongue, and word got around that he was 'difficult'. He had to mark time in several flops, *Hawaii* (1966, George Roy Hill) for example, based on Michener's long, boring novel, and as a substitute Rock Hudson in a Doris Day romp, *Caprice* (1967, Frank Tashlin). A worse example of casting would be difficult to imagine. Harris was so mortified by the outcome that he reportedly cancelled a flight from London when he discovered, on boarding the plane, that *Caprice* was to be shown. His luggage stayed on but Harris caught a later flight – 'imagine being trapped in an aeroplane with 110 angry people!' he scoffed.

His fortunes improved with *Camelot* (1967, Joshua Logan) as King Arthur to Vanessa Redgrave's Guinevere. Memorable tunes and Harris's kingly swagger kept the tills ringing. Richard Burton was popular in the stage production but Harris's version had more firepower. Interestingly, during the 1981 touring revival in the USA, when Burton was forced to abandon the show through illness it was Harris who plugged the gap. In *The Molly Maguires* (1969, Martin Ritt) he was a Pinkerton spy, an agent provocateur sent in to nail the ringleaders in a Pennsylvania miners' strike which occurred during the 1870s. The film was based on fact, and Sean Connery was the miners' leader.

Cromwell got the better of Charles I, but in Ken Hughes' slow-moving film of their conflict, *Cromwell* (1970), the acting contest – if such it was – between Alec Guinness, as the king, and Harris in the title role, levelled the score. David Halliwell noted: '(Harris's) Cromwell was at one extreme snarling cur and at the other hangdog in the soulful manner of Richard Burton, and there was nothing in between'. As a summary of Harris's most discernible acting weakness Halliwell's observation is spot on. All too often his fiercest characters seem to be alight only on the outside, and he contents himself with camouflaging the inner vacuum instead of trying to find ways to fill it.

In *A Man Called Horse* (1970, Eliot Silverstein) Harris played a British aristocrat captured by Seminole Indians who, after a period of ridicule and maltreatment as their prisoner, becomes infatuated with the chief's sister and volunteers to undergo savage initiation rites in order to become betrothed to her, because only a full blood brother can marry into the family of a chief.

Harris's performance is refreshingly subdued, but the film's strength lies in its authentic-looking depiction of the Indian tribal culture, inexplicably harsh in some ways, movingly beautiful in others, where freedom of the plains is counterpointed by frighteningly harsh winters. Its success at the box office helped lure Harris back into repeating the role in *Return of a Man Called Horse* (1974, Irvin Kershner).

Seventies films put a lot of effort into recoup-

Rugger star Richard Harris pleads with widowed landlady Rachel Roberts in *This Sporting Life* (1963)

ing audiences lost to television during the previous decade, by making the backgrounds larger, the action more full-blooded and the characters more colourful than before. Harris's naturally pugnacious personality slipped as snugly into the seventies blockbuster as he had into Rachel Roberts' bed in *This Sporting Life* (1963).

Juggernaut (1974, Richard Lester) was the story of a large luxury liner captained by Omar Sharif which runs into trouble in mid-ocean when several cleverly concealed bombs are discovered on board. Harris and David Hemmings played a couple of buccaneering bomb disposal experts parachuted into the sea nearby and hoisted on board to deal with the crisis. 'Death is nature's way of telling you you're in the wrong job,' Harris confides to his partner as they start work, but a freak wave spares his life as he is about to cut the wrong wire. Hemmings, grappling with a similar device in another part of the ship, is not so lucky.

In *The Cassandra Crossing* (1977, George Pan Cosmatos) Harris was a doctor on board a crowded transcontinental express which is being diverted to a remote, unstable bridge near the Russian border because some of the passengers are thought to be suffering from a deadly contagious disease for which there is no known cure. World governments are so alarmed at the thought of the killer plague spreading that agreement is reached between them for the train to be sealed and then driven over the crumbling bridge which will effectively mean its end. Armed guards in sterile masks are implanted on the train to ensure that no plague carrier ducks out before they reach the assigned destination.

Obviously, since the guards will be plunging into the ravine alongside the passengers, the truth about what's in store for everyone on this particular Awayday has to be kept a secret. But Harris is no slouch when it comes to interpreting ministerial double-talk. He realises what's happening, and marshals a few worthies to try and wrest control of at least part of the train back from the armed guards. This accomplished, a quick uncoupling job is next, and while the front half of the train plummets through the bridge and crashes in flames below as intended, Harris's section grinds to a halt mere yards from where the bridge becomes fresh air.

Though it's really a no-holds-barred adventure caper, *The Cassandra Crossing* poses an interesting question – what would the authorities do if a killer disease struck down a trainload of in-nocents, and there was no hope of containing it by conventional methods? One hopes the authorities would find a more reasonable solution than Intelligence Chief Burt Lancaster advocates. Or failing that, I would hope that the bridges I travel across are better maintained than the one at Cassandra Crossing. The film is packed with familiar stereotypes, with a few babies and dogs thrown in as plague victims, and some of the dialogue, particularly between Harris and Sophia Loren who plays his ex-wife, and between Ava Gardner and Martin Sheen, as a European magnate's wife and her drug-running fancy man respectively, belongs with the remains of the front half of the train. Despite these obvious shortcomings, though, it's a film with energy to spare, and the journey is worth the price of an off-peak ticket.

Harris might be on the wrong side of forty for military service, but even more so were Richard Burton and Roger Moore; so when the three of them appear in commando gear in *The Wild Geese* (1978, Euan Lloyd), one might imagine it's another Dad's Army on manoeuvres. But no, the Old Brigade are deadly serious, as tough mercenaries hell-bent on snatching a kidnapped African leader from his captors' stronghold, conveniently pitched on the edge of a jungle clearing. The raid is successful, but an about-turn by the mercenaries' slimy paymaster (Stewart Granger making a welcome appearance) cuts off the platoon's air-lift out of enemy territory.

Technical adviser on the film was 'Major' Mike Hoare, a real-life mercenary commander, so the running battles and all the carnage are probably authentic. What the film conspicuously avoids is any questioning of the morality of mercenary operations, here conveniently seen on the side of the good guy, a legitimate black African leader ousted from power by ruthless insurgents. But if regarded as simply a big-star adventure yarn unlikely to stir the inner reflexes, *The Wild Geese* has plenty to engage the eye. Best of the three performances comes from Harris, as Burton's right-hand man, a veteran strategist who initially resists the invitation to take up arms again because he wants to do right by his small son after the lad's mother has run off. He fails to complete the return journey, but Burton has already given his word to the boy's guardian, and the film ends with Burton taking up his fatherly duties having first killed the moneybags whose change of allegiance was indirectly responsible for Harris's death.

Richard Harris

b. 1932. Irreverent, extrovert Irish-born actor-singer-poet, not always successful in transferring real-life colour on to the screen. Began as screen 'heavy' opposite American top-liners; stardom came as broody rugby player in *This Sporting Life* (1963). Later improvement as an actor counter-pointed by declining quality of recent films. Gaudy, hell-raiser image conflicts with sensitive quality of his poetry. Previously married to Elisabeth Ogmore (who later married Rex Harrison) and actress Ann Turkel.

1958 *Alive and Kicking* (Lover)
1959 *Shake Hands with the Devil* (Terence O'Brien)
     The Wreck of the Mary Deare (Higgins)
1960 *A Terrible Beauty* (Sean O'Reilly)
     The Long and the Short and the Tall (Corporal Johnstone)
1961 *The Guns of Navarone* (Barnsby)
1962 *Mutiny on the Bounty* (John Mills)
1963 *This Sporting Life* (Frank Machin)
1964 *The Red Desert* (Corrado Zeller)
1965 *The Heroes Of Telemark* (Kurt Strand)
     Major Dundee (Capt Benjamin Tyreen)
1966 *The Bible* (Cain)
     Hawaii (Rafer Hoxworth)
1967 *Caprice* (Christopher White)
     Camelot (King Arthur)
1969 *The Molly Maguires* (James McParlan)
1970 *A Man Called Horse* (Lord John Morgan)
     Bloomfield (also directed)
     Cromwell (Oliver Cromwell)
1971 *Man in the Wilderness* (Zachary Bass)
1973 *The Deadly Trackers* (Sean Kilpatrick)
1974 *99 44/100 Dead* (Harry Crown)
     Juggernaut (Fallon)
1975 *Robin and Marian* (Richard the Lionheart)
1976 *Return of a Man Called Horse* (John Morgan)
     Gulliver's Travels (Gulliver)
1977 *The Cassandra Crossing* (Dr Jonathan Chamberlain)
     Orca, The Killer Whale (Capt Nolan)
1978 *Golden Rendezvous* (John Carter)
     The Wild Geese (Rafer Janders)
1979 *Game for Vultures* (David Swansey)
1980 *Highpoint* (Canadian)

Laurence Harvey

In *The Manchurian Candidate* (1964, John Frankenheimer) Laurence Harvey, the brainwashed ex-Korean GI being manipulated by sinister forces, tells his former buddy Frank Sinatra: 'I am not lovable.' The admission was barely necessary. Whatever else Harvey managed to conjure up as both actor and public figure, lovableness was never in it.

Harvey was at his best playing foxy, smooth, ambitious characters, either needling or cajoling their way to the top, like the hero in the two Joe Lampton films and the fast-mouth agent in *Expresso Bongo* (1959, Val Guest), or poised there and holding on, like the ruthless, amoral playboy in *Darling* (1965, John Schlesinger) or the philandering chemical company boss in *Butterfield 8* (1960, Daniel Mann).

Despite appearances, he was, in fact, Lithuanian by birth, and borrowed the name Harvey from the Knightsbridge store Harvey Nicholls after his agent had assured him that the name epitomised true Englishness. Laurence was, of course, an Anglicisation of his first name

Larushka but, as he was keen to point out, it was something he shared with the greatest stage actor in the world. Other similarities are not immediately obvious.

His early film work was unexceptional – 'messy little films' he called them– including an ambitious fairground fighter in *There Is Another Sun* (1951, Lewis Gilbert), an obnoxious Teddy-boy in *I Believe in You* (1952, Basil Dearden), a young copper in *Man on the Run* (1949, Lawrence Huntingdon), and an amorous French waiter in *Innocents in Paris* (1953, Gordon Parry).

In 1954 came his breakthrough. He starred as a vicious psychopathic gang-leader in *The Good Die Young* (1954, Lewis Gilbert) with American stars Richard Basehart, John Ireland and Gloria Grahame mingling with our own Stanley Baker, Joan Collins and Margaret Leighton. Harvey was thoroughly nasty, and waiting for his come-uppance was like waiting for the dentist to open after a night of howling toothache. Basehart is the gang member who finally takes him out, after a thrilling atmospheric battle along a stretch of live rails, but in doing so is mortally wounded. That same year Harvey was chosen as Romeo opposite unknown Susan Shentall in *Romeo and Juliet* (1954, Renato Castellini) – an experiment more to be applauded for its audacity than its artistic achievement. Harvey mouths his lines like a carpet salesman and Miss Shentall is all wide-eyed innocence; but search as one may, no hint of grand passion emerges.

He played author Christopher Isherwood as a young man adrift among pre-war Berlin low-lifes in *I Am a Camera* (1955, Henry Cornelius), which provided the blueprint for Bob Fosse's Oscar-winning extravaganza *Cabaret* (1978). The vivacious nightclub entertainer in Harvey's film was played by Julie Harris, and the backdrop to their adventures – the rise of Nazism – is better done in that film too. Where Fosse's film improves on its predecessor is in the way he conveys the period's seediness and decadence. The Harvey version expunges all the grime and the feeling that someone somewhere might have screwing in mind. This had to do with the view, popular among many studios at the time, that unless a film could be appreciated by vicars' housekeepers in Middle Wallop its total receipts could be counted in a hat-box.

Room at the Top (1959, Jack Clayton) dragged the British cinema into modern times, or at least, into modern thinking. Its frankness, both visually in the love-scenes and in the amoral attitudes expressed by the central character, broke taboos in a way which was keenly felt throughout the industry. The hero pays with his beating up at the end – so does Albert Finney for an identical reason in *Saturday Night and Sunday Morning* – so that society, not to say the censor of the day, is suitably appeased. These were small concessions for a film with such far-searching and indeed irreversible influence.

Harvey was Joe Lampton, a working-class Yorkshire lad determined to taste the good life which he sees others of independent means enjoying. His problem is that his background equips him only for routine employment, in the town hall audit department, and his social graces are nil. His friendship in the office with Donald Houston, a 'power' in the local drama club, leads to an introduction to Heather Sears, spoilt daughter of the town's leading industrialist, played by Donald Wolfit.

Wolfit warns Harvey about associating with his daughter – the message is delivered by Harvey's sepulchral boss Raymond Huntley – and when this fails, along with crude attempts to buy him off, Miss Sears is sent away. Harvey eases his frustration by having a torrid affair with the wife (Simone Signoret) of a local dignitary, but Miss Sears' return and her subsequent pregnancy put an end to Wolfit's cynical opposition to him.

When, on the insistence of his future father-in-law, Harvey breaks off the affair with Miss Signoret, whose cold unimaginative husband has found out about them and publicly humiliated her, she goes off on a drinking spree and is killed when her car plunges out of control. The way is thus tidily cleared for Harvey to join the elite, which he does by marrying the girl at a posh ceremony. All that's missing is his self-respect, abandoned so callously when he sacrificed love and the woman who desperately needed him for money and social status.

In its time, *Room at the Top* was a daring, controversial film, dealing courageously with topics like infidelity, intercourse and social conflict which, five years before, that is to say when *I Am a Camera* was made, would have been unthinkable. It's a male chauvinist film – the male protagonists are shown as worldly-wise, stubborn and ruthless but admirable for all that; the females, by comparison, notably Signoret and Heather Sears, as weak and too damn willing for their own good – and feminist hackles understandably rise wherever it is shown today. In fairness, they have a point. Women in *Room at the Top* are merely cyphers of their menfolk's success or failure, they have no tangible function of their own. For example, Wolfit's wife is a fussy snob, but she is married to the local bigwig so no-one dares to put her in her rightful place.

Signoret is all-woman but without her lover she has nothing, nor is she capable of giving her nasty crab-like husband the tongue-lashing he deserves. Miss Sears is a shallow little nobody, yet, with a go-getter for a husband and Daddy's accumulated wealth to fire her rockets, she has it made; but hers is a futile existence, unbearable to any bright, thinking woman who wants to have a life of her own. Harvey's performance suggests rascally self-absorption nearing the edge of paranoia. The fact that one is only transiently aware – at no loss of enjoyment of the film, it should be added – that he sounds for all the world like a Bradford talking clock shows how efficiently the film delivers its assorted punches.

In *The Alamo* (1960, John Wayne) he shared honours with John Wayne and Richard Wid-

Doomed lovers Laurence Harvey and Susan Shentall in *Romeo and Juliet* (1954)

mark, as the starchy fortress commander, Travis. Wayne and Widmark are old-time Indian fighters, caught in the sanctuary of the Alamo with a handful of soldiers and their frightened families when the Mexican army masses outside. 'I've never been able to like you but you're one of the other few men to whom I would trust the life of Texas,' gnarled Army veteran Richard Boone tells Harvey as he marshals what assistance he can to repel the Mexican hordes. But before that, Harvey shows a distinct reluctance to face facts. Before the Mexicans actually camp outside the walls hurling cheeky ultimatums because they know the defenders are hideously outnumbered, Harvey brusquely dismisses a report that they are en route in staggering numbers. Widmark believes it, and calls Harvey a 'damn fool' for ignoring the obvious.

Later Harvey redeems himself in Widmark's eyes by taking the initiative when the Mexicans show up in strength to demand an orderly surrender. While the Mexs warble on about the wisdom of quitting, Harvey casually ignites the nearest cannon with his pencil-slim cheroot. 'He sure does know the short way to start a war,' says Widmark admiringly.

He was a Cockney pop music agent in *Expresso Bongo* (1959, Val Guest), a greedy, charmless small-time grafter with ambitions as wide as his padded shoulders. More acid repartee came his way in *The Long and the Short and the Tall* (1960, Leslie Norman) as the bolshie misfit in Richard Todd's wartime Burma patrol. Sensing imminent slaughter by advancing Japanese troops, the platoon releases its remaining venom on to itself. Keith Waterhouse and Willis Hall's authentic-sounding dialogue compensates in part, for the staginess of the setting.

There's a line of dialogue – arguably the worst ever written – which sums up *Butterfield 8* (1960, Daniel Mann). Harvey runs a chemical company – it's actually owned by wife Dina Merrill's family – and has an affair with expensive call-girl Elizabeth Taylor. One night they steal away to his yacht. 'Where are you heading, Captain?' coos the flighty Miss Taylor, to which Harvey replies, 'Out of frustration, bound for ecstasy!'

Miss Taylor becomes annoyed when Harvey tries to buy her off, and pinches his wife's expensive fur coat to teach him a lesson, but fails to return it before Miss Merrill discovers it is missing. That leads to his wife's finding out what's been going on behind her back, and a series of increasingly bitter confrontations between Harvey and the two women – 'I'm a failure as a husband; I'm a failure as a man,' he tells Miss Merrill – leads to a wild proposal of marriage to Miss Taylor, and her death shortly afterwards in a car crash (shades of Signoret and *Room at the Top* here) as, having turned him down, she overspeeds to get away from him. 'Everything about her was struggling towards respectability,' he sighs, as the body is toted away.

The Manchurian Candidate (1962, John Frankenheimer) was Harvey's best film since *Room at the Top*. He was one of a group of Korean prisoners brainwashed by his captors, programmed to respond to a particular playing card. Repatriated with his politically active mother and stepfather, he becomes a tool in their hands, destroying anyone who obstructs their fanatical climb to power. One such victim is Harvey's prospective father-in-law, an influential senator on the opposing side. Programmed to act as a sniper at the Party convention where his stepfather is confidently expecting to win the presidential nomination, his 'masters' are unaware that the effects of the brainwashing are wearing thin, with calamitous results.

This was a slick plausible thriller whose release almost coincided with the assassination of President Kennedy in Dallas in November 1963, an event which inevitably brought its theme into sharper focus. Frank Sinatra played Harvey's prison-camp buddy who tries to avert the sinister chain of events. Harvey's performance is zombie-like but this is excusable for once since the character is supposed to be in a trance.

He was badly miscast in *Of Human Bondage* (1964, Henry Hathaway) as the club-footed medical student lover of waitress Kim Novak. Of the lady in question, he commented, 'a very attractive girl but *why* does she try to act?' – foolhardy words which might easily have rebounded on him, though nobody doubted his sincerity.

He was good in *Darling* (1965, John Schlesinger), as a kinky playboy who enjoys humiliating beautiful women. Julie Christie is one of his victims. He reprised Joe Lampton for

Life at the Top (1965, Ted Ketcheff), showy and contrived compared to the original. Jean Simmons was his wife, Honor Blackman his girlfriend, and Michael Craig the cuckoo in his own nest. One of his last films of any note was *A Dandy in Aspic* (1967, Anthony Mann), an espionage story in which Harvey played a double agent and Tom Courtenay the British MI5-man out to catch him. When the director died in mid-production, Harvey stepped in and steered it to completion.

Exactly what it was that made Harvey a star, apart from his own determination to become one, is a bit of a mystery, and what it was that he brought to films once he had arrived, besides playing grander versions of Laurence Harvey, is equally puzzling.

Harvey was more a behaver than an actor. He struck moods and affected postures, and liked where possible to outrage – during interviews and chat shows he frequently did – but one suspects these were all, to Harvey, mere adjuncts to the 'performance'. Leading ladies tended to be ungenerous about his behaviour – Elaine Stritch spoke up for at least half-a-dozen miffed co-stars when she described acting in a play with him as 'the most horrible experience of my life' – but, in fairness, he gave some of them as spirited a thumbsdown as any he ever got.

By 1971, he was taking brief guest roles, such as a shyster preacher in *W.U.S.A.* (1970, Stuart Rosenberg) with Paul Newman and Joanne Woodward. Not only was the part tiny – he was on-screen no longer than six minutes – it was also irrelevant, as a dubious figure from Newman's past. Asked why he made so few screen appearances around this time, Harvey told a reporter: 'All I was being offered were nude love scenes. I won't lower my trousers for any part, exquisitely divine though such a revelation might be!'

His last film of note was *Night Watch* (1973, Brian G. Hutton), a clever psychological thriller, in which he played a rich smoothie married to Elizabeth Taylor but having his wicked way with house guest Billie Whitelaw. When Miss Taylor starts imagining she sees murders committed in a derelict house next door, and pesters the police with more imagined sightings than a saloon-bar full of UFO enthusiasts at closing time, it starts to look as if Harvey is fixing to have her institutionalised so that he can carry on his affair with Miss Whitelaw more openly.

But having established herself as a rich, pampered crackpot, the kind with whom the long-hours, working-class police inspector wants precious little to do in any event, Miss Taylor savagely murders Harvey and his mistress in the derelict house nearby, exactly as she has described the incident ad nauseum to the police. A creepy neighbour who digs graves in his garden at night proves a useful accomplice, and since the police have already dug up that patch for themselves to reassure the supposedly nervy Miss Taylor that no earlier bodies were planted there, it is unlikely that Harvey's and Miss Whitelaw's final resting places will be disturbed. And Miss Taylor's final call to the police, to report the real killings, before jetting off for a well-earned rest, is firmly but politely wastebinned. Case closed.

Harvey died from cancer in 1973. He was forty-five. A long-time colleague said of him: 'He wanted to be the top of the ladder; he wanted to be great. But to be great you must have compassion and humility, and these were in short supply.'

Laurence Harvey

1928-1973. Raffish, tidy-mannered, eternally poised – even when under siege at the Alamo – Lithuanian-born actor who specialised in cold-blooded opportunist roles, as in *The Good Die Young* (1954), *Room at the Top* (1958), *Expresso Bongo* (1959) and *Darling* (1965). Was married to Margaret Leighton, Joan Cohn, and model Paulene Stone.

1948 *House of Darkness* (Francis Merivale)
1949 *Man on the Run* (Sgt Lawson)
     Landfall (Pilot Officer Hooper)
     The Man from Yesterday (John Matthews)
1950 *Cairo Road* (Lt Mourad)
     The Black Rose (Edmond)
1951 *There Is Another Sun* (Maguire)
     Scarlet Thread (Freddie)
1952 *I Believe in You* (Jordie)
     A Killer Walks (Ned)

     Women of Twilight (Jerry Nolan)
1953 *Innocents in Paris* (François)
1954 *The Good Die Young* (Miles Ravenscourt)
     Romeo and Juliet (Romeo)
     King Richard and the Crusaders (USA) (Sir Kenneth)
1955 *I Am a Camera* (Christopher Isherwood)
     Storm Over the Nile (John Durrance)
1956 *Three Men in a Boat* (George)
1957 *After the Ball* (Walter de Trece)
     The Truth about Women (Humphrey Tavistock)
     The Silent Enemy (Lt Lionel 'Buster' Crabbe)
1959 *Room at the Top* (Joe Lampton)
     Expresso Bongo (Johnny Jackson)
1960 *The Alamo* (USA) (Col William Barrett Travis)
     Butterfield 8 (USA) (Weston Liggett)
     The Long and the Short and the Tall (Pte Bamforth)
1961 *Summer and Smoke* (USA) (John Buchanan)
1962 *A Walk on the Wild Side* (USA) (Dove Linkhom)
     The Wonderful World of the Brothers Grimm (USA) (Wilhelm Grimm)
     A Girl Named Tamiko (USA) (Ivan Kalin)
     The Manchurian Candidate (USA) (Sgt Raymond Shaw)
1963 *The Running Man* (Rex Black)
     The Ceremony (USA) (Sean McKenna)
1964 *Of Human Bondage* (Philip Carey)
     The Outrage (USA) (Husband)
1965 *Darling* (Miles Brand)
     Life at the Top (Joe Lampton)
1966 *The Spy With a Cold Nose* (Francis Trevellyan)
1967 *A Dandy in Aspic* (Alexander Eberlin) (co-director)
1968 *A Winters Tale* (Leontes)
1970 *The Magic Christian* (Hamlet)
1973 *The Night Watch* (John Wheeler)

Jack Hawkins

'I've played every kind of officer except a Wren,' Jack Hawkins once remarked. One suspects that even as a Wren he would have done his usual competent job. You always knew where you were with Big Jack. As British as roast beef, with gentle, expressive eyes and a rich resonant voice, Hawkins' appearance in *Angels One Five* (1952, George More O'Ferrall) gave him his first important screen role – at the age of forty, old for an emerging leading man.

Jack Hawkins as Commander Ericson in *The Cruel Sea* (1952)

In *Angels One Five* Hawkins commanded a wartime fighter station populated by cheery Biggles-types whose favourite off-duty wheeze seems to be climbing over each other. Outwardly, Hawkins is a stickler for regulations – a sentry he attempts but fails to browbeat into letting him through without showing his pass is told, 'You've got your wits about you.' But he's really a big softie, admitting to a fellow-officer's wife at a station knees-up that 'we keep going because we've *got* to keep going', and worrying endlessly about his 'brave chaps'.

But it was the following year, as Commander Ericson in Nicholas Monsarrat's *The Cruel Sea* (1952, Charles Frend), that the Hawkins persona – that of a rugged, sanguine officer-type – became crystallised indelibly in the public's mind.

The Cruel Sea was not just an acting breakthrough for Hawkins. It was a spectacular film on numerous levels, and there was none finer from a British studio depicting the horrors of war and the effects that it has on the survivors. Its depiction of war at sea was both actionful and thought-provoking, and the dreadful toll in death and hardship that must be borne by both sides was graphically realised without resorting to flag-waving or contrived heroics. If any youngsters wonder what it must have been like to be at war with another nation there's a cryptic lesson, and as honest an insight into the subject as one is ever likely to see outside a documentary, contained in *The Cruel Sea*.

Hawkins played a corvette commander patrolling the perilous North Atlantic convoy lanes during the opening years of the War. In one famous scene survivors from a torpedoed British vessel flounder in the water directly above an enemy U-boat. Hawkins orders his ship to plough through them in order to depth-charge the enemy below, knowing that when the depth-charges find their target the unfortunate sailors will be blown out of the water, too.

Later, locked away in his own cabin, the events revive before his tear-filled eyes like a recurring nightmare. 'It's the war, the whole bloody war,' he mutters lamely to a bunch of sympathisers whom he had previously rescued. Shortly afterwards, another horrific memory is added, that of the cries of his doomed engine-room crew as the *Compass Rose,* his ship, plunges to the sea-bed following a direct hit.

The loss of the *Compass Rose* and so many of his crew, hardens his normally ambivalent attitude towards German sailors whom he has previously regarded as simply fellow-professionals under orders. The war has entered its darker phases and there would appear to be no room on board for humanitarian feelings. 'Beforehand there was time to be understanding – now it's simply a business of killing the enemy,' he explains, and he believes every word of it. That is, until a number of German seamen surface near the bows of his new ship, having just been blasted out of a U-boat. Memories of the others that he destroyed prevent him from killing them and instead he gives the order to lower the rescue nets.

On seeing the film author Nicholas Montsarrat described Hawkins' performance as coming closer to the character than the original conception of him. Ericson was arguably the most solid flesh-and-blood character of the British post-war cinema, and it was unimaginable after the event that anyone but Hawkins could have done proper justice to him.

He was at his best playing sympathetic figures of authority. In *The Intruder* (1953, Guy Hamilton) he was an ex-Colonel of the Tank Regiment burgled by a down-and-out former trooper, played by Michael Medwin, whom Hawkins recognises as having served courageously under his wartime command. The film follows Hawkins' pursuit of the truth about the trooper's tangled life, and though its heart was probably in the right place its moral stance shrieked of dated middle-class condescension.

Hawkins' broad catalogue took in numerous kindly father roles, like the would-be emigrant of *Touch and Go* (1956, Michael Truman). As chief designer of an upmarket furniture firm, Hawkins clashes with his boss James Hayter over product stylings. Hayter sees more profits in mass-market designs which Hawkins dismisses as cheap rubbish. His stormy resignation is followed by a decision to resettle in Australia – an idea which encounters little enthusiasm at home. Wife Margaret Johnson is worried about leaving aged parents, and about the family cat, daughter June Thorburn would sooner marry her boyfriend John Fraser. But hating Hayter is stronger than any reasoned argument and, after brusquely turning down his ex-boss's conciliatory gestures, they set off – with Hayter's farewell taunt of 'God Save Australia' ringing in their ears. However, before they have travelled any distance at all, Hawkins about-turns, worn down by the family's subtle but unflagging resistance plus a few last-minute doubts of his own.

He was a crusading newspaper editor in *Front Page Story* (1953, Gordon Parry), a kind of layman's guide to Fleet Street, the type of film which never looks quite as good on screen as it promised to be in script form.

The Bridge on the River Kwai (1957, David Lean) was more his metier, as a British Army major whose small commando unit, augmented by Siam death-railway escapee William Holden, destroys Alec Guinness's infamous rail bridge that would otherwise be a vital link in the Japanese military communications chain across Burma. On the long trek through the jungle, Hawkins and Holden barely see eye-to-eye – the former well-intentioned but humourless, the latter a rather glib, cynical anti-hero not unlike the character Holden won an Oscar for in *Stalag 17* (1953, Billy Wilder).

Tempers flare when Hawkins is injured and, as senior officer, orders the others to abandon him, volunteering to die rather than jeopardise the mission. 'You make me sick with your heroics ... there's a stench of death about you!' sneers Holden, disregarding Hawkins' self-sacrifice and the order that went with it, and Hawkins has to put up with being humped the rest of the way. Ironically, it is Hawkins who survives the assault on the bridge, while Holden dies, cut down by machine-gun fire.

Hawkins created the role of Commander Gideon of the Yard in *Gideon's Day* (1958, John Ford), a character later played on TV by John Gregson. In *Ben Hur* (1959, William Wyler), called by one critic 'a ten-minute chariot race wrapped in four hours of spare celluloid', he was a Roman senator whose life is saved by galley slave Charlton Heston, an act which earns Heston his freedom, and a valuable patron in high places.

One of Hawkins' best performances was in *The League of Gentlemen* (1960, Basil Dearden) as ringmaster of a troop of ex-Army ne'er-do-wells whom he recruits and grooms into a slick bank-raid unit. The wider question, about the dangers to society of men trained for highly drilled and dangerous raids turning their skills against the society which nurtured them, is neatly probed in a mature and literate Bryan Forbes script, although Forbes ultimately cops

Rubber planter Jack Hawkins, wife Claudette Colbert and friendly native Ram Gopal get ready to repel intruders in *The Planter's Wife* (1952)

out by making the gang a ragbag of tarnished souls instead of a consortium of really desperate characters.

By contrast, Hawkins' weakest performance occurred in *Rampage* (1963, Phil Karlson) as a big game hunter who is jealous of Robert Mitchum's effect on his sultry girlfriend Elsa Martinelli, and is killed by a gorilla who enterprisingly takes Mitchum's side.

Hawkins was a shady Foreign Office official mixed-up in kidnapping a Middle Eastern prince in *Masquerade* (1965, Basil Dearden), while at the same time working out a few private deals of his own. Cliff Robertson catches him with his fingers in the till but refuses a share of the proceeds because, as he says, he's 'got scruples', to which Hawkins replies in a knowing sort of way, 'One loses them.' It was a modest adventure drama to which Hawkins, as a gentleman crook who comes out of it all whiter than white, added some livening touches. During an energetic fistfight with Robertson, on whom he has just

pulled a gun, Hawkins, between gasps, declares: 'We're both too old for this sort of thing!' Moments later, Robertson proves him half-right by bouncing his head off a stone pillar.

After *Masquerade*, Hawkins underwent an operation for cancer which resulted in the removal of his vocal chords. 'It's almost impossible to accept that you are suffering from this most dreadful of all diseases,' he wrote in his autobiography *Anything for a Quiet Life*, but he was, although early indications that the surgery had been successful gave cause for optimism.

He went on making films, with actors Charles Gray and Robert Rietty dubbing the voice. His endurance and fortitude became the keynote of a crusade against the common dread and ignorance of cancer. Hawkins was acutely conscious that his training as an actor had given him an advantage in regaining some form of oesophagal speech – using the diaphragm for speech instead of the vocal chords – and he was determined to show others that malignant cancer is by no means the end of the road, that if an actor could keep on talking after his voice had been taken away, then it was within everyone's capabilities to fight back.

'I am not a man of great courage, not by any stretch of the imagination. In fact, I am a very great coward,' he told a journalist in 1967. Subsequent events were to prove that he was no such thing.

In *When Eight Bells Toll* (1971, Etienne Périer), one of the better films he appeared in after the voice operation, Hawkins played a shipping tycoon forced to lend his ships to ruthless gold bullion thieves who have snatched his wife. On the trail of the missing gold is Anthony Hopkins, a shrewd Customs investigator, the sort more usually seen hand-delivering chocolates to pretty ladies in TV commercials.

The film recalls the Bond movies of the early 1960s – notably in its effective use of rugged locales and an equally engaging disregard for human life – but is thankfully free of their technological absurdities.

Hawkins was a sadistic schoolmaster in *Jane Eyre* (1971, Delbert Mann), a narrow-minded religious fanatic who crops Jane's hair off because her natural curls symbolise, to him, sinfulness, and whose harsh treatment of Jane's consumptive classmate hastens the little girl's death. Cigar-chomping George C. Scott played Rochester, an example of woeful casting on a par with Cornel Wilde as Chopin. The film did little for Charlotte Brontë, and even less for Hawkins, whose repertoire of characters could never extend convincingly to miserable bullies.

In 1973, while in the USA, more problems occurred with his throat and a primary growth was discovered and removed in preparation for the fitting of a device in his throat which would help him to speak more naturally. The operation wound, however, refused to heal and following repeated haemorrhages Hawkins was brought back to England. The 'strong, brave man with a great desire to get on with life', as his wife Doreen described him in a touching postscript to his autobiography, lost his fourteen-year struggle against the illness shortly afterwards.

Screenwriter-director Bryan Forbes noted: 'There are few actors who come perfectly equipped to reveal a unique personality, they do not imitate nor are they capable of being imitated. Jack was one such actor, and while he was with us the truth escaped us. We can only be wise after the event. ...'

Jack Hawkins

1910-1973. Hugely popular character star, embodying top qualities of leadership, frequently cast as humane wartime services officer, or someone in authority. Vocal chords removed in 1965 cancer operation, thereafter played burly supports with lines dubbed. Film debut: *Birds of Prey* (1930).

1930 *Birds of Prey*
1932 *The Lodger*
1933 *The Good Companions*
     The Lost Chord
     I Lived with You
     The Jewel
     A Shot in the Dark
1934 *Autumn Crocus*
     Death at Broadcasting House
1935 *Peg of Old Drury*
1937 *Beauty and the Barge*
     The Frog
1938 *Who Goes Next*
     A Royal Divorce
1939 *Murder Will Out*
1940 *The Flying Squad*
1942 *Next of Kin*
1948 *The Fallen Idol* (Detective Ames)
     Bonnie Prince Charlie (Lord George Murray)
1949 *The Small Back Room* (R. B. Waring)
1950 *State Secret* (Colonel Galcon)
     The Black Rose (Tristram Griffen)
     The Elusive Pimpernel (Prince of Wales)
1951 *The Adventurers* (Pieter Brandt)
     No Highway (Denis Scott)
     Home at Seven (Dr Sparling)
1952 *Angels One Five* (Grp Capt Small)
     Mandy (Richard Searle)
     The Planter's Wife (Jim Frazer)
     The Cruel Sea (Commander Ericson)
1953 *Twice Upon a Time* (Dr Matthews)
     Malta Story (AOC)
     The Intruder (Wolf Merton)
     Front Page Story (John Grant)
1954 *The Seekers* (Philip Wayne)
1955 *The Prisoner* (The Interrogator)
     Land of the Pharoahs (USA) (Pharoah)
1956 *Touch and Go* (Jim Fletcher)
     The Long Arm (Supt Tom Halliday)
     Man in the Sky (John Mitchell)
1957 *Fortune Is a Woman* (Oliver Branwell)
     The Bridge on the River Kwai (Major Worden)
     Battle of Britain (short) (voice)

1958	*Gideon's Day* (Insp George Gideon)	1968	*Great Catherine* (British Ambassador)
	The Two-Headed Spy (Gen Alex Scottland)		*Shalako* (Sir Charles Daggett)
		1969	*Oh! What a Lovely War* (Emperor Franz Josef)
1959	*Ben Hur* (USA) (Quintus Arrius)		
1960	*League of Gentlemen* (Norman Hyde)		*Twinky* (Judge Millington-Draper)
1962	*Five Finger Exercise* (USA) (Stanley)		*Monte Carlo or Bust* (Count Levinovich)
	Lawrence of Arabia (General Allenby)	1970	*Waterloo* (General Picton)
1963	*Lafayette* (USA) (General Cornwallis)		*Adventures of Gerard* (Millefleurs)
	Rampage (USA) (Otto Abbott)	1971	*Jane Eyre* (Mr Brocklehurst)
	Zulu (Rev Otto Witt)		*When Eight Bells Toll* (Sir Anthony Skouras)
1964	*The Third Secret* (Sir Frederick Belline)		
	Guns at Batasi (Lieut Colonel Deal)		*Kidnapped* (Captain Hoseason)
1965	*Masquerade* (Colonel Drexel)		*Nicholas and Alexandra* (Fredericks)
	Lord Jim (Marlow)	1972	*Young Winston* (Mr Weldon)
	Judith (Major Lewton)	1973	*Theatre of Blood* (Solomon Psaltery)

Stanley Holloway

Stanley Holloway was Albert the ticket collector with an eye for station buffet waitress Joyce Carey in *Brief Encounter* (1945, David Lean). 'Now look at my Banburys all over the floor,' she flutters, after Holloway makes a playful grab for her across the counter. Theirs was a breezy slice of working-class slap-and-tickle counterpointing the tense middle-class affair between Trevor Howard ('I'm only an ordinary GP') and the fawn-eyed Celia Johnson.

While the central characters ache palpably over the teacups, Holloway's jovial Jack-in-the-box personality keeps life with a small 'l' in perspective. He was a broad-check music hall veteran long before films beckoned, famous for those indestructible monologues like 'Sam and the Musket' and 'Albert and the Lion' and others, delivered in broad Yorkshire dialect.

Holloway's hearty tongue-in-cheek characters were the backbone of numerous 1940s and 1950s comedies. In *Passport to Pimlico* (1949, Henry Cornelius), a sharply observed comedy featuring various London 'types', he was a storekeeper whose discovery of an ancient document annexing a section of Pimlico to the Duchy of Burgundy leads to a declaration of independence by local residents. Border controls and immigration regulations are posted up, along with a barbed wire frontier behind which Holloway's new Burgundians defy and outwit the bureaucrats.

Despite the rousing wartime rhetoric – 'We'll fight them on the tramlines, we'll fight them in the locals ...' – the residents soon discover that their worst enemy is not Whitehall but internal chaos resulting from a relaxation of rationing, clothing coupons (it was early post-war) and other controls. Even when it appears to be firmly grasped, Utopia, it seems, remains as unattainable as ever.

'By Jove, Holland, its a good job we're honest men,' Holloway croons to fellow-lodger Alec Guinness in *The Lavender Hill Mob* (1951, Charles Crichton) – not that stealing gold bullion and converting it into exportable souvenirs seems, on the face of it, particularly honest. The film is a topnotch Ealing comedy, plausible, endearing and articulate, but again it's a Utopian fantasy, inevitably doomed.

Holloway was the sporty old moneybags behind the survival battle of *The Titfield Thunderbolt* (1953, Charles Crichton), delighted to coax his investment along from a reserved stool in the buffet-car. When the branch line's opponents smash the original locomotive, Holloway and local tinker Hugh Griffith, after a drinking spree, pinch another one from a nearby siding and crash it into a tree. After their arrest, Holloway declines bail, being, as he explains, 'in no condition to meet my darling wife'. Told that detainees ordinarily decline offers of custody, Holloway observes chirpily: 'Human nature, my dear sir. No pleasing some people!'

He was deservedly acclaimed as Eliza's dustman father in both the stage and screen versions of *My Fair Lady* (1964, George Cukor),

Stanley Holloway (right) and Nigel Patrick (left) tantalise Patricia Roc with their immaculate table manners in *The Perfect Woman* (1949)

'demonstrating the manner and mien of a brewery horse kicking up its heels in springtime', as one critic put it.

As well as featured roles, Holloway has been good for walk-ons, such as a gravedigger in *The Private Life of Sherlock Holmes* (1970, Billy Wilder), and a deaf caretaker at the gold swindlers' manor house headquarters in *Run a Crooked Mile* (1969, Gene Levitt). One of my favourite Holloway roles was as beauty queen Pauline Stroud's prosaic father in *Lady Godiva Rides Again* (1951, Frank Launder). When naive, small-town waitress Miss Stroud, a minor beauty contest winner, disappears with egocentric movie star Dennis Price, her family fear the worst. Led by Holloway they track her to the supposed love-nest, although in reality it is nothing of the sort, and finding the door locked decide to take matters into their own hands. 'Let's rush it all together – men in front,' Holloway commands, but not before George Cole, as Miss Stroud's discarded boyfriend, has attempted to boost his sagging morale by breaking down the door commando-style, and nearly annihilated himself against the defiant woodwork.

Stanley Holloway

1890-1982. Music hall singer-comedian, in films since 1921. Long catalogue of warm 'human' characters, predominantly in comedies, but serious roles, too. Son Julian also acts.

1921 *The Rotters*
1930 *The Co-Optimists*
1933 *Sleeping Car*
       The Girl from Maxim's
1934 *Lily of Killarney*
       Love at Second Sight
       Sing As We Go
       Road House
1935 *D'Ye Ken John Peel*
       In Town Tonight
       Squibs
       Play up the Band
1936 *Sam Cartoons*
1937 *Song of the Forge*
       The Vicar of Bray
       Cotton Queen
       Sam Small Leaves Town
       Our Island Nation
1939 *Co-operette*

91

Stanley Holloway, 1962

1941 *Major Barbara*
1942 *Salute John Citizen*
1944 *The Way Ahead*
 This Happy Breed
 Champagne Charlie
1945 *The Way to the Stars* (Mr Palmer)
 Brief Encounter (Albert Godby)
1946 *Caesar and Cleopatra* (Belzanor)
 Wanted for Murder (Sergeant Sullivan)
 Carnival (Charlie Raeburn)
 Meet Me at Dawn (Emile)
1947 *Nicholas Nickleby* (Vincent Crummles)

1948 *Snowbound* (Joe Wesson)
 One Night with You (Tramp)
 Hamlet (Gravedigger)
 Noose (Inspector Rendall)
 The Winslow Boy (uncredited)
 Another Shore (Alastair McNeil)
1949 *Passport to Pimlico* (Arthur Pemberton)
 The Perfect Woman (Ramshead)
1950 *Midnight Episode* (Prof Prince)
1951 *One Wild Oat* (Alfred Gilbey)
 The Lavender Hill Mob (Pendlebury)
 The Magic Box (Broker's Man)
 Lady Godiva Rides Again (Mr Clark)
1952 *The Happy Family* (Henry Lord)
 Meet Me Tonight (Henry Gow)
1953 *The Titfield Thunderbolt* (Valentine)
 The Beggar's Opera (Lockit)
 A Day to Remember (Charlie Porter)
 Meet Mr Lucifer (Sam Hollingsworth/
 Lucifer)
1954 *Fast and Loose* (Mr Crabb)
1955 *An Alligator Named Daisy* (General)
1956 *Jumping for Joy* (Jack Montague)
1958 *Alive and Kicking* (MacDonagh)
 Hello London (Guest Appearance)
1959 *No Trees in the Street* (Kipper)
1961 *No Love for Johnnie* (Fred Andrews)
 On the Fiddle (Cooksley)
1964 *My Fair Lady* (Alfred Doolittle)
1965 *Ten Little Indians* (William Blore)
1966 *The Sandwich Man* (Gardener)
1968 *Mrs Brown, You've Got a Lovely Daughter*
 (Mr Brown)
1969 *Run a Crooked Mile* (Caretaker)
1970 *The Private Life of Sherlock Holmes*
 (Gravedigger)
1971 *Flight of the Doves* (Judge Liffy)
1972 *Up the Front* (Vincento)

Michael Hordern

It's no surprise to learn that clergymen are perched among the branches of Michael Hordern's family tree. There is something undeniably ecclesiastical about that morose, equine face, surely among the most expressive in the business. He sees his career as not very dissimilar to theirs. 'Actors and clergymen both adore the sound of their own voices and like good lines, costumes and sets,' he explains.

Hordern's voice is as distinctive as his face –

low, resonant, versatile – and the two dovetail nicely into a commanding presence. As Caryl Brahms once wrote: 'An author can relax when Hordern gets the bit between his teeth, for though the characterisation may not be precisely theirs, it is certain to be viable, valuable and real.'

He was one of Richard Todd's laboratory assistants in *Flesh and Blood* (1951, Anthony Kimmins) and, again with Todd, played a bullied

Michael Hordern (right) helps astronaut Kenneth More into his space-helmet in *Man in the Moon* (1960)

villager sheltering from the excesses of the evil Sheriff in *The Story of Robin Hood and His Merrie Men* (1952, Ken Annakin). He appeared as the ghost of Jacob Marley, Scrooge's former partner, in *Scrooge* (1951, Brian Desmond Hurst) with Alastair Sim, and was King Edward III in *The Dark Avenger* (1955, Henry Levin), starring a burnt-out Errol Flynn.

Hordern played a general in *The Man Who Never Was* (1956, Ronald Neame), a classic wartime secret service movie based on the 'placing' of a corpse on an enemy beachhead. The corpse possesses phoney secret documents, part of an ingenious plan to divert enemy defences away from the real target, Normandy. Hordern scored well as the tetchy father figure to Jon Whiteley in *The Spanish Gardener* (1956, Philip Leacock), with Dirk Bogarde as the title-role character caught up in the emotional cross-fire.

In *Moment of Danger* (1960, Laslo Benedek)

he was a sympathetic copper who knows that Trevor Howard is a jewel thief – thanks to Howard's double-crossing partner Edmund Purdom – but lacks the evidence to make an arrest. Hordern can't figure out why Howard, an ex-seaman of previous good character, is running around with the likes of Purdom, a real bag of snakes. And because he believes that Howard, given a chance, can redeem himself, he warns him against taking revenge into his own hands for having been ditched. Howard dismisses the advice at first, but Dorothy Dandridge helps him to see it Hordern's way.

Hordern was a senior British diplomat in Washington in *Cast a Giant Shadow* (1966, Melville Shavelson), a brief appearance tidily disposed of. When bullish US Army colonel Kirk Douglas, in Washington to receive his umpteenth medal for bravery, makes a jokey reference to the sun never setting on the British

Bungling amateur crook Michael Hordern is ordered back into the dock in *Some Will, Some Won't* (1970), a remake of *Laughter in Paradise* (1951)

Empire, Hordern sniffs, 'Not if we can help it!' In *The Spy Who Came In from the Cold* (1965, Martin Ritt), he was Richard Burton's spy chief, a gloomy bureaucrat with all the warmth of a doused fire – appropriately, the character was called Ashe.

With Burton again in *Where Eagles Dare* (1968, Brian G. Hutton), a comic strip war adventure where the bad guys, ie the Nazis, are popped off like shelled peas, Hordern was the military bigwig behind the raid to spring a bogus American general from a Nazi fortress in the Bavarian Alps. Hordern's problem is that enemy agents are thick on the ground around Whitehall – even three members of the hush-hush seven-man commando raid are German sympathisers in disguise. 'Security is a bloody joke,' he confides to Army boss Patrick Wymark, which, since Wymark too is a high-ranking Nazi, would seem to prove the point.

Yet again with Burton he played Anne Boleyn's father in *Anne of the Thousand Days* (1969, Charles Jarrott), a subtle, ingratiating performance, calculatedly exploiting daughter Genevieve Bujold's spiritedness and beauty to fuel his private ambition.

He can be very good in smallish parts which allow him boundless worry. As director of operations at a London Airport brought to a halt by fog in *The VIPs* (1963, Anthony Asquith), Hordern has none of the problems his grounded passengers have. There was Burton again, a successful tycoon, agonising about losing wife Elizabeth Taylor to the smooth Gallic charm of Louis Jourdan, dear old Margaret Rutherford racked with worry about the upkeep of her stately home, and Rod Taylor facing financial ruin after a business deal has gone sour. Compared to that lot Hordern should have been bouncing with good cheer, but there was none of it. In *The Mackintosh Man* (1973, John Huston), he had a bigger problem in trying to detain and interrogate secret agent Paul Newman in a remote part of Ireland. Hordern's acolytes give Newman a hard time, which he repays when the tables are turned by cracking Hordern's skull.

As one of the critics' circle in *Theatre of Blood* (1973, Douglas Hickox) Hordern incurs Vincent Price's wrath by publishing a review which describes the leading lady as 'having attacked the role with both hands and strangled it to death ...' Price decides to give him a quick refresher course on Shakespeare's *Julius Caesar*, and lures him to a deserted office block where, under Price's erudite direction, a gang of tramps re-enact in earnest Caesar's murder scene – using Hordern for target practice.

Quizzed about his 70-plus films, Hordern is delightfully vague about most of them. Apart from a handful of acknowledged high-spots, including *The Spanish Gardener, The Taming of the Shrew* (1967, Franco Zeffirelli) and 'the ones with Dick Lester', he confesses that the most enjoyable part of filming is 'the money, the locations and the company', admitting with a mischievous chuckle that these are 'all the wrong reasons'.

Michael Hordern

b. 1911. Versatile, resonant-voiced character support, frequently seen as worried official. On stage since 1937. Film debut: *Girl in the News* (1939).

1946 *School for Secrets* (Lt/Cdr Lowther)
1947 *Mine Own Executioner* (uncredited)
1948 *Good Time Girl* (uncredited)
1949 *Passport to Pimlico* (Police Inspector)
1950 *The Astonished Heart* (Ernest)
   Trio (Vicar)
   Highly Dangerous (Rawlings)
1951 *Flesh and Blood* (Webster)
   Tom Brown's Schooldays (Wilkes)

Scrooge (Jacob Marley)
1952 *The Card* (Bank Manager)
The Story of Robin Hood and His Merrie Men (Scathelock)
The Hour of Thirteen (Sir Herbert Lenhurst)
1953 *Street Corner* (Inspector Heron)
Grand National Night (Inspector Ayling)
The Heart of the Matter (Commissioner)
Personal Affair (Headmaster)
1954 *You Know What Sailors Are* (Captain Hamilton)
Forbidden Cargo (Director)
The Beachcomber (Headman)
1955 *The Night My Number Came Up* (Commander Lindsay)
The Constant Husband (Judge)
The Dark Avenger (Edward III)
Storm Over the Nile (General Faversham)
1956 *The Man Who Never Was* (General Coburn)
Pacific Destiny (Commissioner Gregory)
The Baby and the Battleship (Captain)
The Spanish Gardener (Harrington Brande)
Alexander The Great (Demosthenes)
1957 *Windom's Way* (Patterson)
1958 *The Spaniard's Curse* (Judge Manton)
I Was Monty's Double (Governor)
Girls at Sea (Sir Reginald Hewitt)
1960 *Sink the Bismarck* (Commander-In-Chief)
Moment of Danger (Inspector Farrell)
Man in the Moon (Dr Davidson)
1961 *Macbeth* (Banquo)
1963 *The VIPs* (Director)
Dr Syn – Alias The Scarecrow (Sir Thomas Banks)
1964 *The Yellow Rolls Royce* (Harmsworth)

1965 *The Spy Who Came In From the Cold* (Ashe)
1966 *Khartoum* (Lord Granville)
A Funny Thing Happened on the Way to the Forum (Senex)
The Jokers (Sir Matthew)
The Taming of the Shrew (Baptista)
Cast a Giant Shadow (USA) (The British Ambassador)
1967 *How I Won the War* (Grapple)
I'll Never Forget Whatshisname (Headmaster)
1968 *Where Eagles Dare* (Admiral Rolland)
1969 *The Bed Sitting Room* (Captain Bules Martin)
Anne of the Thousand Days (Thomas Boleyn)
1970 *Some Will, Some Won't* (Denniston Russell)
1971 *The Pied Piper* (Melius)
England Made Me (F. Minty)
1972 *Alice in Wonderland* (Mock Turtle)
1973 *Theatre of Blood* (George Maxwell)
The Mackintosh Man (Brown)
1974 *Demons of the Mind* (Priest)
Up Pompeii (Ludicrus)
Juggernaut (Baker)
1975 *Lucky Lady* (USA) (Captain Rockwell)
Mr Quilp (Grandfather/Edward Trent)
Barry Lyndon (Narrator)
Royal Flash (Headmaster)
1976 *The Slipper and the Rose* (King)
Joseph Andrews (Parson Adams)
The Medusa Touch (Atropos)
1979 *Shogun* (Friar Domingo)
1980 *Wildcats of St Trinian's* (Sir Charles Hackforth)

Donald Houston

When council employee Laurence Harvey ogles rich industrialist's daughter Heather Sears for the first time in *Room at the Top* (1959, Jack Clayton), Donald Houston tells him, 'That's not for you, lad,' to which Harvey replies, 'I can look, can't I?' Houston is his treasurers' department colleague, a 'power' in the local amateur dramatic society through whom Harvey meets the two women whose lives he ruins in his own special corrosive way: Heather Sears, whom he

marries, and Simone Signoret, whom he does not – or cannot, since she already has a husband who won't let go, the fish-like Allan Cuthbertson.

Passed over for the more socially-advantageous Miss Sears, Signoret crashes her car and is killed, news of which sends Harvey out on a remorseful bender that ends in a late-night dark-alley thumping after an argument with a gang of teddyboys. Revived next morning by his pal

Rugger supporter Donald Houston (right) about to make an expensive mistake during a day in London in *A Run for Your Money* (1949)

Houston, Harvey can only admit: 'I killed her. I wasn't there but I killed her.' Houston attempts to placate him by insisting that nobody will blame him. 'Nobody but me, that's the trouble,' sighs Harvey.

Donald Houston often played the hero's friend, the sympathetic, companiable good guy. His easy-on-the-ear Welsh charm and clean-cut good looks could have been better used, perhaps, than in the succession of routine supporting roles that Houston has played. He was probably once thought of as having strong leading-man potential, but he lacked that extra dimension an actor needs – and people like Richard Harris and Michael Caine have got – to concentráte the attention.

Houston came to fame as one of the young castaways in *The Blue Lagoon* (1949, Frank Launder). His companion was Jean Simmons, and their exotic island whoopee was hoped, at the time, to be the perfect antidote to post-war

blues, but it was all too fey. He starred in an obscure Ealing comedy *A Run for Your Money* (1949, Charles Frend), as one of a pair of Welsh miners who win a newspaper-sponsored trip to London. This was Ealing's attempt to wring some laughs from the Welsh way of life, along the lines taken by *Whisky Galore* and *The Maggie* (1954, Alexander Mackendrick) with regard to Scotland. But whereas the Scottish-based comedies depicted the Scots as cunning, fun-loving and, collectively, a force to be reckoned with, *A Run for Your Money* sent up the Welsh as a bunch of timid, mindless yokels.

The film never really moved into high gear, and whatever comedy potential existed in a tale of two likable dimwits on a big city jamboree – and one suspects, given the right treatment, it could be quite effective – was lost in a mishmash of spivs, tarts-with-hearts and, in case we had forgotten our two heroes were Welshmen, a rugby match. Alec Guinness did a passable

Lionel Jeffries take-off as a snooty gardening correspondent blackmailed into keeping the lads merry but law-abiding.

Houston was one of the medical student quartet in *Doctor in the House* (1954, Ralph Thomas), a milestone in British comedy, sensibly cast as the rugger aficionado who prefers pitches to patches. Not surprisingly he fluffs his exams, and resigns himself to a further year at medical school along with Kenneth More, an eternal student who cannot afford a pass mark – his grandmother's annuity is timed to end along with his studentship. More has been at the school long enough to know by heart the Dean's welcoming address to each new student intake. As it rumbles to a close, More tells new student Dirk Bogarde: 'That was three minutes shorter than usual.'

Ironically, nine years later, Houston had a small part in the aptly-named *Doctor in Distress* (1963, Ralph Thomas), a hollow reminder of the original. That was a bad year for him – he also made *Carry on Jack* in 1963, a minor spoof on the Hornblower industry, playing a snide ship's officer, a straight man for the ubiquitous 'Carry On' team, which must have taken a lot of living down afterwards. Another low-spot was reached with *My Lover, My Son* (1970, John Newland), in which Houston played a business tycoon whose glamorous wife, Romy Schneider, has an affair with her son, Dennis Waterman – an adult enough theme, treated here with the kind of subtlety one normally encounters in a rugby club bath-house.

Houston was one of Richard Burton's commandos in *Where Eagles Dare* (1968, Brian G. Hutton), but he is, in reality, an enemy agent sent along to thwart the rescue mission. The mission is accomplished, although on the return trip, Houston causes Burton some giddy moments as they slug it out on top of a swaying cablecar.

Possibly his most powerful role occurred in an early B-feature *My Death Is a Mockery* (1952, Tony Young), where Houston played a petty smuggler, wrongly convicted of murder – the killing was accidental – and nervously awaiting the big drop. The film takes a chillingly long look at the condemned cell, and Houston's performance, progressively a mixture of numbed bravado and controlled hysteria, matches its mood exactly. Other films of the 1950s toyed with the same theme, but few had the dispassionate power of this minor classic.

(From left to right) Donald Sinden, Donald Houston, Kenneth More, Suzanne Cloutier and Dirk Bogarde share a spartan dinner in *Doctor in the House* (1954)

Donald Houston
b. 1923. Likable rugged Welsh type, one-time amiable lead and hero's chum, swept to stardom as original *Blue Lagoon* (1949) romantic castaway. On stage from 1940. Most famous stage role in *Under Milk Wood*.

1949 *The Blue Lagoon* (Michael Reynolds)
      A Run for Your Money (Dai Jones)
1950 *Dance Hall* (Phil)
1952 *My Death Is a Mockery* (John Bradley)
      Crow Hollow (Robert)
1953 *The Red Beret* (Taffy)
      Small Town Story (Tony Warren)
      The Large Rope (Tom Penney)'
1954 *Doctor in the House* (Taffy Evans)
      Devil's Point (Michael Mallard)
      The Happiness of Three Women (John)
1955 *The Flaw* (John Millway)
1956 *Doublecross* (Albert Pascoe)
      Find the Lady (Bill)
1957 *The Girl in the Picture* (John Deering)
      Yangtse Incident (Lieutenant Weston)
      The Surgeon's Knife (Dr Alex Waring)

1958 *A Question of Adultery* (Mr Jacobus)
      The Man Upstairs (Sanderson)
1959 *Room at the Top* (Charlie Soames)
      Danger Within (Captain Roger Byford)
1961 *The Mark* (Austin)
1962 *Twice Round the Daffodils* (John Rhodes)
      The Prince and the Pauper (John Canty)
      Maniac (George Bleynat)
      The Longest Day (RAF Pilot)
1963 *Doctor in Distress* (Major Ffrench)
      Carry on Jack (Lieutenant Jonathan Howett)
1964 *633 Squadron* (Group Captain Tom Barrett)
1965 *A Study In Terror* (Dr John Watson)
1967 *The Viking Queen* (Maelgan)
1968 *Where Eagles Dare* (Christiansen)
1970 *My Lover, My Son* (Robert Anderson)
      The Bushbaby (John Leeds)
1973 *Tales That Witness Murder* (Father)
1976 *Voyage of The Damned* (Dr Glauner, Ship's Doctor)
1980 *The Sea Wolves* (Hilliard)

Trevor Howard

When you meet Trevor Howard, the first thing he does is to fill a glass and screw it into your hand like he would a light bulb.

That dour imperturbability which has sustained him through around 65 films and as many years is strongly in evidence, though gentle probing reveals a sad, lonely man underneath.

Howard has been a mainstay of the UK movie industry since shortly after the war, yet stardom of the conventional kind was his only briefly, during the late 1940s when romantic leads were essentially true-blue types in flannels. With the change of style of the early fifties, Howard's reluctance – or inability – to change his spots (he was, it must also be said, clocking up the years) caused him to switch to character parts, where that weathered face and gruff charm found instant appeal. Before that he had caused female hearts to flutter in *Brief Encounter* (1945, David Lean) as the nice married doctor who removes the grit from Celia Johnson's eye and replaces it later with a tear when their futile station buffet romance is shunted into a siding.

The film, which also created director David

Lean's international reputation, is all tender foreplay which cautiously avoids a climax, although the dialogue has, at times, an almost orgasmic urgency: 'You know what's happened, don't you.' 'Yes, I do.' 'I've fallen in love with you.' 'Yes, I know' … etc. Miss Johnson does most of the high tension stuff, while Howard sombrely fetches tea, but it's a good atmospheric movie and deserves its high rating.

His character in *The Passionate Friends* (1949), also for David Lean, could have been modelled on *Brief Encounter*. Howard is again a doctor, and he and Ann Todd are former lovers, each married to someone else, who meet by chance in a Swiss hotel. But their innocent little sightseeing flutter leads to angry recriminations from Miss Todd's jealous banker husband Claude Rains and a foiled suicide attempt. It was really *Brief Encounter* in an Alpine setting, with flashbacks telling how the lovers originally parted – Miss Todd preferred the security of a rich (but annoyingly possessive) husband – and showing the futility of a love that will neither bare its teeth nor go away.

Trevor Howard removes the grit, but later adds a tear to the eyes of prim suburban housewife Celia Johnson in *Brief Encounter* (1945)

In *The Third Man* (1949, Carol Reed), a stylish and visually arresting thriller, Howard is the Vienna-based British military police colonel who is pleased to hear that the notorious Harry Lime, played by Orson Welles, has been bumped off. 'I'm not interested in whether a racketeer like Lime was killed by his friends or in an accident. The important thing is that he's dead,' he tells Joseph Cotten, as expatriate American writer friend of Welles, duped into producing propaganda for a volunteer medical unit which Welles runs (as a cover for his illicit drug traffic activities). But Welles is far from dead, his funeral having been faked to enable him to defect to the Russian zone while the heat is on.

Cotten meets up with Welles – in the famous fairground Big Wheel sequence – whose bland refusal to help a Czech girlfriend now loved by Cotten convinces the writer of Welles' evil duplicity. Cotten is the only one close enough to Welles to be able to lure him back into Howard's eager clutches, which he does, and Welles is finally cornered and killed in the cavernous sewers under Vienna. The vivid night scenes, a canvas of contrasts, plus great performances from a big-name international cast make it a film of remarkable depth.

One reviewer noted: 'Trevor Howard's Calloway is built up, detail by detail, nothing superfluous, nothing exaggerated, until a whole man is put before us.'

In *The Heart of the Matter* (1953, George More O'Ferrall), in what is popularly thought to be his best-ever performance, Howard was a deputy police commissioner in Sierra Leone trapped between a loveless marriage and a doomed affair with a native girl. Rather than cause either of the women further suffering he somewhat gallantly takes his own life. Producer Ian Dalrymple noted that Howard was 'unique in his ability to present the man of action in the round – to suggest even the most confident and straightforward of characters are victims of stress and bewilderment'.

The man of action under stress was present in *The Gift Horse* (1952, Compton Bennett), where Howard played the commander of a wartime destroyer in his first command since resigning the Navy following a mid-ocean collision in suspicious circumstances. The film was a good example of British fifties film-making – strong action, good characterisation, competent performances. One charged scene has Howard going through the ritual of officiating at a shipboard Christmas party even though he has just been notified by telegram of his midshipman son's death in action. Outwardly, everything seems quite normal, yet around the eyes Howard seems to age ten years as the words of the telegram hit him. It was a powerful moment in a movie genre not ordinarily associated with sensitivity.

From the mid-1950s Howard often supported American stars, and acted many of them off the screen. He played José Ferrer's blunt adjutant in *Cockleshell Heroes* (1955), which Ferrer also directed, a colourful war adventure based on actual incidents, in which a platoon of canoeists paddle nonchalantly into enemy docks and attach explosives to the hulls of their ship. A liberal sprinkling of British gallows humour was in evidence, understandable in view of the near-suicidal nature of the mission.

In *Interpol* (1957, John Gilling) he was a baddie, a ruthless narcotics baron, pursued across Europe by New York detective Victor Mature. He was a Nazi in hiding in *Run for the Sun* (1956, Roy Boulting), living quietly and remorsefully in the Mexican outback until a dropout journalist, modelled on Hemingway and played by Richard Widmark, crash-lands and disturbs the sham idyll. Again, Howard was the villain and was killed at the end, but he gave the ex-Nazis a kind of noble, morose dignity that made you want to know more about his former activities.

He was the father in D. H. Lawrence's *Sons and Lovers* (1960, Jack Cardiff) with Wendy Hiller and former American child actor Dean Stockwell making up the family. Howard's was a handsomely earthy performance, reckoned by *Variety* magazine to be 'easily the outstanding feature of the production'.

Another review stated: 'By an almost monastic simplicity of method, Howard can draw a spectator deep into the heart of a character without making one aware until much later that one has been fed an essential psychological detail – the look he gives his waiting wife when he brings the dead son to the surface after the pit explosion

in *Sons and Lovers* tells more about the relationship of this couple than half a page of dialogue.'

Howard has one word for *Mutiny on the Bounty* (1962, Lewis Milestone) – 'flop'. The main cause he says, was co-star Marlon Brando, who usurped control midway through filming and came up with nothing but a morbid preoccupation about his own performance. 'Everything was manipulated in order to give Brando a fifteen-minute death scene,' he told me. It was all the more disappointing because the basic ingredients were all there, including colourful locations, but, compared to the 1935 Charles Laughton version, Howard's performance, as Bligh, was restrained, indeed almost too laconic.

In *Operation Crossbow* (1965, Michael Anderson), a biff-bang wartime sabotage story given a hurried breath of authenticity by including talking heads of Winston Churchill and Duncan Sandys. Howard's role was small but significant, as a senior Ministry scientist who seems unable to accept that the Germans can have advanced their know-how of jet propulsion rocketry to the point where they may be about to launch a terrible offensive against Britain. 'I'm not going to believe your fairy tales until you can show me a photograph of a rocket,' he splutters at a high-level defence meeting. When John Mills, as an Army intelligence general, provides just such a photograph, from aerial reconnaissance, Howard insists its a barrage balloon. 'Whatever it is, you're making a mountain out of a molehill,' he scoffs, to which Mills tartly replies, 'You mean, don't you, a torpedo out of a balloon.'

Luckily for millions of Londoners, Howard's view is ignored, and urgent plans are laid for a team of saboteurs to infiltrate and destroy the enemy rocket sites.

War capers continued in *Von Ryan's Express* (1965, Mark Robson), with Howard as a captured British Army major who is joined behind the barbed wire by Lieutenant Frank Sinatra. Between them a plot is hatched to escape and sabotage an enemy munitions train. It was a lively, red-blooded, boy's-adventure-type story, with Howard and Sinatra comfortable within their established laid-back personae. 'Being in a Sinatra picture does you good,' Howard told me.

In *Triple Cross* (1967, Terence Young), a trueish story about double-agent – and former petty criminal – Eddie Chapman, acted by Christopher Plummer, Howard was a top

Government hawk. The film also starred Yul Brynner, who reappeared with Howard in *The Long Duel* (1967, Ken Annakin), a North West Frontier yarn about natives in revolt at their treatment by their British military administrators and how one British officer, played by Howard, antagonises his fellow-officers by introducing, of all things, diplomacy and courage into his attempts to bring stability to the region. Yul Brynner was a Red Shadow-type rebel leader, driven to insurgency when attempts fail at getting a fairer deal through diplomacy.

Though Howard's ideas are unpopular – 'The British idea of colonising a country is making everything a bad replica of Surrey,' he sighs at one point – the deteriorating situation prompts governor Maurice Denham to give him a special commission to negotiate with the rebels. 'From the point of view of ability, I'm afraid he's the real man for the job,' Howard's commanding officer Laurence Naismith concedes when Denham enquires about his credentials.

From then on Howard and Brynner are eyeball-to-eyeball – and they don't come any more solid than these two in the unflinching stare department – until the rebel leader is eventually cornered in his mountain-side hideout, and kills himself to avoid the disgrace of a public trial, but not before extracting from Howard a promise to adopt his son.

'If they can't fornicate they can't fight,' Howard bellows at the beginning of *The Charge of the Light Brigade* (1968, Tony Richardson), letting rip an aphorism that has been passed down proudly from one generation of soldiers to the next for centuries. Since his men are heavily defeated in the battle that follows, one can only wonder how they fare at other things. Howard's performance as the fire-eating Lord Cardigan, commanding officer of the ill-fated Light Brigade – he survives to pour scorn on his superior officers – is one of the best things in the film and among the best performances he has given. The film is roughly in two parts, beginning at the regiment's London barracks where preparations for war are played out against a silly love story featuring Vanessa Redgrave and the deepening antagonism between Howard and an idealistic young officer, played by David Hemmings, who risks his career by refusing to come to heel on matters of principle.

Howard's attention is diverted by Jill Bennett, as the ripe young wife of a wet junior officer, whose playful self-reproach – 'I must stop look-ing at Lord Cardigan as if I want to be ridden by him' – has an amusing ring of prophecy about it, because, before they get down to making love, the hoary old devil turns her behind to the ceiling and warms it up with a few hearty slaps, saying that flighty young fillies enjoy having their rumps slapped before being mounted. He is talking about horses, of course, but from Miss Bennett's excited giggles you would never know.

He was Sarah Miles' parish priest in *Ryan's Daughter* (1970, David Lean), a glossy, ponderous romantic tragedy set in the west of Ireland during World War I and containing some superb location camera work by Freddie Young. Howard is the first to realise that her marriage to gentle middle-aged school teacher Robert Mitchum is threatened by infatuation for a shell-shocked British Army major, played with a brooding James Dean-like intensity by Christopher Jones. When angry villagers surround and beat her, wrongly suspecting her of being an informer responsible for the capture of patriot-on-the-run Barry Foster, Howard is the only one prepared to defy the mob and snatch her to safety.

Now Magazine nominated *Pope Joan* (1972, Michael Andrew) as 'one of the all-time stinkers', and most discerning observers seemed to agree that this confusing mishmash of medieval

Trevor Howard, 1946

history and religion would have been better left alone. It was brutally and charmlessly done, and told how a simple nun played by Liv Ullman aspired to the Papacy, dressed as a monk, stepping briefly into the near-saintly shoes of her predecessor Pope Leo, alias Trevor Howard.

But all that power goes to the unfortunate girl's head and she succumbs to a short-lived passionate affair with a handsome Italian general which leaves her pregnant and at the mercy of the mob. Liv Ullman was rather negative in the title role, she looked like Peter Pan blown off-course – 'Only the limp solemnity of Liv Ullman quells one's laughter,' wrote Sylvia Miller – and Howard too looked comically wrung-out for a supposedly pious man. Seeing him for the last time stretched out on his death bed, one had the lasting image of a seedy old buffer floored by excessive amounts of cheap liquor.

As the 1970s wore on, Howard found himself slipping over the top as a major star and he was obliged to meet his bills by appearing in largely unworthy material. 'I'm offered more old rubbish than the dustman and expected to make something of it,' he had groaned in 1960, and the words rang true in films like *Ludwig* (1973, Luchino Visconti) where he played composer Richard Wagner, and *Persecution* (1974, Don Chaffey) as Lana Turner's one-time lover – 'Dreadful, dreadful,' he mutters, as if entering a private nightmare just thinking about it. He played senior policemen in *The Offence* (1973, Sidney Lumet), in which he interrogates unbalanced CID inspector Sean Connery, and in *Hennessey* (1975, Don Sharp), a topical thriller about an IRA squad's plan to blow up the Houses of Parliament during the Queen's Speech.

Of his part in *Superman* (1978, Richard Donner) Howard is dismissively vague: 'I can't tell you anything about it, other than I worked on it for about five days with several other actors walking around in silvery suits. It was all utterly insane!'

Meteor (1979) reunited him with Sean Connery in a tail-end seventies disaster movie – or, in this case, near-disaster since the threatened collision between Earth and the stray meteor, which is the basis of the story, never happens. Again, Howard's memory falters when you mention *Meteor* to him. 'Awfully like *Superman*,' he says. 'Another daft film, if you ask me,' which I interpreted as yet another mild self-rebuke. He really does anguish over past mistakes.

Howard supported several big stars in *The Sea Wolves* (1979), notably Roger Moore, Gregory Peck and David Niven. Enemy U-boats are getting information on Allied shipping movements from a radio concealed aboard a German merchant vessel docked in neutral Portuguese Goa, and this major source of irritation to Allied High Command has to be destroyed. Familiar? It's practically a reworking of *The Guns of Navarone*, and the illusion of having heard it all before is compounded by the presence of the two actors from whom we originally heard it – Peck and Niven, survivors of that famous 1961 Navarone caper.

As a vintage-style adventure yarn, *The Sea Wolves* was no worse than dozens of others, but it had an added disadvantage in that everyone looked way past retirement age. As critic Tom Palleine noted: 'It is difficult not to view the crowd jostling round the bar at the Calcutta Light Horse Headquarters as a reunion of character actors who saw active service in the British cinema of the Fifties.'

Sir Henry at Rawlinson End (1980, Steve Roberts) was a watered-down Goon Show parody, shot in black and white (what else?) and apparently made up as it stumbled along. Everyone in the film is mad, but none quite as loony as the booze-raddled Sir Henry – incarnated with considerable cherry-nosed gusto by Trevor Howard, as one critic put it – who lives in a huge mansion, and totters about killing people, ignoring his wife, abusing the servants who are too dotty to notice or even care, and torturing a couple of hapless German POWs incarcerated in a hut on the estate by rasping 'Germany calling, Germany calling' in a strangled Lord Haw-Haw voice over a tin-can loudspeaker system.

In *Windwalker* (1980, Keith Merrill) Howard had one of the most unusual roles of his career as an 80-year-old Cheyenne Indian chief. In a series of flashbacks the old warrior relives his adventurous life – it's an epic story spanning four generations of a Cheyenne family before the coming of the white man, set against a colourful and authentic-looking backdrop of Indian traditions, culture and language.

One critic noted: 'Howard gives Windwalker great warmth and dignity. He is thoroughly convincing.' Another said: 'Trevor Howard is marvellous as Windwalker, despite playing an Indian for the first time in his illustrious career. He seems to merge with his character in body and spirit.' Even Howard talks enthusiastically about the film, an unusual occurrence these days.

Trevor Howard

b. 1916. Much travelled character star. On stage since 1934. Film debut in *The Way Ahead* (1944). Married to actress Helen Cherry.

1945 *Brief Encounter* (Dr Alec Harvey)
    The Way to the Stars (Squadron Leader Carter)
1946 *I See a Dark Stranger* (Lt David Bayne)
    Green for Danger (Dr Barney Barnes)
1947 *So Well Remembered* (Dr Whiteside)
    They Made Me a Fugitive (Clem Morgan)
1949 *The Passionate Friends* (Steven Stratton)
    The Third Man (Major Galloway)
1950 *Golden Salamander* (David Redfern)
    Odette (Captain Peter Churchill)
    The Clouded Yellow (David Somers)
1951 *Outcast of the Islands* (Peter Willems)
1952 *The Gift Horse* (L/C Hugh Fraser)
1953 *The Heart of the Matter* (Harry Scobie)
1954 *The Stranger's Hand* (Major Court)
1955 *Cockleshell Heroes* (Capt Thompson)
1956 *Around the World in Eighty Days* (Fallentin, Member of Reform Club)
    Run for the Sun (USA) (Brown)
1957 *Interpol* (Frank McNally)
    Manuela (James Protheroe)
1958 *The Key* (Chris Ford)
1959 *The Roots of Heaven* (USA) (Morel)
1960 *Moment of Danger* (John Bain)
    Sons and Lovers (Walter Morel)
1962 *Mutiny on the Bounty* (USA) (Captain Bligh)
    The Lion (John Bullit)
1963 *Man in the Middle* (Major Kensington)
1964 *Father Goose* (USA) (Frank Houghton)
1965 *Operation Crossbow* (Professor Lindeman)
    The Liquidator (Colonel Mostyn)
    Von Ryan's Express (USA) (Major Eric Fincham)
    Morituri (USA) (Colonel Statter)

1966 *The Poppy is Also a Flower* (Lincoln)
1967 *The Long Duel* (Freddy Young)
    Triple Cross (Distinguished Civilian)
    Pretty Polly (Robert Hook)
1968 *The Charge of the Light Brigade* (Lord Cardigan)
1969 *The Battle of Britain* (AVM Keith Park)
    Twinky (Grandfather)
1970 *Ryan's Daughter* (Father Collins)
    The Night Visitor (The Inspector)
1971 *Mary, Queen Of Scots* (William Cecil, Lord Burghley)
    Catch Me a Spy (Sir Trevor Dawson)
1972 *Kidnapped* (Lord Advocate)
    Pope Joan (Pope Leo)
1973 *Lola* (Grandfather)
    A Doll's House (Dr Rank)
    Ludwig (Richard Wagner)
    The Offence (Cartwright)
1974 *Craze* (Supt Bellamy)
    Eleven Harrowhouse (Clyde Massey)
    The Count of Monte Cristo (Abbé Faria)
    Persecution (Paul Bellamy)
1975 *Hennessy* (Commander Rice)
    The Bawdy Adventures of Tom Jones (Squire Western)
    Conduct Unbecoming (Colonel Benjamin Strang)
1976 *Aces High* (Lt Col Silkin)
    Eliza Fraser (Prison Governor)
1977 *Last Remake of Beau Geste* (Sir Hector Geste)
    Stevie ('The Man')
1978 *Superman* (First Elder)
1979 *The Shillingbury Blowers* (TV) (Old Saltie)
    Meteor (Sir Michael Hughes)
    The Sea Wolves (Jack Cartwright)
1980 *Hurricane* (Father Malone)
    Sir Henry at Rawlinson End (Sir Henry)
    Staying On (TV) (Tusker)
    Windwalker (The Old Man)

Raymond Huntley

Expressions of joy need considerable encouragement before setting out across Raymond Huntley's face. It's a daunting wasteland of sombre looks and keep-off signs, an acid stomach overlaid with human features. A typical Huntley character has about as much charm as a dentist's drill, and unlike, say, Boris Karloff or Vincent Price in late career, Huntley has resisted the urge to laugh at himself, in films at any rate.

He knows both sides of the executive fence rather well, both as finicky boss and cringing minion, and whether he is making things hot for others, or leading a mongrel's life, that supremely harried expression is unshiftable.

His roles are usually small, but the gloomy face and disdainful manner are like long-time friends – long-time in the sense that Huntley has been frowning on the world at large since well before the war as, for example, a German official in *Night Train to Munich* (1940, Carol Reed), mouthing approved party slogans about Germany being a fine place to live in during negotiations but declaring privately, 'This is a bloody awful country to live in,' when he thinks it's safe to do so.

He was Laurence Harvey's boss in *Room at the Top* (1959, Jack Clayton), first and faraway best of the Joe Lampton sagas. Huntley is a town hall toady uncomfortably perched in mill-boss Donald Wolfit's breast pocket, so that when Wolfit wants Harvey out of the way, it is Huntley who delivers the message. 'Find a girl of your own background ... and you can go a long way in Warmley,' he tells Harvey – a piece of advice which is rightfully ignored.

In *Only Two Can Play* (1962, Sidney Gilliatt), he was Mai Zetterling's husband, another borough beanbag behind whose back Miss Zetterling is having a whale of a time trying to have a whale of a time with Peter Sellers. Things have a habit of going wrong for them, however – even the car they park off the beaten track suddenly honks and flashes while the roof opens and shuts as if visibly protesting at the use to which it is being put. Huntley's air of confident detachment, as if sensing that good luck and Seller's clumsiness are both on his side, is a joy to watch.

In *Passport to Pimlico* (1949, Henry Cornelius), Huntley was a small-minded bank official who leads local council opposition to Stanley Holloway's scheme for turning a Pimlico bomb site into a recreation ground for the community, and disdainfully showers cigar ash over the model Holloway has lovingly made of the proposed site. Discovery of the document which annexes Pimlico to the Duchy of Burgundy and which frees Huntley from the reprimands of his superiors (as a part of Burgundy he would control the bank instead of merely running it for someone else), brings about a remarkable change of attitude. Old enmities are forgotten in the scramble for independence.

He managed the toy department in James Robertson Justice's department store in *Crooks Anonymous* (1962, Ken Annakin). A typical fussy sycophant, Huntley makes the mistake of giving reformed safecracker Leslie Phillips a job as the store's Santa Claus. When the staff gather round to present a commemorative bust of Justice, Phillips, as Santa, is the logical presenter, but all goes badly wrong and the bust of the boss is hopelessly disfigured in the melee. Huntley finds himself summoned to Justice's office to explain himself and to discuss his future – 'Assuming you have one,' bellows Justice ominously.

He was a harrassed magistrate refereeing the industrialists-unionists flare-up in *I'm All Right, Jack* (1959, John Boulting), and a fussy vicar opposed to the effect sexy teacher Agnes Laurent has on Cecil Parker's pupils in *A French Mistress* (1960, Roy Boulting).

More school low jinks occurred in *The Great St Trinian's Train Robbery* (1966, Frank Launder and Sidney Gilliatt), in which the infamous two-and-a-half million-pound snatch finds its way under a few loose floorboards at St Trinian's. Huntley was a top education official parrying demands from outraged schools inspector Richard Wattis to close down the wretched school. Huntley's reasons have nothing to do with education, he's merely on to a good thing with fluttery headmistress Dora Bryan. As with all the St Trinian's films, genuine humour is a low priority and this lame attempt to cash in, by inference, on an event that could never in a million years have a funny side to it, is in the worst imaginable taste.

Films that send up death might not suit every taste either, and *That's Your Funeral* (1972, John Robins), a somewhat frantic comedy about crooks and undertakers, has its share of insensitive moments. Huntley played a bemused undertaker whose inept assistants keep mislaying the merchandise. The trouble stems from the appearance of a second coffin crammed with hashish cigarettes which a gang of smugglers, posing as morticians, have also lost track of. To Huntley's chagrin, losing the corpse of a civic dignitary is not the kind of mistake he can easily keep the lid on. 'I've never known a corpse run me off my feet,' he sighs wearily after a crazy hearse-race around town pursued by the smugglers who think that the coffin in Huntley's charge contains the counterfeit smokes.

Naturally, it is the wrong box which gets cremated, and the fumes from it give the entire funeral party hysterics. *That's Your Funeral* is an odd mixture, tolerably amusing in places and crassly indelicate in others. As Bill Fraser, Huntley's as-

Borough chief Raymond Huntley (right) gives accountant Laurence Harvey a few pointers to success in *Room at the Top* (1959)

sistant says at one point, describing their dim-witted apprentice: 'He doesn't know his hearse from his elbow.' Neither, alas, does the film.

Raymond Huntley

b. 1904. Long-serving icy-faced movie regular, frequently played finicky bosses, snooty officials and servile dogsbodies. On stage from 1922.

1935 *Can You Hear Me Mother*
1936 *Rembrandt*
     Whom the Gods Love
1937 *Knight Without Armour*
1940 *Night Train to Munich*
1941 *The Ghost of St Michael's*
     Freedom Radio
     Inspector Hornleigh Goes to It
     The Ghost Train
     Once a Crook
     Pimpernel Smith
1943 *When We Are Married*
1944 *The Way Ahead*
     They Came to a City
1946 *School for Secrets* (Professor Laxton-Jones)

I See a Dark Stranger (Miller)
1948 *So Evil My Love* (Henry Courtney)
     Broken Journey (Edward Marshall)
     Mr Perrin And Mr Traill (Moy-Thompson)
     It's Hard to be Good (Williams)
1949 *Passport to Pimlico* (Mr Wicks)
1950 *Trio* (Mr Chester)
1951 *The Long Dark Hall* (Inspector Sullivan)
     The House in the Square (Mr Throstle)
     Mr Denning Drives North (Wright)
1952 *The Last Page* (Clive)
1953 *Laxdale Hall* (Samuel Pettigrew MP)
     Glad Tidings (Tom Forester)
     Meet Mr Lucifer (Mr Patterson)
1954 *Hobson's Choice* (Nathaniel Breenstock)
     Orders Are Orders (Colonel Bellamy)
     Aunt Clara (Rev Maurice Hilton)
     The Teckman Mystery (Maurice Miller)
1955 *The Dam Busters* (Ministry Official)
     The Constant Husband (Hassett)
     The Prisoner (The General)
     Doctor at Sea (Captain Beamish)
     Geordie (Rawlins)
1956 *The Last Man to Hang* (Attorney-General)

The Green Man (Sir Gregory Upshott)
1957 *Town on Trial* (Dr Reese)
Brothers in Law (Tatlock)
1958 *Next to No Time* (Forbes)
1959 *Room at the Top* (Hoylake)
Carlton-Browne of the FO (Tufton-Slade)
Innocent Meeting (Harold)
The Mummy (Joseph Whemple)
I'm All Right, Jack (Magistrate)
1960 *Our Man in Havana* (General)
Bottoms Up (Carrick-Jones)
Make Mine Mink (Inspector Pape)
Follow That Horse (Special Branch Chief)
Sands of the Desert (Bossom)
A French Mistress (Rev Edwin Peake)
Suspect (Sir George Gatling)
The Pure Hell of St Trinian's (Judge)

1962 *Only Two Can Play* (Vernon Gruffyd-Williams)
Waltz of the Toreadors (Court President)
Crooks Anonymous (Wagstaffe)
On the Beat (Sir Ronald Ackroyd)
1963 *Nurse on Wheels* (Vicar)
The Yellow Teddy Bears (Malburton)
1964 *The Black Torment* (Colonel Wentworth)
1965 *Rotten to the Core* (Governor)
1966 *The Great St Trinian's Train Robbery* (Minister)
1968 *Hostile Witness* (John Naylor)
1969 *The Adding Machine* (Smithers)
1972 *Young Winston* (Officer)
That's Your Funeral (Emmanuel Holroyd)
1974 *Symptoms* (Burke)

Wilfrid Hyde White

Wilfrid Hyde White was one of the nutty Montpelier brothers – the other was Ronald Squire – who bet each other that anyone could, or could not, live like a king without ever having to break into *The Million Pound Note* (1954, Ronald Neame). Gregory Peck, an impoverished American footloose in London, agrees to put the theory to the test. With an impish face, sardonic mocking eyes and disinctive, drawn-out laugh, Wilfrid Hyde White's Roddy Montpelier is one of the 1950s' most appealing characters.

Mostly, Hyde White's appearances were brief and his acting range limited. But by being minor variations of himself and avoiding long speeches, he has cashed in rather well on a slender talent, playing smooth-tongued crooks, ne'er-do-wells, peers of the realm and cantankerous old coots of varying shades.

In *Mr Denning Drives North* (1951, Anthony Kimmins) he was the only one able to tie in John Mills with the disposal of the body of a blackmailer whom Mills appears to have both motive and opportunity to have killed. Hyde White keeps the audience guessing to the end.

With Robert Morley, he also-starred in *The Adventures of Quentin Durward* (1955, Richard Thorpe), a medieval adventure story set in France. Morley was a conniving monarch and Hyde White his know-all hairdresser.

Again with Morley, he appeared as a jockey club steward in *The Rainbow Jacket* (1954, Basil

Dearden), but had little to do except quiz a teenage jockey who appeared to be going off the rails. It was a poor film but for an actor whose travels in search of work – and sometimes, one is told, to avoid it – are allegedly synchronised to the world's better known race meetings, it must have been a pleasant little number to peel off.

In *Up the Creek* (1958, Val Guest) he played an Admiral of the Fleet who comes aboard to inspect a bizarrely-run ship under David Tomlinson's command, and finishes up treading water after a rocket which Tomlinson is experimenting with in the hold is accidentally detonated.

He was a waspish head surgeon in *Life in Emergency Ward 10* (1959, Robert Day), and, on the other side of the blanket as it were, a cantankerous colonel who gives the hospital staff a miserable time in *Carry On Nurse* (1959, Gerald Thomas). The nurses extract a wicked revenge, however, abandoning the hoary old buffer on all fours, having substituted a daffodil for a thermometer in a most indelicate place.

In *Crooks Anonymous* (1962, Ken Annakin) he is principal of Manderville Hall, a voluntary correction centre run on almost sadistic lines. Each inmate is confronted with his particular weakness and receives aversion therapy in progressively severe jolts, administered by a gleeful Stanley Baxter. Hyde White is himself a reformed thief who has established the academy on an inheritance of a couple of hundred

Bespectacled Wilfrid Hyde White joins Alec Guinness (left) and Sidney James, watched by Jean Collin, in a game of cards in *The Last Holiday* (1950)

thousand pounds to which he has access only while he goes straight and helps others. But when one of his star pupils, Leslie Phillips, comes up with a unique opportunity to nick a quarter of a million pounds, the Christmas takings at a department store where Phillips works, Hyde White is unable to suppress the habits of a lifetime.

Since the early 1960s, Hyde White has filmed regularly in the States. He ran Yves Montand's business empire in *Let's Make Love* (1960, George Cukor), while Montand frivolously squanders on showgirls the fortunes accumulated by illustrious ancestors. He was also, for a time, associated with the marathon TV soap opera *Peyton Place*, replacing George Macready after the veteran American actor withdrew through illness. It was a monumental piece of miscasting, and a chore which Hyde White attacked with the enthusiasm of an alcoholic being woken by bright sunlight.

In *Run a Crooked Mile* (1969, Gene Levitt)

Hyde White was the poetry-loving doctor who brings Louis Jourdan to Switzerland following his 'accident'. Jourdan awakens to find that he has a wife, played by Mary Tyler Moore, whom he has never before set eyes on, and a completely new existence. Hyde White is Jourdan's only logical starting-point in his pursuit of the truth about what's happened, but he disappears as abruptly as he came in. 'Poetry enriches the soul; gambling depletes the bank account,' he sighs, moments before self-administering a poisoned drink.

In real life, the line had a somewhat prophetic ring – Hyde White found himself in financial difficulties in the mid-1970s, and was declared bankrupt in 1978. He has since squared himself with the Receiver. Surfacing in London after one of several hearings he attended, he told a journalist: 'Dear boy, I have always been bankrupt, but *they* have only just discovered it!' It could have been Roddy Montpelier having the last laugh.

107

Wilfrid Hyde White

b. 1903. Imperturbable smooth-faced veteran, noted for toffs and villains and dozens of others in between. On stage from 1922. Long-time USA resident, frequently seen in American films playing impeccable Englishmen. Film debut: *Josser on the Farm* (1934).

1935 *Night Mail*
Admirals All
Alibi Inn
1936 *Murder By Rope*
Scarab Murder Case
1937 *Bulldog Drummond at Bay*
Elephant Boy
Change for a Sovereign
1938 *Meet Mr Penny*
I've Got a Horse
1939 *The Lambeth Walk*
Poison Pen
1941 *Turned Out Nice Again*
1942 *Lady from Lisbon*
Asking for Trouble
1946 *Appointment with Crime* (Cleaner)

1947 *While the Sun Shines* (Receptionist)
1948 *My Brother's Keeper* (Harding)
The Winslow Boy (Watkinson)
1949 *The Passionate Friends* (Solicitor)
The Bad Lord Byron (Mr Hopton)
Britannia Mews (Mr Culver)
Adam and Evelyne (Colonel Bradley)
That Dangerous Age (Mr Potts)
Helter Skelter (Dr Jekyll/Mr Hyde)
Conspirator (Lord Pennistone)
The Third Man (Crabbin)
1950 *Golden Salamander* (Agno)
The Angel with the Trumpet (Simmerl)
The Last Holiday (Chalfont)
Trio (Grey)
The Mudlark (Tucker)
Highly Dangerous (Luke)
Midnight Episode (Mr Knight)
1951 *Blackmailed* (Lord Dearsley)
Mr Drake's Duck (Mr May)
The Browning Version (Frobisher)
No Highway (Fisher)
Mr Denning Drives North (Woods)
Outcast of the Islands (Vinck)

Wilfrid Hyde White (second left) in tough company. With (left to right) Trevor Howard, Herbert Lom and Jacques Sernas in *Golden Salamander* (1950)

1952 *Top Secret* (Sir Hubert)
1953 *The Story of Gilbert and Sullivan* (Mr Marston)
1954 *The Million Pound Note* (Roderick Montpelier)
The Rainbow Jacket (Lord Stoneleigh)
Duel in the Jungle (Pitt)
To Dorothy a Son (Mr Starke)
1955 *John and Julie* (Sir James)
See How They Run (Brigadier Buskin)
The Adventures of Quentin Durward (Master Oliver)
1956 *The March Hare* (Colonel Keene)
My Teenage Daughter (Sir Joseph)
The Silken Affair (Sir Horace Hogg)
1957 *That Woman Opposite* (Sir Maurice Lawes)
The Vicious Circle (Robert Brady)
Tarzan and the Lost Safari ('Doodles' Fletcher)
1958 *The Truth About Women* (Sir George Tavistock)
Up the Creek (Admiral Foley)
Wonderful Things (Sir Bertram)
1959 *The Lady Is a Square* (Charles)
Carry On Nurse (Colonel)
Life in Emergency Ward 10 (Professor Bourne-Evans)

North West Frontier (Bridie)
Libel (Foxley)
1960 *Two-Way Stretch* (Basil 'Soapy' Fowler)
Let's Make Love (USA) (John Wales)
1961 *His and Hers* (Charles Dunton)
On the Fiddle (Trowbridge)
1962 *Crooks Anonymous* (Montague)
In Search of the Castaways (Lord Glenarvan)
1964 *My Fair Lady* (Colonel Pickering)
1965 *You Must Be Joking* (General Lockwood)
Ten Little Indians (Judge Cannon)
The Liquidator (Chief)
John Goldfarb Please Come Home (USA) (Mustafa Gus)
1966 *Chamber of Horrors* (Harold Blount)
Our Man in Marrakesh (Arthur Fairbrother)
The Sandwich Man (Lord Uffingham)
1967 *Sumuru* (Colonel Baisbrook)
1969 *The Magic Christian* (Captain)
Chicago, Chicago (The Governor)
Run a Crooked Mile (Dr Ralph Sawyer)
Skullduggery (USA) (Eaton)
1970 *Fragment of Fear* (Mr Copsey)
1979 *The Cat and the Canary* (Cyrus West)
1980 *In God We Trust* (Abbot Thelonius)

Gordon Jackson

Gordon Jackson was the British POWs' intelligence officer in *The Great Escape* (1963, John Sturges). Outside the wire his intelligence fails him, however, and a momentary lack of concentration cooks his goose. When he is boarding a bus to freedom, having passed himself off successfully as a French labourer, one of the guards catches him out by saying 'Good luck' in English, to which Jackson replies, 'Thank you'. Richard Attenborough, as a fellow-escaper, has little to be thankful about – Jackson's terrible gaffe lands them both in front of a Nazi execution squad.

His film career began, during the war, when he got leave from his draughtsman's bench to appear in the Ealing propaganda movie, *The Foreman Went to France* (1942, Charles Frend) with comedian Tommy Trinder. He had done a few minor acting jobs for BBC Radio in his native Glasgow, and was on the files as a 'raw Scottish

youth', precisely what *The Foreman's* makers were looking for. Later that year, he made another trip south, for *Nine Men* (1943, Harry Watt).

For most of his career, Jackson has been a north-of-the-Border Donald Houston, a stoic, down-to-earth nice guy, commonsense friend of the hero, and all-purpose good sport. In one of his early films, *Pink String and Sealing Wax* (1945, Robert Hamer), he was the respectable son of a Brighton chemist destined to follow in his father's narrow footsteps. Defiantly countering home-life repressions, he gets canned in a public house and, through his infatuation with the landlord's wife Googie Withers, is drawn unwittingly into a plot to murder her husband, Garry Marsh. Miss Withers throws herself into the sea, and Jackson, no longer quite the wide-eyed innocent, returns home to a father now perceptibly softer round the edges.

A serious Gordon Jackson sorts things out with Sally Ann Howes in *Stop Press Girl* (1949)

Jackson thinks now that audiences must have found his accent rather odd. 'There was I, supposed to be the son of a Brighton family, sounding as if I'd been born and bred in Killiecrankie!' he grins.

By the time he made *The Captive Heart* (1946, Basil Dearden), an average POW drama in which he played a Scots Guardsman, Jackson was having so much time away from his drawing board that his employers delivered an ultimatum – he either gave up acting or hung up his set square. Soon after that the engineering industry lost a good man.

Jackson made a favourable impact as the mother-dominated young islander in *Whisky Galore* (1949, Alexander Mackendrick), who is confined to his room by the evil-tempered old shrew and robbed of the chance of going to church after rolling home in the early hours from a Saturday night party.

That same year he made *Floodtide* (1949, Frederick Wilson), cast as a ship-designer who woos and weds the boss's daughter, played by Rona Anderson. Fact and fiction rubbed shoulders in more ways than one for Jackson in *Floodtide* – he was a real-life designer (though not of ships) and he actually did woo and wed Rona Anderson.

His roles during the 1950s and early 1960s came to very little – mostly he was cast as a 'token Jimmie'. In *The Quatermass X-periment* (1955, Val Guest), he played a harassed television producer whose cameras zoom in on the 'thing' during its terminal sojourn in the scaffolding round Westminster Abbey. In *Sailor Beware* (1956, Gordon Parry), a loud stage farce of unremitting tedium, he was the bridegroom's chum, a dour Scot who refuses to flinch within earshot of dreaded ma-in-law Peggy Mount. As pre-nuptial tensions erupt, Miss Mount roars, 'If I get to the wedding at all, I'll be lucky,' to which Jackson, safely out of earshot, mutters, 'If you don't, everyone else will!'

He was a copper in *The Bridal Path* (1959, Frank Launder), helping Sergeant George Cole to capture an amiable hick, Bill Travers, who only wants a wife. He made *Hell Drivers* (1957, Cy Endfield) with Stanley Baker, playing a trucker, and in two more films with Baker in 1959 he played his subordinate. He was the decent, humane platoon sergeant in *Yesterday's Enemy* (1959, Val Guest), who leads a confused old Burmese off to be shot – a necessary precaution for the platoon's own survival – with the words, 'Come on, dad, over here.'

In *Blind Date* (1959, Joseph Losey), he assists Stanley Baker's murder investigation, opting for a safer course than the one his chief instinctively follows. He was an airline pilot in *Cone of Silence* (1960, Charles Frend) whose memory for foreign airfields helps clear the name of veteran pilot Bernard Lee wrongfully suspected of having caused two crashes. In *The Ipcress File* (1965, Sidney J. Furie) he was spectacularly killed during a pause at traffic lights, a lesser spy mistaken for Michael Caine and bumped off at the wheel of Caine's car by bungling assassins.

He was a kilted Scots aviator in *Those Magnificent Men in Their Flying Machines* (1965, Ken Annakin), briefly glimpsed as a competitor. Another brief spot was his ex-Scots Guards engineer who helps Kirk Douglas carve a roadway up a mountain side in *Cast a Giant Shadow* (1966, Melville Shavelson), a sub-Exodus flag-waver about the emergence of the state of Israel. Douglas played with his usual zest a real-life gung ho US Army Colonel who shapes Israeli volunteers into a useful strike force. Jackson's finished roadway is barely wide enough for one truck at a time to make the perilous, gear-crunching ascent, and nobody wants to be first to try it out. Jackson's insistence that it's no worse 'than a

Sunday drive' fails to get them enthused.

He was the shy, weak-willed arts master in love with genteel but fascist-minded fellow-teacher Maggie Smith in *The Prime of Miss Jean Brodie* (1969, Ronald Neame). She allows herself to be taken on boring weekends to his country home for 'sailing, walking the beaches and the pursuit of music', but hankers for the lustier company of uncouth artist Robert Stephens. When one of the weekends together leads to accusations of impropriety, Jackson is more worried about local gossip endangering his choirmaster's job than about its effects on Miss Smith's reputation. As he frets about being interviewed on the affair by the sharp-tongued headmistress Celia Johnson, Miss Smith promises him, rather acidly, that she won't let the headmistress stand him in the corner!

During the 1970s Jackson has worked frequently in television, most memorably in the award-winning *Upstairs Downstairs* as the fussy, genteel butler Hudson, whom he played in 65 episodes before London Weekend Television finally drew the chintz curtains in Eaton Square. For the same company he has also led CI5, a Government controlled anti-terror squad, in *The Professionals*, a rather hysterical comic-strip series to which Jackson brought a welcome note of dour cynicism.

Gordon Jackson

b. 1923. Versatile Scots-born actor, well-known since a juvenile. Film debut: *The Foreman Went to France* (1942). Specialises in sturdy, nice-guy portrayals. Latterly known to TV viewers as *Upstairs Downstairs* butler and spy boss of *The Professionals*. Married to actress Rona Anderson.

1945 *Pink String and Sealing Wax* (David
        Sutton)
1946 *The Captive Heart* (Lt David Lennox)
1948 *Against the Wind* (Johnny Duncan)
1949 *Flood Tide* (David Shields)
        Stop Press Girl (Jock Melville)
        Whisky Galore (George Campbell)
1950 *Bitter Springs* (Mac)
1951 *Happy Go Lovely* (Paul Tracey)
1952 *Castle in the Air* (Hiker)
1953 *Death Goes to School* (Inspector Campbell)
        Meet Mr Lucifer (Hector McPhee)
1954 *The Love Lottery* (Ralph)
        The Delavine Affair (Florian)
1955 *Passage Home* (Burne)
        Windfall (Leonard)

Gordon Jackson as the struggling Scottish farmer in *Greyfriars Bobby* (1961)

        The Quatermass X-Periment (TV Producer)
1956 *Pacific Destiny* (DO)
        Women Without Men (Percy)
        The Baby and the Battleship (Harry)
        Sailor Beware (Carnoustie Bligh)
1957 *Seven Waves Away* (John Merritt)
        Let's Be Happy (Dougal McLean)
        Hell Drivers (Scotty)
        The Black Ice (Bert Harris)
        Man in the Shadow (Jimmy Norris)
1958 *Blind Spot* (Chalky)
        Rockets Galore (George Campbell)
        Three Crooked Men (Don Westcott)
1959 *Yesterday's Enemy* (Sergeant Mackenzie)
        The Bridal Path (Constable Alec)
        Blind Date (Police Sergeant)
        The Navy Lark (Leading Seaman
            Johnson)
        Devil's Bait (Sergeant Malcolm)
1960 *The Price of Silence* (Roger Fenton)
        Cone of Silence (Captain Bateson)
        Snowball (Bill Donovan)
        Tunes of Glory (Captain Jimmy Cairns)
1961 *Greyfriars Bobby* (Farmer)
        Two Wives at One Wedding (Tom)
1963 *The Great Escape* (MacDonald,
            'Intelligence')
1964 *The Long Ships* (Vahlin)

111

Sidney James

Sidney James had the face of a jovial Hallowe'en turnip which its owner once believed would inhibit his acting career. The opposite was probably true. James' impish leer and raucous laugh revitalised many a feeble script. His characters were extrovert, uncomplicated, fastidiously working-class creations, as home-grown, one might suppose, as fish suppers and jellied eels. Yet James was a South African and in his mid-thirties before settling in London.

Thanks to quick acclimatisation, he was giving full-blooded Cockney characterisations in films only a few years afterwards – characterisations indistinguishable from the genuine cor-blimey.

In The Lavender Hill Mob (1951, Charles Crichton), he was one of the lesser villains, a safecracker known as the Wandsworth Boy – the other was Alfie Bass – recruited by Alec Guinness and Stanley Holloway to help with a cheeky bullion robbery. James is the one who brandishes a wad of press clippings about himself to validate his criminal pedigree. Later when the gang are preparing to slip across to Paris for the share-out, James announces sheepishly that his wife won't let him go. So much for the tough-talking Wandsworth Boy. He owned a racetrack snack bar in The Rainbow Jacket (1954, Basil Dearden), anxious to sell it at the right price. The eventual buyer is Bill Owen, a jockey with a tarnished past who philosophically concedes that James' refreshment stall is about as close to the racetrack as he can ever expect to get.

He was one of the opponents of The Titfield Thunderbolt (1953, Charles Crichton), a bulldozer driver who engages the old loco's steam predecessor in a track-side rough-and-tumble. The locomotive wins, but is later nobbled by James' unscrupulous cronies.

A bemused expression, large knitting needles and a quantity of birdseed were his props in Miss Robin Hood (1952, John Guillermin). James was chauffeur to Margaret Rutherford, a pigeon-loving do-gooder who persuades nervy magazine writer Richard Hearne to help her rake back a proportion of distillery tycoon James Robertson Justice's fortune, coined in the first place by swindling Miss Rutherford's family out of a magical whisky formula.

James spent the entire film smothered in a huge scarf which he adds to industriously. Scrambling from the tangled wreckage of the limousine he has just whacked into a ditch, James' sole concern is for the number of stitches dropped. The film seems to have been based on the rather dangerous notion that anything Margaret Rutherford does will raise a laugh and, though she flashes around in that brilliantly eccentric bossy way that endeared her to millions, the film cries out for a stronger plot and better support.

The Square Ring (1953, Michael Relph) was a backstage drama that depicted one night in the life of a group of boxers collecting their bruises at a small-time sports stadium managed by Sidney James. Aging pro Robert Beatty – by boxing standards a real geriatric – wants to prove to the gallery, and to himself, that he still possesses the old fire. Estranged wife Bernardette O'Farrell would prefer him to come to his senses rather than witness them being further scrambled. Dapper, woman-chasing Bill Owen, showy fight-throwing Maxwell Reed, dumb-ox brawler

Bill Travers, punchy veteran George Rose and hapless hopeful Ronald Lewis make up the ill-assorted combatants. Despite the fact that none of them look as if they would last two rounds with a fairground bruiser, and some of the dialogue sounds about as useful as a dented gum-shield, *The Square Ring* was a passably honest attempt to recreate changing room chat and one could almost sniff the liniment.

Competent performances by a stalwart line-up, notably Jack Warner as a seen-it-all swabstick man, and James as the arena manager with a cigar he cannot afford to light, keep the film tottering on its feet till the final bell.

James was gangster Paul Douglas' right-hand man in *Joe Macbeth* (1955, Ken Hughes), secure in his ambitious boss's patronage until James' outspoken son, played by Bonar Colleano, proves to be a threat. At his wife Ruth Roman's insistence, Douglas has Colleano killed and later, when it's James' turn to become dispensable he, too, is eliminated. The familiar Shakespearean plot, reworked into a modern gangland setting, contained more novelty than entertainment value, and its stagey New York setting did not fool anyone.

James' established character, an ambivalent work-shy rogue, provided the perfect counterpoint to Tony Hancock's peevish, pompous suburbanite, with whom he formed a uniquely successful radio sitcom double act, *Hancock's Half Hour*, during the late 1950s.

The partnership transferred to television with moderate success, and established James as a natural light comedian in his own right. He filled the void left by the dissolution of the Hancock partnership in the early 1960s by taking his Railway Cuttings character, with little or no variation, into some of the early *Carry On ...* films, and from 1962 onwards was a regular member of the team.

In *Carry On Constable* (1960, Gerald Thomas) he was a long-suffering desk sergeant; in *Carry On Cabby* (1963, Gerald Thomas) he was the taxi fleet proprietor whose wife, played by Hattie Jacques, sets up a rival firm staffed by sexy chauffeuses. His Mark Antony in *Carry On Cleo* (1964, Gerald Thomas) and Henry VIII in *Carry On Henry* (1970, Gerald Thomas) were both randy rascals under the cloth, and as the former, clad in a toga, he wore conspicuously little cloth.

James returned to TV sitcom in *Bless This House*, a fairly plodding long-run domestic com-

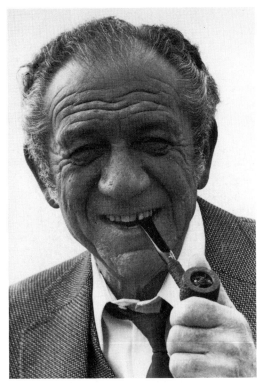

Sidney James, caught in a happy off-duty mood

edy series, later filmed, in which he was the only watchable element, as the father of a dull up-market suburban 1970s family.

Sidney James
1913-1976. Accomplished, makes-it-look-easy film/TV comedy actor, one-time radio partner of Tony Hancock, and *Carry On* regular. Often seen as engaging spiv or shady character with comic overtones. On stage from 1937. Film debut: *Black Memory* (1947).

1947 *Black Memory* (Eddie Clinton)
1948 *Night Beat* (Nixon)
     Once a Jolly Swagman (Rowton)
     The Small Back Room (Knucksic)
1949 *Paper Orchid* (Freddie Evans)
     Give Us This Day (Mundin)
1950 *The Man in Black* (Henry Clavering)
     Last Holiday (Joe Clarence)
     The Lady Craved Excitement (Carlo)
1951 *Talk of a Million* (John C. Moody)
     The Galloping Major (Bookie)
     The Lavender Hill Mob (Lackery)
     Lady Godiva Rides Again (Lew Beeson)

113

Sidney James, with *Carry On* regulars Bernard Bresslaw, Hattie Jacques and Kenneth Williams, gives Kenneth Cope a hair-raising moment in *Carry On Matron* (1972)

1952 *I Believe in You* (Sergeant Brodie)
    Emergency Call (Danny Marks)
    The Gift Horse (Ned Hardy)
    Time Gentlemen, Please (Eric Hace)
    Father's Doing Fine (Taxi-driver)
    Venetian Bird (Bernardo)
    The Yellow Balloon (Barrow-boy)
    Miss Robin Hood (Sidney)
    Tall Headlines (uncredited)
1953 *Cosh Boy* (Sergeant)
    The Titfield Thunderbolt (Harry Hawkins)
    The Wedding of Lili Marlene (Fennimore
      Hunt)
    Will Any Gentlemen (Hobson)
    The Square Ring (Adams)
    The Flanagan Boy (Sharkey)
    Is Your Honeymoon Really Necessary
      (Hank Hamilton)
    Park Plaza 605 (Supt Williams)

1954 *Escape by Night* (Gino Rossi)
    The Weak and the Wicked (Sid Baden)
    The House Across the Lake (Beverley
      Forrest)
    The Rainbow Jacket (Harry)
    Father Brown (Bert Parkinson)
    Seagulls Over Sorrento (Charlie Badger)
    The Belles of St Trinian's (Benny)
    The Crowded Day (Watchman)
    Orders Are Orders (Ed Waggermeyer)
    For Better for Worse (Foreman)
    Aunt Clara (Honest Sid)
1955 *Out of the Clouds* (Gambler)
    A Kid for Two Farthings ('Ice' Berg)
    John and Julie (Mr Pritchett)
    The Glass Cage (Tony Lewis)
    The Deep Blue Sea (Man)
    Joe Macbeth (Bankie)
    A Yank in Ermine (Manager)

1956 *It's a Great Day* (Harry Mason)
    The Extra Day (Barney West)
    Ramsbottom Rides Again (Black Jake)
    Wicked As They Come (Frank Allen)
    The Iron Petticoat (Paul)
    Dry Rot (Flash Harry)
    Trapeze (Snake Man)
1957 *Quatermass II* (Jimmy Hall)
    The Smallest Show on Earth (Hogg)
    Interpol (Joe)
    The Shiralee (Luke)
    Hell Drivers (Dusty)
    The Story of Esther Costello (Ryan)
    Campbell's Kingdom (Driver)
    A King in New York (Johnson)
1958 *The Silent Enemy* (Chief Petty Officer
    Thorpe)
    Another Time Another Place (Jake Klein)
    Next to No Time (Albert)
    The Man Inside (Franklin)
    I Was Monty's Double (Porter)
    The Sheriff of Fractured Jaw (Drunk)
1959 *Too Many Crooks* (Sid)
    Make Mine a Million (Sid Gibson)
    The Thirty-nine Steps (Perce)
    Idol on Parade (Herbie)
    Upstairs and Downstairs (PC Edwards)
    Tommy the Toreador (Cadena)
    Desert Mice (Bert Bennett)
1960 *Carry On Constable* (Sergeant Frank
    Wilkins)
    And The Same to You (Sammy Gatt)
    Watch Your Stern (Chief Petty Officer
    Mundy)
    The Pure Hell Of St Trinian's (Alphonse
    O'Reilly)

1961 *Double Bunk* (Sid Randall)
    Carry On Regardless (Bert Handy)
    A Weekend With Lulu (Cafe Patron)
    The Green Helmet (Richie Launder)
    What a Carve Up (Syd Butler)
    Raising the Wind (Sid)
    What a Whopper (Harry)
1962 *Carry on Cruising* (Captain Wellington
    Crowther)
    We Joined the Navy (Guest appearance)
1963 *Carry On Cabby* (Charlie Hawkins)
1964 *Carry On Cleo* (Mark Antony)
    The Beauty Jungle (guest appearance)
1965 *Three Hats for Lisa* (Sid Marks)
    The Big Job (George Brain)
    Carry On Cowboy (The Rumpo Kid)
1966 *Where the Bullets Fly* (Mortician)
    Don't Lose Your Head (Sir Rodney Ffing)
1967 *Carry On Doctor* (Charlie Roper)
    Carry On ... Up the Khyber (Sir Sidney
    Ruff-Diamond)
1969 *Carry On Camping* (Sid Boggle)
    Carry On Again, Doctor (Gladstone
    Screwer)
1970 *Carry On Up the Jungle* (Bill Boosey)
    Carry On Loving (Sidney Bliss)
    Carry On Henry (Henry VIII)
1971 *Carry On at Your Convenience* (Sid
    Plummer)
1972 *Carry On Abroad* (Vic Flange)
    Bless This House (Sid Abbot)
    Carry On Matron (Sid)
1973 *A King in New York* (Mr Johnson)
1974 *Carry On Girls* (Sidney Fiddler)
    Carry On Dick (Dick Turpin/ Rev Mr
    Flasher)

Lionel Jeffries

It was Lionel Jeffries who, as the Marquis of Queensberry in *The Trials of Oscar Wilde* (1960, Ken Hughes), engineers Wilde's downfall by accusing him of being a sodomite following his son's lame-duck infatuation for the Great Wit. Stung into a High Court defence of the charge, Wilde, played by Peter Finch, is ahead on points until a fatal gaffe in the witness box snatches the verdict from him and wipes him out.

Jeffries' parrot face and bald head have forced the pace in scores of films, yet to many he remains 'old what's-his-name'. From crusty old eccentrics to barmy officers and arrogant villains, Jeffries' versatility has never been in doubt and, though his characterisations are always technically accurate, only with a couple of exceptions has there been very much to get hold of. *The Trials of Oscar Wilde* was one such exception; *Chitty Chitty Bang Bang* (1968, Ken Hughes) was another, in which Jeffries played Dick Van Dyke's father, former batman to James Robertson Justice whose daughter Van Dyke loves – thus completing a cosy circle in an altogether far too cosy film. Like the others,

115

Wombling Free (1976) director Lionel Jeffries (left) lines up one of his stars for a camera shot

Jeffries gets his chance to sing, suspended in a sentry box from a huge balloon and, notwithstanding, displaying a useful baritone voice.

He was an Irish Guards officer in *The Colditz Story* (1954, Guy Hamilton), a Boy's Own adventure yarn based, surprisingly, on fact, and played an inquisitive newspaperman in *The Quatermass X-periment* (1955, Val Guest). In *Blue Murder at St Trinian's* (1957, Frank Launder) he was Gelignite Joe, a diamond robber hiding out after a successful Hatton Garden job. Jeffries' niece, a St Trinian's lass who has rigged an exam and won a trip to Rome, arranges for her crooked uncle to impersonate a new headmistress on the trip. There's a reward of £10,000 for the missing sparklers – incentive enough for the hockeystick horde, when they catch on, to give Jeffries more trouble than he could have imagined.

He was a sailor in charge of all the livestock on board the HMS *Berkeley* in *Up the Creek* (1958, Val Guest), with the tricky job of keeping all the animals out of sight of the new captain, played by David Tomlinson. Jeffries' menagerie is part of a huge floating cottage industry, run on profitable lines by Irish bosun Peter Sellers, which Tomlinson's arrival threatens. In a deadly dull sequel, *Further Up the Creek* (1958, Val Guest), Jeffries played the same character under the same captain, but the profiteering bosun was played by Frankie Howerd.

He was a long-suffering adjutant, and straight man to Anthony Newley's conscripted pop singer in *Idol on Parade* (1959, John Gilling), a clever satire on a topical 1950s theme, the behind-the-scenes efforts of pop singer managements to save their golden-goose protégés from military service. Newley gets conscripted but keeps his rock-star career afloat by maintaining a healthy disregard for Army regulations, represented at their most niggardly by Jeffries. The film made Newley a recording artiste in his own right.

Jeffries took a break from comedy in *The Hellions* (1961, Ken Annakin), as a Jesse James figure in turn-of-the-century Australia, a regular meanie who terrorises the community until police sergeant Richard Todd shows the people how Gary Cooper would have coped with the problem, and before anyone can step in, they are charging off across the moors to zonk the villains.

In *First Men in the Moon* (1964, Nathan Juran), Jeffries was a dotty professor whose discovery of a strange anti-gravity substance answers the problems of fuelling his prototype spacecraft and enables him to make a successful moon landing – sixty years before it actually happened!

Jeffries scripted and directed a couple of pictorially elegant children's films during the 1970s – beginning with *The Railway Children* (1970) from Evelyn Nesbit's novel, and *The Amazing Mr Blunden* (1972) – handled with a combination of maturity and beginner's freshness which suggests that from behind the cameras Jeffries might go on to make the kind of lasting impression which his appearances in front of them have, in the main, sadly failed to do.

Lionel Jeffries
b. 1926. Busy all-purpose character support and director, no established persona, but most memorably crooks and disreputables. Film debut: *Will Any Gentlemen* (1953). Early directorial work with *The Railway Children* (1970) and *The Amazing Mr Blunden* (1972) shows appeal and promise.

1953 *Will Any Gentlemen* (Mr Frobisher)
1954 *The Black Rider* (Brennan)
     The Colditz Story (Harry Tyler)
1955 *Windfall* (Arthur Lee)
     All For Mary (Maître d'Hotel)
     The Quatermass X-periment (Blake)
     No Smoking (George Pogson)
1956 *Bhowani Junction* (Lieutenant George McDaniel)
     The Baby and the Battleship (George)
     The High Terrace (Monckton)
     Up in the World (Wilson)
     Lust for Life (Dr Peyron)
     Jumping for Joy (Bert Benton)
1957 *The Man in the Sky* (Keith)
     Doctor at Large (Dr Hatchett)
     Hour of Decision (Elvin Main)
     Blue Murder at St Trinian's (Joe Mangan)
     Barnacle Bill (Garrod)
     The Vicious Circle (Jeffrey Windsor)
1958 *Orders to Kill* (Interrogator)
     Dunkirk (Colonel)
     Up the Creek (Steady Barker)
     Law and Disorder (Major Proudfoot)
     The Revenge of Frankenstein (Fritz)
     Girls at Sea (Tourist)
     Further up the Creek (Steady Barker)
     Behind the Mask (Walter Froy)
     Nowhere to Go (Pet shop man)
     Life Is a Circus (Genie)
1959 *Idol on Parade* (Adjutant)
     Bobbikins (Gregory Mason)
     Please Turn Over (Ian Howard)
     The Nun's Story (Dr Goovaerts)
1960 *Two Way Stretch* (Sidney Crout)
     Jazzboat (Sgt Thompson)
     Let's Get Married (Marsh)
     The Trials of Oscar Wilde (Marquis of Queensberry)
     Tarzan the Magnificent (Ames)
     Fanny (Monsieur Brun)
1961 *The Hellions* (Luke Billings)
     Operation Snatch (Evans)
1962 *Mrs Gibbons' Boys* (Lester Martins)
     Kill or Cure (Inspector Hook)
     The Wrong Arm of the Law (Inspector Parker)
     Call Me Bwana (Dr Ezra Mungo)
1963 *The Scarlet Blade* (Colonel Judd)
1964 *The Long Ships* (Aziz)
     First Men in the Moon (Professor Cavor)
     Murder Ahoy (Captain Sidney Rumstone)
     The Truth About Spring (Lark)
1965 *You Must Be Joking* (Sgt Major McGregor)
     The Secret of My Success (Inspector Hobart/Baron Van Lukenberg/President Esteda/ Earl of Aldershot)
1966 *The Spy with a Cold Nose* (Stanley Farquhar)
     Drop Dead, Darling (Parker)
     Oh Dad, Poor Dad, Mamma's Hung You in the Closet and I'm Feeling So Bad (USA) (Airport Commander)
1967 *Jules Verne's Rocket to the Moon* (Sir Charles Dillworthy)
1968 *Chitty Chitty Bang Bang* (Grandpa Potts)
1969 *Twinky* (Creighton)
1970 *Eye Witness* (Colonel)
     The Railway Children (wrote – from

Bernard Lee

It's left to Bernard Lee to inject a badly needed touch of earthiness at the end of *Beat the Devil* (1953, John Huston), the Huston-Bogart sailaway farce which left everyone, including its distinguished director, red-faced and rudderless. Lee was the CID inspector investigating a murder in the Colonial Office in which Robert Morley and some other cagey characters are implicated. Morley's coy plausibility is shattered when Jennifer Jones, a respectable but over-imaginative middle-class lady, has them all arrested. Lee handcuffs them two-by-two and prods them aboard a London-bound ship moored in the harbour like some judicial Ark.

Bernard Lee is probably best known for his James Bond film appearances in which he played 'M', Bond's no-nonsense departmental boss, but these represent the tip of a very busy iceberg. His kindly eyes, droll manner and expressly Anglo-Saxon level-headedness were well suited to playing senior detectives, of which his tally might well be the longest in British films. Moral toughness and outward pragmatism combine in a typical Lee characterisation to make up a solid citizen unlikely to become ruffled or led down blind alleys. His detectives were hunters of quiet determination, tenacious predators masquerading as kindly uncles.

An important early role was as a military police sergeant in *The Third Man* (1949, Carol Reed) who co-ordinates the underground sewer chase for wanted drug-trafficker Orson Welles, and is killed by Welles before the net closes on him. In *The Blue Lamp* (1950, Basil Dearden) he was a senior cop directing the hunt for an unhinged young hoodlum, Dirk Bogarde, who has murdered PC Jack Warner while trying to escape with the modest takings from a Paddington cinema. Also with the CID in *Mr Denning Drives North* (1951, Anthony Kimmins) he was the detective who gives John Mills, as an aircraft designer implicated in a manslaughter which looks like

murder, a few feverish turns.

Lee made his share of World War II service dramas, capably handling both officer and other rank types. In *Morning Departure* (1950, Roy Baker) he was a Submarine Command officer liaising with the efforts of a salvage crew to hoist a crippled sub from the seabed. The rescue appears to go well until a prolonged gale forces the exercise to be abandoned, leaving skipper John Mills, Richard Attenborough and two others entombed. When the salvage chief comments: 'It takes all sorts to make a Navy but I've never understood your sort,' meaning it as a compliment, Lee snaps: 'Put it down to the extra half-crown a day!'

In *The Gift Horse* (1952, Compton Bennett), he was an ordinary rating, Richard Attenborough's good humoured chum. He is a casualty during their destroyer's bombardment by German shore batteries as it steams through enemy defences, cheekily brandishing a German flag, intending to cripple with explosives as many moored ships of the Reich as possible.

He was in charge of one of the pocket battleships that hounded the *Graf Spee* in *The Battle of the River Plate* (1956, Michael Powell), and one of the workers meting out rough treatment to non-striker Richard Attenborough in *The Angry Silence* (1960, Guy Green). Ten years later, he was still a thorn in Attenborough's side, although clearly with more justification, as the detective in charge of the murder investigation at *Ten Rillington Place* (1970, Richard Fleischer), chillingly remembered as the address in Notting Hill at which real life mass-murderer John Christie killed and stored his victims.

In *Fire Down Below* (1957, Robert Parrish) Lee was a white-suited medic who treats Jack Lemmon, trapped in the hold of a doomed ship. Lemmon is in real trouble as the burning ship is loaded with explosives, and harbour authorities have ruled that as soon as things start to get out

Bernard Lee (left) courteously informs German skipper Peter Finch that the game is up in *The Battle of the River Plate* (1956)

of hand the ship is to be towed out to sea and scuttled, Lemmon along with it. Characteristically, Lee tries to take the sting out of Lemmon's predicament. After examining his injured legs, the worst prognosis that Lee will make is that Lemmon 'won't be able to go to any dances for a little while'.

Lee is the rule-book airline captain suspected of incompetence in *Cone of Silence* (1960, Charles Frend). The accusation sticks and Lee, whose plane crashed on takeoff killing his co-pilot, forfeits his licence – and his peace of mind. Training officer Michael Craig, an accusing voice at the original court of enquiry, changes his mind after getting to know Lee and his daughter, Elizabeth Seal. Craig becomes convinced that the fault lies in the approved takeoff procedure, but it is not verified in time to save Lee, who dies in a replica crash of the earlier one.

He occasionally played villains, but with little impact, due to the fact that he could mostly be seen at work for the other side. In *The Rainbow Jacket* (1954, Basil Dearden) he was a racetrack racketeer who blackmails ex-jockey Bill Owen into persuading a leading apprentice jockey, whom Owen has befriended, to throw a race.

In *Crossplot* (1969, Alvin Rakoff), an agreeable spy thriller, Lee is the shady Whitehall chief behind an assassination attempt on a visiting dignitary, scheduled to take place at a grand military review. Rather like at the climax of *The Manchurian Candidate*, the intended victim and the power behind the killer occupy the same rostrum, and here, too, it's the baddie who gets it, as sniper Francis Matthews, operating a telescopic rifle concealed in a TV camera, is put off his shot at the vital moment by hero Roger Moore. Matthews' comeuppance only minutes later is far less sophisticated than the technique he was using. Hurrying to get away, he is scuppered by the Household Cavalry.

In *Whistle Down the Wind* (1961, Bryan Forbes) Lee was the widowed farmer, father of three imaginative Yorkshire children who think that a fugitive hiding in the barn might be Jesus Christ. The object of their attention – and affection – is Alan Bates, a bearded criminal.

119

Screen writer/director Bryan Forbes blends fantasy – the children's – and reality into a captivating patchwork, reminiscent at times of, although in no way copying, *The Kidnappers* (1954, Philip Leacock).

Informed, at one stage, that there are no limits to what Jesus can do, tiny Alan Barnes ponders whether the man in the barn, enjoying a well-earned rest from miracle-working, might be persuaded to make him a nice chocolate cake for his birthday. Another witty scene has Bernard Lee, struggling to put on a tight collar prior to slipping into town for a few ales, coming in for some critical flak from his shrewish sister. 'I can hardly breathe in it,' he moans, trying to fix an unhelpful collar-stud, to which the acid and unsympathetic reply is: 'No, but I expect you'll get beer past it, though!'

Bernard Lee

1908-1981. Gruff, reliable, no-nonsense role character actor, whose many credits include policemen, servicemen, father figures and spy chiefs. Mostly shows the honest, hard-working face of officialdom, with only very occasional lapses. On stage since 1924. Film debut: *The Double Event* (1934).

1934 *The Double Event*
1935 *The River House Mystery*
1936 *Rhodes of Africa*
1937 *The Black Tulip*
1938 *The Terror*
1939 *Murder in Soho*
　　　The Frozen Limits
1940 *Let George Do It*
　　　Spare a Copper
1941 *Once a Crook*
1946 *This Man Is Mine* (James Nicholls)
1947 *The Courtneys of Curzon Street* (Colonel Gascoyne)
1948 *The Fallen Idol* (Detective Hart)
1949 *Elizabeth of Ladymead* (John – 1903)
　　　The Third Man (Sergeant Paine)
1950 *The Blue Lamp* (Divisional Detective Inspector Cherry)
　　　Morning Departure (Commander Gates)
　　　Last Holiday (Inspector Wilton)
　　　Odette (Jack)
　　　Cage of Gold (Inspector Gray)
1951 *The Adventurers* (O'Connell)
　　　Calling Bulldog Drummond (Colonel Webson)
　　　Appointment with Venus (Brigadier)

Mr Denning Drives North (Inspector Dodds)
1952 *The Gift Horse* (A. S. 'Stripey' Wood)
　　　The Yellow Balloon (PC Chapman)
1953 *Single-Handed* (Stoker Wheatley)
　　　Beat the Devil (Inspector Jack Clayton CID)
1954 *Father Brown* (Inspector Valentine)
　　　Seagulls Over Sorrento ('Lofty' Turner)
　　　The Purple Plain (Dr Harris)
1954 *The Rainbow Jacket* (Racketeer)
1955 *Out of the Clouds* (Customs Officer)
　　　The Ship That Died of Shame (Sam Brewster)
1956 *The Battle of the River Plate* (Captain Dove)
　　　The Spanish Gardener (Leighton Bailey)
1957 *Fire Down Below* (Dr Sam)
　　　Across the Bridge (Inspector Hadden)
　　　High Flight (Flight Sergeant Harris)
1958 *Dunkirk* (Charles Foreman)
　　　The Key (Wadlow)
　　　The Man Upstairs (Thompson)
　　　Nowhere to Go (Vic Sloane)
1959 *Danger Within* (Lieutenant-Colonel Huxley)
　　　Beyond This Place (Patrick Mathry)
1960 *The Angry Silence* (Bert Connolly)
　　　Cone of Silence (Captain George Gort)
　　　Kidnapped (Captain Hoseason)
　　　Clue of the Twisted Candle (Superintendent Meredith)
1961 *Fury at Smugglers Bay* (Black John)
　　　Partners in Crime (Inspector Mann)
　　　The Secret Partner (Superintendent Hanbury)
　　　Whistle Down the Wind (Mr Bostock)
　　　Clue of the Silver Key (Superintendent Meredith)
1962 *The Share Out* (Superintendent Meredith)
　　　Vengeance (Frank Sears)
　　　Doctor No ('M')
　　　The L-Shaped Room (Charlie)
1963 *Two Left Feet* (Mr Crabbe)
　　　A Place to Go (Matt Flint)
　　　From Russia with Love ('M')
　　　Ring of Spies (Henry Houghton)
1964 *Saturday Night Out* (George Hudson)
　　　Who Was Maddox (Superintendent Meredith)
　　　Goldfinger ('M')
　　　Doctor Terror's House of Horrors (Hopkins)
1965 *The Amorous Adventures of Moll Flanders* (Landlord)

The Legend of Dick Turpin (Jeremiah)
The Spy Who Came in from the Cold
  (Patmore)
Thunderball ('M')
1967 You Only Live Twice ('M')
1969 Crossplot (Chilmore)
    On Her Majesty's Secret Service ('M')
1970 Ten Rillington Place (Police Inspector 'J')
    The Raging Moon (Uncle Bob)
1971 Danger Point (Ship's Captain)
    Diamonds Are Forever ('M')

Dulcima (Mr Gaskain)
1973 Live and Let Die ('M')
    Frankenstein and the Monster from Hell
      (Tarmut)
1974 The Man with the Golden Gun ('M')
1977 The Spy Who Loved Me ('M')
    Beauty and the Beast (USA) (Beaumont)
1979 Moonraker ('M')
    Dangerous Davies, the Last Detective
      (Sergeant Ben)

Christopher Lee

In *Dracula Has Risen from the Grave* (1968, Freddie Francis) a stricken clergyman wails: 'Dear God, when shall we be free of this evil?' Towards the end of his long stint as the slimy Count, Christopher Lee might have pondered the same question. In his witty autobiography *Tall, Dark and Gruesome*, Lee describes how, after fifteen years, he finally ditched the famous cloak: 'The deciding factors were *Dracula AD 1972* [1972, Alan Gibson] and *The Satanic Rites of Dracula* [1973, Alan Gibson]. The former had certain things in its favour, but with the other one . . . I reached my irrevocable full stop.'

Before Dracula, Lee had spent a long time getting nowhere in particular, often as a swarthy villain or silver-tongued 'heavy' for visiting American stars. He was a Spanish man-of-war captain outgunned by a sober Gregory Peck in *Captain Horatio Hornblower* (1951, Raoul Walsh), and aide-de-camp to a wily baron in *The Crimson Pirate* (1952, Robert Siodmak) with Burt Lancaster – Lee describes the film as a 'Boys Own Paper adventure'. He was a lesser painter to José Ferrer's Toulouse-Lautrec in *Moulin Rouge* (1953, John Huston), co-billed for the first time with Peter Cushing, both tucked away out of sight at the tail-end of the credits. He was another artist, wrongly suspected of murder in *Port Afrique* (1956, Rudolph Maté) with Phil Carey, an American B-movie actor, and in *Beyond Mombasa* (1956, George Marshall), with Cornel Wilde, he had a minor role as a white hunter.

After ten years of filming, and still virtually unknown – although he scored well as a sadistic marquis in *A Tale of Two Cities* (1958, Ralph Thomas) with Dirk Bogarde – Lee must have been glad to sink his teeth into Dracula in 1957.

His refined sexuality and expensive-claret bedside manner explained a lot to those of us who grew up on the Lugosi version and could never understand why all those ladies succumbed so willingly to old Door-Knocker Face. In a poor light Lee could be almost dishy and his cultured bark went every bit as deep as that double-pronged bite – a factor, incidentally, central to the spirit of Bram Stoker's original.

That dishiness needed to be toned down for many of the villainous roles, for Lee on his home ground had enough breeding and charm to make the standard hero look legless. In *The Curse of Frankenstein* (1957, Terence Fisher), he was totally unrecognisable as the knobbly creature created in an eerie laboratory by Peter Cushing. They cemented his eyes at the corners to make him inscrutable in *Terror of the Tongs* (1961, Anthony Bushell), in which he was headman of a murderous Chinese secret society. In *The Face of Fu Manchu* (1965, Don Sharp) he was slant-eyed again, and in *The Mummy* (1959, Terence Fisher) he was draped in rolls of frayed, centuries-old bandage, but the film was scarcely a patch on the 1932 Boris Karloff version.

Lee has not always been a villain. In *The Man Who Could Cheat Death* (1959, Terence Fisher), a modest shocker with suggestions of Dorian Gray, he was a doctor colleague of Anton Diffring, alerted to the danger in their midst by recognising the root cause of Diffring's odd behaviour.

'It's not your life you're risking – it's your very soul,' Lee warns Leon Greene in *The Devil Rides Out* (1968, Terence Fisher), as the latter plans to spook a coven at which the devil himself

Christopher Lee as the evil Marquis de St Evremonde in Dickens' *A Tale of Two Cities* (1958), a useful role on his long climb to stardom

has just put in a brief personal appearance. Their objective is to snatch their friend Patrick Mower from the horny clutches of satanic high priest Charles Gray, before Mower is forcibly enrolled as a full member of the club. Gray makes a formidable arch-villain, in a part that might otherwise have been tailored for Lee. The highlight of this neatly composed occult drama, a prolonged duel between the two cultured protagonists, during which Gray throws everything but coffin nails at Lee and his unnerved companions, contains the suggestion of real menace, rare in a Hammer offering.

Christopher Lee

b. 1922. One-time formula villain ideally equipped for Hammer horror pics. A competent, seductive, technicolour Dracula, Fu Manchu, etc. Film debut: *Corridor of Mirrors* (1947). Moved to Hollywood in 1975.

1947 *Corridor of Mirrors* (Charles)
1948 *Scott of the Antarctic* (Bernard Day)

Hamlet (uncredited)
One Night with You (uncredited)
Penny and the Pownall Case (Jonathan Blair)
A Song for Tomorrow (Auguste)
Saraband for Dead Lovers (uncredited)
My Brother's Keeper (uncredited)
1949 *Trottie True* (uncredited)
1950 *Prelude to Fame* (uncredited)
They Were Not Divided (Lewis)
1951 *Captain Horatio Hornblower* (Spanish galleon captain)
Valley of the Eagles (Detective)
1952 *Paul Temple Returns* (Sir Felix Reybourne)
The Crimson Pirate (uncredited)
Top Secret (uncredited)
1953 *Innocents in Paris* (uncredited)
Moulin Rouge (uncredited)
1954 *The Dark Avenger* (uncredited)
1955 *That Lady* (Captain)
Storm Over the Nile (Karaga Pasha)
Cockleshell Heroes (uncredited)
Private's Progress (German Officer)

1956 *Port Afrique* (Franz Vermes)
Beyond Mombasa (Gil Rossi)
Battle of the River Plate (Manola)
Moby Dick (uncredited)
Alias John Preston (John Preston)
1957 *Fortune Is a Woman* (Charles Highbury)
The Curse of Frankenstein (The Creature)
Bitter Victory (Sgt Barney)
Ill Met by Moonlight (uncredited)
1958 *A Tale of Two Cities* (Marquis St Evremonde)
The Truth About Women (François)
Battle of the VI (Brunner)
Dracula (Count Dracula)
Corridors of Blood (Resurrection Joe)
1959 *The Hound of the Baskervilles* (Sir Henry Baskerville)
The Man Who Could Cheat Death (Dr Pierre Gerard)
The Mummy (Kharis)
Treasure of San Teresa (Jaeger)
1960 *The City of the Dead* (Professor Driscoll)
Too Hot to Handle (Novak)
Beat Girl (Kenny)
The Two Faces of Doctor Jekyll (Paul Allen)
The Hands of Orlac (Nero)
1961 *Taste of Fear* (Dr Gerrard)
Terror of the Tongs (Chung King)
1962 *Devil's Daffodil* (Ling Chu)
The Pirates of Blood River (La Roche)
The Devil's Agent (Baron Von Staub)
1964 *The Devil-Ship Pirates* (Capt Robeles)
The Gorgon (Prof Carl Meister)
Dr Terror's House of Horrors (Franklyn Marsh)
1965 *She* (Billali)
The Face of Fu Manchu (Fu Manchu)
The Skull (Sir Matthew Phillips)
Dracula – Prince of Darkness (Count Dracula)
Rasputin the Mad Monk (Rasputin)
1966 *Circus of Fear* (Gregor)
Theatre of Death (Phillipe Darvas)
The Brides of Fu Manchu (Fu Manchu)
1967 *Five Golden Dragons* (Dragon)
Night of the Big Heat (Hanson)
Vengeance of Fu Manchu (Fu Manchu)
1968 *The Devil Rides Out* (Duc de Richleau)
The Face of Eve (Colonel Stuart)
Curse of the Crimson Altar (J. D. Morley)
The Blood of Fu Manchu (Fu Manchu)
Dracula Has Risen from the Grave (Count Dracula)

Christopher Lee watches fellow actors go through their paces in the grounds of Pinewood Studios during outdoor scenes for *Nothing But the Night* (1972) in which he co-starred with long-time Hammer colleague Peter Cushing

The Castle of Fu Manchu (Fu Manchu)
1969 *The Oblong Box* (Dr Neuhartt)
The Magic Christian (Dracula)
Scream and Scream Again (Fremont)
1970 *Julius Caesar* (Artemidorus)
Taste the Blood of Dracula (Count Dracula)
The Private Life of Sherlock Holmes (Mycroft Holmes)
The Scars of Dracula (Count Dracula)
The Crimson Cult (Morley)
The House that Dripped Blood (John Reid)
I, Monster (Marlowe)
1971 *Hannie Caulder* (Bailey)
1972 *The Creeping Flesh* (James Hildern)
Dracula AD 1972 (Dracula)
Deathline (Stratton-Villiers)
Nothing But the Night (Colonel Bingham)
1973 *The Satanic Rites of Dracula* (Count Dracula)
The Three Musketeers (Rochefort)
The Wicker Man (Lord Summerisle)
Island of the Burning Damned (Hanson)
The Creeping Flesh (James)
Raw Heat (Stratton-Villers)

1974 *Diagnosis: Murder* (Dr Stephen Hayward)
   Horror Express (Prof Alex Saxton)
   The Four Musketeers (Revenge of Milady) (Rochefort)
   The Man with the Golden Gun (Scaramanga)
   Dark Places (Dr Ian Mandeville)
1975 *To The Devil a Daughter* (Fr Michael Rayner)
   Killer Force (USA) (Chilton)
   The Diamond Mercenaries (Major Chilton)
   The Keeper (uncredited)
   Whispering Death (uncredited)
1976 *Airport 77* (Martin Wallace)

   Alien Encounter (uncredited)
1978 *End of the World* (Father Pergado)
   How the West Was Won (Grand Duke)
   Return from Witch Mountains (Dr Victor Gamon)
   Caravans (Sardar Khan)
   The Silent Flute (Zetan)
   The Passage (Gypsy)
   Jaguar Lives (Adam Caine)
   Arabian Adventure (Alquazar)
   Bear Island (Prof Lechinski)
1980 *The Salamander* (uncredited)
   Once Upon a Spy (uncredited)
1981 *1941* (Captain von Kleinschmidt)

Herbert Lom

'It's better I die a fool trusting too much than die a tyrant trusting no-one,' declares Mexican president Alexander Knox in *Villa Rides* (1968, Buzz Kulik) shortly before Herbert Lom takes him at his word and bumps him off. Lom has no such finer feelings – he simply wants to rule Mexico. It was a small part but typical of Lom, quiet determination and a kind of controlled ruthlessness made it seem a lot more.

Ever since *Dual Alibi* (1947, Albert Travers), in which he played a trapeze artist who commits murder to recoup a stolen lottery ticket and then tries to implicate his twin brother, Lom's suave cultured voice and swarthy looks have had a special place in British movie villainy. The Lom 'heavy' was no ordinary thug, though. He was always a cut above the rest, an accomplished smoothie in white tuxedo plus carnation and an ornate cigarette holder clamped between pearly teeth. He was more attuned in style to American film noir master crooks – Otto Kruger and Morris Karnovsky types – than the home-grown variety, helped like Kruger and Karnovsky had been by the suggestion of well-heeled mid-European origins.

In *Night and the City* (1950, Jules Dassin), an atmospheric but unremittingly gloomy thriller set in London's sleazier locales – and filmed on location by Jules Dassin, a pioneer in urban location work – Lom and Francis L. Sullivan are rival wrestling promoters conned by small-time crook Richard Widmark, who is having an affair with Sullivan's wife, Googie Withers. The pursuit and eventual killing of Widmark for breaching the criminal code is evocatively captured through the deserted alleys and swirling mists of early morning Thames-side – the chase itself recalling the climax of Dassin's earlier *Naked City* (1949) filmed on the streets of New York.

Lom was one of the thieves in *The Ladykillers* (1955, Alexander Mackendrick), the swarthy one opposed to involving their boarding-house landlady in the bank roll snatch because he happens to dislike old ladies. But he loses the vote and she, unknowingly, becomes their accomplice. The heist is successful but afterwards the gang dispose of each other instead of their considerable hoard. Lom is killed by gang boss Alec Guinness, who prises loose the metal staircase overhanging a railway line along which Lom hopes to make his escape. Instead, trapped like a fly in a web, Lom can only watch bemusedly as Guinness levers him into the path of an oncoming locomotive.

In the third, and generally considered worst remake of *Phantom of the Opera* (1962, Terence Fisher) Lom was the disfigured composer pounding out rhapsodies on his mighty Wurlitzer amid the bowels of the Opera House to the amusement of his idiot dwarf companion. His disfigurement, concealed behind a grey mask that leaves only one shifty eye visible, is the result of an accident with nitric acid which occurred while Lom was revenging the stealing of his best compositions by unscrupulous music publisher Michael Gough. Lom, a tragic mole-like figure, is determined to hear his opera sung beautifully, and to achieve this abducts leading soprano

Heather Sears whom he then tirelessly coaches to the required degree of perfection.

He was a gangster in *No Trees in the Street* (1959, J. Lee-Thompson) whom Sylvia Sims marries in order to escape her slum surroundings – a genuine leap from the frying pan. In *Frightened City* (1961, John Lemont), a dreary, 'clean-up Soho' melodrama, Lom was a mysterious master crook who moulds half-a-dozen grubby Soho gangs into a profitable strong-arm syndicate, but finishes up skewered on the end of a nasty tribal ornament like an underdone kebab. He was a surly mountaineer in *Third Man on the Mountain* (1959, Ken Annakin), a typical slice of Disney heroics in which, to writer James Ullman's eternal shame, a character actually says 'a man must do what he feels he must do'.

Lom has an undeniable flair for comedy, sadly suppressed in an overwhelmingly sombre career, but used to good effect as police commissioner to Peter Sellers' Inspector Clouseau in the Pink Panther series. In *A Shot in the Dark* (1964, Blake Edwards) Sellers' dogged insistence that sexy housemaid Elke Sommer is innocent of murder, a view which Lom does not share, nearly drives him bananas. To bolster sanity, Lom arranges for Sellers – whose sleuthing talent he believes 'has put the science of criminal investigation back a thousand years' – to be transferred to the records office in far-off Martinique. This leads to a heated confrontation between them, with Sellers complaining that he is being victimised for personal reasons. 'Yes, deeply personal,' shrieks Lom, 'I hate you, every little bit of you!'

Herbert Lom

b. 1917. Cultured Czech-born actor, notable for suave unruffled top-drawer villains with occasional comedy – *The Ladykillers* (1955), *Pink Panther* series (1964-77). Has worked in Europe and Hollywood as well as Britain. Film debut: *Mein Kampf, My Crimes* (1939). Won TV popularity during 1960s as Harley Street psychiatrist in *The Human Jungle*.

Herbert Lom shows Phyllis Calvert the world in *The Net* (1953)

1945 *The Seventh Veil* (Dr Larsen)
1946 *Night Boat to Dublin* (Keitel)
      Appointment with Crime (Gregory Lang)
1947 *Dual Alibi* (Jules/Georges de Lisle)
1948 *Snowbound* (Keramikos)
      Good Time Girl (Max)
      Portrait from Life (Hendlemann)
      Lucky Mascot (Peter Hobart)
      The Lost People (uncredited)
1950 *Golden Salamander* (Rankl)
      Night and the City (Aristotle Kristo)
      State Secret (Theodor)
      The Black Rose (Aanemus)
      Cage of Gold (Rahman)
1951 *Hell Is Sold Out* (Dominic Danger)
      Two on the Tiles (Ford)
      Mr Denning Drives North (Mados)
1952 *Whispering Smith Hits London* (Ford)
      The Ringer (Maurice Meister)
1953 *The Net* (Alex Leon)
      The Man Who Watched Trains Go By
        (Julius de Koster)
      Rough Shoot (Peter Sandorski)
1954 *The Love Lottery* (Amico)
      Star of India (Vicomte de Narbonne)
      Beautiful Stranger (Emile Landosh)
1955 *The Ladykillers* (Louis)
1956 *War And Peace* (USA) (Napoleon)
1957 *Fire Down Below* (François the harbour
        master)
      Hell Drivers (Gino)
      Action of the Tiger (Trifon)
1958 *Chase a Crooked Shadow* (Inspector
        Vargas)
      I Accuse (Major du Paty de Clam)
      Intent to Kill (Juan Menda)
1959 *Passport to Shame* (Nick)
      No Trees in the Streets (Wilkie)

Herbert Lom (right) weighs up the opposition in *North West Frontier* (1959) an adventure yarn set in India in the days of the Raj

Malcolm McDowell

In *Aces High* (1976, Jack Gold), timed around the start of World War I, Malcolm McDowell is Peter Firth's house-captain at a posh public school. Firth's hero-worship is so intense that he follows him into the Royal Flying Corps requesting to be posted to the small battle station in France which McDowell commands. The latter is unsettled by Firth's arrival, 'I'm his bloody hero . . . how long can it go on for?' he groans – and there's a good reason. Far from being the Biggles-type daredevil which Firth imagines, McDowell is a heavy drinker and utterly sick of the war, which has inflicted heavy losses on his unit.

Simon Ward played another pilot who boozes all hours to keep his spirits up – unsuccessfully, it seems, since the thought of coming up against even the weediest German, never mind the Red Baron, gives him the jitters. All this is a crushing letdown for the new lad who imagined, after all that propaganda laid on him at school, that our honour in the sky was being defended more stylishly.

Despite an immense disparity in style, *Aces High* looks in places like a Great War version of *The Way to the Stars* (1944), with Firth in the John Mills role of the bushy-tailed new flyer who is aged rapidly by the stress of staying alive. McDowell is excellent as his demoralised senior officer.

He is perhaps most vividly associated with the role of the Establishment's arch-enemy, the sadistic Droog leader in *A Clockwork Orange* (1971, Stanley Kubrick), a futuristic nightmare set incongruously in places to music – remember the superbly choreographed gang-fight which owes more to a 1930s Busby Berkeley musical than any blood-letting Peckinpah ever influenced. Droogs are monsters in natty bowler hats, the ultimate gesture against organised society, who consider murder and rape in much the way Vikings did, that's to say, pleasant everyday diversions. Outraged authorities inflict on McDowell therapy that is every bit as loathsome as his original crimes, hoping thereby to reverse his criminal tendencies.

Made before mass unemployment really hit the young, but accurately anticipating it – the cool young thug and his cronies idle their time in subterranean joints before emerging for the next raid – *A Clockwork Orange* depicts a society scrambling down the tube. If it's intended as a glimpse of the future, one can only hope tomorrow never comes. Or at least, when it does, that it's not quite as disjointed or hysterical as Kubrick's vision of it.

As has happened in a few other films by Kubrick, the visual content here is not matched by any real emotional contact with the central characters. With the awfulness of his life at home, where he is a virtual stranger, and the corresponding rottenness of the authorities, one should be able to feel a measure of sympathy for McDowell along with the outrage that his behaviour arouses. In fact, there is nothing, and one is left at the end with the impression of having watched a parade of elegantly-styled tableaux from around the year 2001 (naturally), strong on pictorial impact but, alas, with no more sociological relevance than *Jason and the Argonauts*.

Playing two paraplegics who fall in love in *The Raging Moon* (1970, Bryan Forbes), McDowell as the sportsman crocked by a freak accident, and Nanette Newman, dying as prettily and as discreetly as any thirties heroine ever did, are individually superb – though if they went out in their wheelchairs jangling collection boxes I suspect they would get nowhere, for they both look far too healthy to be preying on our sympathies. But in this mellow and heart-warming film, stir our sympathies is exactly what they do, and with plenty of effect.

Bryan Forbes' lush evocative camera style, and a sometimes over-deliberate soundtrack score, imply a coyness which, thankfully, McDowell's explosive, despairing performance never allows to settle. The problems – practical as well as emotional – facing paraplegics who plan to marry are turned over in Forbes' customary skilful and literate manner. The consistently radiant Miss Newman has never looked lovelier nor McDowell's fiery temper sounded more justified than in the climactic scene when he struggles, after being told that she has died, to come to terms with the second tragedy to swamp him within so short a time.

McDowell made two important innovative films for Memorial Enterprises, *If . . .* (1968, Lindsay Anderson) and *O Lucky Man!* (1973, Lindsay Anderson). *If. . .*, like the Kubrick film, offers a jaundiced view of modern society, here characterised as a posh public school run by sadists and bigots. McDowell, a rebellious pupil uncowed by the Establishment's harsh attempts to subvert his individuality, retaliates on the whole crazy, archaic system with bombs and mortars. Anderson brilliantly uses a traditionally English setting, complete with its dotty, outmoded customs, mindless tutorial platitudes and bullying prefects, as an allegorical equivalent of what passes for life in industrial Britain today. You can interpret how you like the different levels at work – or mostly in conflict – within the school. At a guess, the weak vacillating teachers represent modern-day management and the prefects, a powerful, self-appointed group of cads and bullies who get away with holding the school (ie the rest of us) to ransom by defending their actions as a traditional right and therefore, in some uniquely English way, entirely legitimate and untouchable – these might be a Tory diehard's view of the hypocrisy of modern trade unionism. McDowell is, again, excellent as the self-contained Mick, in a film which has come to be regarded as a milestone of the 1960s.

O Lucky Man! was another courageous though considerably less successful attempt to convey a similar disenchantment with society of the 1970s. Its style was more ambiguous, and its narrative intermittently confusing, yet the mood of anger and dissatisfaction at the way society functions – expressed by McDowell's contemporary pilgrim progressing from the back seat of an impoverished pop group's converted bus to a seat in a big company's boardroom, and onwards again at nearly the speed of light – was articulately expressed. Nevertheless, the loose-limbed construction of the film, in avoiding a followable story-line, drew accusations of self-indulgence. But to grizzle about lack of plausibility in a film which is itself a protest against the implausibility of real life seems somehow, to me, to miss the whole point.

Slapstick comedy has not been an obvious forte of McDowell's, due to the line-up of sullen, rather intense characterisations he has worked on

Malcolm McDowell and Nanette Newman in a tender moment from *The Raging Moon* (1970)

almost consistently since his first big film, *If . . .* (1968). *Royal Flash* (1975, Richard Lester) changed that, dare one say, in a blinding flash. McDowell was a Zenda-esque monarch with a cocky near-lookalike who is used to fool his enemies into believing he is a lot smarter than he really is. It's all splendid hokum, and McDowell as both king and unwilling impersonator, Alan Bates as a Svengali-like hatcher of dangerous plots – dangerous for McDowell, that is – and Oliver Reed as the bullying rascal for whom it is all being staged, enjoy themselves hugely. Calling it a good film may be an exaggeration, though its infectious knockabout style plus the few hearty chuckles up the sleeve which it snatches at the expense of the old-style swashbuckler genre, make it a pleasant enough analgesic.

McDowell is unmistakably English in looks and, one suspects, temperament, so when he turns up as someone called Max Gunther in *Voyage of the Damned* (1976, Sam Wanamaker) and Captain Von Berkow in *The Passage* (1978, J. L. Thompson), you begin to wonder what's going on. The biggest surprise of recent times was his appearance as the Roman emperor of the title in *Caligula* (1980, Tinto Brass), a mediocre skin-flick financed by *Penthouse,* savaged by the critics and disowned by practically everyone who appeared in it, including McDowell. Compared with *If . . .* and *The Raging Moon,* it scarcely bears thinking about.

Malcolm McDowell

b. 1944. New-wave 'rebel' actor, sprang to fame as public school revolutionary in *If . . .* (1968) and sadistic yobbo in *A Clockwork Orange* (1971). Especially adept at playing tough, smug characters with concealed sensitivities, as for example, the crippled romantic in *The Raging Moon* (1970) and the disillusioned combat flyer-commander in *Aces High* (1976). Married to American actress Mary Steenberger.

1968 *If . . .* (Mick)
1970 *The Raging Moon* (Bruce Pritchard)
      Figures in a Landscape
1971 *A Clockwork Orange* (Alex DeLarge)
1973 *O Lucky Man!* (Mick Travis)
1975 *Royal Flash* (Capt Harry Flashman)
1976 *Aces High* (Major John Gresham)
      Voyage of the Damned (Max Gunther)
1978 *The Passage* (Capt Von Berkow)
1980 *Caligula* (Caligula)

James Mason

There was a time when James Mason's foot on the stairs brought shivers to the lady upstairs, cowering under a bedsheet. Now it's more likely to mean he's sloping off for a quiet forty winks. The passing of years has mellowed the dark jowled brute into an agreeable pensioner; it's hard to imagine him, as *Time* magazine once described him: '. . . swaggering through the title role, barking like Gable and frowning like Laurence Olivier on a dark night . . .'

That was how the critics reacted to him – and audiences even more so – in *The Man in Grey* (1945, Leslie Arliss), during that period when he and Stewart Granger were to the British costume epic what cheese and tomato are to the pizza. Of the two, Granger was more athletic, but Mason's emotional register was always more than Granger could handle.

Audiences had a chance to compare their styles in *The Prisoner of Zenda* (1952, Richard Thorpe), where Granger was both the rightful king and the 'ordinary' Englishman who impersonates him so that the monarchy remains in safe hands. Mason is on the side of the king's rascally half-brother who schemes to usurp the throne. In his sky-blue tunic, gold epaulettes, black thigh-boots and slicked down hair, Mason sneers his way through all the speakable lines while Granger's fixed pearly smile reminds you of a jewellers' display window – and is just as boring to have to peer into for an hour or more. Luckily, Mason is on hand to ease the tedium.

There's a rattling good sword fight between the two near the end but even here, on Granger's home ground, Mason savours the initiative, turning their duel into a frivolous lesson in etiquette. 'I can't get used to fighting with furniture,' Mason tut-tuts as his more nimble adversary dodges behind the umpteenth oak table. With the loyal Ruritanian cavalry thundering over the castle drawbridge intent on wresting the rightful monarch from his evil clutches,

James Mason in his most famous role of the 1940s, the dying fugitive in *Odd Man Out* (1946), seen here with F. J. MacCormack (left)

Mason suddenly remembers he has urgent business elsewhere and leaps into the moat. Granger, not surprisingly, is cut up more by his arch-enemy's abrupt departure than by his swordsmanship, which is a trifle crude to quoth the least.

Mason's appeal, during the days when fashionable young ladies bit their nails nervously at the mention of his name, centred on an ability to curl his lip in anger like a Doberman sensing an intruder's meaty ankle. He could also be downright cruel, as for instance in beating Phyllis Calvert to death and taking a horsewhip to Britain's best loved heroine Margaret Lockwood – he did both in *The Man in Grey*. Any other actor attempting such beastliness to two nationally admired beauties would have prompted questions in the House, but for Mason it was thought an average day's work. The actor himself shrugs off the mean-and-moody tag which put him among the top ten world stars of the 1940s.

'My face falls naturally into a scowl,' he says. It still does, and the marble eyes and cat's-purr voice have not changed much either. Nowadays, he's been known to recite psalms on TV's *Stars on Sunday*. The Man in Grey must be rotating in his grave.

It's a fair estimate of the man's impact in the early days to say that Mason was both admired and hated for himself. He has never resorted to extravagantly made-up characters – the face and the blemishes on view were mostly his own. He prefers it that way, acknowledging perhaps the inevitable; as soon as audiences cottoned on to the fact that it was Mason lurking under the paint and the wigs, the elaborate paraphernalia of disguise would be meaningless.

A Place of One's Own (1945, Bernard Knowles) illustrated the point. Mason played a retired Victorian businessman who buys a haunted country house. Here, the sourness gives way to bafflement – his own no less acute than that of the audience, who had expected at least a minor act of defilement, particularly since Margaret Lockwood – so recently abused by him in *The Man in Grey*, also appeared. He was concert pianist Ann Todd's bullying lover in *The Seventh Veil* (1945, Compton Bennett), boorish enough to restore the fans' faith, and came to a ropey end as a highwayman in *The Wicked Lady* (1945, Leslie Arliss), again with Margaret Lockwood, whom on this excursion he merely half-strangles and rapes.

Odd Man Out (1946, Carol Reed) was an important film of the 1940s. Mason played a dying Republican fugitive, shot during a hold-up, whose movements are eloquently photographed against grim, snow-covered Belfast streets as he tries desperately to shake off the police. Reunited with his faithful girlfriend, he dies with her in a hail of police bullets.

Though a contemporary British situation was used as the basis of *Odd Man Out*, its theme – of a fugitive getting his rightful deserts – had been hugely popular in America since escaped convict Humphrey Bogart had held up a roadside café in *The Petrified Forest* (1936). On the strength of his performance in *Odd Man Out*, Mason was invited to Hollywood. He accepted, pausing only to round up his cats and his family, and deliver a disparaging sermon on the state of the British film industry, accusing Rank of having 'no apparent talent for the cinema or showmanship'.

Mason attributes his outburst, which was seen at the time as a classic case of snarling at the hand which loyally fed him during those early years, as genuine frustration at the monolithic structure of the industry, and anger at the way that so many in the business who had coldly ignored him when he tried to get started were thrusting their unwanted attentions on him as soon as he became box-office.

'Suddenly all these doors that had previously been slammed in my face were opened wide. I resented them, I was still the same young actor to whom the same people had been giving the brush-off,' he says.

His early Hollywood films – 'my first five were total flops'– must have caused him to regret those harsh words about the Rank Organisation, though always he lent depth and dignity to his performances, as, for example, in *Pandora and the Flying Dutchman* (1950, Albert Lewin), in which he was the mysterious Dutchman doomed to sail the seas endlessly until the love of a mortal woman frees him. Ava Gardner was the beautiful woman who provides this valuable service.

Mason's first two American roles of note – as Field Marshal Rommel in *Rommel, Desert Fox* (1951, Henry Hathaway), and World War II's notorious double agent Cicero in *Five Fingers* (1952, Joseph L. Mankiewicz) – drew critical broadsides, not because of his performances which were rivetingly good, but because in both cases the characters expressed strong anti-British sentiments which, after Mason's departing outbursts, were thought to mirror his own.

He was Brutus in *Julius Caesar* (1953, Joseph Mankiewicz), a performance brimming with richness and subtlety, the only one of a distinguished line-up to give Brando a run for his money.

The Man Between (1953, Carol Reed) was Reed's near-miss attempt to amalgamate the themes of *Odd Man Out* and *The Third Man* in an authentic post-war Berlin setting – note even the close similarity (eg repeated use of the word 'man') in the titles. Mason was a ruthless agent working the free zones of the city, helping the Communists to pick off their enemies. He is on the trail of a big fish when he falls in love with Claire Bloom, a British visitor. When Miss Bloom becomes an innocent pawn in the tense political game to make sure Mason honours his agreements with the East, the spy deceives his 'protectors' and organises a daring attempt to whisk her, concealed in a truck, past the armed Communist border guards. But the guards haul him out for questioning, and he dies ensuring her getaway.

In *Botany Bay* (1952, John Farrow) he was a rascally ship's captain ferrying a bunch of convicts to a penal colony in Australia – assisted passages 18th-century style. Alan Ladd was a medical student wrongfully sentenced for being a highwayman – proof of his innocence is on its way before the ship sails, but Mason refuses to delay departure. Most of the film focuses on the clash of wills between the coldly unyielding victim and his sadistic tormentor, with Patricia Medina as a voluptuous thief who stokes the passions of both men.

'So that's how it all ends – not with a bang but with a whimper!' sighs acerbic press agent Jack Carson when he learns that Mason, a faded movie star, has drowned himself at the climax of *A Star Is Born* (1954, George Cukor). Mason's performance as a washed-up matinée idol clinging to a remaining morsel of self-respect neatly charts the pain and devastation of post-stardom

131

oblivion, a condition made more acute by the sudden acclaim of his own discovery, played by Judy Garland, whom he also marries. The seesaw misfortunes of screen notables, passing each other on the way up and down, had been depicted before, but never with quite the same power, which derives in no small way from the restrained playing of the two stars, Mason most noticeably.

In *20,000 Leagues Under The Sea* (1954, Richard Fleischer) Mason was the vengeful Captain Nemo, captain of a Victorian submarine whose interior decor might have been done by the same firm which kitted out the Orient Express. The stars were Kirk Douglas and a lethargic giant squid. At one point Douglas snatches up a concertina and begins to sing, whereupon the squid, quite understandably, turns nasty and begins to crush people.

North By Northwest (1959, Alfred Hitchcock) begins with the kidnapping of adman Cary Grant by superspy James Mason's minders, during which the victim insists he is someone else. When Grant refuses to co-operate, Mason has him pickled in bourbon and put behind the steering wheel of a car which is then accelerated down a steep hill. Grant survives, but his explanation to the perplexed police chief looks less and less convincing when his version of what has happened is contradicted at every turn by the facts that emerge. Apart from several visual goodies, like Grant being chased by deadly cropspraying aeroplanes, and the climactic scramble down Mount Rushmore, this is run-of-the-mill Hitchcock. You know before he starts that Grant's attempts to verify his story of the kidnapping and subsequent misfortunes will lead everyone into ever-diminishing circles, and that Mason's sexy blonde accomplice is most likely a Federal agent. The plot strongly resembles an earlier Hitchcock thriller, *Thirty-Nine Steps* (1935), from John Buchan's story, in which an innocent man, Robert Donat, is pursued by both a deadly spy ring and the police. Both films imaginatively use the countryside and photogenic man-made structures to accelerate the tension, although in the earlier film clumsy back projection robs its key scene, the hunted man hanging on to the outside of a railway compartment as it speeds across the Forth Bridge, of much of its desired impact.

The spy business is eloquently spoofed in *A Touch of Larceny* (1959, Guy Hamilton), a British-made comedy thriller about an Admiralty chief who deceives his Whitehall bosses into believing he has defected to Russia with a top drawerful of state secrets. The point of this deception is to enable him to sue his accusers for defamation and thus make some quick money after he returns home from what appears to have been an innocent shipwreck off a remote Scottish island. Mason wants more than a good financial return for his cheeky scheme, he wants revenge on the system, and the neat, tongue-in-cheek way it's accomplished, in company with that other velvet-voiced master of the stylish put-down, George Sanders, gives this lightweight caper a real touch of class.

In *The Pumpkin Eater* (1964, Jack Clayton), Mason and Peter Finch played one-time buddies turned enemies when movie-writer Finch puts Mason's soft-touch actress wife, played by Janine Gray, in the family way after a brief affair on a film set. This, plus Mason's sly longing for Finch's wife, played by Anne Bancroft, makes for a highly charged 'ménage à quatre' situation, and Harold Pinter's dialogue, based on the novel by Penelope Mortimer, makes the most of these dramatic possibilities.

Exciting air battles dominate *The Blue Max* (1966, John Guillermin), set during World War I. Mason played a German brasshat whose nephew – Jeremy Kemp – is only a few 'kills' short of winning the coveted Blue Max medal for outstanding bravery in dog-fights with the British Royal Flying Corps. The film's strengths are in its aerial combat scenes, dramatically realised by Douglas Slocombe's cameras, James Mason's brief appearance as the ruthless air chief, and Kemp's dandyish pilot officer.

Mason had a good part in *Spring and Port Wine* (1970, Peter Hammond) as a narrow old codger living in the past, unwilling to accept his children's adulthood. His attempts to browbeat wilful daughter Susan George into eating her teatime herrings, by producing the refused items at every meal, spark off a storm in an ale-jar. The formerly tightknit family discovers they are not as tight as they imagined, and for Mason the ultimate realisation that he's living in an age he doesn't understand, is both realistically and movingly captured in Norman Warwick's photography and writer Bill Naughton's ear-to-the-wall dialogue.

In *Eleven Harrowhouse* (1974, Aram Aviakan), a stylish comedy-thriller, Mason is another ordinary little man, a disaffected long-service employee of a powerful diamond syndicate who becomes the inside man in a daring robbery. He throws in his lot with the thieves as a dying gesture – he knows he has not long to live – against the firm which he avows has treated him shabbily. Mission accomplished he contentedly rolls over, thereby denying his irate bosses the satisfaction of putting in the boot. Mason's roles of late have sadly lacked the riveting malevolence of bygone times, which is a dreadful loss to the OAS – the Order of Aging Scoundrels.

A 1980 US television movie *Salem's Lot* gave rise for hope. Mason was an art-dealer in a quiet Mid-west town who pimps for the neighbourhood vampire, a diabolical vision straight out of Nosferatu. People vanish mysteriously, and then pop up again minus their haemoglobin. The story is too contrived and hysterical to make a lot of sense, but Mason's presence as the smooth villain earns it a few extra gongs. In the end it takes a full cylinder of bullets to finish off Mason, who simply will not lie down while there is one more evil twitch left. The Man in Grey would appreciate that.

James Mason, 1962

James Mason
b. 1909. Moody rascal of the 1940s who departed to Hollywood at the height of his fame (1948) and there broadened into a competent character star, with lingering emphasis on smooth, effortless villainy, viz the treacherous Rupert in *The Prisoner of Zenda* (1952), the enemy agent in *North by Northwest* (1959). Among his best roles were the fugitive in *Odd Man Out* (1946), the tragic Humbert in *Lolita* (1962), and the gruff North Country father in *Spring and Port Wine* (1971). Formerly married to actress (later US TV chat-show hostess and sometime textile tycoon) Pamela Kellino.

1935 *Late Extra*
1936 *Twice Branded*
      Troubled Waters
      Prison Breaker
      Blind Man's Buff
      Secret of Stamboul
1937 *The Mill on the Floss*
      Fire Over England
      The High Command
      Catch As Catch Can
      The Return of the Scarlet Pimpernel
1939 *I Met a Murderer*
1941 *This Man Is Dangerous*
      Hatter's Castle
1942 *The Night Has Eyes*

      Alibi
      Secret Mission
      Thunder Rock
1943 *The Bells Go Down*
      The Man in Grey
      They Met in the Dark
      Candlelight in Algeria
1944 *Fanny by Gaslight*
      Hotel Reserve
1945 *They Were Sisters* (Geoffrey)
      A Place of One's Own (Mr Smedhurst)
      The Seventh Veil (Nicholas)
      The Wicked Lady (Capt Jerry Jackson)
1946 *Odd Man Out* (Johnny)
1947 *The Upturned Glass* (Michael Joyce)
1949 *Caught* (USA) (Larry Quinada)
      Madame Bovary (USA) (Gustave Flaubert)
      The Reckless Moment (USA) (Martin Donnelly)
      East Side, West Side (USA) (Brandon Bourne)
1950 *One Way Street* (USA) (Doc Matson)
      Pandora and the Flying Dutchman (Hendrick Van Der Zee)
1951 *Rommel, Desert Fox* (USA) (Field Marshal Rommel)
1952 *Five Fingers* (USA) (Ulysses Diello – 'Cicero')
      The Lady Possessed (USA) (Del Palma)
      The Prisoner of Zenda (USA) (Rupert)

Face To Face (USA) (The Captain)
Botany Bay (USA) (Captain Paul Gilbert)
1953 The Desert Rats (USA) (Rommel)
Julius Caesar (USA) (Brutus)
The Story of Three Loves (USA) (Charles
   Contray)
The Man Between (Ivo Kern)
Charade (USA) (The Murderer, Major
   Linden, Jonah Watson)
1954 Prince Valiant (USA) (Sir Brack)
20,000 Leagues Under the Sea (Captain
   Nemo)
A Star Is Born (USA) (Norman Maine)
The Child (directed)
1956 Forever Darling (Guardian Angel)
Bigger Than Life (USA) (also prod)
   (Ed Avery)
1957 Island in the Sun (Maxwell Fleury)
1958 Cry Terror (USA) (Jim Molner)
The Decks Ran Red (USA) (Capt Edwin
   Rummell)
1959 North by Northwest (USA) (Phillip
   Vandamm)
Journey to the Centre of the Earth (USA)
   (Prof Oliver Lindenbrook)
A Touch of Larceny (Cmdr Max Easton)
1960 The Trials of Oscar Wilde (Sir Edward
   Carson)
1961 The Marriage-Go-Round (USA) (Paul
   Delville)
Escape from Bahrain (USA) (Johnson)
1962 Hero's Island (USA) (co-produced)
   (Jacob Webber)
Tiara Tahiti (Capt Brett Aimsley)
Lolita (Humbert Humbert)
1963 Torpedo Bay (Blayne)
1964 The Fall of the Roman Empire (USA)
   (Timonides)
The Pumpkin Eater (Bob Conway)
1965 Lord Jim (Gentleman Brown)
The Player Pianos (US title:

The Uninhibited) (Regnier)
Ghengis Khan (Kaun Ling)
1966 The Blue Max (Count Von Klugermann)
Georgy Girl (James Leamington)
The Deadly Affair (Charles Dobbs)
1967 Stranger in the House (John Sawyer)
1968 Duffy (Charles Calvert)
Mayerling (Emperor Franz-Josef)
Age of Consent (Australia) (Bradley
   Morahan) (also co-produced)
1969 The Seagull (Trigorin)
1970 Spring and Port Wine (Rafe Crompton)
Kill (Alan)
Cold Sweat (Ross)
1971 Bad Man's River (Montero)
1972 Child's Play (USA) (Jerome Malley)
1973 The Last of Sheila (USA) (Philip)
Frankenstein – The True Story (TV)
   (Dr Palidori)
The Mackintosh Man (Sir Geoffrey
   Wheeler)
1974 Eleven Harrowhouse (Watts)
The Marseille Contract (Jacques Brizard)
1975 Inside Out (Ernest Furben)
Great Expectations (Magwich)
Autobiography of a Princess (Cyril Sahib)
Mandingo (USA) (Warren Maxwell)
1976 Voyage of the Damned (Dr Juan Remos)
Jesus of Nazareth (TV) (Joseph of
   Arimathea)
The Waterbabies (Saul Grimes)
1977 Cross of Iron (Col Brandt)
Heaven Can Wait (Mr Jordan)
The Boys from Brazil (Edward Seibert)
The Passage (Prof John Bergson)
1978 Murder by Decree (Dr Watson)
Bloodline (Sir Alec Nichols)
1980 North Sea Hijack (Admiral Brinsden)
Evil Under the Sun (Odell Gardener)
Salem's Lot (TV) (Richard K. Straker)

Michael Medwin

'I've got some natural cunning,' says Michael Medwin, and anyone who remembers his artful juveniles in films of the 1950s will know what he means. But there was always something more to Medwin than those fizzy-lemonade figures he got branded with as a young actor. His range went far beyond that, but the face remained that of a Sixth Form japer. Twelve years after his screen

debut he was in a film called The Heart of a Man (1958, Herbert Wilcox), billed as Sid The Sausage, enough surely to strike terror into any ambitious actor. For Medwin, it was an experience among many which he reflects on today with good humour.

He made his screen debut in The Root of All Evil (1946, Brock Williams) and was one of The

A scene from the submarine drama *Above Us the Waves* (1955). Donald Sinden (centre) keeps an eye on the target while Michael Medwin plots their course and Harry Towb (left) steers

Courtneys of Curzon Street (1947, Herbert Wilcox). His unexpected break came in *Night Beat* (1948, Harold Huth) as a spiv. It wasn't that Medwin's part was significant, or the film any good, but it got a West End showing by a fluke – another film was withdrawn hurriedly and *Night Beat* was substituted. Medwin claims he was noticed because he was in it for such a short time, and therefore could not be blamed for any of its flaws. Yet he was written about, and made an impact.

By a curious stroke of luck, that same week *Anna Karenina* (1947, Alexander Korda) opened, with Medwin appearing briefly, and again earning press applause, as a bearded doctor. He survived the West End showings but the part vanished except for a mute shot of him when the film was shortened for general release. An actor crony who saw the film in the provinces – then, of course, shorn of Medwin's big scene – remembering the complimentary press notices, told him, 'With the greatest respect, old

man, your couple of seconds were hardly *that* good!'

In *Curtain Up* (1952, Ralph Smart) he was one of the actors rehearsing Margaret Rutherford's play under the exasperated direction of Robert Morley. He had another small part in *Genevieve* (1953, Henry Cornelius) as a flustered expectant father who flags down Kenneth More during his return journey race with John Gregson, an interruption which gains Gregson some valuable minutes. But it was *The Intruder* (1953, Guy Hamilton), with Medwin in the name part, which gave his career its biggest lift.

He played a Tank Corps veteran who becomes a petty thief and, quite by chance, burgles the house of his former Commanding Officer, played by Jack Hawkins, who catches him in the act and recognises him. Hawkins is sufficiently intrigued as to why a courageous and likable serviceman from his own unit should regress to criminality once out of uniform, to carry out his own investigations into Medwin's background and present

135

circumstances. What unfolds is a sad story of chaotic upbringing compounded by folly and bad luck more than real criminal intent. For Guy Hamilton it was a directional debut of considerable promise, though the narrative suffers by showing the working-class trooper's downfall through the eyes of a middle-class do-gooder. With anyone else but Jack Hawkins as the ex-commander, the strong reek of piety would have been scarcely tolerable. Medwin acquitted himself well as the mixed-up fugitive.

He made two films with Dirk Bogarde around this time – *Doctor at Sea* (1955, Ralph Thomas), second of the *Doctor* series, in which he played a randy officer on board a cruise ship, and *The Wind Cannot Read* (1958, Ralph Thomas), where he was a flight officer. He was in numerous war yarns, such as *Malta Story* (1953, Brian Desmond Hurst), again with Jack Hawkins; *Above Us the Waves* (1955, Ralph Thomas), most of which he spent cooped up inside a midget submarine; and *A Hill in Korea* (1956, Julian Amyes), a tough, realistic story about an Army platoon on manoeuvres in Korea, in which Medwin played an irrepressible Cockney conscript – the blueprint, one might imagine, for Medwin's most memorable creation, the crafty Corporal Springer in TV's long-running *The Army Game*.

Medwin denies any direct connection between the two characters, but the similarity is self-evident. The series made him a household name, and was transmitted 'live', something likely to unnerve today's generation of TV actors. Rarely have TV sitcoms looked and sounded so authentic, and as it coincided rather broadly with the tapering-off of National Service in Britain, an entire generation of earlier conscripts readily acknowledged its veracity. Others in the squad, like Alfie Bass's artful dodger, Norman Rossington's genial Scouse and Bernard Bresslaw's well-meaning dumb-head, all added colour to the Army Game, but Medwin, the foxy barrack-room wheeler-dealer, was its undisputed star.

The series was expanded into a single full-length film, *I Only Arsked* (1958, Montgomery Tully), the title taken from a recurring catchphrase of Bresslaw's, his customary defence every time one of his dumb questions was thrown back in his face. But the old gang were curiously off-form, as if canning the whole thing on film destroyed the chemistry between them.

In 1964, Medwin had a small role in *Night Must Fall* (1964, Karel Reisz), in which Albert Finney starred as a murderous psycopath. A year later, Medwin and Finney formed Memorial Enterprises, 'to make films as we wanted them to be made, not as someone else decided for us!' Their first joint venture, *Charlie Bubbles* (1965, Albert Finney), was appreciated by the critics, but failed to get a general release. Finney played a suave novelist returning on a sentimental visit to the industrial North of his origins and finding, sadly, that not only the miles stand between what he was and what he is. The film has a curious unreality, despite the obvious allegory to Finney's own career – working-class lad from Salford making it big in movie-land after heading south – and one sensed he exorcised a few private demons in the making of it, but the end result was less than gripping. This does not, however, explain its failure to get a general release – it was certainly more thoughtful and better lensed than many which make the rounds.

If . . . (1968, Lindsay Anderson) fared better, a satirical look at the corrupting influence of power – as exercised by the Establishment in the shape of a public school. Malcolm McDowell was a rebel pupil, ritualistically flogged for his unwillingness to succumb, who learns that the only way to successfully thwart the evils of the system is to destroy the system, and the people responsible. McDowell and his chums achieve this in a spectacular, surrealistic climax when they attack their one-time tormentors commando-style.

The Sorbonne riots, coinciding with the film's shooting, gave an unexpected – and unsettling – realism to what was clearly intended as an allegorical fantasy, which now ranks among the most original and imaginative productions of the sixties. Medwin calls it a 'near-perfect piece of work'.

McDowell was re-hired to play an ambitious drifter in *O Lucky Man* (1973, Lindsay Anderson), a film of moods and contrasts, unafraid to explore new cinematic language in its method of storytelling but sometimes straining noticeably too hard for its effects. Alan Price's strident yet appreciatively non-vogue music score – he also appears – garnishes the illusion of freshness.

Gumshoe (1971, Stephen Frears) was an affectionate parody of all those grimy Chandleresque thrillers of the forties, with Finney as a Liverpudlian bingo caller whose colourful imagination, fed on endless private-eye stories and Bogart movies, gets him embroiled in a nasty murder mystery, populated by English versions of the familiar shady milieu that made up those earlier private-eye movies. Medwin describes it as 'a good try . . . but one·that I'd like to do again'. One hopes that a new version would be less haunted by the shade of Bogart, and stand more self-assuredly on its own rubber soles.

Medwin produced *Spring and Port Wine* (1970, Peter Hammond) originally as a play, then realised the strong cinematic possibilities in Bill Naughton's earthy look-at-life inside a working-class Northern household. During an eventful week which sees the family at each other's throats – the action is sparked off by daughter Susan George's obstinate refusal to eat some herrings – painful truths have to be exchanged and learnt before reconciliation is possible. James Mason was the dour father who shocks his offspring by admitting there are times when he could cheerfully turn back from the end of t'street and wash his hands of the lot of them. Medwin points out that the 'maturity of perspective' of the writing lifts it above the cosy conventionality of domestic dramas set in the North, and it's not an unfair assessment, though the film falls well short of the fly-on-the-wall spartan realism of TV's *Coronation Street*. The youngsters, notably older daughter Hannah Gordon and Rodney Bewes, are clean-cut and photogenic enough for a TV commercial 'family' – interestingly, both have appeared in TV ads after gaining subsequent stardom within that medium – and the near neighbours are so unpalatably Steptoesque that any contribution they might have made to the dramatic thread of events is effectively stifled.

Medwin enjoys the occasional acting job – he made a brief guest appearance, as a doctor, in David Sherwin's satirical comedy *Britannia Hospital* (1981, Lindsay Anderson) with Malcolm McDowell, Leonard Rossiter and Joan Plowright, a film described as 'a day in the life of a large hospital alternating, as in real life, between incidents of crisis and celebration'. He was also a regular on BBC TV's *Shoestring* series, as the provincial radio station boss, who had to keep a worried eye on his employee, downbeat private-eye Trevor Eve.

Memorial Enterprises continues to flourish, more often than not along a path of its own making, or rather Medwin's making. His reputation as a hard-headed producer, and an innovative story-picker is comfortably established, and the chemistry with Albert Finney, he says, has al-

Michael Medwin, 1976

ways worked well. Neither seems perturbed not to be part of the mainstream commercial cinema, both seemingly preferring to take risks and be liked by the critics rather than involve themselves in junk blockbusters.

As Medwin remarked to me ruefully, 'I'm always saying to Albert, "Don't worry, I'm going to make an absolutely unrelentingly commercial film . . ." but somehow that's not the part of the business that we're into. We didn't make *Star Wars*. We wouldn't want to. That says something about us, doesn't it?'

Michael Medwin

b. 1923. Chirpy unassuming 1950s all-purpose support who later became a TV star in the long-running *Army Game* (as the likably astute Corporal Springer) and respected film mogul through his partnership with Albert Finney in Memorial Films, formed in 1964 'to make the kind of films we want to make.' Notable successes of the partnership include *If . . .* (1968), *O Lucky Man* (1973) and *Spring and Port Wine* (1971). Made brief but engaging return to TV acting, as radio station boss in *Shoestring* (1979-80).

1947 *The Courtneys of Curzon Street* (Edward Courtney)

Black Memory (John Fletcher)
Anna Karenina (Doctor)
1948 An Ideal Husband (Duke of Nonsuch)
Call of the Blood (Student)
Night Beat (Spider)
My Sister and I (co-scripted) (Charlie)
Another Shore (Bingham)
Look Before You Love (Emile)
Operation Diamond (Sullivan)
William Comes to Town (Reporter)
1949 Forbidden (Cabby)
The Queen of Spades (Iloviasky)
For Them That Trespass (Len Stevens)
Trottie True (Marquis Monty)
Boys in Brown (Sparrow)
1950 Someone at the Door (Ronnie Martin)
Shadow of the Past (Dick Stevens)
Trio – Mr Knowall (Steward)
The Lady Craved Excitement (Johnny)
1951 The Long Dark Hall (Leslie Scott)
1952 Curtain Up (Jerry)
Top Secret (Smedley)
Hindle Wakes (George Ramsbottom)
Love's a Luxury (Dick Pentwick)
Miss Robin Hood (Ernest)
1953 The Oracle (Timothy Blake)
Street Corner (Chick Farrer)
Genevieve (Expectant Husband)
Malta Story (Ramsay)
Spaceways (Toby Andrews)
The Intruder (Ginger Edwards)

1954 Bang, You're Dead (Bob Carter)
The Green Scarf (Henri Teral)
The Teckman Mystery (Martin Teckman)
1955 Above Us the Waves (Smart)
Doctor at Sea (Traill)
1956 Charley Moon (Alf Higgins)
A Man on the Beach (Max)
A Hill in Korea (Private Docker)
Checkpoint (Ginger)
1957 The Duke Wore Jeans (Cooper)
Doctor at Large (Bingham)
The Steel Bayonet (Lieutenant Vernon)
1958 I Only Arsked (Corporal Springer)
The Wind Cannot Read (Flight Officer
Lamb)
The Heart of a Man (Sid The Sausage)
1959 Carry on Nurse (Ginger)
1962 Crooks Anonymous (Ronnie)
The Longest Day (Pte Watney)
1963 It's All Happening (Max Catlin)
1964 Night Must Fall (Derek)
Rattle of a Simple Man (Ginger)
1965 I Gotta Horse (Hymie Campbell)
24 Hours to Kill (Tommy)
1966 The Sandwich Man (Sewer Man)
1970 Scrooge (Nephew)
1971 Gumshoe (Produced)
1973 O Lucky Man (Station Technician)
1980 The Sea Wolves (Radcliffe)
1981 Confessions of a Survivor (co-produced)
Britannia Hospital (Doctor)

John Mills

Director David Lean ('I know I'm over-meticulous') extracted three of John Mills' best performances. He was a timid boot-boy, who is elevated to partner and son-in-law of Charles Laughton by Laughton's resourceful spinster daughter Brenda de Banzie, in Hobson's Choice (1953), a sharply observed and consistently amusing slice of early 20th-century Northern low-life. Tired of being a skivvy to her drunken, tyrannical father, and of the neighbourhood's assumption that she is on the shelf, Miss de Banzie gives them all a slap in the eye by marrying the simple but earnest craftsman whose handiwork is a talking-point around their native Salford.

Faced with the ultimatum of making Mills a full partner in the business or losing him to-

gether with Miss de Banzie's organisational skills, Hobson eventually chooses the lesser of the two evils and gives Mills token equality – though darkly maintaining to his boozy fellow-traders that he, Laughton, remains very much in charge. In fact, it is Miss de Banzie who is in charge, sending them toppling in all directions with her verbal shoulder-charges. An engaging scene has the drunken Laughton, pursuing the moon's reflection through several puddles, his anger and confusion giving vent to a full-booted attack on its mocking face.

In Dickens' Great Expectations (1946), Mills' third film for David Lean, he played Pip and won praise for 'becoming more accomplished and sensitive with each performance'. It was a film of extraordinary charm, with Dickensian locales and characters that bustle with life as it surely must once have been. Lean's attention to detail – which delights some and exasperates others – is strongly in evidence. According to Ivan Butler, the early part of the film comes off best but 'to say that . . . is only to compare two standards of excellence'.

Again for Lean, Mills played a village idiot in *Ryan's Daughter* (1971), a sombre, romantic soufflé which somehow got puffed up into a four-course banquet. In fact, it was like a banquet served by the slowest waiters in town who, having diligently taken your order, disappear to work in the café next door. The story was a mixture of political intrigue – it is set in Ireland just before World War I – and romantic turmoil, centring on a naive lass, Sarah Miles, who weds a mild school teacher twice her age, Robert Mitchum and, finding wedlock less exciting than the brochures indicated, cools her ardour in the arms of a suicidal shell-shocked British army officer who has moved in to take command of a nearby garrison.

Mills stole the acting honours as a deformed idiot abused by all and sundry, a sort of cross between Quasimodo and Norman Wisdom. With non-aligned legs, a distorted ear, grotesque teeth, and a nosecap, he hobbled and grimaced his way into filmgoers' affections and picked up an Oscar for his pains – certainly there had to be some pain in getting the disfigurements so convincingly right. The scene where he accidentally stumbles across a brass button in a beach-side cave – scene of the lovers' tryst – and parades with it through the village in a grotesque parody of the English major to whom it belongs, is both intensely funny and deeply moving. Not since Lon Chaney has physical deformity been so expressive.

John Mills' versatility seemed late in developing. A featured screen player since 1932, he was one of several stalwarts who showed wartime audiences how to shape up under stress. He looked more at ease with pips up, but could be likably natural as an ordinary bloke in uniform, too, such as a Cockney seaman in *In Which We Serve* (1942, Noel Coward).

In *The Way to the Stars* (1945, Anthony Asquith) he was a wartime pilot who learns the ropes from room-mate Michael Redgrave, a married flyer. Redgrave's death in action convinces Mills that a combat captain owes it to his crew to keep his life free of emotional distractions – the implication is that Redgrave's concern over a missing cigarette lighter, a gift from his wife, caused the lack of concentration which cost the crew their lives. Mills' budding affair with Renee Asherson is thus temporarily grounded until, in the end, he comes to terms with it. This was one of the best war films of the 1940s, a beautifully modulated and acted story of courage, compassion and quiet optimism. Despite a total absence of flying sequences, the atmosphere within a wartime fighter station and a local hotel – the film's two main settings – was nicely held, and Mills' performance, as the new boy who survives to become a veteran flyer, stands high among several faultless characterisations.

He was a debonair but somewhat stilted Captain Scott in *Scott of the Antarctic* (1948, Charles Frend), a grand-scale homage to the famous British explorer who was beaten to the South Pole by a Norwegian rival and perished on the return trip with two companions in fierce blizzard conditions, only eleven miles from base camp. Despite the film's shortcomings it is difficult to watch the explorers' final ordeal without feeling involved, and even knowing how it ends takes nothing from the poignancy of that final scribbled message.

'I'm so sick of sharing you with a lot of damn submarines,' nags wife Helen Cherry at the beginning of *Morning Departure* (1950, Roy Baker), as Mills, a distinguished submarine commander, sets off on another doomed voyage. He plans to quit the Navy and retire to what First Officer Nigel Patrick whimsically calls 'a place in the country where the flowers stay young while you grow old', but their submarine is lambasted by a mine and drops to the ocean floor. The rescue attempt runs into trouble as storms batter the salvage crews, and finally the whole operation has to be abandoned, leaving Mills and three others tinned up as uncomfortably as sardines.

In *Mr Denning Drives North* (1951, Anthony Kimmins) Mills was a planemaker who tries to put some distance between his family and the corpse of an unsavoury character with whom his daughter has had an association. Mills didn't kill the chap, but manages to spend the entire film behaving as if he did. Nevertheless it was an entertaining who-never-dunnit, neatly wrung in all the right places.

By the mid-fifties some of the steam had gone out of Mills' career, and he played roles that could have been as competently handled by more lightweight actors such as Kenneth More.

John Mills waits for his breakfast egg in *Dulcima* (1971)

Examples are his likably trendy schoolteacher who introduces some fresh thinking, particularly about music, into stuffy Cecil Parker's grammar school in *It's Great To Be Young* (1956, Cyril Frankel), or the murder hunt detective in *Town on Trial* (1957, John Guillermin), climaxed with a lusty scrap between Mills and murder suspect Alec McCowen on top of a church spire.

But he fought his way to the top again, in gutsy character roles such as the shell-shocked near-alcoholic Army captain in *Ice Cold in Alex* (1958, J. Lee-Thompson). Mills and RSM Harry Andrews are put in charge of an ambulance ferrying two nurses from Tobruk to Alexandria, at the height of the British withdrawal across Libya in 1942.

The film takes an uncompromising view of desert warfare, the terrain is arid and full of hidden dangers, and for once the Britishers are not only on the run but behaving rather badly. A portly brigadier flounders in his bath complaining that there's 'never a moment's peace', as German batteries pound their HQ. Mills and fellow officer Richard Leech bitterly wrangle over a woman, and a temporary loss of nerve by Mills indirectly kills one of his passengers. By contrast, the Germans have everything going right for them, and it's a gentlemanly German, Anthony Quayle, who saves the battered vehicle from bogging down in the sand. It was refreshing for a British film of the fifties to view our retreat from Tobruk with such equanimity.

Mills was equally good in the suspenseful *Tiger Bay* (1959, J. Lee-Thompson) as a police inspector scouring Cardiff for a child and her Polish seaman kidnapper, who is also a suspected killer. Mills' daughter Hayley played the threatened moppet, an appealing performance which had a number of hardened reviewers breaking out in superlatives.

Mills' comedy talents have all too rarely been on view, but two notable examples occurred in the mid-1960s. In *The Wrong Box* (1966, Bryan Forbes) he was a rotter who tries to murder his harmless, boring old brother Ralph Richardson in order to become the sole inheritor of a bizarre lottery. At the end of the film he is still attempting to finish Richardson off with a spade, appropriately enough alongside an open grave, having failed all previous attempts with knives and other implements.

In *The Family Way*, (1966, Roy Boulting) he is a gruff, shirtsleeves-and-braces Northerner whose newly-wed son Hywel Bennett has problems consummating matters with child-bride Hayley Mills. The film is broad comedy, but, typically, Mills instils the simple-minded father figure with a real sense of hurt and dismay, particularly at the thought that his lad may not have the necessary equipment. As with *Ryan's Daughter*, this is character acting honed to a sharp point. Marjorie Rhodes played his wife, a down-to-earth old biddy long accustomed to Mills' odd ways yet hopeful, to the end, of improving his less socially-conscious habits.

Observing him tip half a bottle of tomato ketchup on to his dinner and then systematically work it into the contents of the plate until the whole thing looks like a stoat that's been hit by a lorry, Miss Rhodes shakes her head and says reproachfully, 'Eeeegh, anyone'd think you were mixing concrete'. But Mills is already shovelling the stuff into his mouth.

John Mills
b. 1908. Former chorus boy and late twenties revue artiste. In films from 1932 (*The Midshipmaid*). A major character star of enduring popularity since the mid-1940s. Married to playwright Mary Hayley Bell, with both daughters, Juliet and Hayley, successful actresses. Television roles include Professor Quatermass and retired pottery worker in *Young at Heart*, both a mistake.

1932 *The Midshipmaid*
1933 *Britannia of Billingsgate*
       The Ghost Camera
1934 *River Wolves*
       A Political Party
       Those Were the Days
       The Lash
       Blind Justice
       Doctor's Orders

1935 *Royal Cavalcade*
       Forever England
       Charing Cross Road
       Car of Dreams
1936 *First Offence*
       Tudor Rose
1937 *OHMS*
       The Green Cockatoo
1939 *Goodbye Mr Chips*
1940 *All Hands* (short)
       Old Bill and Son
1941 *Cottage to Let*
       The Black Sheep of Whitehall
1942 *The Big Blockade*
       The Young Mr Pitt
       In Which We Serve
1943 *We Dive At Dawn*
1944 *This Happy Breed*
       Victory Wedding (short)
       Waterloo Road
1945 *The Way to the Stars* (Peter Penrose)
1946 *Great Expectations* (Pip Pirrip)
1947 *So Well Remembered* (George Boswell)
       The October Man (Jim Ackland)
1948 *Scott of the Antarctic* (Capt R. F. Scott)
1949 *The History of Mr Polly* (Alfred Polly)
       The Rocking Horse Winner (Bassett)
1950 *Morning Departure* (Lieut Commdr Armstrong, RN)
1951 *Mr Denning Drives North* (Tom Denning)
1952 *The Gentle Gunman* (Terence Sullivan)
       The Long Memory (Davidson)
1953 *Hobson's Choice* (Willie Mossop)
1954 *The Colditz Story* (Pat Reid)
       End of the Affair (Albert Parkis)
1955 *Above Us the Waves* (Commander Fraser)
       Escapade (John Hampden)
1956 *It's Great to Be Young* (Mr Dingle)
       The Baby and the Battleship ('Puncher' Roberts)
       Around the World in Eighty Days (London Cabby)
1957 *Town on Trial* (Supt Mike Halloran)
       Vicious Circle (Dr Howard Latimer)
1958 *Dunkirk* (Corporal Tubby Binns)
       Ice Cold in Alex (Capt Anson)
       I Was Monty's Double (Major Harvey)
1959 *Tiger Bay* (Superintendent Graham)
1960 *Summer of the Seventeenth Doll* (Barney)
       Tunes of Glory (Lt Col Basil Barrow)
1961 *The Singer Not the Song* (Father Keogh)
       The Swiss Family Robinson (Mr Robinson)
       Flame in the Streets ('Jacko' Palmer)
1962 *The Valiant* (Captain Morgan)

Kenneth More

Kenneth More's best film was probably *Reach for the Sky* (1956, Lewis Gilbert), in which he portrayed tin-legged flying hero Douglas Bader. He had waited a long time for something that worthwhile, and when it came he really trowelled on the charm. Charm was a commodity that More had his pockets stuffed with, but his problem had been finding the right excuse to use it. Endlessly cheery types like More run the risk of becoming awful bores, and once or twice he had got dangerously close. But the Bader role gave him something to bite on, a flesh-and-blood personality whose courage and example to others in adversity was truly remarkable.

The film followed Bader's eventful life from before the flying accident which costs him his legs, through his hospitalisation and recovery, insistence on being accepted for wartime RAF service, capture, daring escape from and recapture by the Germans and his term in Colditz. It was a box-office smash.

Long afterwards More reflected: 'Since *Reach for the Sky* there has never been any question of playing a thorough-going villain – fortunately the acting profession is perfectly well endowed with its Christopher Lees and Donald Pleasences – because the public wouldn't swallow it. If they saw me knife someone in the back they'd just laugh.'

He switched to melodrama in Terence Rattigan's *The Deep Blue Sea* (1955, Anatole Litvak), playing a feckless ex-airman lover of judge's wife Vivien Leigh, a role he had previously played on the London stage. Though a performance of obvious sincerity – it won a Best Actor Award at Venice – audiences were indifferent to the idea of More as a weak-knee. Like a visit to the dentist, to his fans it was quickly over and best forgotten. Despite the award, More had his own reasons for wanting to forget it – he disliked the film script which he felt lacked the quality of Rattigan's stage original, a view not shared by his director, who had co-written it.

He was his old self again, as a resourceful butler shipwrecked along with his upper-crust employers in *The Admirable Crichton* (1957, Lewis Gilbert). Cut adrift from the luxuries of home, the genteel family, headed by Cecil Parker, are useless and rely implicitly on More to fend for them, a situation which effectively reverses their former roles. But he rejects the idea of equality because, as he explains to Sally Ann Howes, 'Any satisfaction I might get by being equal to you would be devalued by the footman being equal to me.' Nevertheless, he does establish a hierarchical structure of sorts, with himself as the most pampered member of that tiny society, but rescue of the castaways and reinstatement of the old values are inevitable.

Another better than average role was his humane first officer aboard the *Titanic* in *A Night to Remember* (1958, Roy Baker). Several films have attempted to reconstruct the final, dreadful hours of the doomed liner, none more straightforwardly or realistically than this one. More was the officer through whose vision the tragedy occurs, and most aspects of the human response mechanism – the noble and the

142

Kay Kendall sandwiched between gallant medical students Kenneth More (left) and Dirk Bogarde in *Doctor in the House* (1954)

cowardly, the frail and the foolish – were fairly convincingly represented without the usual moralising.

Attempts to internationalise More failed during the late 1950s, mostly because the actor was too deep-rootedly British. He also had a shrewd idea of what could, and could not, be done with that face, but it did not help matters when, on a trip to the USA in 1957, he lectured American reporters about the likely connection between gangster films and the country's increased delinquency problems, condemning films such as *On the Waterfront* (1954, Elia Kazan) and *Baby Doll* (1956, Elia Kazan) – which the Americans regard as classics – for having been made in the first place. 'I'll stay in Britain and make good, healthy pictures,' he vowed, and they left him to it.

The Thirty-nine Steps (1960, Ralph Thomas) was healthy enough, with lots of outdoors and people scurrying across rugged landscapes, but this weakest of the John Buchan remakes had nothing to commend it but the scenery and a few random visual thrills such as More clinging to the outside of a carriage door to escape his pursuers during a train ride across the Forth Bridge. More's jokey character was out of step with the theme of fifth-columnists infiltrating the establishment, and his Swedish co-star Taina Elg smiled prettily but gave no hint of personality.

Northwest Frontier (1959, J. Lee-Thompson) is light on the kind of items that fire the imagination, unless one worries about what happens to fictitious Hindu princes during the days of the Raj when murderous rebels start closing in. I have managed to keep an open mind on such matters which probably ruined the film for me. On the plus side, there's Kenneth More dispensing cut-price roguish charm as if he had read Errol Flynn's biography carefully, as a British Army captain assigned to rescuing the young prince in an attempt to preserve civil order.

143

Kenneth More as legless flying ace Douglas Bader in *Reach for the Sky* (1956)

More manages to get the lad and a few members of the royal household aboard a creaky old locomotive, and off they chug pursued by rebel hordes. Among the passengers are Lauren Bacall, whose slow-burn eyes are worth at least an extra thousand rounds of ammunition, Wilfrid Hyde White in almost permanent repose and Herbert Lom playing his usual shifty-eyed, sweaty villain.

Lom sneaks on to the train posing as a journalist, but his real purpose is to kill the prince. However, after he has bungled a couple of attempts, More loses patience with him and tosses him into a passing ravine. When Hyde White sleepily enquires what all the noise is about, More breaks the news to him that Lom has 'got off'. Reassured by this, old Wilfrid contentedly drifts back into a coma. *Northwest Frontier* is a bit like Ealing's *Titfield Thunderbolt* with script notes by Kipling.

The break-up of his marriage and the much-publicised affair with pert comedy actress Angela Douglas, 26 years his junior, probably

helped slow down the film offers More received around the mid-sixties. He was considered a family star and the gossip hurt, although to what extent the slump in his career was due to his private life or simply because he had become a victim of the deepening gloom around British studios, is debatable.

Evidence of the extent of his decline was provided by his consent to appear in *The Mercenaries* (1968, Jack Cardiff), an unremittingly violent and altogether mindless cash-in on the Congo troubles. He played an alcoholic doctor conned into serving with Rod Taylor's unsavoury cheque-book army on the promise of free booze. In his autobiography *More or Less,* he recalls: 'Anyone who could remember his lines and pretend to be drunk could do it . . . But I consoled myself with the fact that I was being paid. This was a job. I had to accept that the wheel of fortune turns and whereas I had been lucky in being at the top for years, now I was underneath.'

The following year brought TV fame as Young Jolyon in BBC TV's *Forsyte Saga.* Ironically, perhaps, more people have watched him in this single television role than in all his film work put together.

Kenneth More
b. 1914. Agreeably lightweight actor, ex-Windmill Theatre stage-hand-turned-performer, a major British star of the 1950s, specialising in fortitudinous decent-chap roles, most notably as the screen Bader. Film debut: *Windmill Revels* (1938).

1948 *Scott of the Antarctic* (Lieut Teddy Evans)
1949 *Man on the Run* (Corporal Newman)
     Now Barabbas Was a Robber (Spencer)
     Stop Press Girl (Sergeant)
1950 *Morning Departure* (Lt Commdr James)
     Chance of a Lifetime (Adam)
     The Clouded Yellow (Willie)
1951 *The Franchise Affair* (Stanley Peters)
     No Highway (Dobson)
     Appointment with Venus (Lionel Fallaize)
1952 *Brandy for the Parson* (Tony Rackman)
     The Yellow Balloon (Ted)
1953 *Never Let Me Go* (Steve Quillan)
     Genevieve (Ambrose Claverhouse)
     Our Girl Friday (Patrick Plunkett)
1954 *Doctor in the House* (Richard Grimsdyke)
     Raising a Riot (Tony Kent)
1955 *The Deep Blue Sea* (Freddie Page)

1956	*Reach for the Sky* (Group Captain Douglas Bader)		*We Joined the Navy* (Lt Commdr Badger)

1956 *Reach for the Sky* (Group Captain
     Douglas Bader)
1957 *The Admirable Crichton* (Bill Crichton)
1958 *A Night to Remember* (Herbert Lightoller)
     Next to No Time (David Webb)
     The Sheriff of Fractured Jaw (Jonathan
     Tibbs)
1959 *Northwest Frontier* (Captain Scott)
1960 *Sink the Bismark* (Capt Jonathan
     Shephard)
     Man in the Moon (William Blood)
     The Thirty-nine Steps (Richard Hannay)
1961 *The Greengage Summer* (Eliot)
1962 *Some People* (Mr Smith)

     We Joined the Navy (Lt Commdr Badger)
     The Longest Day (Capt Colin Maud)
1963 *The Comedy Man* ('Chick' Byrd)
1968 *The Mercenaries* (Dr Wreid)
     Oh! What a Lovely War (Kaiser
     Wilhelm II)
     Fräulein Doktor (Colonel Foreman)
1969 *The Battle of Britain* (Group Captain
     Baker)
1970 *Scrooge* (Ghost of Christmas Present)
1976 *The Slipper and the Rose* (Chamberlain)
1977 *Leopard in the Snow* (Sir Philip James)
1979 *The Spaceman and King Arthur* (King
     Arthur)

Robert Morley

'What is operating but manual labour?' asks Robert Morley, a pompous physician, in *The Doctor's Dilemma* (1958, Anthony Asquith). Morley is one of four eminent medics called to the bedside of consumptive ne'er-do-well Dirk Bogarde. Their combined help adds up to very little, alas, for Bogarde dies amid much philosophising. Of the four physicians, Morley manages by a stout waistband to be the wittiest.

But then Morley has always been witty. On film his persona is indistinguishable from the jolly pundit who regales us from time to time on TV chat shows. He can at once be the breezy intellectual and the complete clown, patronising, cherubic and lots more besides in the space of a short conversation. Morley, who has more wobbly chins than a Shanghai drinking club, enjoys poking fun at life's absurdities, among which he generously includes himself.

Morley was born in Folkestone, a then-fashionable upper crust watering hole replete with promenade concerts on Sunday afternoons and bath chairs – not a bad starting point for anyone with an ear for comedy. His father was a gambler and failed tea-rooms proprietor, and the family lived a kind of crazy, shabby-genteel nomadic existence, returning to Folkestone like homing pigeons when all else failed.

An early highspot was his playing of Charles Fox, parliamentary opponent of William Pitt, Britain's prime minister during the Napoleonic Wars, in *The Young Mr Pitt* (1942, Carol Reed). Robert Donat played Pitt but Morley took most of the honours. 'Gloriously foxy' was how the

Sunday Express scored his performance.

Straight after the war he made *I Live in Grosvenor Square* (1945, Herbert Wilcox), which turned out to be dull romantic slop in the worst Miniver tradition, with Morley uncomfortably cast in the role of Anna Neagle's aristocratic grandfather. He rose gamely to the challenge, shrouded in mutton chop whiskers, and managed to look a lot older than Miss Neagle who, in reality, is four years older than Morley. Had the story, about a British officer, Rex Harrison, and a Yank, Dean Jagger, competing for the affections of Miss Neagle, been more inspired, these incongruities might have been more easy to overlook.

He had a small part with Humphrey Bogart in *The African Queen* (1951, John Huston) as Katherine Hepburn's missionary brother. One very funny scene near the start of the film has a famished Bogart sitting down to tea with the prim Miss Hepburn and Morley. The thought of food triggers Bogart's stomach off into a series of loud undignified gurgles. 'Ain't a thing I can do about it,' explains Bogey while Hepburn glares her disapproval. Shortly afterwards, Germans attack the mission – the film is set in Africa during World War I – and Morley's mind gives way. He dies, confused and delirious, muttering: 'Thy will be done, O Lord, I've tried so hard . . .' Bogart obligingly buries him in the shade of his favourite tree.

Had the script been adequate, Morley and Margaret Rutherford could have had some lively moments in *Curtain Up* (1952, Ralph Smart),

Racehorse owner Robert Morley (left) seems unimpressed with boy jockey Fella Edmonds (right) while trainer Edward Underdown (centre) reserves judgement in *The Rainbow Jacket* (1954)

Morley was in good form as a fussy aristocrat with a string of racehorses in *The Rainbow Jacket* (1954, Basil Dearden), an over-cosy, Disney-type look at the racing world. Morley's problem is that despite good stock he has no classic winners. 'Stones, bugs, coughs . . . my horses seem to pick up everything but races,' he laments. But his luck changes with the signing up of a boy jockey who turns out to be a natural.

Unfortunately, the lad is tied in with a veteran jockey with dubious connections which almost ruin his career before it gets properly under way. Bill Owen steps in and saves the boy's licence at the cost of his own long-awaited and promising turf comeback.

Morley filmed several times with Laurence Harvey. He was Harvey's upper-crust father in *The Good Die Young* (1954, Lewis Gilbert), his tutor in *Of Human Bondage* (1964, Ken Hughes), and in *Life at the Top* (1965, Ted Kotcheff) he was a London textile tycoon and business associate of Yorkshire industrialist Donald Wolfit, whose daughter has been put in the family way and married by Harvey. Wolfit grudgingly admits Harvey into his business empire, suspecting with good reason that that was what Harvey had his sights on all along. For his old friend's sake Morley is hospitable to Harvey when he comes south on a business trip, but later, after the marriage starts to come unstuck, Morley gives him the cold shoulder.

He has made his share of stinkers, not surprisingly since, by his own admission, he 'makes a point of never reading a script or turning down a part'. One wishes he would occasionally be more selective, thus avoiding disasters like, for example, *Ghengis Khan* (1965, Henry Levin) where he was the Emperor of China, and *Doctor in Trouble* (1970, Ralph Thomas) in which he played James Robertson Justice's brother, a cruise ship captain. Justice does not appear in the film but there are enough references to his character, Launcelot Spratt, to suggest that he was present at least in spirit. Though carrying in front of him something akin to Justice's bulk, Morley, alas, was given none of his moderately snappy repartee.

He has courageously attempted a number of real-life characterisations, none of which suffered badly for not being on target. He was the Gilbert half of the musical partnership in *The Story of Gilbert and Sullivan* (1953, Sidney Gilliatt), an enjoyable musical biography which bombed at the box-office, and his Great Wit in

but the opportunities were squandered. He played the director of a small provincial repertory company which is rehearsing one of Miss Rutherford's plays. The lady turns up unexpectedly, her arrival resulting in a prolonged clash of ideas and temperaments.

A predictable ragbag of back-stage stereotypes make up the supporting cast: a faded star eating humble pie, a pert ingenue who lacks star quality, a petulant leading ham waiting for that big-time phone call that never materialises, etc. The whole thing is shot entirely within the confines of a small theatre, so that one longed to throw open the doors and let in some ventilation. Kay Kendall played a fledgling actress on the threshold of movie stardom, a situation that would shortly be echoed in real life.

For incongruous casting, *The Adventures of Quentin Durward* (1955), based on the Sir Walter Scott novel, takes a lot of beating. Morley was a medieval French monarch, Robert Taylor a Scottish soldier of fortune, George Cole a fiddling gypsy, and Wilfrid Hyde White a gossipy barber. Nobody seems very certain about the purpose behind it all, but the end result was never in dispute – it was about as exciting as watching bath-water drain away.

Oscar Wilde (1960, Gregory Ratoff) lost by a short quip to the same year's Peter Finch version. He was the press baron who sponsors the London-to-Paris air race in *Those Magnificent Men in Their Flying Machines* (1965, Ken Annakin), a simple part for Morley, dressed up like a dog's dinner and saying things like: 'The trouble with these international affairs is that they attract foreigners!' In *Theatre of Blood* (1973, Douglas Hickox) he was a member of the unlucky critics' circle of whom maniacal thespian Vincent Price decides the world has had enough. Price kills him by force-feeding him with his own pet poodles.

Morley's problem, outsize like everything else associated with him, is that audiences expect him to be funny. His lugubrious appearance has people chuckling long before he speaks, but when his lines veer towards the intentionally serious it is difficult to relate what's being said with what's being seen.

A good illustration of this occurred in *Cromwell* (1970, Ken Hughes), in which Morley played a belted earl supporting Richard Harris, in the title role, against the clumsy, nation-dividing reign of Charles I, played by Alec Guinness. Morley likes Harris' ideas but objects strongly to battles that interrupt mealtimes. At Nazeby, scene of a famous sortie, Harris is dangerously outnumbered by Guinness' men because Morley has gone to ground to reappraise his loyalties. As he explains later to a far-from-subdued Harris: 'If we beat him 99 times we'll still be his subjects. But if he beats us once, we'll all be hanged!'

In *When Eight Bells Toll* (1971, Etienne Périer), an energetic well-photographed spy yarn, he was agent Anthony Hopkins' Whitehall boss, a snobby fellow who blames Hopkins' incompetence on his not having attended a 'proper school'. On one occasion when Hopkins fails to establish contact as prearranged, another top civil servant wonders if the agent may have been hurt. 'Lets hope it's nothing trivial,' sniffs Morley.

He was one of the colourful tricksters in *Beat the Devil* (1953, John Huston), a high-camp adventure with Bogart on the Riviera. Morley and two cronies, wanted in London for questioning by police about the murder of a Foreign Office official, latch on to what appears to be a lucrative uranium swindle. But it's all a high-blown rumour put about by Jennifer Jones. 'They must be desperate characters – not one of them looked at my legs,' complains Miss Jones as the bizarre trio pass her by without a glance.

Vexed because her casual affair with Bogart, a rival swindler, gives him an obvious advantage, Morley keeps her well in his sights, hoping for something nasty to happen to her. On board a cramped steamer taking them all to Africa, Morley spots Miss Jones exercising high in the crow's nest. 'Good morning!' he shouts affably, plucking off his hat, and whispering hopefully to his cronies, 'I hope she breaks her neck!'

Robert Morley

b. 1908. Actor-playwright on stage from 1928. Film debut in 1938 in *Marie Antoinette* (Hollywood). British screen debut in *You Will Remember* (1940).

1940 *You Will Remember*
1941 *Major Barbara*
1942 *This Was Paris*
      The Big Blockade
      The Foreman Went to France
      Partners in Crime (short)
      The Young Mr Pitt
1945 *I Live in Grosvenor Square* (Duke of Exmoor)
1947 *The Ghosts of Berkeley Square* (General Burlap)
1949 *The Small Back Room* (Minister)
1951 *Outcast of the Islands* (Mr Almayer)
      The African Queen (Rev Samuel Sayer)
1952 *Curtain Up* (Harry Blacker)
1953 *The Final Test* (Alexander Whitehead)
      The Story of Gilbert and Sullivan (W. S. Gilbert)
      Melba (Oscar Hammerstein)
      Beat the Devil (Petersen)
1954 *The Good Die Young* (Sir Francis Ravenscourt)
      The Rainbow Jacket (Lord Logan)
      Beau Brummel (George III)
1955 *The Adventures of Quentin Durward* (Louis XI)
1956 *Loser Takes All* (Dreuther)
      Around the World in Eighty Days (Ralph, a Governor of the Bank of England)
1958 *Law and Disorder* (Sir Edward Crichton)
      The Sheriff of Fractured Jaw (Uncle Lucius)
      The Doctor's Dilemma (Sir Ralph Bonnington)
1959 *Libel* (Sir Wilfred)
      Battle of the Sexes (Robert MacPherson)

The Journey (USA) (Hugh Deverill)
1960 *Oscar Wilde* (Oscar Wilde)
1961 *The Young Ones* (Hamilton Black)
    Go to Blazes (Arson Eddie)
1962 *The Road to Hong Kong* (The Leader)
    The Boys (Montgomery)
1963 *Nine Hours to Rama* (P. K. Mussadi)
    Murder at a Gallop (Hector Enderby)
    The Old Dark House (Roderick Femm)
    Ladies Who Do (Colonel Whitforth)
    Hot Enough for June (Colonel Cunliffe)
1964 *Of Human Bondage* (Dr Jacobs)
1965 *Those Magnificent Men in Their Flying
    Machines; or How I Flew from London to
    Paris in 25 Hours and 11 Minutes* (Lord
    Rawnsley)
    The Alphabet Murders (Captain Hastings)
    A Study in Terror (Mycroft Holmes)
    Life at the Top (Tiffield)
    Ghengis Khan (Emperor of China)
1966 *The Loved One* (USA) (Sir Ambrose
    Abercrombie)

Hotel Paradiso (Henri Cot)
Finders Keepers (Colonel Riberts)
1967 *The Trygon Factor* (Hubert Hamlyn)
    Woman Times Seven (Dr Xavier)
1968 *Hot Millions* (Caesar Smith)
1969 *Some Girls Do* (Miss Mary)
    Sinful Davey (Duke of Argyll)
    Twinky (Judge Roxburgh)
1970 *Cromwell* (Earl of Manchester)
    Doctor in Trouble (Captain George Spratt)
    Song of Norway (Berg)
1971 *When Eight Bells Toll* (Uncle Arthur)
1973 *Theatre of Blood* (Meredith Meredew)
1975 *Great Expectations* (TV) (Pumplechook)
    Hugo the Hippo (Voice of the Sultan of
    Zanzibar)
1976 *The Blue Bird* (Father Time)
1978 *Too Many Chefs* (Max Vandervere)
1979 *The Human Factor* (Doctor Percival)
1980 *Loophole* (Godfrey)
    The Great Muppet Caper (English
    Gentleman)

Laurence Olivier

To call Laurence Olivier the greatest Shakespearean actor of the century is merely to repeat the
obvious. Making the Bard box-office is but a tiny
fragment of Olivier's phenomenal achievements. Almost everything he has touched has
been destined to become an event of major proportions, sometimes due to the quality of the
material but mostly because of the actor himself.
Just when you think he must have reached the
end of the barrel, up comes yet another performance startling in its freshness.

Unlike his theatrical activities, Olivier's early
film work is negligible. One suspects he was used
as much for his handsome features – opposite
such divine leading ladies of the period as Gertrude Lawrence, Gloria Swanson and Merle
Oberon – as for his screen presence, as yet unde-
veloped. *Fire Over England* (1937, William K.
Howard) established him opposite Vivien Leigh
as a swashbuckling romantic lead, an Elizabethan
adventurer who goes undercover to Spain to
bring back vital information on the build-up of
the Armada, thus enabling England to be successfully defended. It seems we could have managed without Drake, after all. Whatever merits
the story had to begin with were eased into the

background by the teaming of Olivier and Leigh
in their first film together, as the most photogenic pair of lovers British movies had ever discovered. But it was Merle Oberon, not Miss
Leigh, who was Cathy to Olivier's Heathcliff in
Wuthering Heights (1939, William Wyler),
Emily Brontë's dark tale of unrequited love and
bitter revenge.

During his spell in Hollywood making
Wuthering Heights, Vivien Leigh visited him,
and unwittingly completed the circle which
landed her the co-starring role in *Gone With the
Wind* – Olivier's American agent Myron
Selznick was the brother of the film's flamboyant
producer, then nearing the edge of despair after
testing hundreds of would-be Scarletts. Olivier
made *Rebecca* (1940, Alfred Hitchcock) with
Joan Fontaine, a grimly overwrought production
with none of Hitch's later sardonicism, and then
the clamour from the public could be resisted no
longer – Alexander Korda brought Olivier and
Leigh together again, as Nelson and Lady
Hamilton, in *Lady Hamilton* (1941, Alexander
Korda). However, not all the reviewers were
wowed by the teaming. Respected critic Richard
Winnington noted: 'They are seldom other than

Laurence Olivier and Penelope Dudley Ward in *The Demi-Paradise* (1943)

two modern film stars led in and out of the scenes by the accepted clichés.'

There was nothing modern about *Henry V* (1944, Laurence Olivier) other than a 20th-century cinematic vision of how Shakespeare's rousing tale of love (between Henry and Princess Katherine) and patriotism (the summons to arms and defeat of the French army at Agincourt) could be made interesting and colourful enough, without loss of integrity, for audiences who would sooner be poleaxed than face a page of the Bard's noblest effort. This was achieved by the simple yet inspired device of staging the opening and closing sequences as if at the old Globe Theatre, with the mid-section, including the build-up to Agincourt, the battle and its aftermath, moving 'outdoors'. It's really a film

within a play, merging tantalising segments of Elizabethan drama in action with movement and spectacle on a scale quite unimagined at the time – the time was 1944, remember, and Britain was at war.

Apart from being a classic, the story of a British invasion succeeding in Europe mirrored the turning tide of the war, itself a cause for rejoicing; another was Olivier's performance, towering, like his voice and his authority, over every other ingredient in the film.

Hamlet (1948, Laurence Olivier) was a more vigorous challenge to that authority, in that the story itself – part legend, part fantasy – was previously considered to have little cinematic appeal. There were no stirring battle scenes, no patriotic speeches, no comedy counterpoints. It

149

was a scene of gloom and doom, as the blond Danish prince swears to his father's ghost that he will avenge his murder, the offender being his uncle, the Danish King, now married to his mother. Olivier was 'ruthlessly bold' (his words) in adapting the original play, reducing its full four hours to a more manageable 155 minutes, substituting familiar words for obscure ones, and making it more easy to take in at one sitting. A few purists squealed in horror – 'He has achieved neither first-rate cinema nor first-rate Shakespeare,' declared Richard Winnington – but these critics were felled by a broadside of praise, and the four Academy Awards (best actor, best film, best art director and best set design) picked up by the film underlined the commercial validity of Olivier's interpretation.

The entire British fraternity seemed represented in *The Magic Box* (1951, John Boulting), a Festival of Britain homage to the inventor of cinematography, William Friese-Greene. Olivier played a policeman who unwittingly becomes the first bewildered witness to Friese-Greene's invention. He was the middle-aged restaurant manager driven to embezzlement and ruin by an unhappy love affair in *Carrie* (1952, William Wyler), a satisfying performance despite the curious casting. He had accompanied Vivien Leigh to Hollywood while she made *A Streetcar Named Desire* with Brando, and while there he got the offer to appear in *Carrie*. What decided him to accept was not the story but the fact that the director was William Wyler, who had previously worked with him on *Wuthering Heights*, and whom Olivier had wanted to direct *Henry V*. A close rapport and mutual respect existed between the two.

He was the highwayman Macheath in *The Beggar's Opera* (1952, Peter Brook), again a considerable challenge involving acting, singing and dancing, performed, as C. A. Lejeune noted, 'without any touch of self-consciousness, as though all these exercises were a joy, and the player's impression of ease, of relaxation, is irresistibly communicated to the audience.'

'Dogs bark at me as I pass,' he complains, as *Richard III* (1955, Laurence Olivier), and no wonder, for the character is the very essence of evil – cunning, pitiless, a fiend without scruple, whose obsession to rule England drives him to hack down anyone in his path. Since several of his family have a prior claim – brother Edward, and a couple of princely cousins – they are swiftly disposed of, but his methods inevitably create

enemies who unite along with their followers under the banner of Henry Tudor, and in the battle which follows, Richard is cornered and killed by a group of the people he has tyrannised.

Richard III is one of the great historical films. The power of Olivier's acting is matched by his coherent direction, and though he bends a few details for the sake of clarifying the narrative, scene after scene leaves you stunned by the sheer brilliance of its construction. Olivier enlivens the murder and mayhem by making Richard a raffish, vain creature, listing his deformities with the kind of nonchalant arrogance that roadhogs use to tot up their brushes with the law, sardonically letting his audience in on the next move. Olivier sees to it that the character functions on several levels – he arouses interest because he is bold and colourful; revulsion because he is so grotesque; admiration for his cunning; and anticipation because he is someone around whom dramatic events happen. He makes Richard a heartless, smarmy-voiced monster, yet defies you not to like him, and it's a measure of Olivier's artistry that you do like him, even while he is curdling your stomach.

Olivier was a monocled Ruritanian Grand Duke in *The Prince and the Showgirl* (1957, Laurence Olivier), co-starring Marilyn Monroe. The film is set in 1911, with the Duke, a solitary, stuffy figure, in London for King George V's Coronation. He meets a dizzy chorus girl – that's Monroe – who proceeds to show him a different perspective on life. Monroe, then on honeymoon with Arthur Miller, had gushed beforehand about the project like a teeny-bopper invited backstage to meet her current heartthrob – 'I'd like to continue my growth in every possible way!' Simply getting in front of the cameras on schedule and in a condition to work would have been growth enough for Olivier. He had agreed to do it to help raise cash and prestige for his next Shakespearean project, *Macbeth*, but neither the cash nor the Shakespeare film he had set his heart on materialised.

He supported Burt Lancaster and Kirk Douglas in Shaw's *The Devil's Disciple* (1959, Guy Hamilton), and according to the London *Evening Standard* made the two American stars 'look like stupid oafs who have wandered back from a western'. As General Burgoyne, the British commander-in-chief of New England during the

(*Opposite*) Laurence Olivier expresses righteous indignation in *Hamlet* (1948)

150

War of Independence, Olivier is on the losing side, historically speaking, but neatly redresses the balance by acting the American pair into an 18th-century cocked hat. Lancaster and Douglas, two stars whose egos are usually to the fore, accepted their upstaging with good humour. 'It's not my ambition to be a great actor like Mr Olivier, nor would I be capable of becoming one,' said Lancaster.

A remarkable transformation occurs in John Osborne's *The Entertainer* (1960, Tony Richardson), with Olivier as a seedy, fourth-rate vaudeville comic with a gin-rinsed wife and a fading career. It's a guided tour of defeat and despair, and Olivier piles on the pathos, the enforced heartiness and greasepaint in near-equal amounts.

In *Term of Trial* (1962, Peter Glenville) he was a drab North Country schoolteacher with marriage and career problems. During a school trip to Paris, one of the pupils, Sarah Miles – an impressive screen debut – who is infatuated with him but resentful when she gets no encouragement, complains that he has assaulted her. The film shows the catastrophic effects of this malicious accusation on the teacher's already fragile existence. Simone Signoret, fresh from her success as Laurence Harvey's discarded lover in *Room at the Top*, played Olivier's nagging wife. It was a curious role for Olivier who, like Jack Hawkins, was at his least convincing, always thoroughly ill-at-ease, when trying to play ordinary little men.

The same can be said for *Bunny Lake Is Missing* (1965, Otto Preminger), in which he played a CID Inspector investigating the disappearance of a toddler from a Hampstead nursery school. Olivier is baffled at first because, despite the mother's anguished protestations, no evidence can be found that the child – if it exists – ever attended the school. Is the whole episode a guilt-ridden illusion by the so-called mother, or is something really sinister going on under the inspector's nose? Olivier plods from one clue to the next in a wryly bemused, downbeat manner, but in order to get inside the skin of a doleful Scotland Yard man, he has to completely shroud his massive authority, which might be good acting but most people would sooner watch him motoring along at high speed, exercising his exceptional talents at full stretch. What's missing in *Bunny Lake* is not just a child, but Olivier at anything near his normal idling speed.

Khartoum (1966, Basil Dearden) united Olivier with one of his greatest admirers, Charlton Heston, on opposite sides in the Sudan conflict of the 1880s. Heston was General Gordon, an experienced colonialist, who is despatched by Gladstone to the troubled region to effect the evacuation of troops and civilians before they can be massacred by the fanatical supporters of the religious leader, the Mahdi, played by Olivier.

Heston's problems are heightened by his government's refusal to become offically involved – if anything goes wrong, he is on his own. His attempts to reach an understanding with the Mahdi are unsuccessful, the mob seize Khartoum and – one suspects to the immense relief of the British Government – the general is killed, taking their secret with him. Heston's portrayal is a repeat of all his others, and Olivier's is disappointingly superficial; he more than anyone should know that growling and posturing do not make a performance; in the words of *The Times*: 'No real feeling of a real man ever comes over.'

From the late 1960s, Olivier has lent valiant support to lots of films which make you wish he had been the star. He was a Russian prime minister in *The Shoes of the Fisherman* (1968, Michael Anderson); a First World War field marshal in *Oh! What a Lovely War* (1969, Richard Attenborough) – old chums Ralph Richardson, John Gielgud, Jack Hawkins, John Miles and Michael Redgrave popped in and out like a sheepdog's tongue; an air chief marshal with Trevor Howard, Nigel Patrick, Michael Redgrave and Ralph Richardson in *The Battle of Britain* (1969, Guy Hamilton); a rotten headmaster in *David Copperfield* (1969, Delbert Mann), again with Redgrave, Richardson, Richard Attenborough, Edith Evans and Wendy Hiller; a pre-Revolution Russian count in *Nicholas and Alexandra* (1971, Franklin Schaffner), with Jack Hawkins and Redgrave; the Iron Duke in *Lady Caroline Lamb* (1972, Robert Bolt), with John Mills and Ralph Richardson – it seems Olivier's participation drew other notables in swarms.

In recent years, despite indifferent health, he has worked consistently in big-budget dramas, taking – or at least sharing – responsibility for each film's success. He and Michael Caine play convoluted games in *Sleuth* (1973, Joseph L. Mankiewicz), Anthony Shaffer's sophisticated comedy-thriller about the revenge of a distinguished mystery writer on his wife's lover which, despite the inspired mugging of its stars, never loses its staginess.

He was a real nasty, a bald-headed German war criminal, in *Marathon Man* (1976, John Schlesinger), setting about Dustin Hoffman with dentist's tools in the now-famous torture sequence. Olivier has come to New York from exile in South America to seize a cache of diamonds, left behind by Jewish concentration camp victims. Hoffman, a history student with ambitions to be a top-class marathon runner, stands in his way. After his dentist's chair ordeal, Hoffman spunkily turns the tables on his torturer, after first putting the hoard of diamonds well beyond his reach.

In a neat switch of allegiances, he turned up as an aging Nazi-hunter in *The Boys from Brazil* (1978, Franklin Schaffner), with Gregory Peck as the latest object of his dogged pursuit, war criminal Josef Mengele, still fomenting murder and tyranny from the seclusion of his Paraguayan stronghold.

Laurence Olivier

b. 1907. Revered actor-lord whose work in Shakespeare and the classics has influenced several generations. On-screen, has directed vivid and fluent versions of Shakespeare (*Henry V* (1944), *Hamlet* (1948), *Richard III* (1955)) in which he also played the title characters, and has created a long catalogue of momentous performances on film. Formerly married to Jill Esmond and to Vivien Leigh. Since 1961, has been married to Joan Plowright.

1930 *Too Many Crooks*
The Temporary Widow
1931 *Friends and Lovers*
Potiphar's Wife (US title: *Her Strange Desire*)
The Yellow Passport (US title: *The Yellow Ticket*)
1932 *Westward Passage*
1933 *No Funny Business*
Perfect Understanding
1935 *Moscow Nights* (US title: *I Stand Condemned*)
1936 *As You Like It*
1937 *Fire Over England*
The Divorce of Lady X
1939 *Q Planes* (US title: *Clouds Over Europe*)
1939 *Wuthering Heights* (USA)
Twenty One Days (US title: *Twenty One Days Together*)
1940 *Rebecca*
Conquest of the Air

Pride and Prejudice
1941 *Lady Hamilton* (US title: *That Hamilton Woman*)
49th Parallel (US title: *The Invaders*)
1943 *The Demi-Paradise*
1944 *Henry V* (Henry)
1948 *Hamlet* (Hamlet, Prince of Denmark)
1951 *The Magic Box* (Holborn Policeman)
1952 *Carrie* (USA) (George Hurstwood)
The Beggar's Opera (Captain Macheath)
1953 *A Queen Is Crowned* (Documentary narration)
1955 *Richard III* (Richard III, also prod/dir)
1957 *The Prince and the Showgirl* (Charles, Prince Regent; also prod/dir)
1959 *The Devil's Disciple* (General Burgoyne)
1960 *The Entertainer* (Archie Rice)
Spartacus (USA) (Crassus)
1961 *The Power and the Glory* (USA) (The Priest)
1962 *Term of Trial* (Graham Weir)
1965 *Othello* (Othello)
Bunny Lake is Missing (Inspector Newhouse)
1966 *Khartoum* (The Mahdi)
1968 *The Shoes of the Fisherman* (Kamenev)
Romeo and Juliet (Prologue and Epilogue narration)
1969 *Oh! What a Lovely War* (Field Marshal Sir John French)
The Dance of Death (Edgar)
The Battle of Britain (Air Chief Marshal Sir Hugh Dowding)
David Copperfield (Mr Creakle)
1970 *Three Sisters* (Chebutikin, the Doctor) (also directed)
1971 *Nicholas and Alexandra* (Count Witte)
1972 *Lady Caroline Lamb* (Duke of Wellington)
1973 *Sleuth* (Andrew Wyke)
1974 *Love Among the Ruins* (USA) (Arthur Granville-Jones)
1976 *Marathon Man* (Szell)
1977 *The Seven-Per-Cent Solution* (Professor Moriarty)
A Bridge Too Far (Dr Spaander)
The Betsy (USA) (Loren Hardeman Sr)
1978 *The Boys from Brazil* (Ezra Lieberman)
1979 *Jesus of Nazareth* (TV) (Nicodemus)
1980 *The Jazz Singer* (USA) (Cantor Rabinovitch)
1981 *Clash of the Titans* (Zeus)
Brideshead Revisited (TV) (Lord Marchmain)

Peter O'Toole

'Stardom is insidious,' Peter O'Toole once told writer Philip Oakes. 'It creeps up through the toes. You don't realise what's happening until it reaches your nut. And that's when it becomes dangerous.'

Dangerous or not, Peter O'Toole handles it rather well, possibly because he has little respect for it. His unsuccessful bookmaker-father had many brushes with the fickle finger of fate, and his experiences were not entirely lost on young Peter. The movie actor and reformed drunkard – reformed for medical reasons, he hastily points out in case you should think he has discovered something better – remains wholesomely unaffected by his huge popularity.

O'Toole's natural ebullience – he attributes it to a Yorkshire upbringing by Irish parents – registers clearly in films which give it elbow room. He is an actor who generates excitement without having to work up a sweat. Like Denholm Elliott, he has played his quota of anguished souls, but with O'Toole, underneath the haunted expression you can detect mockery in close attendance. It would be unfair to suggest that he takes either his profession, or his success, lightly, yet he is capable of looking beyond both, and retains a healthy disregard for those who would seek to impose on him a less earthy attitude to life. When O'Toole the performer falls flat on his face, as he has done several times, the guilty hand propelling him forward and the foot waiting to bring him down are usually his own.

He struck gold – in view of its setting, one should perhaps say oil – as T. E. Lawrence in *Lawrence of Arabia* (1962, David Lean). Prior to this, he had supported Peter Finch in *Kidnapped* (1959, Robert Stevenson) and Aldo Ray in *The Day They Robbed the Bank of England* (1960, John Guillermin), but Lawrence (O'Toole describes him as a 'brave, brilliant, slightly crazy Englishman') thrust him into the big league. Lean's customary meticulousness, and a heavyweight cast from both sides of the Atlantic, made it a striking film on a number of levels. Vying for attention beside the top-notch performances were the breathtaking locations – filmed on the spot in the Middle East – always a bonus in Lean's cautiously made epics. Neither O'Toole nor Omar Sharif, both relative newcomers, are intimidated by the other fine elements in the film. Few more spectacular stardom-ascents are on record.

He was Henry II in *Becket* (1964, Peter Glenville), with Richard Burton as the archbishop who falls foul of Henry's murderous aides for simply doing his job according to the Roman way. O'Toole is excellent as the loudly degenerate monarch whose rage against Burton's archbishop turns inward when he discovers that a death-wish expressed in the heat of the moment has been stealthily and tragically turned into reality by a quartet of power-hungry nobles who think that getting rid of Becket will win them some king-sized favours.

O'Toole was Conrad's Far East wayfarer in *Lord Jim* (1964, Richard Brooks), an actionful hotch-potch which never actually came to the boil. *What's New Pussycat* (1965, Clive Donner) also failed, by attempting to be more significant than the sum of its diverse ingredients. Leslie Halliwell called it 'a product of the wildly swinging sixties when it was thought that a big budget and stars making fools of themselves would automatically ensure a success'. Woody Allen wrote the script, and, understandably in view of more recent triumphs, declines to comment on *Pussycat* these days. Peter Sellers and O'Toole camp it up like a couple of pier-end clowns at the end of a long season who recognise there's nothing whatever to be gained from gentlemanly restraint.

By the late sixties, O'Toole had got into the tedious habit of looking wild and roaring. His characters varied from the comically daft to the dangerously mad, not so much larger than life as functioning in an orbit somewhere outside it. Roaring became a trade-mark, a substitute for having to convey extremes of emotion in more artistic forms. He applied it unreservedly in *The Lion in Winter* (1968, Anthony Harvey), as an older but scarcely wiser Henry II than in *Becket*, here hankering for an escape from his barren marriage to Eleanor of Aquitaine, played by Katherine Hepburn.

The gross antics continued with barely a pause for breath in *Country Dance* (1969, J. Lee-Thompson), written by James Kennaway, author of *Tunes of Glory* which it vaguely resembles. Here, instead of a Scottish regiment CO, the central character going boisterously mad is a Scottish landowner, played by O'Toole, whose incestuous love for his sister, Susannah York, is the root cause of his problem. Miss York is married to Michael Craig, manager of a neighbouring estate, but their relationship is on the rocks, partly because he is a bloodless soul, a well-reasoning pillar of the community, and partly because of O'Toole's and, to a lesser extent, Miss York's, hangups.

The focal point of the story is a dance organised by the local Conservative Party to introduce their soppy, Bertie Wooster-type candidate, whom the raucously inebriated O'Toole loudly calls a 'piss-pot'. The three protagonists all quarrel bitterly, amid much ranting and posturing and grand, flowing language which no-one can believe in for a minute, but the incident which pushes O'Toole over the edge is not the thought of Miss York taking up again with Craig, distressing though that prospect is for him, but her admission the morning after the dance that she has availed herself of the local stud.

As a film, it's all rather too hysterical and boneless, preferring to toy with its thorny theme of unnatural love rather than grasp it courageously. Despite all the shouting and crazy – mostly tiresome – behaviour, only for a few brief moments at the very end does O'Toole get near to conveying anything like real torment or terror. By no coincidence are those extraordinarily moving closing minutes also his most subdued in the entire film.

Wide-scale puzzlement followed the announcement that O'Toole was going to tackle the Robert Donat part in a musical remake of *Goodbye Mr Chips* (1969, Herbert Ross) opposite, of all people, Petula Clark. Yorkshire's wild Irishman and Britain's favourite wartime schoolgirl-turned-songbird seemed close to the real-life pairing of the raunchy Wolf and Little Red Riding Hood. But this was a sad, subdued O'Toole as the middle-aged schoolmaster, and Miss Clark fizzles as the musical comedy actress wooed and brought back to his stuffy school, where she fits in about as comfortably as a chunk of grit in an open tooth socket. In the Donat version, she dies in childbirth early in the film, but the remake has her flattened by a buzz-bomb whilst entertaining troops in war-time London three-quarters of the way through.

Under Milk Wood (1971, Andrew Sinclair) reunited O'Toole, as the blind Captain Cat, with Richard Burton. Dylan Thomas' pungent homage to Welsh village life is an acquired taste, and neither Burton nor Elizabeth Taylor – both, incidentally, functioning at half-strength –

Peter O'Toole, 1960

could do justice to it. One recalls the Donald Houston stage version in London during the mid 1950s and revived several times, with ten times the affection.

In *The Ruling Class* (1972, Peter Medak), O'Toole returned to ancestral homes, batty earls and gross antics. He is another deeply disturbed baronet, who inherits his title, after the previous incumbent, Harry Andrews, hangs himself clad in a ballerina skirt and be-ribboned regimental jacket. O'Toole thinks he is God, and when anyone near him exclaims 'My God', he reacts as though it were a personal summons. Asked how he can be certain he is The Man Himself, O'Toole explains that whenever he prays, 'I'm talking to myself'. All this irreverent blarney may have had some point, but the difficulty is finding it. Towards the end the film's tone of loose-limbed satire – if such it was – takes an unexpected grisly turn, as if the producers belatedly recognised they had a turkey on their hands, and decided to go out on a note of high camp. O'Toole's familiar fire-eating performance suggests nothing of the fragile but complex struggle for the character's sanity which might have made this a film worth watching.

After an enforced lay-off through illness, O'Toole came back to two Roman epics – *Caligula* (1980, Tinto Brass) and *The Antagonists* (1981, Boris Sagal) – each derisory for a different reason. The former was a trashy, lurid sexploita-

155

tion movie financed by *Penthouse*; the latter a lengthy US TV mini-series hacked down to a tolerable length for cinema distribution – one reviewer talked about O'Toole 'grimacing like a man with terminal constipation'. In *The Stuntman* (1980, Richard Rush) he played a movie director.

One of O'Toole's most refreshing performances was in the TV film *Rogue Male* (1975, Clive Donner), Geoffrey Household's elegant political thriller about a British aristocrat whose failed attempt to assassinate Hitler before the War results in his arrest, torture and escape, aided by a sympathetic freighter captain. But after he slips into Britain, O'Toole's embarrassed Upper House connections, clamouring for appeasement, abandon him to the mercies of a cultured hit-man.

O'Toole's *Macbeth* at the National Theatre (1980) was scuffed up by the critics but O'Toole defended his performance vigorously, apparently amazed that they could all be so clumsily out of sync with his own ideas. He once declared: 'If I hadn't become an actor I probably would have become a criminal.' After *Macbeth* a lot of people were saying he had accomplished both.

Peter O'Toole
b. 1932. Emotive, individualistic star who invites acting challenges which he then sometimes refuses to rise to. Enjoys playing wild-eyed, slightly mad figures which allow him to give full rein to his formidable vocal and emotional regis-

ter. Very effective as *Lawrence of Arabia* (1962). Formerly married to Sian Phillips.

1959 *Kidnapped* (Robin Oig MacGregor)
1960 *Savage Innocents* (1st Trooper)
  The Day They Robbed the Bank of England (Capt Fitch)
1962 *Lawrence of Arabia* (T. E. Lawrence)
1964 *Becket* (King Henry II)
  Lord Jim (Lord Jim)
1965 *What's New Pussycat* (Michael James)
1966 *The Bible – In the Beginning* (The Three Angels)
  How to Steal a Million (Simon Dermott)
1967 *The Night of the Generals* (General Tanz)
  Casino Royale (Piper)
1968 *Great Catherine* (Capt Charles Edstaston)
  The Lion in Winter (King Henry II)
1969 *Goodbye Mr Chips* (Arthur Chipping)
  Country Dance (Sir Charles Henry Arbuthnot Pinkerton Ferguson)
1971 *Murphy's War* (Murphy)
  Under Milk Wood (Captain Cat)
1972 *The Ruling Class* (14th Earl of Gurney)
  Man of La Mancha (Cervantes/Don Quixote)
1975 *Man Friday* (Robinson Crusoe)
  Rosebud (Larry Martin)
1980 *Caligula* (Tiberius)
1981 *The Antagonists* (Flavius Silva)
1975 *Rogue Male* (TV) (The Earl)
1979 *Zulu Dawn* (Lord Chelmsford)
1980 *The Stuntman* (Eli Cross)

Cecil Parker

In *The Iron Maiden* (1962, Gerald Thomas), PR man Jim Dale has an idea. 'Why don't we call it Swift,' he suggests to his boss, aircraft chief Cecil Parker, as they rack their brains for a name for his latest airliner. Parker's face dissolves into weary resignation. 'You'll get a swift something else in a minute,' he grunts as Dale retreats out of range.

Parker's plane takes to the air like a bird, but on the ground he's surrounded by lame ducks, as he frequently was in a career that contained more suppressed outrage than a wrestler's shorts.

He was a product of the old school, a relic of gentler times, a nobly despairing figure who al-

ways had good reason to regret, but seemed curiously incapable of abandoning, his dangerously high expectation of others. He could be snooty, smug, narrow, petulant or bossy, but this was usually redeemed by the fact that he suffered more discomfort than he caused.

In *The Iron Maiden* Parker badly needs to sell his plane to a flashy American airline boss who happens to be combining a business trip with a European vacation, along with his dreadful, bourgeois family. Parker force-feeds them on uppercrust bonhomie and cosy hobnobbing with the gentry, most of which, thanks to his chief designer's single-minded attachment to an old

Cecil Parker (right) with Stewart Granger as Paganini in *The Magic Bow* (1946)

traction engine, go badly wrong for him. The film matches the aged traction engine's performance – it was mostly an uphill struggle to sustain momentum, and even on the straight there was a tendency to creak and splutter.

In *The Man in the White Suit* (1951, Charles Crichton), a richly observed Ealing satire, Parker was boss of a textile factory where industrial chemist Alec Guinness, obsessed with creating an indestructible fabric, signs on as a labourer in order to have after-hours access to the firm's research laboratories.

Guinness achieves an apparent breakthrough, but is prevented from conveying the results to Parker personally by an implacable Teutonic butler who seems to have more arms than an octopus conducting a symphony. Eventually, through tycoon's daughter Joan Greenwood, Guinness establishes contact and Parker is impressed, but when fellow industrialists oppose the invention Parker throws in his lot with them. Textile workers, too, angrily denounce the new fabric as a threat to job security – but they need not have worried, for Guinness's invention turns

out to be not a patch on what he expected.

Parker looked every inch a diplomat, a role that he returned to several times. In *His Excellency* (1952, Robert Hamer), as a stuffy resident official of a strike-torn Mediterranean colony, he gloomily contemplates the arrival of the island's inexperienced new governor Eric Portman, a gruff dockland Socialist. Parker's misgivings are well-founded – his new boss's liberal attitude towards strikes is interpreted as weakness and cunningly exploited by a bunch of unsavoury power-snatching radicals. In the end, to keep law and order, Portman has to submerge his feelings and send in the troops, but not before he has lectured the anarchists on being 'no more fit to govern themselves than a load of blue-bottomed baboons'.

An African colony on the eve of self-government provided the setting for *Guns at Batasi* (1964, John Guillermin), in which Parker was the outgoing British governor. As an unscrupulous rebel leader waits to seize power, Parker admits to retiring military chief Jack Hawkins that 'the situation is delicate'. The black guerilla leader who threatens to turn the constitution on its end was previously detained by Parker for acts of political subversion. During his term of detention, one of his assigned duties had been to tend the Government House lawns. 'Lousy gardener,' sighs Parker. 'I hope he makes a better president!'

In *I Believe in You* (1952, Basil Dearden), Parker was a do-good probation officer coping with delinquency 'like some visiting Bishop', according to Raymond Durgnat.

He was a starchy new head of a grammar school in *It's Great to be Young* (1956, Cyril Frankel), whose high expectations suffer a severe jolt when liberal-minded history teacher John Mills, who is also in charge of the school orchestra, takes a pub piano job to pay for new instruments. Parker demands Mills' resignation for dragging the school's name into disrepute, which provokes a spontaneous demonstration of pupil power, a nose-thumbing sit-in aided and encouraged by neighbouring school-kids whose bombardment of food and other goodies strikes chords of the *Passport to Pimlico* solidarity demo. It all ends with the predictable climb-down by Parker, and peace is restored to the strains of Mills' freshly revived orchestra.

In another fussy headmaster role in *A French Mistress* (1960, Roy Boulting), he believes that sexy French teacher Agnes Laurent is his daughter – the result of a youthful Alpine holiday indiscretion. When his son, Ian Bannen, falls in love with her, Parker tries wilfully to obstruct the affair without being spotted but Bannen fails to take the hint. Eventually, an exasperated, guilt-ridden Parker has to come clean about Agnes being the lad's half-sister.

'It can't be and I *love* her,' wails Bannen, to which Parker warns: 'It can be, and you mustn't!' The only solution seems to be to send Miss Laurent packing, a move which provokes the inevitable strike action by the pupils. When a small boy cheekily recites the terms of their resumption of studies, Parker informs fellow-teachers: 'When I kill this boy, you are witnesses to the fact that I was provoked beyond endurance!'

He was nicely cast in the excellent *The Ladykillers* (1955, Alexander Mackendrick) as the smoothest of Alec Guinness's payroll gang, a genteel ex-major who consorts with crooks to pay his aged, invalid mother's welfare bills. At least, that's the sob story he concocts to prevent their landlady reporting the gang to the police. When the ploy fails, Parker is elected by the others to get rid of

her. Alone with his unsuspecting victim, Parker pretends he cannot go through with it, and confesses to her, 'These men are criminals and I am one of them, but a spark of decency remains . . .' What he hopes is that she will keep quiet long enough to let him debunk with all the loot.

He was a wicked but slightly potty, medieval despot preoccupied with, in his own words, 'laughter, gaiety, wit and wenches' in *The Court Jester* (1955, Norman Panama, Melvin Frank), a Hollywood send-up of the Robin Hood story – which is now dangerously close to becoming a send-up itself. Danny Kaye is a simple simon who conceals the real infant king from the baddies who want him dead, until help arrives in the form of a green-cloaked crusader and hordes of merrie men. Basil Rathbone, as a power-hungry nobleman, parodies his evil-sheriff image and there's an entertaining take-off of a classic Errol Flynn swordfight when Kaye, hypnotised in and out of being the world's best swordsman by the snap of a finger, changes back and forth from deadly duellist to timid rabbit before Rathbone's disbelieving eyes.

Parker was head of the pre-World War I household shipwrecked with perfect butler Kenneth More in *The Admirable Crichton* (1957, Lewis Gilbert). They have taken a tropical cruise to avoid the scandal of the arrest of one of Parker's daughters for being a suffragette, but the ship goes down in a fierce storm and for two years the little group – who have managed to reach land in a rickety lifeboat – are obliged to fend for themselves as the tropic isle's only inhabitants. More's keen survival instincts and physical resource promptly establish him a natural leader, while Parker and the others acknowledge a grudging dependence. Before long, More is installed in a hilltop cane house – a desert island equivalent of his former boss's stately home – and Parker is fussing over the odd jobs. 'You're not much help but you're a nice cheerful thing to have around,' chirps Cockney maid Diane Cilento, with whom Parker, by this time, is hopelessly in love.

While Parker is away on official duties as GOC of a Scottish regiment in *The Amorous Prawn* (1962, Anthony Kimmins), wife Joan Greenwood decides to turn the regimental HQ into a classy hotel-retreat for salmon fishing, in an attempt to boost their savings towards a retirement cottage. Ian Carmichael is a short-back-and-sides batman who doubles as a maître d'hotel, with a veneer of refinement about as

The headmaster and the organ salesman. Cecil Parker (left) about to explode over Bryan Forbes in *It's Great to be Young* (1956)

thin as the shine on his brasses. To avoid embarrassing questions from her well-to-do clientele, Miss Greenwood poses as a widow, which makes her fair game for philandering American tourist Robert Beatty.

When Parker returns prematurely, due to a dust-up at the War Office over his retirement grant – 'Forty years of loyal service and *this* is all their gratitude!' – he is in no mood to reject the offer of extra money which his wife's cheeky commercial venture is so obviously capable of earning. Unaware that Parker is Miss Greenwood's husband – it's more expedient to pass him off as a brother-in-law – Beatty confides to him, as a fellow man-of-the-world, that he is in love with her and toasts her beauty: 'To Dodo, for the way she makes you feel like one of the family.' Parker admits wryly, 'I've often felt that way myself.'

Cecil Parker
1897-1971. Versatile actor with polished, upper crust appearance, specialised in harassed fair-minded figures of authority. Equally suited to drama and comedy. On stage from 1922. Film debut: *The Woman in White* (1928)

1928	*The Woman in White*
1933	*The Golden Cage*
	Cuckoo in the Nest
1934	*Silver Spoon*
	Flat No 3
	Nine Forty-Five
	The Office Wife
	Little Friend
	The Blue Squadron
	Lady in Danger
	Dirty Work
1935	*Me and Marlborough*
	Crime Unlimited
	Her Last Affaire
	Foreign Affaires
1936	*Jack of All Trades*
	Men of Yesterday
	The Man Who Changed His Mind
	Dishonour Bright
1937	*Dark Journey*
	Storm in a Teacup

1938 *Housemaster*	*The Ladykillers* (The Major)
The Lady Vanishes	*The Court Jester* (USA) (King Roderick)
Old Iron	1956 *It's Great to be Young* (Mr Frome)
The Citadel	1957 *True As a Turtle* (Dudley)
Bank Holiday	*The Admirable Crichton* (Lord Loam)
1939 *She Couldn't Say No*	1958 *A Tale of Two Cities* (Jarvis Lorry)
The Stars Look Down	*Happy Is the Bride* (Arthur Royd)
Sons of the Sea	*Indiscreet* (Alfred Munson)
The Spider	*I Was Monty's Double* (Colonel Logan)
1940 *Two for Danger*	1959 *The Night We Dropped a Clanger* (Sir
Under Your Hat	Bertram Bukpasser)
1941 *The Saint's Vacation*	*The Navy Lark* (Commodore Stanton)
Dangerous Moonlight	*Wreck of the Mary Deare* (Chairman)
Ships With Wings	1960 *Follow That Horse* (Sir William Crane)
1946 *Caesar and Cleopatra* (Britannus)	*A French Mistress* (Mr Crane)
The Magic Bow (Germi)	*The Pure Hell of St Trinian's* (Professor
1947 *Hungry Hill* (Copper John)	Canford)
Captain Boycott (Capt Charles Boycott)	*Swiss Family Robinson* (Captain)
The Woman in the Hall (Sir	1961 *On the Fiddle* (Group Captain Bascombe)
Hamar Barnard)	*Petticoat Pirates* (Commander-in-Chief)
1948 *The First Gentleman* (Prince Regent)	1962 *The Amorous Prawn* (General Fitzadams)
The Weaker Sex (Geoffrey Radcliffe)	*Vengeance* (Stevenson)
Quartet (Colonel Peregrine)	*The Iron Maiden* (Sir Giles Trent)
Under Capricorn (The Governor)	1963 *Heavens Above* (Archdeacon Aspinall)
1949 *Dear Mr Prohack* (Arthur Prohack)	*The Comedy Man* (Rutherford)
The Chiltern Hundreds (Benjamin	*Carry on Jack* (First Sea Lord)
Beecham)	1964 *Guns at Batasi* (Deputy Commissioner
Tony Draws a Horse (Dr Howard Fleming)	Sir William Fletcher)
1951 *The Magic Box* (Platform Man)	1965 *The Amorous Adventures of Moll Flanders*
The Man in the White Suit (Alan Birnley)	(Mayor)
1952 *I Believe in You* (Henry Phipps)	*A Study in Terror* (Prime Minister)
His Excellency (Sir James Kirkman)	1966 *Circus of Fear* (Sir John)
1953 *Isn't Life Wonderful* (Father)	*A Man Could Get Killed* (USA)
1954 *For Better, For Worse* (Mr Purves)	(Sir Huntley Frazier)
Father Brown (The Bishop)	1967 *The Magnificent Two* (Ambassador)
1955 *The Constant Husband* (Llewellyn)	1969 *Oh! What a Lovely War* (Sir John)

Leslie Phillips

'The public wants comedy to forget the news, the taxes, the rates; people need laughter around them,' says Leslie Phillips, sounding like one of his doctor impersonations. And when Phillips loomed into view, moustache twitching like Bugs Bunny on heat, laughter was usually not far behind.

Refreshingly for a successful comedy actor, he has never pretended he wants to abandon the clown's tunic for More Meaningful Things. 'I'm making no claim on the heavy stuff like we comedy actors are supposed to,' he chirps. 'I can

go on forever in comedy. It gives me a terrific lift, and I often think how lucky I am to get this feeling.'

Comedy is unquestionably his forte, most frequently as a silly-ass smoothie. Before 1960 he attempted to be all-purpose, but it was a doomed struggle. Moustacheless, he was an air traffic controller in *The Sound Barrier* (1952, David Lean) with nothing to do but stare at Nigel Patrick's vapour trails. *The Limping Man* (1953, Charles De Latour) gave him slightly more to do, as a detective. In *Les Girls* (1957, George

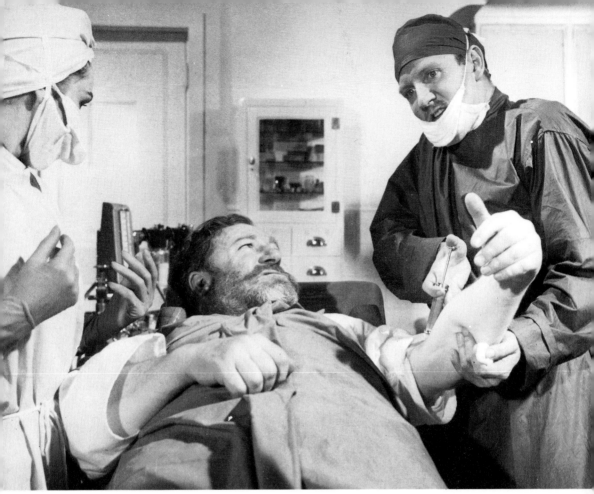

Leslie Phillips (right) injects more than a touch of humour in *Doctor in Love* (1960). James Robertson Justice takes it in the right vein!

Cukor) he was an aristocrat married to one of Gene Kelly's girl dancers.

Phillips made three early *Carry On* films and three *Doctor* tail-enders – all tedious and for-mula-written. He was a randy schools inspector in *Carry On Teacher* (1959, Gerald Thomas), a hospital patient in *Carry On Nurse* (1959, Gerald Thomas), and a copper on the beat in *Carry On Constable* (1960, Gerald Thomas).

In *Doctor in Clover* (1965, Gerald Thomas) he was in love with beguiling French physio-therapist Elizabeth Ercy, and in *Doctor in Trouble* (1970, Ralph Thomas) passion, again, lands him in the sea up to his neck when, seeing off his tweety-pie actress girl-friend Angela Scoular on a holiday cruise, he fails to disembark and gets caught up with the usual shipboard stereotypes. He was Dr Burke to Michael Craig's Dr Hare in *Doctor in Love* (1960, Ralph Thomas), about two nice-guy GPs on the loose in suburbia.

James Robertson Justice did his familiar Spratt routine without a blink, driving his car like a fire-engine ('I haven't stopped at a red light since Cairo in 1922,' he growls, hurtling through yet another one) and supervising arrangements for his own appendectomy. The film had a macabre postscript – both Virginia Maskell and Carole Lesley, who played the doctors' girlfriends, were to die in tragic circumstances.

Phillips supported Stanley Baxter in *The Fast Lady* (1962, Ken Annakin), a lumpy comedy that made too much of Baxter's lugubrious personal-ity and not enough of the comic potential of the trials of an inept learner-driver. Baxter needs his licence to impress girl friend Julie Christie's car-mad bigwig father James Robertson Justice, and Phillips is Baxter's raffish chum whose well-meaning help is an invitation to disaster.

Crooks Anonymous (1962, Ken Annakin) reunited several of the *Fast Lady* team in an

161

amusing but over-the-top farce about a successful thief, Phillips, who volunteers for reform therapy at Wilfrid Hyde White's self-correction academy for the sake of romance. Showgirl Julie Christie has threatened to ditch him unless he mends his ways, but when the temptation of a quarter of a million-pound pre-Christmas take from the department store where he works is thrust his way, love almost loses by a light finger.

He sold slimming biscuits in *The Magnificent Seven Deadly Sins* (1971, Graham Stark) from an office converted into an anorexic's nightmare. Filing cabinets, desk drawers, even a hollow desk lamp were stuffed with mouth-watering goodies. Not even a scantily-clad Julie Ege can divert his attention from food. What is intended as an intimate evening at her opulent apartment becomes an frantic search for calories as Phillips' taste buds go on the rampage. And when Julie vanishes into the bedroom as a prelude to some slap and tickle, Phillips gleefully helps himself to the contents of her pressure-cooker.

When he eventually rests his head on the divine Miss Ege's pillow, the muffled groans she hears have nothing to do with passion – he is writhing with indigestion, with his doctor's recent shrill warnings of the consequences of over-eating echoing in his ears. Proof, indeed, that nobody should expect to eat his cake – and have it!

Phillips was TV's original *Man at St Marks* in 1964, an unusual choice in view of his established libidinous personality. One had the strangest feeling that he might be concealing a blue movie inside his cassock. His successor Donald Sinden, a different type of film smoothie, wore the cloth more imposingly. Phillips reverted to his familiar capers in 1966, in the TV series *Foreign Affairs*, as a raunchy diplomat married to Jan Holden. Most of his attention in recent times has concentrated on the theatre, in amorous farces designed to give the brain a night off.

Leslie Phillips

b. 1924. Former child actor, later suave but accident-prone 'silly-ass' light comedy actor. *Carry On . . .* and *Doctor* series veteran noted for roving-eye roles in slapstick and farce. Frequently seen in recent years in sexy stage romps. Film debut: *Lassie from Lancashire* (1935).

1938 *The Citadel*
1949 *Train of Events* (uncredited)

1951 *Pool of London* (Harry)
1952 *The Sound Barrier* (Air Traffic Controller)
1953 *The Limping Man* (Inspector Cameron)
1955 *Value for Money* (Robjohns)
1956 *The Gamma People* (Howard Meade)
       The Big Money (Receptionist)
1957 *The Barretts of Wimpole Street* (Harry Bevan)
       Brothers in Law (Shopman)
       The Smallest Show on Earth (Robin Carter)
       High Flight (Squadron Leader Blake)
       Just My Luck (Hon Richard Lumb)
       Les Girls (Sir Gerald Wren)
1958 *I Was Monty's Double* (Major Tennant)
1959 *The Man Who Liked Funerals* (Simon Hurd)
       Carry On Nurse (Jack Bell)
       The Angry Hills (Ray Taylor)
       Carry On Teacher (Alastair Grigg)
       This Other Eden (Crispin Brown)
       The Night We Dropped a Clanger (Squadron Leader Thomas)
       The Navy Lark (Lieutenant Poulter)
       Please Turn Over (Dr Henry Manners)
1960 *Carry On Constable* (Tom Potter)
       Inn for Trouble (John Belcher)
       Doctor in Love (Tony Burke)
       Watch Your Stern (Lieutenant Commander Bill Fanshawe)
       No Kidding (David Robinson)
1961 *A Weekend with Lulu* (Tim)
       Very Important Person (Jimmy Cooper)
       Raising the Wind (Mervyn)
       In the Doghouse (Jimmy Fox-Upton)
1962 *Crooks Anonymous* (Dandy Forsdyke)
       The Fast Lady (Freddie Fox)
       The Longest Day (RAF Officer)
1963 *Father Came Too* (Roddy Chipfield)
1965 *You Must Be Joking* (Husband)
       Doctor In Clover (Dr Gaston Grimsdyke)
1966 *Maroc T* (Raymond Lowe)
1970 *Some Will, Some Won't* (Simon Russell)
       Doctor In Trouble (Dr Simon Burke)
1971 *The Magnificent Seven Deadly Sins* (Dickie, in the Gluttony episode)
1972 *Not Now Darling* (Gilbert Bodley)
1973 *Don't Just Lie There* (Sir William Mainwaring-Brown)
1975 *Spanish Fly* (Mike Scott)
1976 *Not Now Comrade* (Commander Rimmington)

Donald Pleasence

'I always think I'm much better looking than I turn out on screen,' says Donald Pleasence. He is entitled to his illusions. On film or across a room Pleasence is a chilling sight. He has the kind of piercing stare that lifts enamel off saucepans and when he is nasty, which is most of the time, he can be very convincing.

Like Robert Newton, Pleasence is a potent combination of eyes and voice. The eyes are mournful but they can also be sinister or seedy or just plain nutty. The voice rarely rises above a cultured purr and sounds like blood slushing over the edge of a cauldron. He declines to be called a star, preferring the description 'feature player who is occasionally given star billing', which says it all. Pleasence is a skilful, sensitive performer whose range has been influenced more by his appearance than anything else. 'I was slotted into the beady-eyed business, and find it immensely enjoyable,' he explains.

So, too, have his audiences, for nobody can accuse him of holding anything back. At excavating holes in people's skulls with a solitary glance, Pleasence can have few equals.

In the James Bond film *You Only Live Twice* (1967, Lewis Gilbert) he was arch-villain Blofeld, feared boss of SPECTRE and would-be world supremo, engaged by Red China to foment a global war by setting the USA and the Soviets at each other's throats. SPECTRE achieves this by the simple device of a monster rocket skulking around in outer space and gobbling up any manned capsule foolish enough to venture into orbit. Naturally, America and Russia blame each other. But we have already been let into the secret – that it's only slippery old Pleasence, badly scarred and wonky-eyed and with a liking for cuddly white cats.

When the Chinese protest to Pleasence for jacking up the price of starting World War III by a few million dollars, and yelp about extortion, Pleasence calmly replies: 'Extortion is my business, gentlemen.' After he dunks an inefficient female aide in a giant pool of piranha fish to show the kind of chap he is, the Chinese decide to waive all further protests.

In *James Bond in the Cinema* John Brosnan points out the unsuitability of Pleasence to playing Blofeld and rates his performance a 'disappointment'. The facial disfigurement was a studio afterthought aimed at giving Pleasence,

literally, a distinguishing mark to help audiences forget his previous lengthy catalogue of weak, snively creations. On later Blofelds – Telly Savalas, Charles Gray – the device was considered unnecessary.

But long before that, Pleasence had been beavering away in a succession of small but highly charged, predominantly villain roles that were difficult to ignore. He was a vicious rabble-rouser in *A Tale of Two Cities* (1958, Ralph Thomas), committed to making the nobs pay, notably the hated Christopher Lee. In *The Flesh and the Fiends* (1960, John Gilling) he was a 19th-century grave-robber who really digs his profession. In *Circus of Horrors* (1959, Sidney Hayers) he gives half his rundown circus to face-surgeon Anton Diffring in gratitude for transforming his disfigured little daughter into a bright-eyed gamine. Diffring inherits the whole show when Pleasence is crushed to death by an overweight Russian bear. Pleasence was an embittered headmaster in *Spare the Rod* (1961, Leslie Norman), whose preference for antiquated whack 'em techniques strikes the wrong note with the new teacher Max Bygraves.

He made a couple of arty films around the mid-1960s, both heavy going. In Pinter's *The Caretaker* (1963, Hall Bartlett) he was a shabby old tramp and in *Cul-de-Sac* (1966, Roman Polanski) he played a sexual fruitcake whose bizarre hideaway is invaded by a couple of malevolent gangsters.

In *The Great Escape* (1963, John Sturges), he was James Garner's cell-mate, a timid fussy civil servant shot down during a reconnaissance flight which he had no business being on in the first place. 'Tea without milk is so uncivilised,' he complains to Garner, who is nicknamed the Scrounger for his knack of being able to charm or steal off the Germans anything that's needed for the planned escape. When Pleasence, whose job it is to forge visas and other documents, wants a camera, Garner blithely asks, 'What kind?' Shortly before the breakout Pleasence's sight fails, but Garner gamely volunteers to look after him. They snatch a light aircraft and head for Switzerland, but engine trouble forces them down on the German side of the border and Pleasence is spotted and shot by an enemy patrol.

He has acted in numerous American films,

Donald Pleasence (right) looking very 'off-the-peg' beside an elegant Oliver Reed in *Tomorrow Never Comes* (1979)

such as *Soldier Blue* (1970, Ralph Nelson) in which he played a nasty gun-runner, and *The Greatest Story Ever Told* (1965, George Stevens), where he went round stoking up trouble for Max Von Sydow, the film's gaunt and uninspired Jesus. In *Fantastic Voyage* (1966, Richard Fleischer), a sci-fi adventure about pumping a miniaturised team of medics into a VIP's bloodstream to repair brain damage, Pleasence was a baddie, implanted to sabotage the job. While the others are outside their capsule, Pleasence seizes control and drives off along a getaway artery, but star repairman Stephen Boyd scores a direct hit on the vehicle with his laser gun. The crashing capsule damages the host subject's tissues, and Pleasence, trapped in the pilot's cabin, is slowly devoured by white corpuscles, the bloodstream's natural vigilantes.

He was a royal toady in *Henry VIII and His Six Wives* (1972, Waris Husein), a big screen adaptation of Keith Michell's TV success, gleefully weeding out opponents to Henry's divorce, smug in the delusion that with the king's patronage he can literally get away with murder. When a confession is needed, Pleasence is there with a knot-

ted rope. Not surprisingly, he clocks up a few enemies in high places, and an alliance of nettled privy counsellors extract their revenge in the traditional way.

During the early 1970s, Pleasence made two engaging films with Michael Caine. In Robert Louis Stevenson's *Kidnapped* (1971, Delbert Mann), he was the young hero David Balfour's niggardly Uncle Ebenezer, a crafty old skinbag who is aware that he is dying before the doctor, rushed to his bedside, knows it. As Davie and the physician retire to an adjoining room, to finalise burial arrangements, Pleasence yells at his nephew, 'Don't let him charge you too much!'

In *The Black Windmill* (1974, Don Siegel), an above-average spy thriller whose opening credits defy anyone to read them, he was Caine's boss, director of subversive warfare, a tetchy individual who, according to department chief Joss Ackland, needs to consult his doctor if he 'hasn't solved his *Times* crossword by ten in the morning'. When a kidnap gang seize Caine's son and Pleasence refuses to meet the ransom demand, Caine is forced to take matters into his, as usual, competent hands. He steals half a million pounds in diamonds from his employers and sets off to Paris, where he believes the boy is being kept, to arrange the handover, but the lad is imprisoned much nearer home, in an old windmill near Brighton. Villain of the plot turns out to be Pleasence's boss, played by Joseph O'Connor, whose sexy young wife has depleted his resources in every way imaginable. Typically, Pleasence gives a knockout performance as the twitchy spymaster who keeps fiddling with his moustache, and continuously dabs his face with paper tissues which are then fed into the shredder beside his desk.

Donald Pleasence
b. 1921. On stage since 1939. Specialises in high tension menace. Film debut: *The Beachcomber* (1954).

1954 *The Beachcomber* (Tramp)
     Orders Are Orders (L/Cpl Martin)
1955 *Value for Money* (Limpy)
1956 *1984* (Parsons)
     The Black Tent (Ali)
1957 *The Man in the Sky* (Crabtree)
     Manuela (Evans)
     Barnacle Bill (Bank-teller)
1958 *A Tale of Two Cities* (Barsad)

Heart of a Child (Speil)
The Wind Cannot Read (Doctor)
The Man Inside (Organ Grinder)
The Two Headed Spy (General Hardt)
1959 *Look Back in Anger* (Hurst)
Killers of Kilimanjaro (Captain)
The Battle of the Sexes (Irwin Hoffman)
1960 *The Shakedown* (Jessel)
The Flesh and the Fiends (William Hare)
Hell Is a City (Gus Hawkins)
Circus of Horrors (Vanet)
Sons and Lovers (Pappleworth)
The Big Day (Victor Partridge)
Suspect (Brown)
The Hands of Orlac (Coates)
A Story of David (Nabal)
1961 *No Love for Johnnie* (Roger Renfrew)
The Wind of Change (Pop)
Spare the Rod (Jenkins)
The Horsemasters (Major Pinsky)
What a Carve Up (Everett Sloane)
The Inspector (Sergeant Wolters)
1962 *Doctor Crippen* (Doctor Crippen)
1963 *The Caretaker* (Davis)
The Great Escape (Blythe, 'The Forger')
1965 *The Greatest Story Ever Told* (USA)
(The Dark Hermit)
The Hallelujah Trail (Oracle Jones)
1966 *Cul-de-Sac* (George)
Matchless (USA) (Andreanu)
Eye of the Devil (Père Dominic)
Night of the Generals (Gen Kahlenberge)
Fantastic Voyage (USA) (Dr Michaels)
1967 *Will Penny* (USA) (Preacher Quint)
You Only Live Twice (Blofeld)
1969 *The Madwoman of Chaillot* (Prospector)
Arthur Arthur (unbilled)
1970 *THX 1138* (USA) (SEN 5241)
Soldier Blue (USA) (Isaac Cumber)
Mister Freedom (Doctor Freedom)

1971 *The Pied Piper* (Baron)
1972 *Kidnapped* (Ebenezer Balfour)
Innocent Bystanders (Loomis)
Henry VIII and His Six Wives (Thomas
Cromwell)
Death Live (Inspector Colquhoun)
1973 *Wedding in White* (Jim)
Raw Meat (Inspector Calhoun)
From Beyond the Grave (Peddler)
Tales That Witness Madness (Tremayne)
1974 *The Black Windmill* (Cedric Harper)
The Mutations (Nolter)
Barry Mackenzie Holds His Own (Erich,
Count Plasma)
The Count of Monte Cristo (Danglars)
1975 *Hearts of the West* (USA) (A. J. Nietz)
From Beyond the Grave (Underwood)
I Don't Want to Be Born (Dr Finch)
Escape to Witch Mountain (USA)
(Deranian)
Trial by Combat (Sir Giles Marley)
1976 *A Choice of Weapons* (Sir Giles Marley)
The Devil's Men (Father Roche)
The Last Tycoon (Boxley)
1977 *The Eagle Has Landed* (Heinrich
Himmler)
The Uncanny (Valentine De'Ath)
Oh God (USA) (Dr Harmon)
1978 *Halloween* (USA) (Dr Sam Loomis)
Dracula (Jack Seward)
1979 *Telefon* (USA) (Nicolai Dalchimsky)
Blood Relatives (Doniac)
Tomorrow Never Comes (Dr Todd)
Sergeant Pepper (USA) (B. D. Brockhurst)
Jaguar Lives (General Villanova)
Labyrinth (France)
The Monster Club (Pickering)
All Quiet on the Western Front (Kantoreck)
Escape to New York (USA) (US President)
1980 *Halloween II* (Loomis)

Dennis Price

Dennis Price was consistently our best-ever cultured swine. Behind that gentlemanly disdain
lay a sadly underrated self-effacing light-comic
talent. The trouble was that Price rarely took
anything very seriously, least of all his own
career which meandered along under its own
steam while the actor scanned the horizon for
other amusements. After a well-publicised

bankruptcy, Price withdrew to the Isle of Sark,
returning only when work required his presence
and then with little enthusiasm.

An ex-Gainsborough smoothie, nastier than
Granger but lighter than Mason, he adopted the
pose of an English George Sanders – refined,
self-centred, caddish, contemptuous of a world
inhabited by inferiors. Everything about Price

Dennis Price, Marie Lohr (centre) and Phyllis Calvert in *The Magic Bow* (1946)

was deceptive. He could be penniless and still manage to look as if he owned the bank. But behind all that grand talk and those lordly ways there skulked, in his characters, the most ordinary of shabby, grasping souls.

He played the daddy of all murderers in *Kind Hearts and Coronets* (1949, Robert Hamer), through which his measured but laconic attitude to humour, and to life, was most graphically depicted. Price was a relative of the rich and influential D'Ascoynes – all played by Alec Guinness – but his branch of the family has been disinherited, and thus impoverished, because Price's mother, daughter of the seventh Duke, eloped with an Italian tenor. The family's callous treatment of her, and Price's resultant poverty, makes him want to kill every member, a feeling that intensifies when childhood sweetheart Joan Greenwood rejects him for a rich oaf.

One by one the Guinness characters succumb to his deadly overtures, which include drowning, shooting, poisoning, detonating and bring-

ing down with an arrow. His final victim dodges the net, but only by collapsing and dying of his own accord – on hearing about the others. It's not the Guinness murders for which Price is eventually convicted but for killing Miss Greenwood's oafish husband, a crime which, ironically, he did not commit. And that's not the end of the story by any means.

Kind Hearts and Coronets fairly sparkles throughout. Price's witty voice-over narration of the events leading to the condemned cell, particularly his references to the actual murders, is matched blow for blow by Robert Hamer's stylish images.

Price was the poet Byron in *The Bad Lord Byron* (1948, David Macdonald); a mediocre music hall artiste in *Charley Moon* (1956, Guy Hamilton); an English major in *Oh Rosalinda* (1955, Michael Powell); a psychiatrist in *The Millionairess* (1960, Anthony Asquith); and a gay photographer – corrupt again, but making an enjoyable meal of it – in *No Love for Johnnie* (1961, Ralph Thomas) – characters elevated

166

beyond their book value by Price's cut-glass portrayals.

In *The Naked Truth* (1957, Mario Zampi), he publishes a sleazy scandal magazine as a prop to blackmailing several prominent figures, who include randy artistocrat Terry-Thomas, glutinous TV personality Peter Sellers, and famous authoress Peggy Mount. Determined to keep their nasty secrets locked away, the victims join forces against Price, and after a few disasters manage to get him into their clutches.

In *I'm All Right, Jack* (1959, John Boulting), again with Terry-Thomas and Sellers, he was one of the capitalist swindlers, boss of a missile factory profiteering from a specially-engineered strike.

Price was the police inspector investigating *The Haunted House of Horror* (1969, Michael Armstrong), a trite melodrama about a bunch of Carnaby Street mods who attempt to leaven their boredom by holding a midnight seance in a deserted manor house. Later, one of them is mutilated in a frenzied knife attack. Twenty years previously similar grisly goings-on are rumoured to have happened – could the ghost of the original crazed killer have been activated by the kids' apparently harmless caper? In the hands of an imaginative scriptwriter, perhaps, but this weak exploitation movie contained no surprises. Price plodded around with the wounded air of a five-star hotel guest who had just lost his trousers in a revolving door – as well he might, for having lent his name to such junk.

He was an obnoxious adjutant in *Tunes of Glory* (1960, Ronald Neame), reunited with Alec Guinness as his commanding officer. In *Tamahine* (1963, Philip Leacock) he was the lah-di-da headmaster of a public school into whose serene, well-ordered world pops his orphaned, Polynesian-born god-daughter Nancy Kwan, a frisky, fun-loving lass who unselfconsciously sets the campus alight and ends up marrying the headmaster's son. In *Theatre of Blood* (1973, Douglas Hickox), Price was a dramatic critic whose career is cut short on the end of a spear. It's a tricky business at any time writing about actors, but Price makes the mistake of panning the work of his namesake, mad Vincent, whose anger comes across a little more pointedly than the unfortunate Dennis might have wished.

In one of his earlier films, *Lady Godiva Rides Again* (1951, Frank Launder), Price played a character one imagines might have been close to

the bone, a movie star pursued by adoring females. Price's problem is that none of his conquests share his sophisticated, amoral attitude to life. When beauty queen Pauline Stroud, enticed to his yacht for a dirty weekend, turns out to be another simple-minded, small-town bosom on pretty legs, Price can scarcely conceal his distaste. 'I can't stand fans who dote on every word and gesture,' he quibbles, dismissing her as if she were a troublesome housefly.

Dennis Price

1915-1973. Refined but slightly wooden romatic lead of the 1940s, developed via *Kind Hearts and Coronets* (1949) into effortless, entertaining, decadent, light comedy actor, seen in several of the best Boultings satires. Late career involvement in obscure horror pics and worse considered a sad waste. Definitive Jeeves in TV's *World Of Wooster*. On stage from 1937. Film debut: *A Canterbury Tale* (1944).

1945 *A Place of One's Own* (Dr Selbie)
      The Echo Murders (Dick Warren)
1946 *Caravan* (Sir Francis Castleton)
      The Magic Bow (Paul de la Roche)
1947 *Hungry Hill* (Greyhound John)
      Dear Murderer (Richard Fenton)
      Holiday Camp (Squadron Leader
        Hardwicke)
      Jassy (Christopher Hatton)
      Master of Bankdam (Joshua Crowther)
      The White Unicorn (Richard Glover)
1948 *Easy Money* (Joe Henry)
      Snowbound (Neil Blair)
      Good Time Girl (Red Farrell)
      The Bad Lord Byron (Lord Byron)
1949 *Kind Hearts and Coronets* (Louis Mazzini)
      The Lost People (Captain Ridley)
1950 *The Dancing Years* (Rudi Kleiber)
      Murder Without Crime (Matthew)
1951 *The Adventurers* (Clive Hunter)
      The Magic Box (Assistant)
      The House in the Square (Tom Pettigrew)
      Lady Godiva Rides Again (Simon Abbott)
1952 *Song of Paris* (Matthew Ibbetson)
      Tall Headlines (Maurice Fletcher)
1953 *Noose for a Lady* (Simon Gale)
      Murder at 3 am (Inspector Lawton)
      The Intruder (Leonard Pirry)
1954 *Time Is My Enemy* (Martin Radley)
      For Better for Worse (Debenham)
1955 *That Lady* (Mateo Vasquez)
      Oh Rosalinda (Major Frank)

Dastardly Dennis Price woos Valerie Hobson in *Kind Hearts and Coronets* (1949)

1956 *Private's Progress* (Bertram Tracepurcel)
      Charley Moon (Harold Armytage)
      Port Afrique (Robert Blackton)
      A Touch of the Sun (Hatchard)
1957 *Fortune is a Woman* (Tracy Morton)
      The Naked Truth (Nigel Dennis)
1958 *Hello London* (guest appearance)
1959 *Danger Within* (Captain Roger Callendar)
      I'm All Right Jack (Bertram Tracepurcel)
      Don't Panic Chaps (Captain Edward Von
          Krisling)
1960 *School for Scoundrels* (Dunstan
          Dorchester)
      Oscar Wilde (Robbie Ross)
      Piccadilly Third Stop (Edward)
      The Millionairess (Dr Adrian Bland)
      Pure Hell of St Trinian's
          (Gore-Blackwood)
      Tunes of Glory (Major Charles Scott)
1961 *No Love for Johnny* (Flagg)
      The Rebel (Jim Smith)
      Five Golden Hours (Raphael)

      Double Bunk (Leonard Watson)
      Watch It Sailor (Lt/Cdr Hardcastle)
      Victim (Calloway)
      What a Carve Up (Guy Broughton)
1962 *Go to Blazes* (Withers)
      Play It Cool (Sir Charles Bryant)
      The Pot Carriers (Smooth-Tongue)
      Behave Yourself (short)
      The Amorous Prawn (War Minister
          Prawn)
      Kill or Cure (Dr Crossley)
      The Wrong Arm of the Law (Educated
          Ernest)
1963 *The Cool Mikado* (Ronald Fortescue)
      The VIPs (Commander Millbank)
      The Cracksman (Grantley)
      Doctor in Distress (Blacker)
      Tamahine (Charles Poole)
      The Comedy Man (Tommy Morris)
      A Jolly Bad Fellow (Jack Hughes)
1964 *The Horror of It All* (Cornwallis)
      Murder Most Foul (Harris Tumbrill)

The Earth Dies Screaming (Quinn Taggett)	*Venus in Furs* (Kapp)
1965 *A High Wind in Jamaica* (Mathias)	1971 *Twins of Evil* (Dietrich)
Curse of Simba (Major Lomas)	1972 *Tower of Evil* (Laurence Bakewell)
Ten Little Indians (Dr Armstrong)	*The Adventures of Barry McKenzie* (Mr Gort)
1966 *Just Like a Woman* (Salesman)	*Alice's Adventures in Wonderland* (King of Hearts)
1967 *Jules Verne's Rocket to the Moon* (Duke of Barset)	*Pulp* (Mysterious Englishman)
1969 *The Haunted House of Horror* (Inspector)	*Go for a Take* (Dracula)
The Magic Christian (Winthrop)	*That's Your Funeral* (Mr Soul)
1970 *Some Will, Some Won't* (Benson)	1973 *Theatre of Blood* (Hector Snipe)
The Horror of Frankenstein (Grave Robber)	*Son of Dracula* (Van)
The Rise and Rise of Michael Rimmer (Fairburn)	1975 *Horror Hospital* (Mr Pollack)
	Helter Skelter (guest appearance)

Basil Radford

'I think of myself as a matador and the audience as the bull,' Basil Radford once said. As the lovable old bull of British film comedy, Radford did his own share of stamping and snorting. Irascible, tweedy, cricket-loving, Radford was, according to Charles Barr, 'the epitome of the Whitehall mind'. He certainly came close to the popular idea of a civic toady neatly parcelled in red tape.

Radford was the actor who more than anyone gave pinstripes a bad name. Richard Wattis and, to a lesser extent, Terry-Thomas came along afterwards and cashed in on the type of fussy, myopic, bungling minor official that Radford had played to perfection. Radford gave pomposity a box-office value and that was no mean achievement.

His successful partnership with Naunton Wayne took nothing away from either's individual accomplishments, but each is probably better remembered for the films they made together than for their independent appearances. As the *News Chronicle* so charmingly put it: 'They were as inseparable in the public mind as mild and bitter or mustard and cress.'

They were British diplomats in *The Lady Vanishes* (1938, Alfred Hitchcock), agreeably chirpy in the face of dangers they never quite seem to acknowledge. The dangers, like the characters, reappeared in *Night Train to Munich* (1940, Carol Reed), famous for the scene where Radford, unable to get his copy of *Punch* from a mid-German station bookstall, settles grumpily for a copy of *Mein Kampf*. 'They give it to all the bridal couples, don't they,' he tells Wayne, who tut-tuts, 'I don't think it's *that* kind of book, old man.' Later, when they are obliged to make a hasty exit from the train in borrowed German uniforms, the original owners of the uniforms are left trussed like chickens and one of them has the dreaded book, open at a suitable page, strapped to his face.

Radford's most famous character was arguably Captain Waggett, the killjoy Home Guard official in *Whisky Galore* (1948, Alexander Mackendrick), eternally thwarted by devious islanders in his efforts to recoup a large consignment of booze shipwrecked off the Hebridean coast. 'Once you let people take the law into their own hands it's anarchy, *anarchy*,' he preaches to long-suffering wife Catherine Lacey. But unfortunately for Radford, the islanders – 'A happy people with few and simple pleasures,' croons the voice-over as a dozen children in diminishing sizes scamper from a humble croft – are prone to interpret the law somewhat liberally if it means keeping hold of a quantity of shipwrecked Scotch.

The resourcefulness of the mop-up operation (cots, cash registers and hot water bottles are among containers used to hide the stuff) halts Radford in his tracks as surely as the barbed wire with which they snag his car. His sad, humiliating recall to the mainland is cleverly counterpointed by the islanders' giving expression to their glee.

Rebellion against authority figured strongly in *Passport to Pimlico* (1949, Henry Cornelius), with Radford and Naunton Wayne as a pair of dim Whitehall johnnies getting their fingers burnt on a constitutional hot potato, when a bunch of residents demand self-government following the discovery of an ancient scroll which apparently bestows upon them that right.

Like the *Whisky Galore* islanders, the Pimlico residents – or Burgundians, as they prefer to be called – outwit officialdom at every turn. But it all ends amicably when they tire of the novelty of being foreigners, with Radford and Wayne invited to the celebratory lunch to mark their surrender. On the way to the festivities, Wayne contemplates the possibility of the meal extending, with luck, to two courses. 'Hope so,' says Radford gloomily. 'I haven't had a decent feed since that deadlock in Moscow . . .'

One of his last films was *Chance of a Lifetime* (1950, Bernard Miles, Alan Orbiston), a modest but caring anecdote about how Radford copes with a rash of industrial unrest at his small agricultural firm, triggered off by the dismissal of a troublemaker. When he agrees to step down and let the union bulletheads take over responsibility, they are at first delighted but soon discover that pacifying banks and suppliers of raw materials is trickier than they had imagined.

When resources dry up, the new 'bosses' become the target of the same kind of insults and recriminations previously levelled at Radford, who unknown to them is beavering away behind the scenes trying to keep the firm on the rails. In the end, the workers recognise somewhat shamefacedly that their traditional 'them-and-us' mentality is a recipe for certain failure, and Radford is invited back to lead a vigorous assault on their dwindling markets.

Despite the cosiness with which all the problems are tidied up at the end, the film delivers its message with an appreciable degree of honesty, and, bearing in mind the state of modern-day industrial relations, it seems amazing how little either management or unions have learnt in the intervening decades. The mailed-fist attitudes

Home Guard officer Basil Radford (right) and Army sergeant Bruce Seton review plans to thwart the islanders in *Whisky Galore* (1948)

which tripped up Radford's firm seem to have softened very little. Perhaps *Chance of a Lifetime* should be made obligatory viewing in every industrial dispute before anyone calls for a show of hands.

Basil Radford

1897-1952. Imperturbable English gent-type actor, often bumptious diplomat or military top brass. Successful partnership on film with Naunton Wayne. On stage from 1922. Film debut: *There Goes the Bride* (1932).

1933 *Just Smith*
     A Southern Maid
1936 *Broken Blossoms*
     Dishonour Bright
1937 *Jump for Glory*
     Young and Innocent
     Captain's Orders
1938 *Convict 99* ·
     The Lady Vanishes
     Climbing High
1939 *Let's Be Famous*
     Trouble Brewing
     Jamaica Inn
     Spies of the Air
     Secret Journey

Just William
The Girl Who Forgot
She Couldn't Say No
1940 *The Flying Squad*
     Night Train to Munich
     Room for Two
     Crooks Tour
     The Girl in the News
1942 *Unpublished Story*
     Flying Fortress
1943 *Dear Octopus*
     Millions Like Us
1944 *Twilight Hour*
1945 *The Way to the Stars* ('Tiny' Williams)
     Dead of Night (George Parratt)
1946 *The Captive Heart* (Major Dalrymple)
     A Girl in a Million (Prendergast)
1948 *The Winslow Boy* (Esmond Curry)
     Quartet (Henry Garnet)
     Whisky Galore (Capt Paul Waggett)
1949 *It's Not Cricket* (Major Bright)
     Passport to Pimlico (Gregg)
     Stop Press Girl (Engine Driver, Bus
          Driver, Fred, Projectionist, Pilot)
1950 *Chance of a Lifetime* (Dickinson)
1951 *The Galloping Major* (Major Arthur Hill)
     White Corridors (Civil Servant)

Ralph Richardson

In *Tales from the Crypt* (1972, Freddie Francis), Ralph Richardson was the crypt-keeper who presides over the salutary warnings given to five individually dislikable people. 'I assure you I do have a purpose,' he insists. Presumably it was to prove that even an actor of Sir Ralph's peerage would act the fool occasionally if the money is good enough.

Richardson is best in smallish colourful roles which engage his natural eccentricity and intuitive sense of theatre. He attacks his roles with relish, and loftily dismisses the idea that fun diminishes art. The real-life Richardson, a motorbike-mad senior citizen in primrose coloured socks and a fluorescent crash-lid presents as enduring – and endearing – an image as anything he has done on film.

He has been around a long time, in films since the mid-1930s, with much of his pre-war work in the major productions of the period – eg *Things*

to *Come* (1936, William Cameron Menzies), *The Citadel* (1938, King Vidor), *The Four Feathers* (1939, Zoltan Korda). His first major post-war role was in *The Fallen Idol* (1948, Carol Reed), adapted from Graham Greene's short story *The Basement Room*, and first of the Reed-Greene collaborations.

Richardson played an unhappily married embassy butler suspected of killing his wife after his affections transfer to typist Michele Morgan. The impressionable ambassador's son who idolises the butler as a kind of father-substitute, believes Richardson is responsible for his wife's death, and first absconds then lies to the police to protect his idol, unaware that his behaviour is helping to fix a noose around Richardson's neck.

Set during a weekend in the embassy when the boy's parents are away, the tragic events are portrayed through the boy's eyes, with plenty of low camera shots and elaborate, gloomy room sets to

Ralph Richardson, 1962

ments of hell, but the audience is denied a glimpse of this till the 'evil vision' nears expurgation in the shape of dearly-bought triumph making its final flirtation. And when we are let into his awful secret, the dread that all the pain and the loss may in the end be for nothing, as replacement test pilot John Justin goes after the big prize, the anguish is crosshatched across his face like vapour-trails across the sky.

Through the film's theme of supersonic flight, Lean uses contemporary conflict to pose a question that is, in effect, timeless: are experiments that risk life worth the end results? Miss Todd and Richardson articulate both sides of the argument with considerable fire and honesty, but it is in the superb flying sequences where the film's vitality is most memorably tracked.

Denholm Elliott was again Richardson's son in *The Holly and the Ivy* (1952, George More O'Ferrall), in which Richardson played a Norfolk clergyman who, during a strained Christmas reunion, is served up with a series of unpalatable truths about his siblings. This is a modest little film, good on atmosphere, and its depiction of an unremittingly gloomy rural middle-class family, whose outward calm at the beginning is revealed as merely cosmetic and whose skeletons need very little bidding before popping out of the closet, appears nicely judged throughout.

Richardson was Laurence Olivier's conniving aide in *Richard III* (1955, Laurence Olivier), Shakespeare's weighty historical tome pruned and trimmed into a thrifty and visually appealing confection. Olivier was in lusty form, as the excitable, treacherous English prince who uses Richardson, as a shady duke, to help nobble more direct heirs to the throne than he.

The villains disagree, however, on how Richardson will be rewarded for his services and their acrimonious parting – as Richardson doggedly reminds the evil king of his pledge, whilst sensibly recognising the dangers of getting too far out on a limb, and Olivier sulks and threatens, all pretence at fair-mindedness and humility dramatically discarded the moment he wears the crown – is a scene that stays in the memory. The film, it must be said, is only intermittently brilliant although the eve-of-battle 'ghost' sequences and Olivier's acrobatic death spasms contain sufficient impact to help one overlook their obvious theatricality.

Richardson has played numerous historical figures, such as Gladstone in *Khartoum* (1966,

convey his deepening fear and bewilderment. Richardson played the tragedy's centrepiece 'flawlessly', helped by Greene's articulate script and Reed's ability to expand fine words into vivid images.

He was the steely-minded aircraft chief obsessed with proving his supersonic flight theories in *The Sound Barrier* (1952, David Lean), an exhilarating tribute to the early jetmen. It's a film which has lost none of its original appeal, and contains the flavour of the period – those halcyon, pre-computer days when chief designers probably were lovable, crumpled figures like Joseph Tomelty – held tightly in place like a relic under glass.

Richardson's hopes of having the world of supersonic flight by the tail fin suffer numerous setbacks – first, his son Denholm Elliott is killed attempting a solo flight, and then debonair son-in-law test pilot Nigel Patrick, who has married Richardson's daughter, Ann Todd, becomes a hole in the ground when the plane refuses to level off after a record-challenging dive – but the old tycoon battles on, apparently unmoved by the realisation that he is despatching members of his family like Red Star parcels.

Inwardly, of course, he is suffering the tor-

Basil Dearden); barrister Sir Edward Carson, a key figure in the trial of *Oscar Wilde*, the Robert Morley version (1960, Gregory Ratoff); and George III in *Lady Caroline Lamb* (1972, Robert Bolt), a trashy account of the celebrated 19th-century scandal involving a top peer's lady and the poet Byron. Richardson was the orphaned Omar Sharif's sanguine foster father Gromeko – and latterly his father-in-law when Sharif marries his daughter, played by Geraldine Chaplin – in *Doctor Zhivago* (1965, David Lean). Once more with Olivier, he played Mr Micawber in Dickens' *David Copperfield* (1969, Delbert Mann).

A comedy high-spot was *The Wrong Box* (1966, Bryan Forbes), with Richardson and John Mills as brotherly rivals to a tontine of £100,000, due to be collected by whoever outlives the other. Richardson survives numerous dastardly attacks, including a train crash staged by fiendish nephews Peter Cook and Dudley Moore, and Mills' energetic homicidal assaults with knife and poker. The film ends without a solution being offered, although by then both old codgers have carried their ludicrous tug-of-war to quite lunatic extremes.

If one of Richardson's many impeccable brief cameos is asked to stand as a reminder of his magnificent sense of occasion, it could be his sardonic British Defence Minister in *The Battle of Britain* (1969, Guy Hamilton). When suave German ambassador Curt Jurgens attempts to secure British neutrality over the Nazis' planned attack on Poland with honeyed words and worthless guarantees authorised by Hitler, our man-on-the-spot Richardson responds stonily: 'Experience shows that the Führer's guarantees guarantee nothing!'

A less conciliatory approach by Jurgens fails just as dismally. Warned of the consequences to the British nation of interfering, Richardson tartly points out that the last little corporal who tried to bring an invading army across the Channel 'came a cropper'. The time to begin dictating to Britain, he tells a somewhat startled Jurgens, was when the Nazis were marching up Whitehall – 'And even then, we won't listen!' he adds, defiantly.

Ralph Richardson
b. 1902. Internationally respected, distinctive-voiced classical stage actor/director, pre-war cinema leading man, later dependable support progressing on to eccentric smallish roles. On stage from 1921. Film debut: *The Ghoul* (1933).

1933 *Friday the 13th*
1934 *The Return of Bulldog Drummond*
     Java Head
     The King of Paris
1935 *Bulldog Jack*
1936 *Things to Come*
     The Man Who Could Work Miracles
1937 *Thunder in the City*
1938 *South Riding*
     The Divorce of Lady X
     The Citadel
     Smith (short)
1939 *Q Planes*
     The Four Feathers
     The Lion Has Wings
     On the Night of the Fire
1940 *Health for the Nation* (short) (voice)
1942 *The Day Will Dawn*
     The Silver Fleet
1943 *The Volunteer*
1946 *School for Secrets* (Professor Heatherville)
1948 *Anna Karenina* (Alexei Karenin)
     The Fallen Idol (Baines)
1949 *The Heiress* (USA) (Dr Austin Sloper)
1951 *Outcast of the Islands* (Captain Lingard)
1952 *The Sound Barrier* (John Ridgefield)
     The Holly And The Ivy (Rev Martin Gregory)
     Home at Seven (also directed) (David Preston)
1955 *Richard III* (Duke of Buckingham)
1956 *Smiley* (Reverend Lambeth)
1957 *The Passionate Stranger* (Roger Wynter/ Sir Clement)
1960 *Our Man in Havana* ('C')
     Oscar Wilde (Sir Edward Carson)
     Exodus (USA) (General Sutherland)
1962 *Long Day's Journey Into Night* (USA) (James Tyrone Senior)
     The 300 Spartans (USA) (Themistocles)
1964 *Woman of Straw* (Charles Richmond)
1965 *Dr Zhivago* (USA) (Alexander Gromeko)
1966 *Khartoum* (Mr Gladstone)
     The Wrong Box (Joseph Finsbury)
1969 *Oh! What a Lovely War* (Sir Edward Grey)
     The Battle of Britain (Minister)
     The Looking Glass War (Leclerc)
     David Copperfield (Mr Micawber)
     Midas Run (Henshaw)
     The Bed Sitting Room (Lord Fortnum)
1970 *Eagle in a Cage* (USA) (Sir Hudson Lowe)

James Robertson Justice

James Robertson Justice's screen character was like a giant panda – cuddly to look at but peppery within. The crinkly, benign eyes could suddenly turn very nasty indeed. But when he was jolly he was everyone's favourite uncle, and when he chortled it rumbled and shook his 250-pound frame like the onset of an earthquake.

Justice was a canny Scot who refused to take either himself or the trade he practised seriously. He described himself as a terrible actor with no right whatever to stardom, and remained genuinely mystified by the eagerness of producers to pay him, by his reckoning, astronomical sums simply to go before the cameras and be himself. 'If the public wish to see me that's their affair,' he would growl if quizzed on the subject.

His most famous role was Sir Lancelot Spratt, the liverish, steam-rolling chief surgeon of the long-running *Doctor* series, and most of his screen performances after the first and way-ahead best of the series, *Doctor in the House* (1954, Ralph Thomas), were variations of Spratt in one guise or another. He was, however, Spratt-like before taking office at St Swithin's, and the film which, in all likelihood, clinched the Spratt role was *The Voice of Merrill* (1952, John Gilling),a tense, low-budget but highly original thriller with a literary setting. Justice was a successful but difficult playwright whose bored, glamorous wife, Valerie Hobson, has an affair with a morose, failed writer, Edward Underdown. Commissioned by BBC radio to broadcast a series of short stories, but anxious to conceal from listeners that he is the author, Justice agrees, at Miss Hobson's insistence, to let Underdown do the broadcasts under an assumed name, Merrill.

The Merrill broadcasts are hugely popular, and Miss Hobson sees them as her lover's big chance to become successful, since his own efforts have failed miserably. Gambling on her husband's re-

luctance to debate the matter in public, she goads Underdown into claiming authorship of the stories – he agrees only out of fear of losing her – but her gamble goes amiss and then, to safeguard Underdown's ill-acquired reputation, she is obliged to get rid of Justice. But is it the poisoned medicine which she leaves for him to take which polishes him off, or did the belligerent old goat, warned he might pop off anytime if he overdoes things, pass on through natural causes?

It was an ably constructed thriller, with Justice levelling all before him like a mechanical shovel, as when Miss Hobson unwisely brings up the subject of Underdown's literary accomplishments. 'Don't compare a down-and-out hack with one of the field marshals of English literature,' he storms. The field marshal referred to is, of course, himself!

Doctor in the House consolidated half-a-dozen reputations including Justice's. In one scene, surrounded by a gaggle of students, Justice is laying down the law about the curious behaviour of human blood, and the scientifically approved term, bleeding-time, when he spots Dirk Bogarde daydreaming. 'You – what's the bleeding-time?' he barks, whereupon Bogarde, jolted back to reality, snatches a guilty look at his watch and replies, 'Ten past ten, sir.' Later, however, he saves Bogarde's bacon when the student is hauled before the establishment's prim-and-proper dean, played by Geoffrey Keen, for having been caught in the nurses' quarters, for which he can be expelled.

Keen wants to come down heavily on Bogarde until Justice reminds him of 'another student' who had once induced a nurse to play Lady Godiva on a cart horse. Pressed by a member of the hospital board to identify the earlier miscreant, Justice merely says, 'I expect I'm the only person who hasn't forgotten!' But under his ac-

Doctor James Robertson Justice waits with an anxious Gabrielle Blunt to pick up the pieces while her boyfriend stands up to his bossy mother in *Whisky Galore* (1948)

cusing stare Keen undergoes an abrupt change of heart and Bogarde escapes with a nominal fine.

Justice's performance, or rather, the impact of the Spratt character on audiences, caused red faces at Rank Studios because the follow-up, *Doctor at Sea* (1955, Ralph Thomas), set on board a cruise ship, had made no provision for Spratt. But they overcame the problem by casting Justice as the ship's captain and making the character indistinguishable from the bolshie head surgeon of St Swithin's.

The captain is a crusty bachelor, deaf to the romantic overtures of Brenda de Banzie whose father owns the shipping line. 'Steamship lines do like their commodores to be married,' she coos but Old Bristleface is having none of it. He is oblivious to any attempt to make him jealous – when Miss de Banzie enquires rather cheekily if she can borrow one of his dishier officers, Hubert Gregg, Justice growls: 'Madam, as far as I'm concerned, you can keep him!'

The *Carry On* team paid a nice tribute to him in *Carry On Doctor* (1965, Gerald Thomas). In one scene, Justice's framed portrait stares down

from a hospital corridor wall at surgeon Kenneth Williams trying to appease angry matron Hattie Jacques with an explanation of why he was caught kissing Nurse Barbara Windsor in his quarters the previous evening. One cannot help wondering what Spratt would have made of them all.

Justice was one of the fated explorers in *Scott of the Antarctic* (1948, Charles Frend), and the island doctor in *Whisky Galore* (1948, Alexander Mackendrick). In the latter film, when Gordon Jackson decides to stand up for his right to marry Gabrielle Brune, in defiance of his cantankerous mother's wishes, he and Miss Brune hitch a ride home in Justice's car. As Jackson climbs out and braces himself for the inevitable confrontation, Miss Brune asks Justice to stay on in case Jackson needs patching up.

Justice played a burly seadog under Gregory Peck's command in *Captain Horatio Hornblower* (1951, Raoul Walsh), a stodgy compilation of three C. S. Forester novels, tolerable only if you like that sort of thing. He reappeared with Peck in *Moby Dick* (1956, John Huston), as a rival

175

whaler with a vicious hook on the end of one arm – 'Better than flesh and blood,' he roars merrily.

In *Miss Robin Hood* (1952, John Guillerman) Justice was an unscrupulous distiller who cheats Margaret Rutherford out of a fortune by snatching a winning whisky formula that has been the property of her family for generations. Maggie retaliates with an Entebbe-style raid on Justice's premises, aided though scarcely encouraged by timid magazine writer Richard Hearne. With binoculars, focused through a window of his secret laboratory, they observe Justice brewing a quantity of the stuff, and eagerly tasting it. 'Like Jekyll and Hyde,' mutters Hearne as Justice's dazed eyes celebrate with the optical equivalent of a victory roll.

During 1952-53 Justice made three actioners for Walt Disney Productions, each time supporting – yes, literally – Richard Todd. All three – *The Story of Robin Hood and His Merrie Men* (1952, Ken Annakin), *The Sword and the Rose* (1953, Ken Annakin) and *Rob Roy the Highland Rogue* (1953, Harold French) – might have been made from discarded Tarzan scripts. Todd went

James Robertson Justice, 1965

through his sub-Errol Flynn routines without a flicker of shame, while Justice, never a pretty sight in drag, looked more ill-at-ease than a country curate held in a vice raid.

James Robertson Justice
1905-1975. Burly, bearded temperamental Scots-born actor, noted for liverish chief surgeon character in *Doctor* film series. Film debut: *For These In Peril* (1944).

1948 *Vice Versa* (Dr Grimstone)
    My Brother Jonathan (Eugene Dakers)
    Against the Wind (Ackerman)
    Scott of the Antarctic (Petty Officer 'Taff' Evans)
    Quartet (Branksome, in the 'Facts Of Life' episode)
    Whisky Galore (Dr MacLaren)
1949 *Stop Press Girl* (Mr Peters)
    Christopher Columbus (Martin Pinzon)
    Poet's Pub (Professor Benbow)
    Private Angelo (Feste)
1950 *Prelude to Fame* (Sir Arthur Harold)
    My Daughter Joy (Professor Keval)
    The Black Rose (Simeon Beautrie)
1951 *Blackmailed* (Mr Sine)
    Pool of London (Trotter)
    Captain Horatio Hornblower (Quist)
    The Voice of Merrill (Jonathan Roach)
1952 *The Story of Robin Hood and His Merrie Men* (Little John)
    Miss Robin Hood (McAllister)
1953 *The Sword and the Rose* (Henry VII)
    Rob Roy the Highland Rogue (Duke of Argyll)
1954 *Doctor in the House* (Sir Lancelot Spratt)
1955 *Out of the Clouds* (Captain Brent)
    Above Us the Waves (Admiral Ryder)
    Doctor at Sea (Captain Hogg)
    Storm Over the Nile (General Burroughs)
    An Alligator Named Daisy (Sir James)
    Land of the Pharoahs (USA) (Vashtar)
1956 *The Iron Petticoat* (Colonel Skiarnoff)
    Moby Dick (Captain Boomer)
    Checkpoint (Warren Ingram)
1957 *Doctor at Large* (Sir Lancelot Spratt)
    Seven Thunders (Dr Martont)
    Campbell's Kingdom (James MacDonald)
1958 *Orders to Kill* (Commander)
1959 *Upstairs and Downstairs* (Mansfield)
1960 *Doctor in Love* (Sir Lancelot Spratt)
    A French Mistress (Robert Martin)
    Foxhole in Cairo (Captain Robertson)

1961 *Very Important Person* (Sir Ernest Pease)
      The Guns of Navarone (Jensen)
      Raising the Wind (Sir Benjamin)
      Murder She Said (Ackenthorpe)
1962 *A Pair of Briefs* (Mr Justice Hadden)
      Crooks Anonymous (Sir Harvey
          Russellrod)
      Guns of Darkness (Hugo Bryant)
      Dr Crippen (Captain Kendall)
      The Fast Lady (Charles Chingford)
1963 *Mystery Submarine* (Rear-Admiral
          Rainbird)
      Doctor in Distress (Sir Lancelot Spratt)
      Father Came Too (Sir Beverly Grant)
1965 *You Must Be Joking* (Librarian)

      The Face of Fu Manchu (Sir Charles)
      Doctor in Clover (Sir Lancelot Spratt)
      *Those Magnificent Men in Their Flying
          Machines* (narrator)
      Up from the Beach (Beachmaster)
1967 *The Trygon Factor* (Sir John)
      Two Weeks in September (McClintock)
      Hell Is Empty (Angus McGee)
1968 *Mayerling* (Prince Edward)
      Chitty Chitty Bang Bang (Lord
          Scrumptious)
1969 *Zeta One* (Major Bourdon)
1970 *Some Will, Some Won't* (Sir Charles
          Robson)
      Doctor in Trouble (Sir Lancelot Spratt)

Peter Sellers

'I'm not essentially a funny man, I'm really only an instrument for somebody's writing,' Peter Sellers once said. It was a typically candid self-appraisal, but wide of the mark. His reliance on good scripts was undeniable, but not total. Sellers was a magnificent clown who, given the chance, could radiate merriment from inside a paper bag.

The one-time radio mimic and founder anchor-man of the Goons – whose near-surrealistic humour was like a new language, adored by the faithful who understood it and avoided by those who did not – switched to the big screen as a solo performer in 1951, but returned to the arms of his irreverent Goon buddies in *Down Among the 'Z' Men* (1952, Maclean Rogers), a barrack square comedy involving atomic formulae and rotten spies, tripe even by early 1950s standards. A second Goon film, *The Case of the Mukkinese Battlehorn* (1956, Joseph Sterling) proved to be 30 minutes of rapturous self-indulgence and little else.

Despite the world acclaim, justifiably earned, Sellers remained in essence a vocal performer, and the debate on his ability to project a character body and soul, to be rather than simply pretend to be, is now, alas, indefinitely adjourned. No-one would question for a moment his extraordinary range of voices, nor that unique talent for absorbing all kinds of garbled dialects. Yet the face he presented was often as much a tribute to the skills of the studio make-up department as evidence of Sellers' ability to project in visual terms what he accomplished so adroitly –

and, it appeared, so effortlessly – in the vocal department.

An early role was the Teddy Boy gang member in *The Ladykillers* (1955, Alexander Mackendrick). When their landlady discovers that Alec Guinness's genteel string ensemble are, in reality, a bunch of unsavoury gangsters, nasty old Herbert Lom wants to abduct her in a fast car before she can shop them to the police. But before they can hustle her off, the house fills up with members of her ladies circle. Pressed on all sides by twittering old ladies, Sellers whispers despairingly to Lom: 'What d'you think we should do – hire a bus?'

The Naked Truth (1957, Mario Zampi) was a kind of radio show with visuals, in which Sellers, as Dennis Price's extortion victim, adopts several disguises in a series of progressively frantic and slapstick attempts to thwart the blackmailer. All Price's victims have nasty secrets they desperately want to keep suppressed – Sellers, outwardly a jovial, Wilfred Pickles-type quiz show personality, is, in fact, a seedy rent-book racketeer.

Up the Creek (1958, Val Guest) was a routine shipboard farce, with Sellers as a crafty Irish bo'sun who transforms his ship's company – 'a sorry bunch of desperadoes' is Captain David Tomlinson's view of them – into a hotbed of private enterprise. The engine room becomes a same-day laundry; a bakery is set up to accommodate local demand; livestock are prodded around the deck by a dour Lionel Jeffries. The

Peter Sellers, 1957

film puffs hard but to little purpose, and Sellers is wasted as the fast-mouth seaman, the kind of role that Ronald Shiner used to do in his sleep.

Naked Truth co-star Terry-Thomas joined Sellers in three other comedies. *Tom Thumb* (1958, George Pal) was a hollow panto-farce, aimed one suspects at the under-fives, with Sellers and Terry-Thomas, as a pair of mindless woodland rogues, empty and grotesque as Hallowe'en turnips.

Terry-Thomas was a dim foreign office type caught in colonial brouhaha in *Carlton-Browne of the FO* (1959, Jeffrey Dell). Sellers played the prime minister of a foreign part that Britain wants to retain for strategic reasons, and poor old T-T has to defend Britannia's interests whilst keeping the simple but wily Sellers in check.

Another multi-role challenge surfaced again in *The Mouse That Roared* (1959, Jack Arnold), a tame comedy about an obscure principality's cunning plan to escape insolvency by declaring war on the mighty United States, and, when defeated, claiming massive injections of financial relief. Sellers played three parts – the hero, the principality's haughty grand duchess, and its double-dealing prime minister.

The plan misfires, however, when the cheeky invasion coincides with a nuclear bomb escape drill, and the raiders unwittingly overrun New York while its citizens are barricaded, unsuspectingly, in fallout shelters.

The film seemed undecided whether to opt for pungent satire or play safe as a leisurely spoof. In the end, it achieved neither, and Sellers' characters were disappointingly skin-deep, like comic faces painted on balloons.

High spot of his 1950s film work was *I'm All Right, Jack* (1959, John Boulting), a sharp-eyed satire on modern trade unionism with Sellers as a speech-mangling, doom-laden shop steward, accurate down to the last exasperating detail. The actor, it was said, had serious reservations about the script, complaining about its lack of funny lines, but it became, undeniably, the turning point for Sellers. Critic Tom Milne wrote: 'Far too many punches are pulled . . . to give this performance the sharp context it needs; but the mousetrap brilliance of its execution is enormously enhanced by the unexpected glimpse of a lonely, wistful Sellers behind the shop steward's implacable mask'.

He was a petty, vicious Brummie car thief in *Never Let Go* (1960, John Guillerman), a dubious choice of film for Sellers and one that riled audiences who had gone along expecting a good laugh. In its only memorable scene, suspecting a girlfriend of duplicity he sadistically crushes her fingers.

The Millionairess (1961, Anthony Asquith) was a reworking of Shaw's play in which Sellers did his by-then familiar Indian send-up, partnered by Sophia Loren, an odd choice for a Shavian heroine, but a safe box-office bet in any tongue. They also made a hit record together ('Doctor, I'm in Trouble') and there were rumours of an off-screen romance, strenuously denied by the Loren camp.

An example of the way that intelligent adult British comedy might have gone – if the money had not run out – was seen in *Only Two Can Play* (1962, Bryan Forbes), the screen version of Kingsley Amis' *That Uncertain Feeling*, described by one critic as having the funniest script 'since the heyday of Ealing'. Sellers played a randy, accident-prone Welsh librarian driven to seek escape from a tedious existence in the sexy embrace of roving-eyed, married socialite Mai Zetterling. The polarising influences in his life are neatly rolled back: in one corner, amiable, dowdy wife Virginia Maskell plus a string of aggravating kids, and in the other, blonde swinger Zetterling; the grim Swansea lodging house with its evil wallpaper, primitive plumbing and meddlesome landlady versus Zetterling's plush love-nest.

The more Sellers struggles against Fate, the more its grip strangles him. Even a part-time assignment as local drama critic disappears when, applauding a production in absentia – he is parked in a field with Miss Zetterling at the time – he omits to mention anywhere in his glowing report that midway through the evening the theatre burnt down.

The first of Sellers' collaborations with director Stanley Kubrick, *Lolita* (1962), was a slow-tempo serving up of Nabokov's contemporary shocker about a sex-nymph's destruction of her weak-willed stepfather. James Mason was the New England professor embroiled with the nymphet whilst married to her blowsy mother Shelley Winters, and Sellers was a rival for her affections, a sinister playwright shot by Mason in a jealous tantrum.

Doctor Strangelove (1963, Stanley Kubrick) was a three-role virtuoso performance, creating the illusion of three different actors playing, in turn, a weak-willed US President, his volatile Germanic nuclear adviser – whose artificial arm insists, against its owner's wishes, on executing periodic Nazi salutes – and an RAF Group Captain who is something of a buffoon. The film was a horrific comedy about nuclear invasion, in which a demented Commie-hating US general sets in motion an all-out H-bomb attack on Russia and then, to thwart any attempt by his government to reverse his decision, severs all communications with the outside world – not that there's likely to be much of any sort of world left after Russia's deadly counter-offensive is launched.

Neither the US President nor his Russian counterpart can actually save the world yet, it seems, any one of a number of loonies in high places can wilfully authorise its destruction – that appears to be the nub of Kubrick's message which is forcibly relayed in a series of witty, but profoundly disturbing, images such as Sellers grovelling on the newly hooked up Hot Line to Moscow. 'One of our base commanders, er, ordered our planes to attack your country – Dmitri, LET ME FINISH . . .!' And the US bomber pilot, played by ex-Western movie villain Slim Pickens, sits astride the 25 megaton bomb as it falls, whooping and hollering like a maniac rodeo star. The film ends with Vera Lynn singing 'We'll Meet Again' over a nuclear mushroom cloud.

'Someone has been murdered here. Please let it be Clouseau!' gasps police chief Herbert Lom on arrival at the scene of a killing in *A Shot in the Dark* (1969, Blake Edwards), first of the 'Pink Panther' series that made Sellers, as the thick, impetuous, trench-coated Sûreté policeman, a millionaire. The series offered him a welcome sanctuary when critics, whose darling he had been for a decade, rounded on him after a string of Hollywood-made flops that left the actor bruised and disconsolate. Clouseau also gave Sellers an opportunity to experiment with physical comedy, and the result was a tantalising mixture of Jacques Tati and Buster Keaton.

The undistinguished roles resulted in the main from misjudgments over how to internationalise Sellers. 'Hollywood did little to develop or extend his genius,' said John Boulting who knew him well, and that was putting it mildly. The flops included an Italian crook with Victor Mature in *After the Fox* (1966, Vittorio de Sica); a timid, second-rate matador in *The Bobo* (1967, Robert Parrish), co-starring his then wife Britt Ekland; a middle-aged misfit company executive in *Hoffman* (1970, Alvin Rakoff) – 'claustrophobic, tasteless and boring' according to Leslie Halliwell; an Indian film actor in *The Party* (1968, Blake Edwards); an eccentric multi-millionaire in *The Magic Christian* (1969, Joseph McGrath) – in which he also shared the writing credits; and a brief guest appearance in *Woman Times Seven* (1967, Vittorio De Sica) as the seducer of grieving widow Shirley MacLaine as they return from having just interred her dead husband.

He was back on form as an egotistical, randy TV gourmet who finds fluffy-brained pick-up Goldie Hawn a troublesome handful in *There's a Girl in My Soup* (1970, Roy Boulting), a breezy adult comedy fashioned on the lines of *Only Two Can Play*, but relying too heavily on symbols of the period – TV, the media, rockstar hippie life-styles – to deserve serious comparison with the earlier movie.

In *Soft Beds, Hard Battles* (1973, John Boulting) Sellers played six different characters, high-ranking clientele of a wartime French brothel. The portrait gallery included a buck-toothed French president, a Japanese general, an aging French general, a British intelligence officer, a wire-spectacled Gestapo boss, and Adolf Hitler. It was an example of conveyor-belt characterisation at its least satisfying, and the novelty of its raunchy bordello setting soon wore off.

His best performance for years occurred in *Being There* (1980, Hal Ashby), a timely reminder of the great performances of old, and a welcome return to the kind of grass roots acting, rudimentary in style and simple in execution, of which he had once been such a charismatic exponent.

In complete contrast, the last film completed before his death, from a heart attack in 1980, was *The Fiendish Plot of Fu Manchu* (1980, Piers Haggard), a rather silly, ill-judged affair about which one critic was moved to write: 'The few laughs it gathers hardly compensate for the sheer ineptitude of the film as a whole.' *Fu Manchu* aptly summarised the strange paradox that Sellers could be – both in real life and on the screen – one day, a finely tuned and extraordinarily gifted performer in complete control, the next, as hopelessly off-pitch as a Saturday night reveller attempting Lohengrin.

Peter Sellers

1925-1980. Temperamental ex-radio Goon whose 1950s comedies gave notice of a formidable talent, later frivolously squandered in a succession of mediocre films. Most memorable roles include the bolshie shop steward in *I'm All Right, Jack* (1959), the quirky *Dr Strangelove* (1963) and the inept Inspector Clouseau in several Pink Panther films. Formerly married to Ann Howe, Britt Ekland and Miranda Quarry. Wife at the time of his death was actress Lynne Frederick.

1951 *Penny Points to Paradise* (The Major/Arnold P. Fringe)
       Let's Go Crazy (short) (Groucho/Guiseppe/Cedric/Izzy Gozzunk/Crystal Jollibottom)
1952 *Down Among the 'Z' Men* (Major Bloodnok)
1954 *Orders Are Orders* (Private Goffin)
1955 *John and Julie* (PC Diamond)
      The Ladykillers (Harry)
1956 *The Case of the Mukkinese Battlehorn* (short) (Inspector Quilt/Henry Crun/Sid Crimp/Sir Jervis Fruit)
      The Man Who Never Was (Voice of Winston Churchill)
1957 *The Smallest Show On Earth* (Percy Quill)

A disguised Peter Sellers (left) and a disgusted Terry-Thomas plan revenge on a blackmailer in *The Naked Truth* (1957)

Insomnia Is Good for You (short)
(Hector Dimwiddie)
The Naked Truth (Sonny MacGregor)
1958 *Up the Creek* (Chief Petty Officer
Doherty)
Tom Thumb (Tony)
1959 *Carlton-Browne of the FO* (Amphibulous)
The Mouse That Roared (Tully
Bascombe/Grand Duchess Gloriana/
Count Mountjoy)
I'm All Right, Jack (Fred Kite)
The Running, Jumping, Standing Still Film
(Producer)
The Battle of the Sexes (Mr Martin)
1960 *Two Way Stretch* ('Dodger' Lane)
Never Let Go (Lionel Meadows)
1961 *The Millionairess* (Dr Ahmed el Kabir/
Parerga)
Mr Topaze (Albert Topaze)
1962 *Only Two Can Play* (John Lewis)
The Waltz of the Toreadors (General Leo
Fitzjohn)
The Road to Hong Kong (Indian Doctor)
Lolita (Clare Quilty)
1963 *The Dock Brief* (Morgenhall)
The Wrong Arm of the Law (Pearly Gates)
Heavens Above (Rev John Aspinall)
Dr Strangelove (Dr Strangelove/Group
Captain Lionel Mandrake/President
Mervyn Muffley)
1964 *The Pink Panther* (Inspector Jacques
Clouseau)
The World of Henry Orient (USA)
(Henry Orient)
A Shot in the Dark (Inspector Jacques
Clouseau)

1965 *What's New Pussycat* (Fritz Fassbender)
1966 *The Wrong Box* (Doctor Pratt)
After the Fox (USA) (Aldo Vanucci)
1967 *Casino Royale* (Evelyn Tremble)
The Bobo (Juan Bautista)
Woman Times Seven (Jean, in the
'Funeral' sequence)
1968 *The Party* (USA) (Hrundi Vakshi)
I Love You, Alice B. Toklas (Harold Fine)
1969 *The Magic Christian* (Sir Guy Grand)
A Shot in the Dark (Inspector Jacques
Clouseau)
1970 *Hoffman* (Benjamin Hoffman)
There's a Girl in My Soup (Robert
Danvers)
1972 *Alice's Adventures in Wonderland* (TV)
(King of Hearts)
1973 *The Blockhouse* (Bouquet)
The Optimists of Nine Elms (Sam)
Soft Beds, Hard Battles (General
Latour/Major Robinson/Schroeder/
Adolf Hitler/Prince Kyoto/French
President)
1974 *The Great McGonagall* (Queen Victoria)
1975 *The Return of the Pink Panther* (Inspector
Jacques Clouseau)
1976 *Murder By Death* (Sidney Wang)
The Pink Panther Strikes Again (Inspector
Jacques Clouseau)
1978 *Revenge of the Pink Panther* (Inspector
Jacques Clouseau)
1979 *The Prisoner of Zenda* (Prince
Rudolph/Sidney Frewin)
1980 *Being There* (Chance Gardner)
The Fiendish Plot of Dr Fu Manchu (Fu
Manchu/Nayland Smith)

Robert Shaw

'They are ready to die for you and you ask more?' asks an incredulous German tank officer in *Battle of the Bulge* (1965, Ken Annakin), when Colonel Robert Shaw curtly dismisses the assembled troops as 'mere boys'. Cold-eyed Shaw does ask more. In fact, anything less than a compulsion to die for the Fatherland is deemed treasonous by Shaw's dotty standards. So single-minded is he that when a hostess, Barbara Werle, is provided for him by his CO on the eve of battle, Shaw can scarcely adjust his turrets low enough to be civil to her.

With the carnage at its height, and the Allies clearly on the offensive ('We're not in a pillow-fight, Joe,' comments US commander Henry Fonda to fellow-brass hat Dana Andrews), poor old Shaw seems unable to grasp the simple fact that his side is losing. The war, he predicts, will go on and on. 'But when do we go home?' asks a battle-weary German. 'This *is* our home,' replies Shaw, glancing fondly at the tangled metal and pock-marked hills. Not everyone, alas, shares his ambition. 'You would murder the whole world to stay in that uniform,' accuses a disillusioned aide shortly before a well-aimed Allied rocket puts an end to Shaw's capers.

He picked the winning side in *Battle of Britain* (1969, Guy Hamilton) as Skipper, a no-non-sense squadron leader. 'Skipper hates Jerries,' murmurs an admiring erk as Shaw, with the light of battle in his eyes, heads for another sortie. Scanning the skies for bandits was old hat to Shaw – he began his movie career as Richard Todd's co-pilot in *The Dambusters* (1955, Michael Anderson).

He was a member of Victor McLaglen's hardy salvage crew in *Sea Fury* (1958, Cy Endfield) who resents new crewman Stanley Baker's swift elevation to First Officer. The ship dices with a Dutch rival to reach each wreck first – it's a first come, first paid arrangement. Back in port, Old Vic is rather enamoured of a local Spanish wench who has been tricked into becoming his fiancée by her unsavoury father, but prefers to spend her time with Baker.

When Shaw spots them together, he con-siders it his duty 'as an officer and a friend' to tell McLaglen – but before the fists can fly, a cargo ship loaded with volatile drums is reported in difficulties in rough seas. Old animosities are set aside in the dash to head off their Dutch rivals. Baker finally wins the admiration of his ship-mates, and McLaglen's, by leaping aboard the dangerously listing vessel and saving it from de-struction, which guarantees everyone a fat pay-day.

In *From Russia with Love* (1963, Terence Young) Shaw played the po-faced blond villain Red Grant, the muscle end of SPECTRE's plot to steal a Russian cipher machine and arrange it so that the Russians think British intelligence is to blame. SPECTRE intends then to resell it back to the Russians, who will pay handsomely for its return. Shaw is chosen by the evil Lotte Lenya – a name which, by itself, conjures up murky goings-on, although it is the actress's name and not the character she plays – to dis-pose of James Bond, alias Sean Connery. In his excellent book on the Bond films, John Brosnan comments: 'Shaw manages to invest Grant with much of that unsettling menace that [Ian] Flem-ing so chillingly described in his novel.'

Shaw and Connery – again to be on opposing sides, as the Sheriff of Nottingham and Robin Hood respectively in *Robin and Marian* (1976, Richard Lester) – finally square up, aboard the Orient Express, where Shaw masquerades as another British agent. But the penny drops when he mistakenly orders red wine with his fish in the restaurant car. Later, back in their com-

Robert Shaw as Henry VIII with Paul Scofield as Sir Thomas More in *A Man for All Seasons* (1966)

partment, Shaw gets the better of Connery and mutters acidly, 'You may know the right wines but you're the one on your knees.'

Thanks to a gas bomb concealed in a brief-case, Connery redresses the balance, and in one of the most physical fight sequences ever staged in a British film, he finally disposes of Shaw by garotting him with one of the villain's more chilling murder devices, a length of chicken wire concealed in his wristwatch.

Shaw was Henry VIII to Paul Scofield's Thomas More in A Man for All Seasons (1966, Fred Zinnemann), a stylishly-mounted if rather narrow-focus view of events leading to More's trial and execution for treason. Shaw makes only one relatively brief appearance early on but such is the impact that his presence casts a shadow over the remainder of the film. He visits Scofield in an attempt to secure his support for divorce and remarriage, an attempt which runs the full gamut from feigned niceties – 'Thank God I have a friend for my Chancellor' – through numerous threats – 'I will have no opposition' – to uncontrollable anger – 'See how you've maddened me, I hardly know myself'. But nothing can shift Scofield. It was a vigorous, swaggering, heavyweight performance that neatly counter-pointed Scofield's probing study, and was a fair illustration of Shaw's tough uncompromising acting style.

During the 1970s, Shaw became a major star through Hollywood blockbusters like Jaws (1975, Steven Spielberg) – in which he was eaten by a killer shark – and The Sting (1973, George Roy Hill), in which he played the dour gang boss whose arranged murder of Robert Redford's black associate prompts the elaborate re-taliatory rip-off, accomplished with split-second timing and engaging good humour by Redford and Paul Newman. He played the chauffeur in love with Sarah Miles in The Hireling (1973, Alan Bridges), and Lord Randolph Churchill,

the proud, syphilitic father of Winston, in Young Winston (1971, Richard Attenborough). Always with Shaw there was an aura of controlled violence.

Robert Shaw
1927-1979. Actor-playwright-novelist with a forceful personality and rugged physique who specialised in he-man roles. Married to Mary Ure, who died in 1975.

1955 The Dambusters (Flight-Sergeant Pulford)
1956 A Hill in Korea (Lance Corporal Hodge)
1958 Sea Fury (German)
1962 The Valiant (Lieutenant Field)
       Tomorrow at Ten (Marlow)
1963 From Russia with Love (Red Grant)
       The Caretaker (Aston)
1964 The Luck of Ginger Coffey (Ginger)
1965 Battle of the Bulge (Colonel Hessler)
1966 A Man for All Seasons (Henry VIII)
1968 Custer of the West (USA) (General Custer)
1969 The Battle of Britain (Squadron Leader Skipper)
       The Royal Hunt of the Sun (Francisco Pizarro)
1970 The Birthday Party (Stanley Webber)
       Figures in a Landscape (MacConnachie) (also scripted from Barry England's novel)
1971 Young Winston (Lord Randolph Churchill)
       A Town Called Bastard (Priest)
1973 The Hireling (Leadbetter)
       The Sting (USA) (Doyle Lonnegan)
       A Reflection of Fear (Michael)
1974 The Taking of Pelham 123 (USA) (Blue)
1975 Jaws (USA) (Quint)
1976 Diamonds (Charles/Earl Hodgson)
       Robin and Marian (Sheriff of Nottingham)
1977 The Deep (Romer Treece)
1978 Force Ten from Navarone (Major Mallory)
       Avalanche Express (General Marenkov)

Ronald Shiner

I met Ronald Shiner only once, at a charity function where he and other celebrities were fund-raising the night away. While the others hawked autographs and harangued the punters to buy signed pictures, Shiner stayed contentedly perched on a barstool dispensing wise-

cracks and supping ale at an impressive rate of knots. He collected more cash and bigger laughs than most, which was par-for-the-course Shiner, a past master at achieving results and having a good time into the bargain.

Shiner never made anything seem like work

Teacher's pet Jacqueline Pierreux gives headmaster Ronald Shiner a different kind of French lesson in *Top of the Form* (1953)

yet he was one of the hardest-working actors in the business, particularly on stage where, during the 1940s and 1950s, his name was synonymous with long runs.

He looked like a slimmed-down, shifty-eyed version of Stanley Holloway, with a beak like a toucan and the survival instincts – some might say the inner sensitivities – of a rhino. He was often the crafty NCO or cheeky spiv, a sharp-witted schemer barely half-a-pace ahead of the posse. Even when they caught up with him Shiner always managed to fast-mouth his way out of trouble, leaving everyone else in disarray while he scarpered, usually with that huge infectious grin splitting his face in half.

His big films occurred within the short space of five years, from *Worm's Eye View* (1951) to *Dry Rot* (1956), both originally long-run Whitehall stage farces. It's difficult for me to be objective about farces – most of them seem to me to be about as funny as a punctured lung. But the Whitehall Theatre's receipts during the 1950s and 1960s are a salutary lesson to anyone misguided enough, which I certainly am not, to attempt to analyse their popularity.

Worm's Eye View (1951, Jack Raymond) catalogued the misadventures of a troop of airmen billeted on to a seaside boarding house, with Shiner in chirpy form marshalling the erks

into outwitting their landlady. It was good-natured enough, but, oh, those cretinous airmen! On stage, it had clocked up 2,000 performances, and the screen version, filmed on a shoestring, did quite well, too. *Reluctant Heroes* (1951), from the same stable, was another formula-written service caper, no better or worse than *Worm's Eye View*, with Shiner as a Bilko-type drill sergeant out to prove that his squad can take care of itself on manoeuvres.

In *Top of the Form* (1953, John Paddy Carstairs), Shiner played a racing tipster, on the run from a heavy mob, who shakes off his pursuers by assuming the identity of a schoolmaster. He finds himself in charge of a school trip to Paris where – as if there wasn't enough improbability to be getting on with – he helps the class foil a jewel theft attempt on a Paris museum.

Paris was again the setting for *Innocents in Paris* (1953, Gordon Parry), in which Shiner was one of a party of British tourists who descend on the French capital in search of fun and romance. It was a forerunner of *Airport*-type dramas where a group of dissimilar types are thrown together for whatever reason, and the plot examines the chemistry between them and possible outsiders. With people like Alastair Sim and Margaret Rutherford along for the ride it could hardly be dull, although the film failed to live up to its promise.

In *Laughing Anne* (1953, Herbert Wilcox) Shiner was tidily in character, but strangely misplaced, as a sympathetic Cockney seaman in Joseph Conrad's steamy tale of female duplicity. Margaret Lockwood played the tart who abandons roughneck boxer Forrest Tucker for ne'er-do-well steamship captain Wendell Corey, with tragic results. But it was back to grass roots in *Dry Rot* (1956, Maurice Elvey), one of the more successful of all Whitehall farces, replete with shabby bookies, switched favourites and doped runners.

Shiner's last film, *The Night We Got the Bird* (1960, Darcy Conyers), was a dreary, mindless concoction, involving a ludicrous parrot, supposedly Shiner in reincarnated form, after he has been killed in a car crash whilst escaping from some gangsters. When Shiner's widow, Dora Bryan, decides to marry Brian Rix, a goofy, North Country junk-dealer, the parrot starts making trouble for them, squawking insults and defiance, till he gets caught in an Air Ministry pigeon basket and is launched into space in a moon rocket.

Ronald Shiner

1903-1966. London-born comedy actor, occasionally serious, graduated from pre-war bit roles to stardom as Cockney character. Played in numerous film versions of long-running stage farces (*Reluctant Heroes, Dry Rot, Worm's Eye View,* etc.). On stage from 1921. Film debut: *My Old Dutch* (1934).

1934 *Doctor's Orders*
1935 *It's a Bet*
     Royale Cavalcade
     Gentleman's Agreement
     Once a Thief
     Squibs
     Line Engaged
1936 *Excuse My Glove*
     King of Hearts
1937 *The Black Tulip*
     Beauty and the Barge
     Dreaming Lips
     Dinner at the Ritz
1938 *They Drive by Night*
     A Yank at Oxford
     Prison Without Bars
1939 *The Mind of Mr Reeder*
     Trouble Brewing
     The Flying 55
     The Missing People
     I Killed the Count
     The Gang's All Here
     Discoveries
     Come on George
     The Middle Watch
1940 *Let George Do It*
     Bulldog Sees It Through
     Case of the Frightened Lady
     Salvage With a Smile (short)
     Old Bill and Son
1941 *The Seventh Survivor*
     Major Barbara

     Black Sheep of Whitehall
     South American George
1942 *The Big Blockade*
     They Flew Alone
     Those Kids from Town
     Sabotage at Sea
     King Arthur Was a Gentleman
     The Balloon Goes Up
     Unpublished Story
     Squadron Leader X
     The Young Mr Pitt
1943 *Get Cracking*
     Thursday's Child
     The Gentle Sex
     Miss London Limited
     The Butler's Dilemma
1944 *Bees in Paradise*
1945 *I Live in Grosvenor Square* (Paratrooper)
1946 *George in Civvy Street* (Fingers)
1947 *The Man Within* (Cockney Harry)
1949 *Forbidden* (Dan Collins)
1951 *Worm's Eye View* (Sam Porter)
     The Magic Box (Fairground Barker)
     Reluctant Heroes (Sergeant Bell)
1952 *Little Big Shot* (Henry Hawkwood)
1953 *Top of the Form* (Ronnie Fortescue)
     Innocents in Paris (Dickie Bird)
     Laughing Anne ('Nobby' Clark)
1954 *Up to His Neck* (Jack Carter)
     Aunt Clara (Henry Martin)
1955 *See How They Run* (Wally Winton)
1956 *Keep It Clean* (Bert Lane)
     Dry Rot (Alf Tubbs)
     My Wife's Family (Doc Knott)
1957 *Carry On Admiral* (Salty Simpson)
     Not Wanted on Voyage (Albert Higgins)
1958 *Girls at Sea* (Marine Ogg)
1959 *Operation Bullshine* (Gunner Slocum)
     The Navy Lark (Chief Petty Officer Banyard)
1960 *The Night We Got the Bird* (Cecil Gibson)

Alastair Sim

In *The Doctor's Dilemma* (1958, Anthony Asquith), consumptive artist Dirk Bogarde, an incorrigible scrounger, is putting the bite on people left, right and centre. After he dies, physician Felix Aylmer remarks to Alastair Sim that the poor chap is in another world. 'Probably borrowing his first five-pound note,' adds Sim ruefully.

Sim's eyebrows were extraordinary. They enjoyed unrestricted travel up and down that pleasantly rumpled faced like hedgehogs scampering over an unmade bed. When they shot up

Alastair Sim, 1947

in amazement it seemed they would go into orbit, and when they plummetted down in reproachful scowl they made his eyelids redundant. He was best known as a fussy eccentric, and every mannerism in his huge workbox of tricks was sharpened to a fine edge. He looked at times like a turkey startled by bright sunlight – with much twitching and croaking and rolling of those big button eyes. But he could also chortle like a schoolboy peering through a crack in the gym-mistress's changing room – swooping to a low, rapturous chuckle that fizzed and splashed like vintage champagne.

His Inspector Hornleigh films (1939-41) brought him into contact with screenwriters Frank Launder and Sidney Gilliatt, later to make several of Sim's tastiest successes, such as *Green for Danger* (1946, Sidney Gilliatt – but set two years previously, during the height of the enemy's flying bomb raids). In this tense whodunnit, filmed against authentic, contemporary backgrounds, Sim was a detective investigating the mysterious death of a patient on an operating table, in a hospital threatened with destruction at any moment by flying bombs.

The backdrop for *Hue and Cry* (1946, Charles Crichton) was equally authentic – London's riverside bomb sites – but the story was pure

escapism in which hordes of children, led by Harry Fowler, capture some crooks who have been using a comic-book serial to pass coded information. Sims played the fussy, reclusive author whose work is unwittingly used as a kind of bush telegraph for London's underworld. He is appalled to discover the truth but sternly urges Fowler to leave matters alone. 'Remember what happened to Nicky the Nark in "The Case of the Creeping Death",' he tells Fowler, recalling a gruesome fate from an earlier serial.

The Happiest Days of Your Life (1950, Frank Launder) was like a sneak preview of the later St Trinian's adventures, a sharply observed comedy about a girls' school being billeted on to a boys' school, due to a Whitehall mix-up. Margaret Rutherford was the pushy old mother-hen in charge of the girls, and Sim, naturally, was the outraged academic fighting gamely to preserve some kind of status quo. The film gives both leading players a superb platform for their highly individual comic skills. No sooner have the girls arrived than Miss Rutherford throws down the challenge, informing Sim that her pupils are used to milk and biscuits before bed and enquiring, 'Have you any digestives?' Recovering his poise Sim wastes no time pointing out that, should there be any digestives or indeed biscuits of any kind, they will be consumed entirely by his boys.

A familiar retinue of British comedy stalwarts made up the opposing members of staff. Among Sim's teachers were Guy Middleton and Richard Wattis, while Miss Rutherford's angular gym mistress was Joyce Grenfell, who has difficulty co-ordinating the simplest movement. Asked to summon assistance after their arrival by sounding the school gong, Miss Grenfell almost swipes it off its moorings and draws this famous withering reprimand from her headmistress: 'A tap, Gossage, I said a tap! You're not introducing a film!'

Sim had a marvellous part, as a beneficiary in the will of a rich prankster, in *Laughter in Paradise* (1951, Mario Zampi). He was one of four relatives on whom the deceased, who departs chortling to his grave, plays a penultimate cruel jape – each gets £50,000 only on condition they fulfil a particular clause in the will. Sim, a respectable but impoverished writer of trashy crime novels, has to spend 28 days in jail for whatever minor offence he favours.

Efforts to ingratiate himself with the local constabulary, followed by failed attempts at shoplifting and house-breaking at the home of one of his relatives ('I couldn't *possibly* rob someone I didn't know!'), leave Sim dismally contemplating his loss of inheritance. When eventually he musters the courage to heave a brick through a shop-window, the magistrate he is dragged before happens to be his prospective father-in-law, crusty old A. E. Matthews, whom he has to insult in order to get his original lenient sentence bumped up to the stipulated 28 days.

The final joke, as Sim discovers on regaining his freedom, is that the crazy old fool died penniless. Though swindled of their promised riches, each of the victims has benefited from the experience in other ways, so the joke is good-naturedly received, especially by George Cole, as a timid bank-clerk, who in the course of robbing his employers – as his clause of the will demanded – unwittingly thwarted a real robbery and ended up a hero.

With Joyce Grenfell as Sim's toothy, long-suffering fiancée – they have been engaged for 10 years – and Ernest Thesiger as the harassed executor among the familiar faces chipping in nicely-rounded cameos, this a delightful farce whose individual scenes, which employ the actors' familiar mannerisms to their fullest comic effect, work well despite an overburdened plot.

All the players deserve high praise, notably Sim and Cole, whose dispirited attempts to honour – or, in this case, dishonour – the terms of their inheritance must rank among the funniest scenes ever played by either.

In *Lady Godiva Rides Again* (1951, Frank Launder), Sim played a movie mogul with cash-flow problems. When beauty queen Pauline Stroud visits his office, hopeful of a walk-on part, Sim has nothing to offer but a sip of his glass of milk. 'There was a time when I would not have been able to resist pursuing you around this desk,' he tells her – in effect, a harmless piece of morale-boosting for both of them. He came close to the popular conception of *Scrooge* (1951, Brian Desmond Hurst), miserly and dark-jowled to begin with, all sweetness and good humour after wrestling with various phantoms.

Sim was a Treasury official mixing drinks with a Russian counterpart in *Innocents in Paris* (1953, Gordon Parry), a minor comedy about a group of Britishers on a weekend trip to the French capital. The Russian blankly refuses to have anything to do with Sim's proposed disar-mament conference, until at the end of a night of balalaikan revelry, the near-legless Russki discovers, under Sim's persistent tutelage, the pleasures of the word 'yes'.

In *The Belles of St Trinian's* (1954, Frank Launder), first of the Ronald Searle comedies which Sim and George Cole were to dominate, he played the fussy, impoverished headmistress Miss Fritton, and her no-good, equally money-shy brother Clarence, a curious piece of casting which came off surprisingly well.

As with all the other St Trinian's capers, the plot is secondary to screaming hordes of black-stockinged tearaways running amok, with a bit of amiable crookery thrown in. It's too farcical for words, but Sim's drag act is deliciously executed, and some of the older girls, notably Belinda Lee, look not at all bad in their sexy suspenders.

In *The Green Man* (1956, Robert Day), Sim was a semi-retired assassin brought out of mothballs to bump off a troublesome, inept politician, played by Raymond Huntley, during an adventureful weekend at a quiet country inn. A highlight of this charming, modestly-made comedy thriller is the flashback sequences, alive with the subtlety and craftsmanship employed by Sim in the disposal of earlier victims.

In *Left, Right and Centre* (1959, Sidney Gilliatt), a patchy satire on behind-the-scenes electioneering, Sim was right-wing candidate Ian Carmichael's crusty, aristocratic uncle driven by lack of funds to turn his crumbling mansion into a hive of commercialism. He appeared again with Carmichael in *School for Scoundrels* (1960, Robert Hamer), as headmaster to Carmichael's inept student, teaching him the rudiments of one-upmanship and turning him into a lady-killing cad.

After an absence from the screen of around ten years, Sim returned as a long-suffering bishop in *The Ruling Class* (1971, Peter Medak). Informed that nephew Peter O'Toole – who thinks he's God – is proposing marriage to Carolyn Seymour, Sim gives the famous sad eyes a disapproving roll and says: 'I hear she's some sort of entertainer!' The wedding, at which Sim officiates, is a disaster. O'Toole, being God, refuses to keep to the approved responses. Asked by Sim, 'Wilt thou love this woman?' O'Toole replies, 'From the bottom of my soul to the tip of my penis.' It's all too much for Sim who sinks exhaustedly to his knees imploring God's – the real One's, that is – forgiveness.

Alastair Sim

1900-1976. Rumpled-faced, Scots-born character player, equally adept at drama and comedy but most affectionately associated with the latter, in 1950s laughter-makers like *The Happiest Days of Your Life* (1950), *Laughter in Paradise* (1951) and *Innocents in Paris* (1953) to which his gloomy features and kill-joy figure added a note of extra piquancy.

1935 *Riverside Murder*
      The Private Secretary
      A Fire Has Been Arranged
      Late Extra
1936 *Troubled Waters*
      Wedding Group
      The Big Noise
      Keep Your Seats Please
      The Man in the Mirror
      The Mysterious Mr Davis
1937 *Strange Experiment*
      Clothes and the Woman
      Gangway
      The Squeaker
      A Romance in Flanders
      Melody and Romance
1938 *Sailing Along*
      The Terror
      Alf's Button Afloat
      This Man Is News
      Climbing High
1939 *Inspector Hornleigh*
      This Man in Paris
      Inspector Hornleigh on Holiday
1940 *Law and Disorder*

Her Father's Daughter (short)
1941 *Inspector Hornleigh Goes to It*
      Cottage to Let
1942 *Let the People Sing*
1945 *Waterloo Road* (Dr Montgomery)
1946 *Green for Danger* (Inspector Cockrill)
      Hue and Cry (Felix H Wilkinson)
1947 *Captain Boycott* (Fr McKeogh)
1948 *London Belongs to Me* (Mr Squales)
1950 *The Happiest Days of Your Life* (Wetherby Pond)
      Stage Fright (Commodore Gill)
1951 *Laughter in Paradise* (Deniston Russell)
      Scrooge (Ebenezer Scrooge)
      Lady Godiva Rides Again (Movie Producer)
1952 *Folly to Be Wise* (Captain Paris)
1953 *Innocents in Paris* (Sir Norman Barker)
1954 *An Inspector Calls* (Inspector Poole)
      The Belles of Trinian's (Miss Fritton/ Clarence)
1955 *Escapade* (Dr Skillingsworth)
      Geordie (The Laird)
1956 *The Green Man* (Hawkins)
1957 *Blue Murder at St Trinian's* (Miss Fritton)
1959 *The Doctor's Dilemma* (Cutler Walpole)
      Left, Right and Centre (Lord Wilcott)
1960 *School for Scoundrels* (Stephen Potter)
      The Millionairess (Julius Sagamore)
1971 *The Ruling Class* (Bishop Lampton)
1975 *Rogue Male* (TV) (The Earl)
      Escape From The Dark (USA) (Lord Harrowgate)
      Royal Flash (Mr Greig)

Terry-Thomas

He was our most successful TV comic of the late 1940s and early 1950s, yet everything about him suggested bad taste. That apart, Terry-Thomas' gaudy waistcoats, flashy cigarette holders and affected mannerisms were just the ticket to make a drab, ration-book Britain perk up and take notice.

He was never a stand-up comic in the music hall sense, but the super-refined twittish character he adopted had at least one foot planted squarely in vaudeville. He looked for all the world like the posh half of a comedy duo whose partner had failed to turn up. Like Norman Wisdom, he successfully adapted his small screen character to films, and after a hesitant start was offered, in *Private's Progress* (1956, John Boulting), exactly the role he needed, that of the effete, eternally scornful CO.

He became a Boultings regular, and appeared diversely as a wide-boy defended by fledgling barrister Ian Carmichael in *Brothers in Law* (1957); an objectionable university duffer with literary aspirations in *Lucky Jim* (1957); an obstreperous policeman in *Happy Is the Bride* (1958); and the name part in *Carlton-Browne of the FO* (1959, Jeffrey Dell), a blundering diplomat

Terry-Thomas and Shirley Eaton plot the downfall of a scandal magazine publisher (Dennis Price) in *The Naked Truth* (1957)

sent to quell an uprising within a former colony precipitated by its unscrupulous prime minister Peter Sellers.

He was the personnel manager of Dennis Price's factory in *I'm All Right, Jack* (1959, John Boulting), the *Private's Progress* commanding officer now demobbed and floundering in the acrimonious world of modern-day industrial relations. Once again the bane of his life was Peter Sellers, a union leader whom Terry-Thomas regards as 'an absolute shocker, the type who sleeps in his vest'. Calling unexpectedly on Sellers in an attempt to solve the factory's strike problems, he encounters a scene of total domestic chaos, with a dishevelled Sellers morosely darning his socks and lamenting the fact that wife, Irene Handl, has left him in retaliation for having called the strike. 'Do you think she'll come back?' Sellers asks. T-T's eyes sparkle – 'Mine didn't, thank God,' he says.

He was a titled victim, along with Sellers, of blackmailer-publisher Dennis Price in *The Naked Truth* (1957, Mario Zampi), a rumbustious performance, all leers and grimaces – not dissimilar, in fact, from his grossly overdone panto villain in *Tom Thumb* (1958, George Pal) with Sellers as his dumb partner.

In *Blue Murder at St Trinian's* (1957, Frank Launder), Terry-Thomas was a crafty motor-coach proprietor who does a deal with local education official Richard Wattis for the hire of two derelict old buses to transport the St Trinian's horrors to Rome. As the clapped-out vehicles begin the journey from St Trinian's, tour organiser George Cole peers at the rusted chassis and wonders if they will ever get to Rome. 'Well,' replies T-T chirpily, 'We've come all the way from Wantage!'

En route, he meets undercover policewoman Joyce Grenfell who, he understands, is shortly to

189

inherit some money – reason enough to ply her with raffish charm. Cornered in a high-class café, Miss Grenfell confesses, 'I don't know whether it's the music or the atmosphere or what, but I feel utterly defenceless,' to which Terry-Thomas can only mutter, 'Good show.'

Back home, however, the discovery that her police superintendent boyfriend has been reduced to the ranks brings Miss Grenfell gushingly to his side. As her promised wealth recedes from Terry-Thomas' grasp, she tries to atone for the wrong she has done him by confessing how wretched she feels. 'I feel an absolute Charlie,' admits T-T, glumly.

He was a dastardly villain in *Those Magnificent Men in Their Flying Machines* (1965, Ken Annakin), sabotaging other competitors' chances by spiking their drinks with a mild poison, and hacking bits off their fragile flying machines. Terry-Thomas is determined to win the race at all costs, aided in his scurrilous endeavours by insolent manservant Eric Sykes.

Having stabbed his main rivals in the back, so to speak, T-T is making excellent time but runs out of fuel. Expertly, he sets his aeroplane down on a Paris-bound train, but overlooks the small fact that trains occasionally disappear into tunnels. *Those Magnificent Men . . .* was a sparkling period comedy, and the huge assembled cast performed with the drilled precision of cavalry mounts.

Terry-Thomas was one of only a handful of British movie eccentrics to achieve wide acceptance in America, and went on to film in Hollywood, but here what was lacking most of the time was material tailored accurately enough – as the Boultings' scripts had been – to his outsize personality. In *Bachelor Flat* (1962, Frank Tashlin) he played a clownish English professor prone to losing his trousers; in *How to Murder Your Wife* (1965, Richard Quine), he was Jack Lemmon's very proper English butler, discreetly assisting Lemmon, a bachelor-type comic strip writer, to get rid of a foreign dolly-bird whom he has allegedly married whilst in a drunken daze; he played a mortician in *Strange Bedfellows* (1964, Melvin Frank), a marital mix-up comedy with Rock Hudson and Gina Lollobrigida; and was a villain along with Lionel Jeffries in *Jules Verne's Rocket to the Moon* (1967, Don Sharp) – not very good and not very Jules Verne, either. About his role in *It's A Mad, Mad, Mad, Mad World* (1963, Stanley Kramer), an all-star manic compilation of stunts and slapstick that would

have benefited from an occasional pause for breath, Robin Bean wrote in *Films and Filming*: 'Terry-Thomas supplies his best caricature of what the English think the Americans think the English are like' – a fair explanation of why most of his transatlantic films disappointed.

Terry-Thomas
b. 1911. Popular gap-tooth, gaudy-waistcoat comic of early TV vintage. Screen success as likable, upper-class oaf in numerous Boultings satires. Appeared in Hollywood comedies, as archetypal silly Englishman. Film debut: *A Date with a Dream* (1948).

1948 *A Date with a Dream* (Terry)
     The Brass Monkey (Himself)
1949 *Helter Skelter* (Announcer)
     Melody Club (Freddie Forrester)
1956 *Private's Progress* (Major Hitchcock)
1957 *Brothers in Law* (Alfred Green)
     Lucky Jim (Bertrand Welch)
     Blue Murder at St Trinian's (Captain
       Romney Carlton-Ricketts)
     The Naked Truth (Lord Mayley)
     The Green Man (Bought flower)
1958 *Happy Is the Bride* (Police Constable)
     Tom Thumb (Ivan)
1959 *Too Many Crooks* (Billy Gordon)
     Carlton-Browne of the FO (Cadogan de
       Vere Carlton-Browne)
     I'm All Right, Jack (Major Hitchcock)
1960 *School for Scoundrels* (Raymond Delauney)
     Make Mine Mink (Major Albert Rayne)
1961 *His and Hers* (Reggie Blake)
     A Matter of Who (Archibald Bannister)
1962 *Operation Snatch* (Lieutenant Piggy Wigg)
     Kill or Cure (J. Barker-Rynde)
     Bachelor Flat (USA) (Professor
       Bruce Patterson)
     The Wonderful World of the Brothers Grimm
       (Ludwig)
1963 *The Mouse on the Moon* (Spender)
     The Wild Affair (Godfrey Dean)
     It's a Mad, Mad, Mad, Mad World (USA)
       (J. Algernon Hawthorne)
1964 *Strange Bedfellows* (USA) (Mortician)
1965 *Those Magnificent Men in Their Flying
       Machines; or How I Flew from London to
       Paris in 25 Hours and 11 Minutes*
       (Sir Percy Ware-Armitage)
     You Must Be Joking (Major Foskett)
     How to Murder Your Wife (USA) (Charles)
1966 *Our Man in Marrakesh* (El Caid)

The Sandwich Man (Gardener)
1967 Jules Verne's Rocket to the Moon (Sir Harry Washington-Smythe)
I Love A Mystery (Gordon Elliott)
1967 Arabella (Fellini Hotel Manager/ General Sir Horace Gordon/Duke Moretti/Insurance Manager)
1968 Don't Raise the Bridge, Lower the River (H. William Homer)
1969 Monte Carlo or Bust (Sir Cuthbert Ware-Armitage)
1971 The Abominable Doctor Phibes (Dr Longstreet)
1972 Doctor Phibes Rises Again (Lombardo)
1973 Robin Hood (Voice of Sir Hiss)
The Vault of Horror (Critchit)
1975 Spanish Fly (Sir Percy de Courcy)
Bawdy Adventures of Tom Jones (Mr Square)
Side by Side (Max Nuggett)

Richard Todd

Even in his 1950s heyday, a lot of people would have thought twice before crossing a busy road to see Richard Todd. Yet he was enormously popular. With clean-cut, chiselled features you could cut your hand on, nicely proportioned shoulders and more virtue up front than a van-load of Bibles, Todd looked as if he had come off a drawing-board instead of having been born the usual way. Wisely, he made the most of what he had, which could be summed up as an inability to sit still while there was a horse to leap astride, a swollen river to swim, or a tree to vanish into.

His first big success was as a dour Scots Guards corporal in *The Hasty Heart* (1949, Vincent Sherman). The setting is a wartime Burma field hospital, and Todd, unknowingly, is riddled with some fatal disease. He is arrogant and dismissive, more difficult to handle than a Scots football fan at closing time, but everyone else, including fellow patient Ronald Reagan and nursing sister Patricia Neal, knows that his number is up so tolerance prevails. Looking every inch a stage weepie – which it originally was – the story rumbles on towards a predictable climax, with Todd learning of, and coming to terms with, his condition, but not before a rather pathetic attempt to woo Miss Neal – 'I've good teeth,' he insists. Todd's playing is in tune with the sombre mood of the piece and his faltering, change-of-heart address at the end works reasonably well, but some of the earlier writing lacks conviction.

He was another terminal case in *Flesh and Blood* (1951, Anthony Kimmins), a consumptive medical student who discards pushy girlfriend Ursula Howells for some peace and quiet – only to find his action has precisely the opposite effect. Miss Howells rounds on him like a demented fishwife, hollering, 'I wish you'd die!' to which poor Todd, semi-convulsed in yet another coughing fit splutters, 'I'm . . . doing . . . my . . . best!' She gets her wish, but Todd reappears as his own grandson, an even worse cad with the ladies. 'Do you think I'd have let you kick me around all this time without adoring you', trills Glynis Johns, pacifist daughter of an ammunitions tycoon when, after she has carried out a chequered pursuit of the rotter, he grudgingly proposes to her.

Walt Disney picked Todd for three costume actioners during 1953-4, as if determined, at all costs, to establish him as Errol Flynn's successor. His *Robin Hood* (1952, Ken Annakin) was, alas, a pale echo of Flynn's prewar classic. The villains – Hubert Gregg in the Claude Rains part and an emerging Peter Finch as the evil Sheriff – had all the best lines, while Todd, whose performance had comic-strip vigour but no real guts, got stuck with possibly the worst Maid Marian of all time, little known (and destined to remain so) Joan Rice.

In *The Sword and the Rose* (1953, Ken Annakin) and *Rob Roy the Highland Rogue* (1953, Harold French) only the costumes, and Miss Rice were changed. Disney brought in his *Flesh and Blood* co-star Glynis Johns, plus Robin hoodlums James Robertson Justice and Michael Gough. Todd risked being adversely compared with Errol Flynn for a second time as Raleigh to Bette Davis' Elizabeth I in *Virgin Queen* (1955, Henry Koster), which did nothing for Todd, but reminded audiences how far ahead of his imitators the charismatic Flynn had been in his heyday.

Todd rose to the bait as wartime flying ace Guy Gibson in *The Dambusters* (1955, Michael

Anderson), a pleasantly restrained performance projecting strength of character without showiness. Todd had not been an easy actor to accommodate dialogue-wise, but the hero of the Mohne and Eder dam raids settled on his shoulders like an expensively tailored jacket, and the film, whose over-reverence for its subject was its only obvious flaw, was hugely successful.

Several factors helped to maximise its impact. There was Todd's remarkable physical resemblance to Gibson, and Michael Redgrave's to Dr (later Sir) Barnes Wallis, the bouncing bomb's dogged inventor; there was the near-documentary feel of the early experimentation sequences, the squadron briefings and the raid itself; the despairing loss as well as the triumph expressed by Redgrave as the dreadful death toll becomes known, due as much to the dangers of low flying in the dark in a target zone surrounded on all sides by steep hills as to the enemy's defending battery stations; and there was the stirring theme music by Eric Coates, impossible to

hear then or now without the spirits being stirred.

Nothing much stirred watching *D-Day Sixth of June* (1956, Henry Koster), which used the Normandy landings as backdrop for a turgid love triangle involving Todd as a British colonel, Dana Wynter as his girlfriend, a cross between Mary Poppins and a toothpaste commercial, and Robert Taylor as a married GI captain who fills in for Todd while the lad is engaging the Hun elsewhere.

Even though it means putting the china doll-like Miss Wynter in storage for a while, Todd is no shrinking violet when the call-to-arms comes. 'I have a singular theory – the quicker more of us go, the quicker more of us'll come back,' he tells Miss Wynter. Her grumpy old retired defence chief dad is in agreement – 'A bit of cold steel now is worth twenty Americans later,' he urges, before killing himself because he is too old to kill others.

Miss Wynter's tally falls short of twenty Americans, presumably because not enough of

Richard Todd (left) as Wing Commander Guy Gibson and Michael Redgrave as bouncing bomb inventor Barnes Wallis watch the bomb being put to the test in *The Dambusters* (1955)

them looked like Robert Taylor. Their dreary, lukewarm affair has to be heard to be believed. Apologising for her father's dismissive attitude towards US troops – they meet originally when Taylor is sent along to smooth out an incident involving her father and a group of GIs – Miss Wynter explains rather grandly: 'We [meaning the British] are not much good at being thankful. We haven't had an opportunity to be thankful to anyone, except maybe God, in several hundred years.'

Later, on a dance floor, she ticks him off: 'Don't be cross but would you mind *awfully* not calling me Honey.' Sitting in a café overlooking the Thames, the watchful Taylor acknowledges the presence of the moon. Miss Wynter coos, 'Please God, let him be looking at it,' apparently unaware that any soldier staring at the moon is unlikely to notice an enemy sniper creeping up behind him.

In the end, Miss Wynter loses both of them. Taylor is badly wounded in action and shipped home to the USA, and Todd is killed when he trips over a land mine on the newly-liberated beachhead.

It took the filming of a real-life heroic naval incident, the escape from Chinese waters of the RN frigate *Amethyst* in 1949, after months of blockading, as *Yangtse Incident* (1957, Michael Anderson), to restore Todd's prestige after *D-Day Sixth of June*. Todd played the ship's commander, the redoubtable Commander Kerans – a part which suited his sharp-eyed, closed-mouth style comfortably – and the tension of the wait in Communist waters followed by the ship's nimble getaway down the Yangtse River under cover of darkness, was graphically conveyed without the need to resort to expensive special effects.

In *Danger Within* (1959, Don Chaffey), a wartime POW drama, Todd was a paratroop colonel who heads the obligatory escape committee, plagued on this occasion by the presence of a mysterious traitor. He appeared against type in *Never Let Go* (1960, John Guillermin), as a seedy cosmetics salesman whose car is nicked by sadistic Birmingham car-thief Peter Sellers. In the conflict that follows, Todd is the underdog but he comes through in a way that Sellers could never have anticipated. This was an intriguing – but not altogether successful – pairing of two stars playing outside their familiar selves.

By the early 1960s, he was beginning to run out of steam. He played a Gary Cooper-style lawman in *The Hellions* (1961, Ken Annakin), urging the inhabitants of a remote 19th-century South African township to find their backbone and repel Lionel Jeffries' outlaw gang. In *The Longest Day* (1962, Ken Annakin) he risked reminding us of his earlier Normandy landings caper, in a small role as a British Army major, again refreshingly brisk and stiff-upper-lip among hordes of laconic Americans.

In one of his later films, *Asylum* (1972, Roy Ward Baker), a modest Amicus horror compilation, Todd's was the first story, a loony tale in which he and lover-doll Barbara Parkins bump off and dismember his troublesome wife, Sylvia Sims. He packages the assortment of odd limbs in neat brown paper packs, and stores them in a freezer till he can get around to final disposal. But the victim refuses to rest in pieces. Like a well-drilled football squad, the gory parcels gang up to inflict a nasty surprise on Todd and his girlfriend.

Richard Todd

b. 1919. Energetic, handsome leading man, popular during 1950s as unblemishable, upright hero of costume and wartime actioners. Best remembered as Robin Hood (1953) and Dambuster Guy Gibson (1955). On stage from 1936. Film debut: *For Them That Trespass* (1948).

1948 *For Them That Trespass* (Herb Logan)
1949 *The Hasty Heart* (Cpl 'Lachie' McLachlin)
1950 *Stage Fright* (Jonathan Penrose)
      Portrait of Clare (Robert Hart)
1951 *Flesh and Blood* (Charles Cameron/
      Charles Cameron Sutherland)
      Lightning Strikes Twice (USA)
      (Richard Trevelyan)
1952 *The Story of Robin Hood and His Merrie
      Men* (Robin Hood)
      Twenty Four Hours of a Woman's Life
      (Young Man)
      The Venetian Bird (Edward Mercer)
      Elstree Story (Documentary)
1953 *The Sword and the Rose* (Charles Brandon)
      Rob Roy the Highland Rogue (Rob Roy
      Macgregor)
1955 *The Dambusters* (Wing Commdr Guy
      Gibson)
      Virgin Queen (Sir Walter Raleigh)
1956 *D-Day Sixth of June* (John Wynter)
1957 *Saint Joan* (Dunois)
      Yangtse Incident (Lt Commdr Kerans)
      The Naked Earth (Danny Halloran)
      Chase a Crooked Shadow (Ward Prescott)

Peter Ustinov

One of Peter Ustinov's school reports declared : 'He shows great originality which must be curbed at all costs!' The advice went unheeded and the world – not just the cinema – became a more colourful place. The actor's bravura personality is merely the outward guise of a man whose mind is irresistibly and eloquently tuned to life's more amusing aspects. On film he is a natural jester, a clown by design, Bunteresque in both shape and inclination, an unspoken 'Yaroo' never far from those mocking lips. But comedy, to Ustinov, is not simply the business of making audiences laugh, but a means of telling the world about its condition ('fatal, but not serious') and discussing the human predicament, all of which he achieves masterfully.

Ustinovian fantasies may seem, on the surface, remote from real life but the deeper you scratch the more relevant the message to contemporary existence can become. But you have to look for it, and even then he glories in the idea that you may fail. At such times he appears to be saying, 'I'm sure you believe that you understand what you think my message is, but please realise that what appears to be the point I'm making may not necessarily be what I meant!' At least, I think that's what he appears to be saying!

Private Angelo (1949, Peter Ustinov) was Ustinov's first film of note, though he had previously appeared as the Dutchman accused by the Nazis of the Reichstag incident in *Mein Kampf, My Crimes* (1941, Norman Lee); one of Will Hay's pupils in *The Goose Steps Out* (1942, Will Hay, Basil Dearden); and a Dutch priest who assists an RAF crew in trouble in *One of Our Aircraft Is Missing* (1941, Michael Powell, Emeric Pressburger). *Private Angelo* was mostly

his own work, that's to say he co-wrote it with Michael Anderson, and also produced, directed and starred – early evidence of the multi-faceted film-maker at work. Private Angelo is a dumb Italian army private who hates combat, and deserts in order to become a British prisoner-of-war. What happens is that he spends the war being chased by both sides. The comedy is patchy, but clearly what Ustinov wants to do is make us reflect on the sad truth that, in war, it is the uniforms that matter. War is uniforms fighting each other with real people inside.

The film that made him, at least in terms of international recognition, was *Quo Vadis* (1951, Mervyn Le Roy), an expensive and recurringly vulgar peep-show at what Hollywood moguls believed might have been ancient Rome. Apart from the lions and people wearing bedsheets it might have been a dissection of Hollywood itself. Compare Ustinov's performance, as the Emperor Nero, with Rod Steiger's bullying neurotic film producer in Clifford Odets' Hollywood exposé *The Big Knife*, made only two years later, and there is hardly any difference.

Ustinov's role, like Steiger's in the later film, is a supporting one, but when he gets into full flight, as the slack-jawed loony emperor, poor old Robert Taylor and Deborah Kerr, whose love story is supposed to provide the centrepiece, might just as well go for a dip in the Tiber. Taylor is a victorious legion commander, and Miss Kerr a cultured former slave who is also a Christian. At first Taylor mocks the idea of a single, all-powerful God though, after witnessing the tastelessness and moral decay of his home crowd every night, the notion gains on him.

Ustinov, meanwhile, wants to rebuild Rome

to his own grand design and, as existing buildings have to be got rid of first, he sets Rome ablaze, craftily blaming the Christians for the carnage that results. A massive backlash against the Christians leads to hundreds of arrests and scores of deaths at a series of so-called 'games', presided over by the gloating emperor. Having grown to hate Taylor the way madmen in Roman epics despise sane people, Ustinov chains him to a post so that he can watch the decorously-dressed (in a fetching see-through blue chiffon) Miss Kerr being disembowelled in the arena by a killer bull. Against all odds, though, her faithful slave manages to snap the creature's neck, and the film ends with a gloomy, terrified Ustinov contemplating the choice of killing himself or having the angry mob storming the palace gates do it for him. The reason for all this unseemly mob outrage is not their suddenly being denied a glimpse of Miss Kerr's tasteful insides, but because Taylor has blown the whistle on who really did burn Rome.

Ustinov's performance is showy and overdone, but the actual character is an attention-seeking, spoilt-brat monster-child, so that it's hard to say where the line ought to have been drawn. My own view is that he got it about right; and the film, too, has several pluses, such as the way it conveys the tyranny, treachery and decadence of 'Rome at the top'.

Ustinov was a cunning Arab hotelier in *Hotel Sahara* (1951, Ken Annakin), safeguarding his property against successive cycles of militia, as the changing tides of war turn arrogant winners into shamefaced losers. Ustinov deploys the visible charms of fiancée Yvonne de Carlo to win over each wave of invaders whilst, at the same time, resourcefully ensuring that her honour remains intact. All in all, a clever rather than inspired comedy that gave Ustinov adequate opportunity to show off his zany lugubrious personality.

In *The Magic Box* (1952, John Boulting) he played a cigar-chewing movie distributor, a guest appearance neither more nor less significant than the dozens of others this film attracted. He was George IV in *Beau Brummel* (1954, Curtis Bernhardt) – an odd choice for that year's Royal Film Performance since it dealt with madness among the Hanoverian princes. The film, though, was less concerned with historical accuracy than sketching pretty images, so that any offence to the present Royal Family was scarcely possible. Stewart Granger played Brummel, the

Peter Ustinov, 1965

Regency dandy who befriends and later quarrels with the king. Their relationship is kept ambiguous – one is never sure whether Brummel was an avaricious social climber or a man of honour. Ustinov soon grows weary of the battle to sustain either sympathy or interest with anything passably artistic and resorts to the usual ragbag of mannerisms.

In *We're No Angels* (1954, Michael Curtis), Ustinov, Humphrey Bogart and Aldo Ray are three Devils Island escapees who take refuge in a run-down general store, and later befriend the family who run it. Each is a ruthless jailbreaker, but it's Christmas Eve and the addled shopkeeper and his nice family are so helpless that the fugitives can't bring themselves to rob them. When an obnoxious cousin arrives and starts throwing his weight around, Bogart and his pals eagerly spring to the shopkeeper's defence. Aldo Ray's pet snake poisons the cousin and his equally nasty son, and altogether the trio provide the impoverished family, whom they now regard as their own, with a Christmas to remember. When Bogart returns with a turkey concealed in his ill-fitting prison suit, his innocent explanation, that it followed him back against his will, fools no-one. Earlier, before their change of heart, Ustinov and Ray insist that the family must be murdered so that no wit-

195

nesses remain to tell tales. Bogart eventually agrees. 'You're right,' he avows. 'We'll bash their heads in, gouge their eyes out, cut their throats, *after* we wash the dishes!'

Kirk Douglas, who produced as well as starred in *Spartacus* (1960, Stanley Kubrick), knew what he was doing when his company drafted Laurence Olivier, Charles Laughton and Ustinov in support. Douglas' affection for British quality actors is well known and here he scooped the main board of directors of Scene-stealers Incorporated. It was a sensible investment in view of the dollars he planned to squander on this sprawling epic – $12 million, making it for those times the costliest film ever produced. If only for the performances of those three, Douglas shrewdly acknowledged, the eventual outcome must at least be watchable regardless of any other merits the film might have.

Spartacus, played by Douglas, leads a rebellion of slaves from a gladitorial school against their Roman masters. The rebels are quickly augmented by others freed along the way, and no mercy is shown as, in battle after battle, the slaves triumph. Unwisely, though, they allow themselves to be drawn into a bloody conflict with the main body of the Roman army, and the uprising, once it is thought to be a threat to Rome itself, is brutally crushed. Spartacus is taken prisoner, and he and thousands of his supporters are crucified on poles erected the length of the Appian Way. Ustinov played a wily slave-trader who specialises in the supply of nubile ladies for the aristocracy, a wryly jovial figure wise in the ways of cleaning up a few extra denarii.

In *The Sundowners* (1960, Fred Zinneman) he was a whimsical sheep drover, drifting across Australia with his sheep-shearing buddy Robert Mitchum. Ustinov works for Mitchum but it's an association of equals, with Ustinov tagging along for the companionship as much as the meagre pay-outs. Mitchum's wife, played by Deborah Kerr, and his teenage son hanker for a permanent home but Mitchum's wanderlust, like Ustinov's, still has miles and miles of outback to run.

The Sundowners is a handsomely photographed 'outdoors' adventure but it is also a love story of epic proportions, sensitively expressed in telltale nods and glances between the rugged but weak-willed Mitchum and his loyal, down-to-earth 'missus', Miss Kerr. Her anguish, when she discovers that he has bought drinks all round with their slender bank roll, followed by a sudden, tight-lipped resolve to face their misfortunes as best they can together, is but one highlight of many. Ustinov makes the sidekick a colourful, articulate, eternally bemused figure who dreads the idea of the landscape around him suddenly standing still, an educated man fleeing from educated men's values.

Romanoff and Juliet (1961, Peter Ustinov) offers typically Ustinovian solutions to the world's problems. It's an adaptation of the old 'Romeo and Juliet' story, in which the warring families are senior diplomats on the Russian and American benches at the United Nations Assembly. When the daughter of the American delegate falls in love with the son of his Russian counterpart, neither realises that a third onlooker stands to benefit from their romance. That's Ustinov, president of a tiny, impoverished mid-European republic which holds the casting vote in a crucial UN debate, but which relies substantially on both super-powers for its revenues and therefore cannot risk offending either. Bringing the two sides together by means of a gingerly engineered love-match seems the most sensible way out of the dilemma.

This is a tame little fantasy, anxious to please and succeeding in the main, though it transfers rather woodenly in places. It's at its best poking sly fun at the differences in attitude between East and West, an area in which Ustinov's connections with both camps – Russian grandparents, lengthy periods of residence in California – were undoubtedly useful.

He cast himself as the decent-minded captain – 'I could find no-one else at the price' – in *Billy Budd* (1962, Peter Ustinov), Herman Melville's 18th-century naval drama in which the essence of goodness, the unsullied young seaman of the title, and the embodiment of evil, a cruel master-at-arms, are drawn into a series of tense and ultimately tragic confrontations. A newcomer to films, Terence Stamp, played the innocent Billy and Robert Ryan, the veteran Hollywood tough-guy, proved an unusual but competently-played adversary.

Highpoint of the film is a scene where the two appear to be edging towards compromise – Stamp acknowledging the existence of evil, Ryan conceding that good has an equal right to exist – but the opportunity is lost, the master-at-arms is killed when Billy lashes out at him in a fit of justifiable rage. Despite the strong humanitarian case that can be put in Billy's defence, Navy

Regulations demand the boy's execution, and the captain reluctantly orders him to hang.

Ustinov won his second Academy Award in *Topkapi* (1964, Jules Dassin), as an insufferable Englishman named Arthur, recruited by a group of international jewel thieves to drive them to freedom after a daring but disaster-prone raid on the high security Topkapi Palace Museum in Istanbul. Ustinov is seen here as another of life's born losers, a lowly tourist guide in an obscure Greek town, duped into joining the gang because their offer includes a chance to drive a swish limousine – a sop to his vanity which he is unable to resist. Reminiscent of Dassin's earlier, more famous, robbery film *Rififi* (1954), the audacious snatch – of a jewel-encrusted dagger – is carried out by the same method as the one in *Rififi*, by lowering the thief down through the ceiling because the museum's floor is wired for sound. This one, however, is played for laughs instead of suspense, with Ustinov in excellent form as the charmless stooge.

He took a small part, as a heavily-beribboned, whiskery Bavarian prince in *Lady L* (1965, Peter Ustinov). The character – target of a rather clumsy assassination attempt in which he manages to catch in his hands the bomb intended to kill him – has nothing whatever to do with the main plot, a romantic pastiche in which the common-born Corsican wife of an English aristocrat also happens to be the wife of his chauffeur, a European political hothead. Ustinov, the writer, finds enough gaps in Romain Gary's original plot-line to plug in a few lip-smackin' wheezes of his own, and it is these, rather than the adulterous carryings-on of Sophia Loren, David Niven and Paul Newman, as the star-studded 'ménage à trois', which rouse the film to semi-life.

In *The Comedians* (1967, Peter Glenville) Ustinov was a South American ambassador whose wife, Elizabeth Taylor, has an affair with a melancholy drifter, played by Richard Burton – 'a fine actor with a wayward quality women find hard to resist', according to Ustinov. Graham Greene adapted the screenplay from his own novel about political oppression and voodoo in a Caribbean republic, but, alas, not even his talented pen, nor the Burton-Taylor ensemble, nor, indeed, Ustinov or Alec Guinness – the latter cast as a mysterious British-born guns expert who joins a group of revolutionaries seeking to overthrow a corrupt, nightmarish regime – can make other than a stodgy pie of these potentially exciting individual ingredients.

Hot Millions (1968, Eric Till) is a delightfully English farce about a cheeky embezzler trapped by a computer who responds, after serving his prison sentence, by using the dreadful machines to expand his criminal activities into a lucrative international operation. Ustinov was the likable swindler whose horizons are first curtailed but then later joyously expanded by electronic wizardry. Like the Alec Guinness gold-bars thief in *The Lavender Hill Mob* (1951), Ustinov absconds to Rio de Janeiro to enjoy his ill-gotten gains with Cockney wife Maggie Smith, but when the moment of retribution arrives, and his victims descend on Rio intending to re-possess what is rightfully theirs, Ustinov's threatened bacon is saved by his wife's ingenuity. She has gambled a bundle of their 'hot millions' on the stock market, and comes up a surprise winner – with enough profit to settle all outstanding grievances and still have plenty for themselves.

Peter Ustinov

b. 1921. Prolific, versatile actor-writer-director whose erratic comedy style – some thunder-flashes, some damp squibs – beguiles or infuriates according to individual tastes. Has bolstered his weak writing spells with a chain of sly, scene-stealing performances – *Quo Vadis* (1951), *We're No Angels* (1954), *Spartacus* (1960), *The Sundowners* (1960) – but love or hate him, he is consistently inventive, in both comedy and drama fields. Previous wives were Isolde Denham and actress Suzanne Cloutier. Now married to Helene du Lau d'Allemans.

1941 *Hello Fame*
      Let the People Sing
      Mein Kampf, My Crimes
      The Goose Steps Out
      One of Our Aircraft Is Missing
1942 *The Way Ahead* (co-scripted)
1945 *The School for Secrets*
1947 *Vice Versa* (scripted and directed)
1949 *Private Angelo* (scripted, co-directed) (Private Angelo)
1950 *Odette* (Arnaud)
1951 *Quo Vadis* (Emperor Nero)
      Hotel Sahara (Emad)
1952 *The Magic Box* (Film distributor)
1954 *Beau Brummel* (Prince of Wales)
      The Egyptian (Kaptah)
      We're No Angels (Jules)
1955 *Lola Montez* (Ringmaster)

Jack Warner

'I'm an old-fashioned sort of chap; I do routine things in a routine way,' says pipe-smoking CID Inspector Jack Warner to Brian Donlevy, alias the humourless professor in The Quatermass X-Periment (1955, Val Guest). Donlevy is opposed to Warner's investigating the disappearance of a sick astronaut, but bulldog Jack refuses to be fobbed off. By the time he gets his man, though, he would need a mechanical shovel to pick him up – the poor chap has turned into a huge mass of porridge-like substance.

Good-humoured coppers, easy-going fathers, honest-to-goodness working-class types – Warner specialised in solid citizenry, and his reassuring presence has held together scores of blue-collar melodramas and comedies. Of all the characters he played – really it was the same character – two became household names, Joe Huggett and PC George Dixon. The Huggetts first appeared in Holiday Camp (1947, Ken Annakin), as a typical working-class London family on vacation, coping with the hardships of the period with resilience and good humour. The characters – father Jack Warner, mother Kathleen Harrison, daughters Jane Hylton, Susan Shaw and Petula Clark – were drawn faithfully from London life, and the humour, like the people, was warm and self-effacing. Even Warner's crusty old boss Clive Morton had a heart ticking away behind the watchchain.

Spivs tended to be of the Ronald Shiner variety and the daughters' assorted boyfriends were either agreeably smooth-chinned or harmless cretins. What permeated through them, as

indeed through contemporary comedies like Passport to Pimlico (1949, Henry Cornelius) as well, was a marvellous sense of community, evoking a Cockney London that no longer exists.

In The Blue Lamp (1950, Basil Dearden) Warner, as PC George Dixon, postpones his retirement for five years and shortly afterwards is shot dead confronting an unnerved gunman, Dirk Bogarde, during a raid on a Paddington cinema. Warner's murder, early in the film, alienates Bogarde from London's criminal milieu within whose closed ranks he had hoped to vanish. Cop killers are tossed back – that's the code of the streets – and Bogarde is eventually run to ground at a dog-track after much siren-bashing and breakneck chases. The killer's alienation from fellow thug Patric Doonan (a lesser villain nervous of firearms), from girlfriend Peggy Evans who is intimidated by Bogarde's violent outbursts, and from society as a whole is graphically illustrated when, with the police net tightening, Bogarde can be seen plunging desperately through the crowds, all of whom are moving, like humanity itself, in the opposite direction.

The Dixon character was later exhumed for BBC Television by screen writer Ted Willis, who had co-written the original story with Ian Read, and the series ran for a marathon 434 episodes spread over 21 years (1954-1975), with Warner's jaunty 'Evenin' all' becoming the police slogan to end all slogans.

His first post-war copper was the one leading the chase after escaped Dartmoor prisoner John

Jack Warner shares a retirement joke with (left to right) Bruce Seton, Jimmy Hanley, Clive Morton and Meredith Edwards in *The Blue Lamp* (1949). The Warner character reappeared as *Dixon of Dock Green* in the long-running television series

McCallum in *It Always Rains on Sunday* (1947, Robert Hamer). McCallum shelters in the Bethnal Green home of one-time girlfriend Googie Withers, now trapped in a dull marriage to Edward Chapman. McCallum's reappearance awakens Googie's passions all over again, but she is wasting her time – McCallum, a hardened criminal, merely wants to use her. The film is a grimly authentic canvas of London's East End on a drab Sunday morning, shot against a backdrop of market stalls, mobile snack bars and railway sidings. In *Emergency Call* (1952, Lewis Gilbert), a pacy drama about a race against time to track down a donor with a rare blood group to provide a transfusion for a dying child from a random cross-section of metropolis low-life, Warner played the police inspector heading the search, Anthony Steel was the doctor-in-charge, and Earl Cameron was the embittered boxer who eventually saves the child.

Warner was an over-the-hill Test cricketer with a problem son in *The Final Test* (1953, An-

thony Asquith), and switched to boxing as a sympathetic cornerman in *The Square Ring* (1953, Basil Dearden). He was the naval officer in charge of the escape committee in *Albert RN* (1953, Lewis Gilbert), again with Anthony Steel, and in *The Ladykillers* (1955, Alexander Mackendrick), played a kindly police superintendent who dismisses landlady Katie Johnson's colourful version of what her lodgers have been up to – bank robbery – as senile ramblings.

Jack Warner

1894-1981. Former music hall comedian and long-serving all-purpose character actor – brother of radio stars Elsie and Doris Waters – specialising in warm-hearted Cockney portrayals. Two most memorable creations were family man Joe Huggett in the 'Huggett' film series, and PC Dixon, a character in Ealing's *The Blue Lamp* (1949) later resurrected for long-life TV series *Dixon of Dock Green*. On stage from 1927. Film debut: *The Dummy Talks* (1943).

Richard Wattis

Richard Wattis was mostly glimpsed as a disaster-prone official or dogsbody, blinking owlishly behind horn-rimmed specs. The worries of the world were always draped across those beanpole shoulders, and the balding dome was set in a permanent furrow. Wattis was a stalwart of the British film comedy school, where his alternately goofy, dyspeptic, snide, outraged, browbeaten, servile, snooty characterisations were briefly seen but favourably remembered.

He might have been the supercilious twit to end them all, and a rotten killjoy, but he was never malicious or underhand, even when drastic measures were needed to extricate him from the results of his own folly. At school – public, no doubt – he might have been the unpopular swot but never the form-room sneak.

When that bubble of pomposity was punctured, as it always was, Wattis would assume a sly, little-boy-lost air which fooled no-one but was usually just enough to gain him social readmittance on the most meagre terms. It was a measured caricature, perfected over many years, which to anyone who has regular dealings with council chambers, ministry offices or tax officials, had an uncomfortable reality. Wattis looked like a form that needed filling in, and his characters were about as cuddly as a binful of fish-heads.

It would be a waste of space to catalogue his many appearances other than checklist a few highlights. He was a St Trinian's regular, a harrassed education official expressly responsible for the hideous schoolgirls. In *Blue Murder at St Trinian's* (1957, Frank Launder), he gleefully hands over responsibility to another official, Peter Jones, with the advice: 'There's only one thing to do, old man – open a vein!'

But his escape is short-lived, and it is Wattis who supervises their trip abroad. At one point a water polo match regresses into outright warfare, both in and out of the pool, and ends with Wattis being fished from the battle zone on a stretcher, specs halfway down his nose, his bowler and briefcase bobbing in the water.

That same year he made *The Abominable Snowman* (1957, Val Guest), abominable in every sense of the word. Wattis was scientist Peter Cushing's assistant, and the two of them are dallying in Tibet hoping to catch a yeti off-guard. The opportunity comes in a shared expedition with blustery old Forrest Tucker whose motives are mercenary – he wants to sell a yeti to a zoo, and since no zoo yet has one his price is likely to be steep. But so, too, are the snowy slopes that have to be negotiated before the ill-assorted party get within grunting range of the creature.

Wattis, sensibly, remains behind to console Cushing's wife and go through his familiar droll boffin routine. Midway through the film, a character slumps to the floor and Cushing informs us, 'He's in a complete trance!' By then, weren't we all!

In *Innocents in Paris* (1953, Gordon Parry) Wattis was an embassy secretary, in *The Intruder* (1953, Guy Hamilton) a schoolteacher, in *Lease of Life* (1954, Charles Frend) a solicitor, in *Simon and Laura* (1955, Muriel Box) a harrassed TV station controller, in *The Prince and the Showgirl* (1957, Laurence Olivier) a fussy diplomat, in *Libel* (1959, Anthony Asquith) a sombre judge, in *The VIPs* (1963, Anthony Asquith) an overworked reception manager at Heathrow Airport, in *Chitty Chitty Bang Bang* (1968, Ken Hughes) the principality's befuddled secretary. These, as always, were brief vignettes, like welcome seasoning added to a sometimes indifferent stew.

Wattis became a TV regular in the Eric Sykes-Hattie Jacques sitcom series *Sykes* as their snooty, petty-minded, nosey parker neighbour. Sykes, like Spike Milligan, a comedy writer with an acute sense of the absurd when not writing his own lines, created in the Wattis character a suburban monster of frightening proportions.

Richard Wattis

1912-1975. Lanky, balding, bespectacled comedy performer, often seen as goofy official or browbeaten underdog. British comedy regular with scores of credits. Played minus familiar specs, for once, in *Hobson's Choice* (1954). Was Eric Sykes' nosey neighbour in long-running TV sitcom. Film debut: *The Happiest Days of Your Life* (1950).

Richard Wattis, 1961

1950 *The Happiest Days of Your Life* (Arnold Billings)
1951 *Appointment with Venus* (Executive)
1952 *The Importance of Being Earnest* (Seton)
     Mother Riley Meets the Vampire (PC Freddie)
     Top Secret (Barnes)
     Made in Heaven (Vicar)
1953 *Top of the Form* (Willoughby-Gore)
     Appointment in London (Pascal)
     Innocents in Paris (Secretary)
     Background (David Wallace)
     Blood Orange (Macleod)
     The Intruder (Schoolmaster)
     Park Plaza 605 (Theodore Feather)
1954 *Hobson's Choice* (Albert Prosser)
     Doctor in the House (Salesman)
     The Belles of St Trinian's (Manton Bassett)
     Lease of Life (Solicitor)
     The Crowded Day (Mr Christopher)
1955 *The Colditz Story* (Richard Gordon)

See How They Run (Rev Lionel Toop)
The Time of His Life (Edgar)
A Yank in Ermine (Boone)
Simon and Laura (Controller)
An Alligator Named Daisy (Hoskins)
1956 *Jumping for Joy* (Carruthers)
     The Man Who Never Was (Assistant)
     Eye Witness (Anaesthetist)
     It's a Wonderful World (Harold)
     The Iron Petticoat (Clerk)
     The Silken Affair (Worthington)
     A Touch of the Sun (Purchase)
1957 *The Prince and the Showgirl* (Northbrook)
     Second Fiddle (Bill Turner)
     The Abominable Snowman (Peter Fox)
     Barnacle Bill (Registrar of Shipping)
     Blue Murder at St Trinian's (Bassett)
1958 *The Inn of the Sixth Happiness* (Mr Murfin)
1959 *The Captain's Table* (Prittlewood)
     Left, Right and Centre (Harding-Pratt)
     The Ugly Duckling (Barclay)
     Libel (Judge)
     Follow a Star (Dr Chatterway)
1960 *Your Money or Your Wife* (Hubert Fry)
     Follow That Horse (Hugh Porlock)
1961 *Very Important Person* (Woodcock)
     Nearly a Nasty Accident (Wagstaffe)

201

Naunton Wayne

Naunton Wayne was once asked by a journalist to provide some interesting facts about himself. 'There's absolutely none, old chap, absolutely none,' confessed Wayne. Despite this apparent handicap Wayne enjoyed a useful career as a leading light comedy actor during the 1940s and 1950s, often in partnership with Basil Radford.

Like Richard Wattis, he excelled at playing pinstriped characters, but Wayne's were infinitely more impish and good-humoured, coping with the minor insanities of others with tact and resignation. That look of splendid imperturbability took a lot of wiping off, and compared to obtuse Basil Radford, Wayne represented the sober voice of common sense.

Their partnership began in Hitchcock's *The Lady Vanishes* (1938, Alfred Hitchcock), a spy thriller set aboard the Trans-Continental Express and starring Michael Redgrave and Margaret Lockwood. Radford and Wayne were natty, eccentric Englishmen. They reappeared as the same duo in *Night Train to Munich* (1940, Carol Reed), 'a delectable mix of comedy and suspense', again with Margaret Lockwood. The film is directed tellingly at the Nazis, but considering the film's vintage they are seen in a surprisingly reasonable light. When, for instance, ss officer Paul Henreid boasts that 'a nation is behind the Führer', a wise old industrialist enquires, 'Yes, but how *far* behind ?'

As daffy Britishers adrift in Germany on the day war is declared, Radford and Wayne react to the war announcement in precisely the way one might expect seasoned diplomats to do – Radford is more worried about the fate of his golf-

clubs, loaned to a colleague in Berlin, than that of his country, which he knows instinctively will weather whatever comes. Wayne, on the other hand, is rather mystified by what's happening. He cannot adapt to being prodded and badgered by their new enemies and wonders why 'everything we sit on seems to be required'. It's a cleverly done, but not over-done propaganda film, which cuts the enemy tidily down to size with clever satire. There's a nice touch at the end when arch rivals Henreid and Rex Harrison battle it out at a deserted cable car station on the Swiss border. Henreid has lost, but still has the option of finishing off British agent Harrison. He chooses not to, with a half-admiring shrug.

In *Passport to Pimlico* (1949, Henry Cornelius), Radford and Wayne were Whitehall officials plagued by the discovery that a section of London within their jurisdiction belongs to Burgundy. The delighted residents force the ministry to recognise their independence, but soon there is a problem over dwindling foodstuffs, and the worried rebels appear to have no option but to concede to ministry demands for removal of the barriers.

'We can't let them starve to death,' declares Radford but, whilst agreeing with his colleague's humanitarianism, Wayne glumly points out that they can't not let them starve to death, either. The New Burgundians agree to discuss surrender but before Radford and Wayne can whisk away their leaders for a top-level parley, outside sympathisers bombard the rebels with food supplies and urge the tiny principality to fight on. When Radford and Wayne show up in their posh

Ministry men Naunton Wayne (extreme right) and Basil Radford (second right) meet passive resistance from New Burgundians Stanley Holloway (centre) and Raymond Huntley in Ealing's classic comedy *Passport to Pimlico* (1949)

limousines they are met not by the hungry, dispirited citizens they expected, but by a jubilant, derisive mob who are in no mood for surrender.

Wayne made numerous films in his own right. Probably the best known of these was *The Titfield Thunderbolt* (1952, Charles Crichton), in which he was a village lawyer who throws in his hand with a local consortium striving to save an old branch line railway from the Beeching – or someone similar's – axe.

Rural England had never looked so mouthwatering on film before, and Douglas Slocombe's colour cameras – it was Ealing's first film in colour, incidentally – accentuated the warmth and appealing simplicity of village life. The film's sympathies are clearly on the side of conservationists – the rival bus company which wants the railway out of business is run by a couple of stooges, and the British Rail officials who will determine its ultimate fate are, one feels, made deliberately anonymous in that they

are not played by well-known actors like Radford or Richard Wattis who would, by their mere presence, have unconsciously exhorted the audience to have mixed loyalties.

On the eve of the fateful test run, the bus company thugs manage to derail the locomotive, but the conservationists – led by the local vicar – fight back by borrowing from the local museum an antique but nicely preserved puffer which promises to be the answer to all their problems.

But it's not all smooth running to the finishing line. The rivals have drained a water tower along the way and the puffer is in danger of exploding unless it is topped up. But, never fear, the entire village population willingly turns out to give the stricken loco a push, and to rush to it supplementary supplies of water from a nearby pond in various makeshift containers – a scene reminiscent of the hiding away of the stolen whisky in Ealing's earlier *Whisky Galore.*

Wayne is a passenger on the trial run, but

203

though he supports the venture has no intention of rolling up his sleeves to help it survive. 'I didn't pay my fare to become a beast of burden,' he moans, when asked to lend some muscle.

Another scene vividly recalls his chum Radford in *Whisky Galore*. Wayne has overheard the conniving busmen plot to destroy the locomotive. Later the same night, clad in pyjamas, he ponders his next move. Finally, he decides. 'In my position one daren't risk making a fool of oneself,' he tells wife Nancy O'Neil, as he thrusts a leg back into his trousers. Her weary smile suggests that she knows only too well that's precisely what he is going to do.

Naunton Wayne

1901-1970. Light comedy actor specialising in mild-mannered types. Paired with Basil Radford in several comedy classics. On stage from 1920. Film debut: *The First Mrs Fraser* (1932).

1933 *Going Gay*
    For the Love of You
1938 *The Lady Vanishes*
1939 *A Girl Must Live*

1940 *Night Train to Munich*
    Crooks' Tour
1943 *Millions Like Us*
1945 *Girl in a Million* (Fotheringham)
    Dead of Night (Larry Potter)
1948 *Quartet* (Leslie)
1949 *It's Not Cricket* (Capt Early)
    Passport to Pimlico (Straker)
    Stop Press Girl (Fireman, Conductor, Fred's Boy, Projectionist, Co-Pilot)
    Obsession (Supt Finsbury)
1950 *Double Confession* (Inspector Tenby)
    Trio (Mr Ramsay)
    Highly Dangerous (Hedgerley)
1951 *Circle of Danger* (Reggie Sinclair)
1952 *The Happy Family* (Mr Filch)
    Tall Headlines (Inspector)
    Treasure Hunt (Eustace Mills)
    The Titfield Thunderbolt (Blakeworth)
1954 *You Know What Sailors Are* (Capt Owbridge)
1959 *Operation Bullshine* (Major Pym)
1961 *Double Bunk* (Officer)
    Nothing Barred (Lord Whitebait)

Acknowledgements

Stills from the following films are by courtesy of The Rank Organisation: *The Informers; The League of Gentlemen; Checkpoint; Miracle in Soho; Whistle Down the Wind; The Shout; The Thirty-nine Steps; The Lady Vanishes; House of Secrets; Doctor in Love; Nothing But the Night; Doctor At Sea; The Captain's Table; The Heroes of Telemark; Maroc 7; Bad Timing; A Town Like Alice; No Love for Johnnie; The Ipcress File; Deadlier Than the Male; Genevieve; Sea of Sand; A Night to Remember; Revenge; Great Expectations; To Paris With Love; This Sporting Life; Romeo and Juliet; The Planter's Wife; The Perfect Woman; Man in the Moon; Doctor in the House; Brief Encounter; Room at the Top; Golden Salamander; Stop Press Girl; Carry On Matron; Wombling Free; The Battle of the River Plate; A Tale of Two Cities; The Net; North West Frontier; Odd Man Out; Above Us the Waves; Reach for the Sky; The Demi-Paradise; Hamlet; The Magic Bow; Tomorrow Never Comes; The Naked Truth; Top of the Form.*
EMI kindly provided stills from: *Ice Cold in Alex;*

Violent Playground; The Hasty Heart; The Lavender Hill Mob; Wings of Danger; Laughter in Paradise; Top Secret; Billy Liar; Frankenstein and the Monster from Hell; I Was Monty's Double; Aces High; The Cruel Sea; Some Will, Some Won't; A Run for Your Money; The Last Holiday; The Raging Moon; Dulcima; The Rainbow Jacket; It's Great to be Young; Kind Hearts and Coronets; Whisky Galore; The Dambusters; The Blue Lamp; Passport to Pimlico.

My thanks must also go to Columbia Pictures Organisation for stills from *Gumshoe* and *A Man for All Seasons*; Metro-Goldwyn-Mayer for *Where Eagles Dare*; the Walt Disney Organisation for *Greyfriars Bobby*; and to the Press Association for providing photographs of Peter Ustinov and Richard Wattis. I am especially grateful to Mickie Meade and Graham Howell of Rank Film Distributors, and Jack Middleton of EMI Films, for all their help in connection with this book.

Index

205

208